4th Edition

Auburn vs. Alabama

BRAGGIN' RIGHTS

By Bill Cromartie

Gridiron Publishers
P.O. Box 724201
Atlanta, GA 31139

.Braggin' Rights by Bill Cromartie
Copyright © 1994 by William Kelly Cromartie

All rights reserved. No part of this book may
be reproduced in any form, except for quotations
in a review, without permission of the publisher.

Printed in the United States of America

Library of Congress Cataloging-in-Publication data:
1. History. University of Alabama — Football —
2. History. Auburn University — Football —
3. History. College sports — United States —
4. History. Football — United States —
Library of Congress Catalog Number: 93-078021

ISBN 0-932520-54-5

Published in Atlanta, Georgia

1st Edition: 1978
2nd Edition: 1982
3rd Edition: 1993
4th Edition: 1994

Jacket photograph by Wendall Adams & Associates,
Atlanta, Georgia

GRIDIRON PUBLISHERS
P.O. Box 724201
ATLANTA, GA 31139
(404) 431-0962

Table of Contents

Dedication
Foreword by Coach Ralph "Shug" Jordan
Foreword by Coach Pat Dye
Acknowledgment
Introduction by Coach Terry Bowden
1893 — "Remember The Victory That You Have Won This Day" ■ 13
1893 — "If You Can't Discuss Football, You Are Simply Not In It" ■ 26
1894 — No, You Can't Play ■ 30
1895 — The Heisman Comes To Auburn ■ 35
1900 — Mercy ■ 38
1901 — "Auburn Tigers Win The Game From Alabama Team" ■ 41
1902 — Shop Hands Upset Votaries ■ 47
1903 — Upset No. 2 ■ 51
1904 — Fierce ■ 56
1905 — Mass Muscle And Chain Lightning ■ 59
1906 — Axed By Auxford ■ 62
1907 — They Tied Up And Called It Quits ■ 69
1908-1948 — A 41-Year Time Out Over $34.00 ■ 74
1948 — Unwrap The Bandages, Boys ■ 91
1949 — 14-13 ■ 97
1950 — The Red Elephants Remembered ■ 103
1951 — A Return To Auburn, Forever ■ 107
1952 — Alabama-Auburn All Even ■ 113
1953 — Second Field Goal Puts Alabama First ■ 117
1954 — Turnabout's Fair Play ■ 123
1955 — "Yiieeee!" ■ 128
1956 — "Nobody Asked For A Refund" ■ 132
1957 — "We're No. 1!" ■ 137
1958 — The Shug & Bear Show ■ 146
1959 — Some Changes ■ 155
1960 — X vs. Y ■ 159
1961 — Tide Rolls To No. 1 ■ 163
1962 — Joy And Desperation ■ 169
1963 — "Tick Clock! Tick! Darn You, Tick!" ■ 173
1964 — Back To Tuscaloosa ■ 181
1965 — It Stayed In Tuscaloosa ■ 189
1966 — Victories vs. Votes ■ 193

1967 — AU Couldn't Believe It. Neither Could UA ■ 197
1968 — A Fifth (Straight) For Bear ■ 203
1969 — Bear's Longest Football Day — Ever ■ 207
1970 — Pat Escapes Panicsville ■ 216
1971 — The Biggest Game Of All ■ 222
1972 — "Punt, Bama, Punt!" ■ 230
1973 — Revenge ■ 243
— Time Out For A Trip To Tuscaloosa ■ 247
1974 — No AU Luck At All ■ 249
1975 — An Auburn Era Ends ■ 255
1976 — Back To The Blackboard ■ 259
1977 — Auburn Can't Hide From Intensified Tide ■ 263
1978 — "Too Many Chinks In Auburn's Armor" ■ 269
1979 — The December Fumble Fest ■ 274
1980 — Bear Sees Another Change ■ 280
1981 — 315 In The Beartrap ■ 285
1982 — Bedlam In B'ham ■ 291
1983 — The Pat & Bo Show ■ 298
1984 — "We Beat The Sugar Out Of Auburn" ■ 306
1985 — The Boy From Red Bay ■ 313
1986 — Ho-Hum. Another Thriller. ■ 321
1987 — Long Seasons End In Auburn's Favor ■ 330
1988 — Bye-Bye, Ol' Iron Bowl, As We've Known It ■ 338
1989 — Home Sweet Home? Yes! Yes! Ohh, Yes! ■ 344
1990 — Oct.: No. 2 In America. Dec.: No. 2 In Alabama ■ 358
1991 — Bama's Big "D" Pays Big Dividends ■ 363
1992 — Tuscaloosa Is Again Titletown ■ 368
1993 — "The Miracle Season" ■ 377
Appendix, Records Section ■ 407
Epilogue — by David Housel, Auburn Athletic Director ■ 426

*To Auburn Fans Everywhere.
War Eagle!*

FOREWORDS

By Ralph "Shug" Jordan, 1978

When I came to Auburn as head coach in 1951, the Auburn-Alabama series had been resumed for only three seasons following a 41-year lapse from 1907 to 1948.

At the time it meant more to Auburn people to beat Georgia and Georgia Tech than it did to beat Alabama.

However, that changed in a hurry. I can truthfully say that Paul Bryant's return to Alabama in 1958 did more to change Auburn's thinking than anything else.

At that time, Auburn was in the middle of a five-year winning streak over Alabama. We had also won the national championship in 1957. The Alabama game was just the last on the schedule.

Now, both sides spend the entire year preparing for the two hours they face each other. The Auburn-Alabama game now means as much as an entire season. Bowls, polls and season records don't count.

It's easy for me to recall all the games, but several naturally stand out more than the others.

The 40-0 victory that cinched the 1957 national championship was probably the biggest ever for Auburn at that time.

Auburn teams made rallies from 10 to 17 points behind to win in 1969 and 1970. Those games with Pat Sullivan and Terry Beasley were some of the most exciting in the series.

Perhaps the most heartbreaking loss for us was in 1967 when we dominated the game, only to lose 7-3 on a great run by Kenny Stabler.

We had to wait five years to block two punts to get over the 1967 game. However, the 17-16 victory in 1972 will remain as the most memorable victory to Auburn people everywhere.

By Pat Dye, 1994

The Auburn-Alabama game is probably too big. It affects too many lives for too much of the year.

We made a decision early on not to let the outcome of any one game, even the Alabama game, affect how we felt about ourselves, our program, and the season as a whole.

It doesn't matter who wins the game in a particular year, Auburn's always going to have a good football program, and Alabama's always going to have a good football program.

In traditional rivalries, you can expect to win about half the time, which is what we did. We won six and lost six. I'll never forget those six wins. I'll never forget those six losses, either. Each one will always stay with you in a particular kind of way.

There was a fundamental change in the Auburn-Alabama game after the 1987 season, and I believe it has been good for the rivalry. From 1948 thru 1987, tickets were split evenly, half for Auburn and half for Alabama. That meant every play was a big down. A one-yard gain would be just as big for the defense as a 15-yard gain would be for the offense. On every snap of the ball, one side of the stadium would be on its feet cheering.

Since 1988, the visiting team has been allotted 10,900 tickets and the home team keeps the rest. That means more Auburn fans will see the game in odd years and more Alabama fans will see it in even years. That's good for the fans and for the game.

Moving the game to Auburn has also been good — good for Auburn and good for the rivalry. When you visit the other team's campus, you can't help but have a greater appreciation of the other school and its fans.

I've been a part of 21 Auburn-Alabama games, nine as an assistant coach at Alabama and 12 as head coach at Auburn, and I know, from having been on both sides, there's nothing quite like an Auburn-Alabama football game. It has always been special and it always will be. It certainly gets the blood running.

ACKNOWLEDGEMENT

We want to thank David Housel and the Auburn Athletic Department for their generous cooperation and support in the publication of this Special War Eagle Edition of "Braggin' Rights."

INTRODUCTION

By Coach Terry Bowden

Even though I grew up in the state of Alabama, the 1993 game was my first Auburn-Alabama game. I had grown up following the rivalry, but was always too busy watching my father's team or coaching my own to attend any of the Auburn-Alabama games.

When I became head coach at Auburn, people on both sides told me that there was absolutely nothing like an Auburn-Alabama game and that I had better be prepared for the experience of my life when Alabama came to Auburn on November 19.

I thought about that as the season progressed, but to be honest, we were wrapped up in trying to be as good as we could be every week, I really didn't think about Alabama that much until the end of the season.

Normally the campers and fans don't begin arriving until Thursday. That week, however, they began pulling in on Tuesday. By Wednesday afternoon, the camper lot was virtually full and fans were everywhere. I began to realize then what people were talking about when they said the Auburn-Alabama game was special.

By Friday, the excitement and emotion were so intense you could almost reach out and touch it. We had to take the team out of town on Friday to keep the players from getting too involved with the emotional aspect of the game.

The Tiger Walk was special the entire year, but before the Alabama game, it was almost unbelievable. Our players had to walk single file down the street from Sewell Hall to the stadium. I've never seen so many people ready to play a football game. There must have been 30,000 people lining the street shouting encouragement to our team.

We played well, and with the tremendous support of our fans, the Auburn people, we were able to come back and defeat the defending national champions 22-14 and finish the season with a perfect 11-0 record.

SERIES WIN NO. 1 — This photograph of the Auburn football team was taken in February 1893, following its first win over Alabama. The game was Auburn's fifth all-time gridiron fray and third victory. The three wins had been over Georgia, Georgia Tech and Alabama, and that fact is noted on the football being held by Tom Daniels. The inscription reads: "93 Champions Ala. & Ga." Also notice the cup that team manager W.F. Feagin (in suit and tie) is holding on his knee. It is the silver cup (inset) presented to Auburn in Birmingham in honor of its 32-22 victory over Alabama.

First row—Rufus Dorsey, Coach G.H. Harvey, W.R. Shafer and Feagin.
Second row—Robert Foy, L. Buckalew, A.F. McKissick, J.C. Durham, Tom Daniels, J.V. Brown, S.A. Redding and W.M. Riggs.
Back row—D. Wills, R.M. Stevens, Loveless, Shackelford and A.V. Herren.
This photograph was taken on the steps of Samford Hall, then only five years old. (Photo courtesy of Auburn University Archives)

1893
GAME 1

"Remember The Victory That You Have Won This Day"

On Wednesday morning, February 22, 1893, the *Birmingham News* posed these three questions to its sportsminded readers:

"Do you play football?"

"Do you understand the game?"

"Did you ever see a game played?"

"These and a number of other questions are asked daily," continued the story, "for Birmingham is absorbed in the great contest, which is to come off at Lakeview Park this afternoon between the students of Alabama's two great rival seats of learning.

"It's not merely of local interest, but the whole State has its eyes turned to Birmingham and is eagerly awaiting to learn who will be the vanquishers.

"Never before was there such enthusiasm over an athletic contest in the State."

There was definitely cause for excitement. After all, it was the day of the big game, the day Auburn and Alabama would come face to face for the very first time on the gridiron. And to show the importance attached to the gala event, it was scheduled on George

Alabama's 1893 team that lost to Auburn in series' first game. 1-Abbott, 2-Bayle, 3-Mgr. Bush, 4-Pratt, 5-Coach Beaumont, 6-Cape, 7-Smith, 8-Savage, 9-Bankhead, 10-Little, 11-Henderson, 12-Grayson, 13-McCants, 14-Walker, 15-Frazer, 16-Ferguson, 17-Kyser. (Photo courtesy University of Alabama Archives)

Washington's birthday, which in 1893 was allowed to fall on Wednesday, February 22nd, where it belonged.

The game was also an early indication that, no matter how small the detail, Auburn and Alabama agreed only on one thing—to disagree. Auburn's football records indicate the game was the 1893 season opener, while Alabama considers the meeting the final game on its 1892 schedule.

Either way, the two schools wasted little time during their football infancy to "get with it." Auburn wanted some of Alabama; Alabama wanted a piece of Auburn.

Auburn was serious enough about the date that it hired a "big-time Eastern coach" just for this one game. F. M. Balliet, a former University of Pennsylvania player who was living in that state, was contacted and asked to come and coach the squad against a rival never before met. Balliet accepted, hopped a Southbound train and headed for the small village located in East Alabama.

Auburn had played its first football game a year earlier (February 20, 1892) in Atlanta, and defeated the University of Georgia, 10-0, launching the South's oldest gridiron series. It would be nine months before Auburn played again; but they more than made up for the long layoff by scheduling three games within a four-day period—all in Atlanta. On November 22, the Orange and Blue lost their first football game ever, 34-6 to Trinity, now Duke University. The next day, Auburn met North Carolina and suffered the most lopsided defeat in the school's history—64-0. After a day's rest, the Auburn boys were at it again, and rebounded with a 26-0 victory over Georgia Tech. This latter game was the beginning of the second longest rivalry in the South.

When it came time to face Alabama for the first time, Auburn's brief football history showed an even split in its four games—two wins and two losses.

Football at Alabama had begun just three months before the initial confrontation with Auburn. "Tuskaloosa," as the press often called the team back in those days, thumped a Birmingham high school team, 56-0, on November 11 at Lakeview Park and football at the University of Alabama was on its way.

Twenty-four hours later, the college lads were back on the field, ready for a game against the Birmingham Athletic Club. In 1893, a touchdown was worth four points, a conversion two points, and a field goal five points. The University lost 5-4, on a phenomenal 65-yard goal by J.P. Ross just before the end of the game. The field goal was listed as a collegiate record at one time and Birmingham newspapers of that time featured its distance in accounts of the game.

A month later, revenge came in the form of a 14-0 win against this same Athletic Club. That brought Alabama to its date with Auburn, and the University's three game football history showed two wins against one loss.

Auburn had played all of its games in Atlanta; Alabama had played nowhere but in Birmingham.

At 10 o'clock that morning many years ago, the Alabama crowd, which numbered a reported 220, arrived at the train station in Birmingham. "There were 150 students," the *News* correspondent wrote, "and they filed out in their bright uniforms. They were as handsome a lot of young fellows as ever trod the depot platform."

According to the reporter, Auburn brought along six more fans than Alabama.

"The athletes from the Druid City had scarcely gotten out of the station when the special from Auburn rolled in with 226 lovers of the

Auburn's J.C. Dunham was the first ball carrier in the series.

Auburn's Rufus Dorsey scored the first touchdown in the series.

Frank Savage scored the first touchdown for Alabama in the series.

'pig skin' aboard. There were fully 100 cadets aboard, and as they lined up on the platform they presented a handsome appearance. Having been cooped up in the coach for several hours, they stretched themselves and crowed out quite lustily the clarion notes of their college call."

No, there were no "Roll Tide" or "War Eagle" cries that day. Those famous yells would come later.

The *News* reporter undoubtedly had an eye for the girls. He noticed that the lassies had not been left behind. "It is hard to decide which of the colleges had the prettiest young women to wear their colors. Both Universities brought a charming lot of young ladies with them . . . Miss Delma Wilson, one of Birmingham's most charming young women, will present the trophy to the victors this afternoon at the grounds. Miss Wilson has selected as her Maids of Honor, Miss Sara Regan, who wears Auburn colors, and Miss Mamie Morrow, who wears those of Tuskaloosa."

The Caldwell Hotel headquartered Alabama's followers, while the Auburn entourage was housed at the Florence Hotel. Both buildings were draped in the colors of their guests. It was also reported that many of the merchants decorated their store fronts, and residents their homes, with the colors of the day — crimson and white and orange and blue.

At the depot, other football specials continued to arrive from Montgomery, Selma, Anniston, Eufaula and many other points in the State.

By 2 o'clock, the whole city was on the move. Quoting from the *News*, "Every private vehicle, stable turn out, and public hack was filled with people on the way to Lakeview Park. The dummies and electric cars were crowded with lovers of the manly sport of football. Men and women who heretofore have jeered at such exhibitions of brawn and muscle were eager to see the contest. Little children just beginning to tottle about were anxious to see the big boys fight. Every train which arrived at the station brought in football enthusiasts from all parts of the State, and there were a thousand visitors in the city. All came to see the great game.

"The crush around the ticket window (notice — ONE window) was simply fearful, as the crowd was too big to be handled by one man, and tickets had to be sold on the inside. The vast surging throng kept its temper and the women took being jostled about good naturedly . . . As soon as the crowd got on the inside the men unaccompanied by ladies made a rush for both sides of the grounds and soon were ranged a dozen deep around the ropes, which were put up around the grid-iron . . . The East side of the field had been set apart for carriages, and soon from one end to the other it was filled with vehicles of all descriptions gaily decorated in blue and gold and white and red.

"Both the grandstands were literally packed with people, making a most artistic picture as the colors of the schools in conjunction with the many-hued costumes of the women blended artistically... The bleachers were filled with as jolly a lot of men as ever sat on hard planks, and from their faces and their merry talk, it was evident that they had come out to make a happy afternoon of it."

At 3 o'clock, the teams entered the playing field for warm-ups. Alabama appeared first, dressed in solid white uniforms, red stockings and a large red "U of A" on its sweaters.

Moments later, here came Auburn, decked out in blue sweaters with an orange "A", white pants and blue stockings.

It was reported that the 2,000 people in attendance went absolutely wild with excitement. Alabama "shouted themselves hoarse," while Auburn "yelled until they were 'blue' in the face."

At 3:30, the big crowd quieted down a bit as both teams, warm-ups completed, went to their respective sidelines. With the toss of the coin and the kickoff just moments away, the fans realized that all of their pre-game whooping and hollering and banner waving and bragging suddenly meant nothing. Now, it was up to the boys on the field.

And the boys on the field showed off with a dazzling display of offensive know-how, with Auburn coming out on top in a high-scoring affair, 32-22.

The first "braggin' rights" championship was draped in Orange and Blue.

One has to remember that in 1893, the forward pass was still about 15 years away. In that era of ground-pounding football it was virtually unheard of for a losing team to score as many as 22 points. It would be 52 years later before Alabama registered that many points in a losing cause; 73 years for Auburn.

THE GAME

Team captains, fullback Tom Daniels of Auburn, and guard W. G. Little of Alabama, met at midfield. The coin toss went in favor of Auburn, and they wanted the football. Alabama chose to defend the South goal.

Even though the old *Birmingham Age-Herald* recorded a rather detailed play-by-play of that first game, there was no mention of who fielded the opening kickoff. However, the ball was brought out to the Auburn 46-yard line. On first down, according to the *Age-Herald*, "A flying wedge was formed and the ball was passed (snapped) to J. C. Dunham, who makes a gain of 10 yards."

Dunham, then, was the first ball carrier from scrimmage in the Auburn-Alabama football series. The whole swinging thing had started.

That placed the ball on Alabama's 54-yard line (a football field measured 110 yards in 1893.) On the next play, Shackelford rambled for another 10 yards. W. M. Riggs was stopped for no gain, but S. A. Redding and L. Buckalew each picked up five yards, and another first down, at Alabama's 34. (According to the rules, a team got only three downs to gain 10 yards.) Rufus Dorsey slammed to the 24, and Buckalew bucked to the 19. Here, Alabama braced. They stopped thrusts by Dunham and Cape for no gain and took possession of the ball.

Eli Abbott could muster only one yard in two tries. Brockman Bankhead sliced a short punt of only 10 yards, and Auburn was in business at the Alabama 30-yard line. Dunham was stopped at the line before Redding ran for 10. Dorsey then broke through and raced the final 20 yards for the first score of the series. Daniels missed the conversion, but Auburn had grabbed a 4-0 lead. (In 1893 touchdowns counted four points; conversions two.)

Alabama came right back with a drive to Auburn's four-yard line. However, the golden opportunity for at least a tie game was fumbled away by William Walker.

After a six-yard run by Buckalew, Daniels darted 65 yards all the way to Alabama's 35. "Applause was deafening at this play, and the game was delayed a few moments as to clear the field of the crowd who began to get on the field," reported the *Age-Herald*. Nine plays later, Dorsey slipped in from the one for his second touchdown of the game. Again, Daniels' conversion was off target. Auburn now led, 8-0.

Alabama returned the ensuing kickoff out to its 51-yard line. Sparked by Walker's 12-yard run and Burr Ferguson's 15-yard gain, the Crimsons, in nine plays, banged down to Auburn's 10-yard line. From there, Frank Savage scored, and Alabama had its first touchdown against Auburn. Bankhead's conversion kick was perfect and the score was now 8-6.

But not for long. Auburn came right back down the field, and from the Alabama 25, Riggs ran around right end but was hemmed up very near the goal. No problem. He lateraled the ball to Shackelford, who scored. Daniels, this time, made the conversion and Auburn

Birmingham Age-Herald, Feb. 23, 1893. The first Alabama-Auburn game was front page news.

was out front, 14-6.

With about three minutes left before intermission, Alabama got back in the game with its second touchdown. D. H. Smith registered on a 20-yard run, and G. H. Kyser's kick was good. The Crimsons trailed, but again by only two points, 14-12.

Auburn was at it again, but the whistle blowing the first half to a close stopped them. Halftime score: Auburn 14, Alabama 12.

Alabama took the second-half kickoff and was on the move when disaster struck. On a line buck, the ball popped right in the hands of Auburn's Dorsey, who sped 65 yards for his third touchdown of the game. Daniels was good on the conversion and it was now 20-12.

There was no rest. On Auburn's next series, a fumble gave Alabama the ball at the enemy 35. In just one play, Little covered the distance on a scoring run. Kyser's successful conversion made it 20-18.

The Orange and Blue then blew open the close contest. Daniels recorded two touchdowns, kicked both conversions and suddenly Auburn had a 32-18 advantage.

Late in the game, Smith scored his second touchdown of the day, Kyser missed the conversion, and the final score of the first series game was posted: Auburn 32, Alabama 22.

Reported the *News*, "A marked feature of the playing was almost a total lack of punting on each side. The game was an offensive one as neither side cared to be on the defensive . . . The reason the Auburn team never punted was the fact that they found they could make better gains by runs . . . Auburn snapped the ball quicker than Tuskaloosa, as Balliet, their coach, put them on this method, which is very swift . . . Goal kicking on both sides was good, but Tuskaloosa's was the best."

As for Coach Balliet, he soon departed and left a unique record in Auburn football history—the only coach with a perfect record—one win, no losses and no ties. That's 1.000.

The *News* story continued, "As the boys would pile up on one another the ladies would get alarmed, fearing that they would have their bones broken, but their gentlemen friends would kindly assure the timid sympathetic women that the athletic youths could have been dropped from the top of the grand stand to the ground without sustaining any injury."

Individual efforts were also recorded, and the *News'* scribe typed this about some of Auburn's standouts: "Redding was a fine tackler. As a running tackler he had no superior in the South . . . Brown's work did much towards the defeat of the Tuskaloosa boys . . . Dunham had only two days practice, but no one would have ever

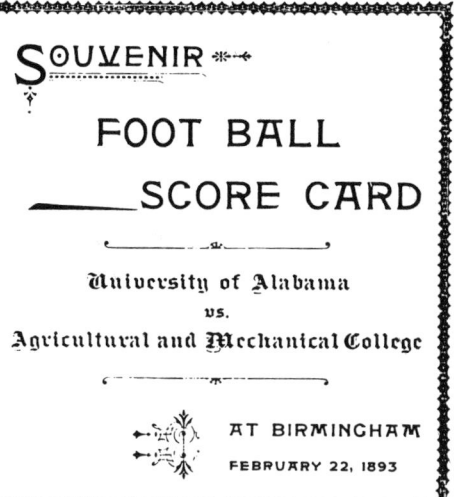
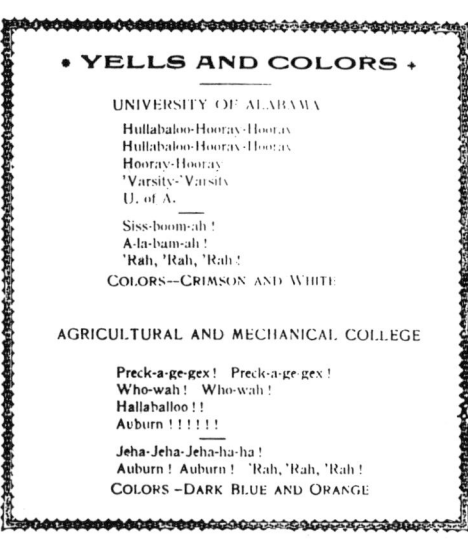

David Rosenblatt, Auburn University Department of Archives, recently discovered this rare memorabilia—the game program from the first Auburn-Alabama meeting in 1893. Notice the notes opposite Auburn's roster. Smith H. (Harry) was scratched from the game because he was "sick." Auburn's team, according to the notes, consisted of three Sigma Nu fraternity members, three Kappa Alphas, two Phi Delta Thetas and one Kappa Sigma. Also notice that, back in those days, linemen were listed as "rushers."

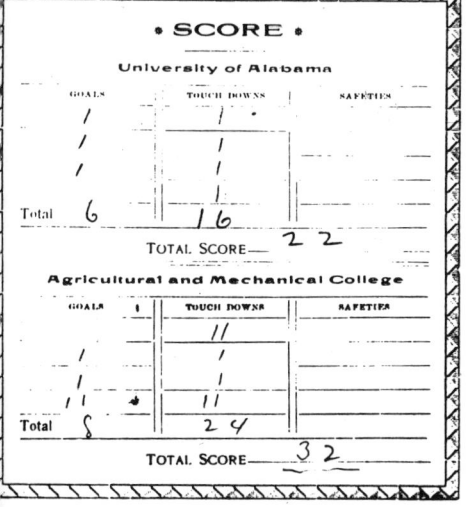
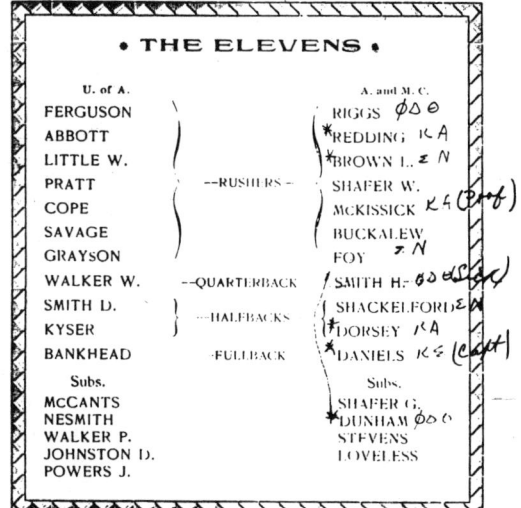

known it by his playing ... Daniels, the Captain, was simply a phenomenon. He played everywhere and is a brilliant runner, tackler and is very tricky."

Some of the Alabama players also impressed the reporter: "Abbott excels in rushing, and is hard to down on the run. He is Tuskaloosa's best all-round player ... Little, the Captain, has no superior in holding the line. He is good-natured, keeps his temper and does good head work ... Ferguson caught the crowd by his hard playing. When he tackled Daniels and threw him, every woman who wore red and white, wanted to kiss him ... Smith is as fleet as a deer and is one of the best ground gainers on the team."

Auburn operated from the T-formation as far back as 1893 as this old photograph shows. Notice the nose guards (or face masks) that the fullback and right halfback are wearing. This picture was taken on the playing field behind Samford Hall. Langdon Hall is under construction. (Photo courtesy of Auburn University Archives)

AUBURN WON!

BLUE AND GOLD WERE THE WINNING COLORS.

Tuskaloosa Fought Desperately, But Auburn Was the Strongest, and Won by 32 to 22.

IT WAS A GLORIOUS STRUGGLE

The Montgomery Advertiser

After the game, Captain Daniels and the Auburn team gathered around the Misses Wilson, Regan and Morrow for the presentation of the cup. As Miss Wilson gave the trophy to Daniels, she was quoted as saying, "Gallant and victorious Captain, in the name of the City of Birmingham, I present this cup. Drink from it, and remember the victory that you have won this day."

The *News* reported, "A series of cheers rent the air, and then the sun went down, blotting out the day on which the greatest football game was ever played in the State of Alabama."

It was perhaps unwitting, but the *Age-Herald* reporter, looking at the day's end, injected a partisan tone in his report. He wrote: "The sky had a gold tint at sunset in honor of Auburn."

The cup that was presented to the winning team back in 1893 is alive and well and is today resting in Auburn's athletic trophy case but whatever happened to Delma and Sarah and Mamie?

1893
GAME 2

"If You Can't Discuss Football, You Are Simply Not In It"

The City of Montgomery offered a $600 bonus for Auburn and Alabama to divide if they would agree to play the series' second game in the State Capital. Both teams agreed, and the contest was scheduled for the last day of November, at Riverside Park.

A reporter from the *Daily Advertiser* wrote this about the game day: "The day dawned dark. Up to 9 o'clock the fog was heavy and the sky indicated rain with its leaden hue. It did seem that the day was going to be disagreeable and a sad disappointment to all. However, as it advanced, the mist began to clear away and the sky to grow bright.

"About noon 'Old Sol', for the first time, made his appearance in splendor and warmth. From then on he showed himself much to the delight of the thousands who were anxious to witness the game at the park."

The Auburn special arrived at 10:30, and it was reported that the Orange and Blue players and fans were not at all timid in their cheering. The women who were brought along "added zest to the party."

At 12:40, the Alabama team pulled in, and as they filed from their special, they were greeted by the Auburn boys, who shouted their yells with the greatest of vigor. In response, the Bama boys began to cheer with just as much force and noise.

After topping Alabama back in February, autumn rolled around and Auburn cracked Vanderbilt 30-10, and fought Sewanee to a 14-14 tie. Both Tennesee teams were Southern supers back in the Gay Nineties. Auburn, then, was unbeaten (2-0-1) when they readied themselves for Alabama.

The Crimsons meanwhile came to their second meeting with Auburn winless. They had been beaten twice by the Birmingham Athletic Club, 4-0 and 10-8, and by Sewanee, 20-0.

As did Birmingham, Montgomery worked itself into a frenzy over the big game.

An *Advertiser* reporter wrote, "The streets were now lined with people moving up and down in restless, aimless wandering ... Everybody had either red and white or orange and blue streamers to show which was his or her feelings ... Buggies filled with bevies of pretty girls and parties of boys rushed between Union Station and The Square, their gaudy college colors fluttering in the wind."

The crowd began to make its way toward the park. "The grandstand was well filled and the railing about the gridiron was crowded five or six deep to say nothing of the hundreds of vehicles that brought up the background," reported the *Daily Advertiser.*

Finally it was game time; time to play ball.

As it turned out, it didn't really seem to matter whether Auburn and Alabama met in Birmingham or Montgomery, because not only did Auburn make it two straight over their Tuscaloosa rivals, but they had defeated Alabama for the second time in 1893, as well. The Orange and Blue, led by the runs and conversion kicks of team Captain Rufus Dorsey, routed the Crimson, 40-16.

Auburn took an early advantage by winning the toss of the coin and receiving the opening kickoff at 2:56 in the afternon. They drove the ball down close to the Alabama goal, but fumbled. Tuscaloosa recovered and rammed it out to the 34-yard line before a fumble lost the team eight yards and possession.

Auburn then called upon four different running backs for one carry each, and the plan resulted in a quick touchdown. Snow Perkins popped for five yards to the Alabama 21; Arthur Redding then ran for three; Robert Foy battled for eight more, and Dorsey darted around right end from the 10-yard line to a score. Dorsey kicked the goal, and Auburn grabbed an early 6-0 lead.

Alabama took the ensuing kickoff and marched right in for a score, with J. I. Burgett covering the final 35 yards. G. H. Kyser's conversion was no good, and the Tuscaloosa team trailed, 6-4.

Auburn bounced right back when J. C. Dunham went in for a touchdown. Dorsey's kick made it 12-4.

Alabama took the kickoff but fumbled on its own 52-yard line. After recovering, Auburn put on a 10-play drive that registered two touchdowns—neither counted. Auburn was penalized both times because of a forward pass, and the forward pass was an illegal play in 1893.

Alabama then took over but was forced to punt. Auburn stormed down the field and scored again, with Dunham recording his second touchdown of the day. Dorsey was perfect with his third placement to make it 18-4 late in the first half. (1893 rules called for two, 30-minute halves.)

Alabama received the second-half kickoff and rammed it home for a score. M. P. Walker made the touchdown and Kyser kicked the goal. Auburn 18, Alabama, 10.

Soon after the Alabama score, Auburn was on the attack again with a Perkins scoring run, plus another Dorsey conversion. Auburn's next possession led to a Redding touchdown. The conversion by Dorsey was missed, but Auburn still had a commanding lead of 28-10. The score mounted to 34-10 on J. V. Brown's 10-yard run and Dorsey's conversion.

Later in the game, the two teams traded touchdowns. Alabama's David Grayson tallied on a 45-yard run, and Kyser's placement made the score 34-16. Auburn quickly retaliated with the use of successful "flying wedge" and "Pennsylvania interference" plays and scored its seventh touchdown of the game. Dorsey made the four-pointer, along with his sixth conversion, giving him a personal game total of 20 points.

Alumni of both colleges had purchased a handsome trophy for the victors, and the prize belonged to Auburn. Governor Jones presented it to team Captain Dorsey, and the winners gave out a mighty cheer.

Auburn had its second straight conquest of Alabama, with a combined score of 78-38, and it was reported that the Orange and Blue whooped it up in grand style for the remainder of their stay in the State Capital City.

In those early and sometimes informal days of college football, there were no organized conferences or official championships. Yet the Auburn team declared themselves the 1893 Southern Champions. Their logic for this declaration was that they had handed Vanderbilt its only loss of the year, and Vanderbilt had defeated Sewanee twice, while Auburn and Sewanee had tied.

What better reasons were there for Auburn not to be champs?

As for the $600 pot Montgomery was to give the two colleges, losing Alabama got $350, and winning Auburn received $250. Newspaper accounts gave no reasons why the money wasn't split equally, although a possible explanation is that the Tuscaloosa team had a greater distance to travel in order to reach Montgomery.

Some of the *Daily Advertiser's* post-game comments were: "Redding (Auburn fullback) strikes the line like a cyclone . . . The sympathies of the crowd were nearly equally divided . . . Dunham (Auburn quarterback) plays like an accurate machine . . . The livery stables had every rig and horse available hired out . . . Lots of sweet and pretty girls were out in all their glory . . . Glenn (Auburn guard) weeded a wide row . . . The ribbon clerks did a rushing business."

But the one in particular that best expresses the mood of that day and time was, "If you can't discuss football, you are simply not in it."

1894

GAME 3

No, You Can't Play

The 1894 game produced the first official gripe of the series. It came from Auburn. The Orange and Blue issued a pre-game protest that four of Alabama's better players were not students of that school and that the Auburn people fully expected those four not to play.

Two of the athletes in question—Eli Abbott and J. E. Shelly—were allowed to participate and this duo scored all three touchdowns, as Alabama posted its first series victory by a score of 18-0. The game was played at Riverside Park in Montgomery on Thanksgiving Day before 3,000 lovers of the game.

There was considerable talk in Montgomery on game day about Alabama using outsiders, or "ringers". Team managers, Mr. Dewberry of Alabama and Mr. Riggs of Auburn, met that morning to discuss the controversy.

The *Montgomery Advertiser* reported, "It was understood by manager Riggs that Alabama would play Kirkpatrick and Devin, both well-known players from the University of North Carolina. Manager Dewberry understood that Auburn would play Hall of Pennsylvania, and Dorsey of last year's Auburn team, neither of whom is a member of the current team."

Auburn also objected to Abbott (Alabama's coach from 1893-1895) and Shelley as members of the Crimson and White playing squad.

Kirkpatrick, Devin, Hall and Dorsey presented certificates, signed by the Presidents of their respective colleges, stating that they were bona fide students. Even so, they were not allowed to play. For reasons never explained, Abbott and Shelley were permitted to participate, and this promoted the official protest from Auburn, which was in the form of a letter to the Editor of the *Montgomery Advertiser*.

The letter read as follows:

We, the college football team of the A. and M. College of Alabama, do hereby protest against the following men of the University team in view of the fact that they are not bona fide students, but are grown men who have been out of school and have engaged in regular business for several years—Abbott and Shelley—and under the circumstances we play the game under protest.

W. M. Riggs, Manager
James V. Brown, Captain

The raging controversy, although, did little to dampen the spirit and enthusiasm of the locals and out-of-towners who wanted to see the big game.

Auburn opened its 1894 season with a 20-4 loss to Vanderbilt. Their next game still remains in the gridiron record books of Georgia Tech as well as Auburn. The Orange and Blue crushed Tech, 94-0, and that score represents Auburn's largest victory margin ever, as well as Tech's all-time worst defeat. Auburn's third game of the season was a disappointing 10-8 loss to Georgia. Alabama was next.

In their season opener, the Crimsons had journeyed outside the State for the first time and lost, 6-0, to Mississippi in Jackson. The defeat was Alabama's sixth straight, and it would be 61 years before a streak of that nature would occur again for an Alabama football team. They went on to top Tulane 18-6, and Sewanee 24-4. Auburn was next.

On the day of the contest, the *Advertiser* reported, "Early in the morning the streets began to take on life. As the day advanced, activity became more marked . . . The weather could not have been more favorable. It did seem that the Almighty had recognized the significance of the Day of Thanksgiving and favored His people with a type weather that made every soul happy. The day was cloudless. Not a semblance of a frown was seen on the face of the sky. As to

The 1894 Alabama team that notched the school's first win over Auburn, 18-0. First row: Walker and McCants. Second row: Mgr. Dewberry (standing), Peter, Cahalan, Devin (Coach), Dew and Bankhead. Third row: Nesmith, Abbott, Slone, Thompson, Burr and McIntosh. Back row: Davis, Pratt, Kirkpatrick (Coach) and Shelly. (Photo courtesy of University of Alabama Archives)

the atmosphere, it was just cool enough for an overcoat to make one comfortable."

The story continued, "At 10 o'clock the crowds began to congregate at the Union Station to meet the special trains bearing Auburn and Tuscaloosa. . . . As early as 1 o'clock the people started to make their way to Riverside Park, the place for the battle. They went out in gaudily decked vehicles, horseback, on the electric cars and afoot."

At 3 o'clock, Auburn's J. C. Dunham kicked off to Samuel Slone and the third game of the series was underway. The contest quickly settled into one of short plunges, fumbles and kicks. Possession of the ball changed rapidly, as in the first half alone, Alabama had 10 chances and Auburn nine.

Just before intermission, Shelly went over from short range and the scoreless tie had been broken. "At this point," reported the *Advertiser*, "the Alabama 'vocators' went wild. Hats and sticks tied with crimson and white streamers, found local habitation in the crisp atmosphere. Shelly was the hero . . . order was finally restored and (Allen) McCants kicked the goal." The score was 6-0, and Alabama had its first lead ever over Auburn in a football game.

Alabama kicked off to start the second half and soon recovered a fumble about midfield. A penalty of five yards and a run that lost two more momentarily set the Crimson back. However, M. F. Callahan got off a stunning run of 45 yards to Auburn's three-yard line. Abbott scored from there, and after McCants' conversion, the score became 12-0.

One particular play in the second half caught the ears of an *Advertiser* reporter and he wrote, "The loud crack of two heads (helmets were not yet in use) coming in contact was heard in the scrimmage. It was a fearful sound and was the craniums of Abbott and Harvey. No damage resulted, other than the shaking up of their brains, possibly."

As the game progressed, Auburn just couldn't get untracked and never seriously threatened the Alabama goal line. With five minutes left to play, the Tuscaloosa boys added their final touchdown of the day on a dazzling 75-yard run by Abbott. McCants added his third conversion and the final score was posted: Alabama 18, Auburn 0.

The series now stood 2-1-0 in Auburn's favor and the Orange and Blue had out-scored Alabama, 72-56.

The public wasted no time in discovering the potential of this new game of football as an occasion for wagering. "There was considerable betting on the game and much money changed hands after the contest," reported the *Advertiser.* "Alabama was the favorite. Odds were offered on that team, but found a limited number of takers. Some even money was put up. The biggest registered during the day was $100 to $60 on Alabama. The betting, of course, was done on the quiet."

As for Auburn's gripe, a reporter for the *Advertiser* observed, "It is a noticeable fact that the two men who did the best playing for Tuscaloosa—Abbott and Shelly—are the very men against whom Auburn entered her protest . . . The Auburn men wish it to be distinctly understood that they played a regular college team."

Thus, the Alabama-Auburn football series had seen its first major disagreement.

There would be more.

Today's Heisman Trophy is named for this man. A confident, young John Wilhelm Heisman shown as Auburn's coach in 1895, and in his later years at the helm at Georgia Tech.

1895
GAME 4

The Heisman Comes To Auburn

Auburn became the fourth stop on the coaching circuit of the man for whom today's Heisman Trophy is named—John Wilhelm Heisman. After Heisman's collegiate playing days at Brown and Pennsylvania, he coached at Oberlin in 1892, Buchtel in 1893, and again at Oberlin in 1894. From there he headed South for Auburn.

Heisman would stay at the Polytechnic Institute for five years (1895-99) before packing his bags for Clemson and a four-year stint. He then bid farewell to the South Carolina countryside and moved to Atlanta and Georgia Tech. There, Heisman would retire from coaching in 1919, after 16 years at the Tech helm.

By 1905, because of deaths and serious injuries, the game of football came very close to being abolished in the United States. Numerous rule changes, many the ideas of Heisman himself, were adopted in 1906 and the game was given a fresh breath.

Football historians have written that it was only because of Heisman's influence and innovations that the game survived and developed into the immensely popular participant and spectator sport it is today.

Heisman arrived as Auburn's fourth coach in the school's three-year football history. Even though he lost his first game, 9-6, to a strong Vanderbilt team, this stern intellectual wasted no time in pointing Auburn's football program in the right direction. But that was nothing exceptional for this man.

Heisman's second game was against a winless Alabama eleven that had managed only two touchdowns in games against Georgia, Tulane and LSU. Heisman continued Alabama's winless streak, as Auburn exploded for a 48-0 victory.

When November 23 and the time for the fourth game of the series arrived, neither team had won a game.

Throughout Heisman's coaching career, he was never bashful about bashing the opposition. When he had an opportunity to pile up the points, he did. Later in his career, he was on the winning side (in 1916) of college football's most famous score: Georgia Tech 222, Cumberland 0. Today's Auburn fans often take exception to that score as being "most famous." Some will argue that college football's most famous score is 17-16 (1972). Others pick 14-13 (1949) for this distinction.

The *Birmingham News* had this to say about the 1895 game, "It was apparent to the spectators that when the two teams came on the field, Auburn greatly outclassed the University team in the matter of size and when the playing began it was a battle of seasoned veterans against fresh recruits. The University boys put up a plucky game, but it was to no avail. . . . Auburn drove through the University line for touchdown after touchdown."

The game was played in Tuscaloosa, and even though the hometown Crimsons got crushed, nobody could accuse the hosts of being spoilsports. The *News* said, "The University boys gave a brilliant hop in the red 'Mess Hall' in honor of their victorious rivals. In the elaborate decorations of the hall, the Orange and Blue of the visitors was as much in evidence as the Crimson and White of the home team."

The Birmingham, Montgomery and Tuscaloosa newspapers had only brief accounts and no details or statistics on the game. The *Mobile Register* gave generous coverage to the Yale-Princeton and Penn-Harvard games, but failed even to mention the Alabama-Auburn game.

Other than newspaper clippings, the Athletic Departments of Auburn and Alabama have no details of that particular game. Lost forever, then are the names of the Auburn players who scored those 48 points against Alabama back in 1895.

Auburn later defeated Georgia, 16-6, to finish the season with a 2-1-0 record. Alabama was 0-4-0. The Orange and Blue now led the series 3-1-0, and had outscored its intrastate rivals, 120-56.

The Auburn team that defeated Alabama 48-0 in 1895.

Even though no specific reason was given, it took the two teams only four games to disagree on agreeing to play each other. It would be five long years before another Alabama-Auburn game would come off.

Heisman left Auburn in 1899. His trophy would return 72 years later.

The Crimson=White.

VOL. VIII. University of Alabama, November 29, 1900. No. 5

Alabama Defeated

FORMAN SCORES ONE TOUCHDOWN FOR 'VARSITY.

Auburn's Line Crossed for the First Time This Year, at Montgomery.

1900
GAME 5

Mercy

The last time Auburn and Alabama had met, the Orange and Blue won by a 48-0 score. Five years later they met again, and even though the score wasn't the same, Auburn's margin of victory was. This time it was 53-5, in a game played at Riverside Park in Montgomery on November 17.

The winners unleashed three backs who galloped and pranced up and down the football field all afternoon. F. R. Yarbrough carried the ball 20 times and piled up a phenomenal 308 yards; W. L. Noll rushed for 203 yards in 21 attempts, and Thomas, in 10 snaps, gained 105 yards. If that wasn't enough, four other Auburn players registered 19 yards in eight cracks. Those totals—635 yards in 50 rushes—averaged out at almost 13 yards per try.

Noll and Yarbrough scored three touchdowns each. Yarbrough also added eight conversions for a total of 25 points, and his feat is still on the book as a series record for one game.

Based on today's scoring system, the 1900 game would have ended 61-6. During the five-year period the intrastate rivals had decided to "cool it", Alabama had performed under a different coach each season and had played only eight games, winning six and losing two. Six of the games were against athletic clubs from Birmingham, Tuscaloosa and New Orleans. In 1898, the school abolished football altogether and going into the 1900 game against Auburn, Alabama's all-time grid record stood at 11-13-0.

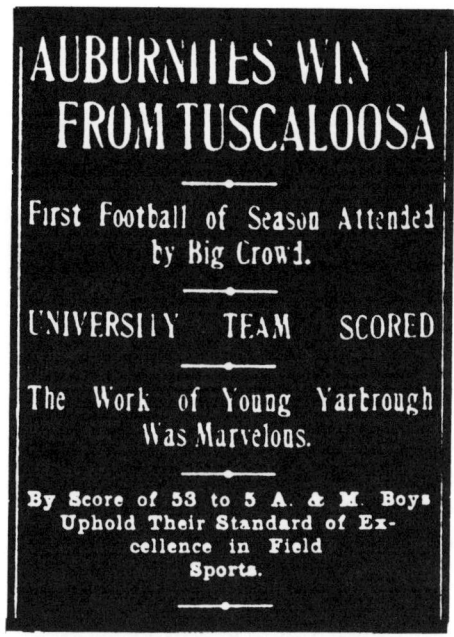

The Montgomery Advertiser

The same period saw Auburn, under Coach John Heisman, post a 12-4-2 record, and in the process amass a total of 440 points to only 95 for all opponents. The school's all-time record, going into the Alabama game stood at 18 wins, nine losses and four ties.

When time arrived for the fifth game of the series, Auburn was unbeaten and unscored upon after two games, having blanked the University of Nashville 28-0, and Tennessee 23-0. Following the thrashing of Alabama, Auburn closed the season with a 44-0 crushing of Georgia. Auburn had completed its first perfect season.

Alabama had a 2-1-0 record, with wins over Taylor School 35-0, Ole Miss 12-5, and a 6-0 loss to Tulane. After the Auburn mismatch, the Crimsons lost to Clemson 35-0. This was definitely a bleak era in Alabama football.

Auburn was the overwhelming favorite. "Of the Auburn team nothing need be said," reported the *Montgomery Advertiser.* "The people of Montgomery have seen them before, and it is sufficient to say that yesterday the brilliancy and dash of the team was kept up to the Auburn standard.... That college has been playing football for years and years and it has come to pass that Auburn ranks among the kingpins of the South in that line."

Alabama never had a chance.

Auburn kicked-off to open the game, forced a fumble and went 43 yards in six plays. Thomas scored from the six-yard line and Yarbrough kicked his first conversion to make it 6-0. The hammering had begun.

Soon, it was 12-0, and here is the way an *Advertiser* reporter saw the second touchdown. "The ball was given to Yarbrough again, and, like a whirlwind, he broke through the Crimson and White line and with the entire Tuscaloosa team at his heels, he flew past yard line after yard line of the gridiron until seventy-five of the chalked lines had been crossed. . . . Yarbrough then kicked his own goal, which he had won so brilliantly."

A few minutes later, Noll scored from seven yards out and Yarbrough's point-after made it 18-0. According to the *Advertiser*, "The Tuscaloosa contingent looked just a trifle weary, for it began to appear as if nothing could withstand the steady rushes and tremendous onslaughts of the team that Coach (Billy) Watkins had labored so hard and with so much success to make a winner."

A Noll run of eight yards, another Yarbrough PAT and the score was 24-0. But here, Alabama got on the scoreboard when J. R. Forman's 25-yard scamper to the two set up C. M. Plowman's touchdown burst. The conversion by W. E. Drennen was missed. Moments later, the first-half ended and the score was 24-5, Auburn.

In the second half, Yarbrough tallied on runs of seven and eight yards; Noll registered on a long 55-yarder; Sloan returned a punt 25 yards for another score, and Blevens scooted across from the three—all for Auburn.

The *Advertiser* reported, "The team work of Auburn was something beautiful. The men worked together like clockwork. This matter of teamwork is something that Tuscaloosa is a bit lacking in."

Auburn now had a 4-1-0 series lead, with 173 points to Alabama's 61.

1901
GAME 6

"AUBURN'S TIGERS
Win The Game From Alabama Team"

The above headline appeared in the *Birmingham News* on Saturday, November 16, 1901. Its significance is that it was the first time in the series that the Auburn football team was referred to as "Tigers," at least journalistically. Furthermore, it was only the second time that the press had used the nickname.

According to David Rosenblatt and Bill Sumners of the Auburn University Archives, who completed a study on this subject, in 1978, the first time the name "Tigers" appeared in a newspaper story was in the *Birmingham Age-Herald* on November 11, 1900, in describing a 23-0 Auburn victory over Tennessee.

"THE AUBURN TIGERS DEFEAT TENNESSEANS," read the headline.

Actually, the nickname "Tigers" goes back as far as 1895. Rosenblatt and Sumners discovered a "Yell Book" of that year, and included as one of the cheers was: "Who Rah, Rah! Who Rah, Rah! Rah! Rah! Tig-e-r! Auburn!"

As a result of the research by Rosenblatt and Sumners, it is their opinion that the name "Tigers" was never officially adopted as the Auburn symbol; rather, it slowly crept into use and was accepted.

But in 1895, someone (more than likely a student) writing yells for Auburn used the nickname "Tigers" among the school's cheers.

Another significant fact attached to the 1901 Auburn-Alabama game is that it almost didn't happen. An agreement to play wasn't

The Birmingham News

reached until the week the game was actually played. According to press accounts, Thomas Bragg, Auburn football manager, had been trying since summer to arrange a game with Alabama. However, the Crimsons would not make a commitment. Auburn accused Alabama of being afraid to play because of the previous year's 53-5 drubbing.

On Saturday, November 9, Georgia and Alabama met in Tuscaloosa and Bragg went to the game to try and work out a date with J. D. McQueen, manager of the Alabama team.

Bragg hand-delivered a letter to McQueen. It read, in part: *Last summer, I, as manager of the Auburn Football Team did all in my power to arrange for a date for the University team to meet Auburn. Auburn failed on every effort, but kept a date open for you until about the middle of October. . . . After we had suffered a severe defeat (44-0 to Vanderbilt), I received a letter from you begging for a game on any day, I think, between November 9 and November 16. . . . Auburn never selects weak teams to play. After we are defeated we always leave the field with a satisfaction that we played the best game we were capable of playing. . . . I would like very much to accommodate you by signing a contract this afternoon for a game on our campus, or on your campus. . . . There are only six dates left that we can accommodate you. . . . I hope that you will accept, or the public understand the real condition of affairs.*

Alabama had a game scheduled the following Saturday (November 16) in Tuscaloosa against Mississippi State, and for that reason could not accept Auburn's proposal. Also, Auburn had dates with LSU on November 23 and with Georgia on Thanksgiving Day, and the Auburn faculty would not permit a game after Thanksgiving.

This meant there were no weekend dates left for an Alabama-Auburn encounter.

After Georgia and Alabama battled to a scoreless tie (the first tie in Alabama's football history), McQueen wrote a letter and gave it to Bragg. The letter stated, . . . *your offer would force my team to play three games within seven days, as we have just met Georgia, and have another game on November 16. Of course, any one who has ever seen a game of football knows that no team can afford to play three games within so short a time. It is due to that fact, and not to any ducking down on our part that I have declined to meet Auburn.*

It is not known whether McQueen himself changed his mind, or whether it was changed for him. By University authorities? By alumni? Perhaps by the players themselves? In any event, on Monday, Alabama officially accepted Auburn's challenge and the game was scheduled to be played at Tuscaloosa in four days—on Friday, even though Alabama had a game the next day.

With that background the sixth game of the series was played, and as the headline reads, Auburn won "Seventeen to Nothing."

Considering the teams' records at game time, it seems unlikely that Auburn should wear the favorite's cloak. The Tigers had lost to Nashville University 23-5, plus that lopsided loss to Vanderbilt. Meanwhile, Alabama hadn't surrendered a point, thrashing Mississippi 41-0 and tying Georgia 0-0.

"Alabama had the best team they have had in years and had been extremely anxious to meet Auburn," reported the *News*. "When the Auburn boys arrived, however, it was seen that as a whole they considerably outweighed the University boys. This fear for Alabama

The Montgomery Advertiser headlining Alabama-Auburn activities in 1901.

NO GAME WITH AUBURN

TUSCALOOSA COULD NOT GIVE A SATISFACTORY DATE.

Letter from Aburn's Men Offering a Game and the Statement of Manager McQueen Explaining His Position.

For several months past an effort has been made to get a game between the Tuscaloosa and Auburn teams, and yesterday morning the climax was reached, the result being that there will be no game between the two institutions this season.

Sunday, November 10.

WILL MEET AFTER ALL

Date Offered Auburn by Tuscaloosa for Friday Inside Time Limit.

Tuesday, November 12.

NEWS OF THE SPORTS

AUBURN AND TUSCALOOSA MEET TODAY IN FOOTBALL.

Ruhlin and Jeffries Fight in San Francisco Tonight and Tomorrow Yale Meets Princeton on the Gridiron.

Friday, November 15.

TUSCALOOSA SCORED 0

WHILE AUBURN ROLLED UP 17 POINTS

Matt Sloan Makes First Two Touchdowns and Kicks Two Goals, Guinn Making 35-yard Run for Third Touchdown—Stickney Hurt

Saturday, November 16.

The old baseball and football field located on the quadrangle at the University of Alabama. Auburn and Alabama met here twice (1895 and 1901) in football with the visitors winning both times. This photo was taken in 1907 and is courtesy of U. of A. Archives.

was borne out when the game progressed. It seemed absolutely impossible for the Alabama boys to break the heavy line of the Auburn team."

Alabama did not get into Auburn's territory all day.

By intermission, the Orange and Blue had an 11-point lead—all resulting from two touchdowns by Matt Sloan, plus a Matt Sloan conversion. W. H. Guinn's 35-yard scoring run in the second half and Sloan's kick concluded the afternoon's scoring.

"The game was practically featureless," said the *News.* "It was steady work with the grim determination on the part of both teams to do the best they could. There were no trick plays and only once was there any attempt to slug. In the last half of the game, the alleged slugging of Parsons by an Auburn man, and a return slug by an Alabama man caused some excitement."

The disappointment of their defeat by Auburn apparently didn't linger too long with the Alabama boys, for the next day they wallopped Mississippi State 45-0. And Alabama had played three football games in a seven-day period and came out all even—one win, one loss and one tie. Two weeks later, the Crimsons and Tennessee fought to a 6-6 tie. Alabama was 2-1-2 for the season.

Auburn went on to defeat LSU 28-0, before ending the autumn with a 0-0 knot with Georgia, and a 2-2-1 record.

After their first decade of football competition, Auburn was 24-11-5; Alabama 15-17-2. In addition, Auburn held a 5-1-0 series advantage and had outscored Alabama, 190-61.

"You've come a long, long way, baby." Tennis and its dress on the Alabama campus in the early 1900's. As shown in the bottom photo, the old tennis court is long gone. (Top photograph courtesy of the University of Alabama Archives)

1902

GAME 7

Shop Hands Upset Votaries

Let's go back in time and allow a reporter of the *Birmingham News* to tell it as it was that autumn afternoon some 80 years ago. One of the headlines that accompanied his story read:

"BLACKSTONE VOTARIES
NEVER ENOUGH FOR
TECHNIC SHOP HANDS"

Before an expectant mass of 2,000 spectators gathered at West End Park Saturday afternoon, upon a neutral and fortified gridiron, the plucky tiger-clad eleven from the technic shops of the eastern Alabama hills administered a crushing and remorseless reverse to the Blackstone votaries from historic Tuscaloosa.

The Technic Shop Hands? The Blackstone Votaries? It's possible though that "Crimson Tide" and "War Eagles" would have sounded just as strange to that writer as his colorful nicknames sound three quarters of a century later.

In any event, Auburn beat Alabama and the final score was 23-0.

A case can be made for this 1902 game being regarded as the first bona fide "upset" in the series. Alabama had played two games before their duel with Auburn and the Crimsons had won by overwhelming scores of 57-0 and 81-0. Meanwhile, Auburn had met only one opponent and the winning margin of 18-6, while decisive, was far from impressive.

As the two teams came onto the gridiron that October 18 in Birmingham, the *News* reporter observed the pre-game feeling and wrote, "Greeted by the vibrating shouts of a thousand wearers of the Orange and Blue, the light Auburn team trotted upon the field

CRIMSON--WHITE LAID LOW BY AUBURN'S ORANGE AND BLUE

Blackstone Votaries Never Enough For Technic Shop Hands

REVERSE WAS CRUSHING.

Rooters From Historic Old University Saw Their Football Eleven Routed.

FAST LAYOUT FROM AUBURN.

The Birmingham News

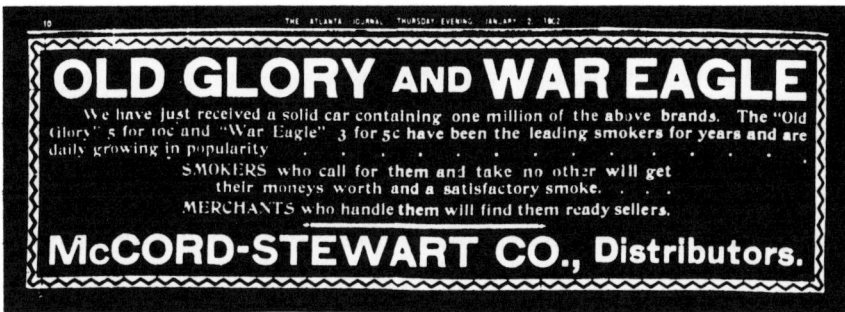

The *Atlanta Journal*—Jan. 2, 1902
"WAR EAGLE!" Nobody is really certain who originated this Auburn battle cry, or why, or when or where. There is one thing for certain, though, there was a War Eagle cigar as far back as 1902, and they sold three for a nickle in Atlanta in those days.

with confident action.... Later the University squad appeared amid inspiring ovations from every quarter of the field. They presented a heavy, towering aspect of brawn and strength that forbode certain defeat by the foxy kid opponents."

The question still remains, was it an upset? Alabama had piled up its 138 points against a Birmingham High School team, and a squad representing a tiny junior college from Marion, Alabama. Auburn had beaten Georgia Tech.

Auburn won the toss and elected to defend the west goal; Alabama wanted the football. Our friend from the *News* typed, "A sharp, quivering whistle rends the air and one second later the pigskin is trapped with a mighty force by (James) Webb of the Auburns and sent reeling through a parabola, falling and fumbled by a University man 35 yards from the center of the field."

The seventh game of the series had begun.

Alabama recovered its bobble on the kickoff, but fumbleitis had set in. On third down, the Crimsons dropped the ball again, and this time Auburn recovered at the 23-yard line. In four plays the Plainsmen worked it to Alabama's four, but quarterback Zac Smith fumbled and the University found it. Three plays later, though, it was Auburn's ball again as F. G. Sitckney fumbled at the 12.

That was a costly mistake for Alabama.

Ed Lacey hit two and four yards, and Webb rushed for five to the one-yard line. From there, H. A. Allison plunged over for a 5-0 lead. The conversion attempt, by Zac Smith, failed.

Five minutes before intermission, Auburn scored again. After taking a punt at the enemy 42, Webb went to the 40 and Lacey to the 32. Webb lost four, but came back for five. Then Lacey broke loose for 18 yards all the way to the Alabama 13-yard line. Allison took it to the 10, and Bill Patterson took it in. Smith's point-after was perfect and his team led, 11-0.

At the half, Auburn had operated 42 plays from scrimmage, while Alabama had run only 13.

Midway through the second half, Alabama reached Auburn's 29-yard line only to lose the ball on downs. Four plays later and Auburn had its third touchdown of the afternoon. The *News* reporter told how it happened: "Allison is sent through a wagon opening in Tuscaloosa's line, gives (J. R.) Forman an effective stiff arm and cleverly eludes (G. T.) McCorvey, sprinting down an open field for the longest and most spectacular run of the game, a touchdown over the measure of 75 yards. A tumultuous uproar follows and the rooters of the Orange and Blue are busied for five minutes collecting and readjusting their apparel."

After Smith's conversion, Auburn led 17-0. The *News* reporter wrote, "... (Alabama's) mouths were surreptitiously hushed and an equal number of waving colors lay damp with enthusiasm and drooping in desperate hopelessness."

Auburn's next possession resulted in another score—a 70-yard drive in 15 plays. The big gainers were a 20-yarder by Webb and a 10-yarder by T. A. Ward. Allison shot over from the two-yard line, his second touchdown of the game, and Smith's kick concluded the scoring.

The final 23-point difference could have been worse, considering that Auburn ran 78 plays, Alabama only 26.

Webb, with 125 yards in 22 carries, was the leading ground gainer, followed by Allison who had 118 yards in 19 attempts. Auburn rushed for 369 yards in all.

The Alabama-Auburn squabble was over for another year, but each team had five games remaining on their respective 1902 schedules.

Alabama, in order, lost to Georgia, beat Mississippi State, lost to Texas, beat Georgia Tech and lost to LSU. The Crimson finished the season 4-4-0.

Auburn managed only one touchdown in its final five games. There was a scoreless tie with Tulane and consecutive losses to LSU, Sewanee, Clemson and Georgia. The Tigers finished in 1902 with a 2-4-1 mark.

Considering the later developments of the 1902 season, perhaps it can be argued that the Technic Shop Hands' victory over the Blackstone Votaries was indeed the first upset of the series.

1903
Game 8

Upset No. 2

If Auburn's win over Alabama in 1902 was the first upset in the series, then by applying the same standards, the 1903 contest became the second time a consensus underdog emerged with a triumph. It was Alabama's turn to beat the odds.

Auburn had warmed up for its encounter with Alabama with blank jobs of the Montgomery Athletic Club, 26-0, and Howard College, 58-0. Alabama, on the other hand, was not only winless, but also scoreless, having lost to Vanderbilt, 30-0, and to Mississippi State, 11-0.

Thus, Auburn had scored 94 points and surrendered none; Alabama had scored no points and surrendered 41.

On game day, the *Montgomery Advertiser* reported, "The most sanguine of the alumni of the honored institution (Alabama) thought that their team had, perhaps, a fighting chance for the championship of the state, but, responses were few in the betting odds of 5 to 1, which were frequently made by the Auburn supporters."

The contest was played at Montgomery's Highland Park on Friday, October 23, and won by Alabama 18-6, before a reported crowd of 1,900. It was to be the last Alabama-Auburn football game to be fought in the state's capital city, and in fact, the last to be played anywhere except Birmingham. It is perhaps another unique feature of the Alabama-Auburn series in comparison with other major col-

The *Montgomery Advertiser*, October 24, 1903

lege series, that none of the games was ever played in the hometown of one of the participants—in this case, Auburn.

Auburn kicked off to start the game and Alabama wasted no time in showing its superiority. Nineteen plays and 79 yards later, Tuscaloosa was in the end zone. Six different running backs got into the act and W. M. McMahon accounted for 24 yards in three carries. J. V. Boyles registered the touchdown. Truman Smith tacked on the point-after and Alabama jumped out front with a 6-0 lead.

Auburn bounced right back for a touchdown, but in the officials' eyes combined more trickery and razzle-dazzle than was allowable. According to the *Advertiser,* "On the next play a fake kick was attempted. (W. G.) Boyd received the ball and went around right end. He was tackled by (W. S.) Sherrill, but passed the ball back to (Zac) Smith, Auburn's quarterback. Smith, with admirable interference by Ed Lacey, charged down the field to the ten-yard line, where Captain W. S. Wyatt of the University, attempted a tackle. He got Smith but the ball was passed to Lacey, and the touchdown was made. Auburn yells immediately began, but were brought to a sudden hush . . ."

The referee brought the ball back to the point of the first lateral and ruled that Smith had interfered with Sherrill (by holding) on Sherrill's tackle of Boyd. Instead of a tie game, Alabama maintained a 6-0 lead and hung on tenaciously for the remainder of the first half.

After intermission, Auburn took the kickoff but could get nowhere and punted. Alabama mounted an offensive drive from its own 38-yard line. McMahon went for 12, B. A. Burks for five and Hall for 10, and just that quick, the scrimmage line was at the Auburn 45. The playing field was 110 yards long. That distance, however, was covered in just one play on a breakaway run by Smith. The score became 12-0 when the same Mr. Smith was true with his conversion kick.

Taking the ensuing kickoff, the Orange and Blue, sparked by Lacey's 40-yard run, got a touchdown they could keep. Boyd burst over for the score and also added the conversion. Suddenly, Auburn was back in the game, 12-6.

But not for long. A reporter for the *Advertiser* wrote, "Boyd kicked off and McMahon returned 20 yards. By mass plays the University reached the 25-yard line, where the perpetual hammering of the Auburn line by the tackle-back formation continued. Truman Smith was again sent over for a touchdown, kicking his own goal."

The game ended with Auburn battling on Alabama's 25-yard line. "When the timekeeper blew his whistle signaling the close of the game, the big wire netting which had kept the crowd from surging

VICTORY PERCHED ON CRIMSON-WHITE; AUBURN'S ORANGE-BLUE TRAILED IN DUST

University Took Football Game From the Polytechnic.

DEFEAT WAS DECISIVE

Tuscaloosa Eleven Outplayed the Former Champions.

Crowd of 1,200 Persons Gathered at Highland Park Gridiron to Witness Contest—Yates, Tuscaloosa Tackle, Injured by Moon.

The Montgomery Advertiser

over the field during the game, restrained them no longer. Every alumnus of the University present dashed on the gridiron and sent up a triumphant yell of 'Old Alabama,'" observed the *Advertiser*.

Coach W. B. Blount was carried from the field on the shoulders of his victorious team. The final score in the eighth game of the series was a surprising 18-6 in favor of Alabama—its first win over Auburn in four games in the past nine years.

The series now stood 6-2-0, Auburn. The Orange and Blue had scored 213 points, Tuscaloosa 77.

Losing coach Billy Bates told an *Advertiser* reporter, "There was absolutely no excuse for the repeated bucks of Tuscaloosa being so uniformly successful. True, five of our best men were out of the game, but even then Auburn should have won and I firmly believe that if the game were to be played over today we would win, 20-0."

Coach Blount said, "I am free to confess that the result of the game was as much a surprise to me as anybody else.... we adhered strictly to the Yale game, relying entirely on straight football.... The victory, I think, is the result of the indomitable spirit of the Alabama team. They came to Montgomery imbued with the determination to win, and win they did in signal fashion."

Gwinn, Oates, Reddon and Fortune were cited for their line play that repeatedly opened big holes in the Auburn line for Alabama backs to buck through.

Following the big game with Alabama, Auburn went on to defeat LSU and Georgia Tech, but lost to Sewanee and Georgia, finishing the 1903 season with a 4-3-0 record.

Alabama followed with victories over LSU and Tennessee, but was beaten by Sewanee and Cumberland. That gave the Crimsons a 3-4-0 record for the year.

According to the records, it would be almost half a century—48 years in fact—until a University of Alabama football team would suffer another losing season. It was a period which saw the inauguration of seven U.S. presidents, World War I, The Roaring Twenties, Prohibition and Repeal, the Great Depression, World War II, the advent of the Atomic Age, and war in Korea. It was a period of globe shaking events, both disasters and triumphs. At Alabama at least, the latter included an unprecedented era of winning football.

1904
Game 9

Fierce

The 1904 Alabama-Auburn clash "Resulted in as fierce and game a struggle as was ever seen on the local gridiron," reported the *Birmingham News.*

Why such a fierce match?

"It was distinctively a state game, as both Auburn and Alabama without question have a right to battle for the honors of the State Championship. The University of Alabama, last year for the first time in a number of years, succeeded in wrestling the title of supremacy from Auburn and the fierce desire of the Tigers (notice that the name "Tigers" crops up again) to win back their lost championship," the *News* said.

Auburn 29, Alabama 5. Or was it 29-6?

Auburn entered the game unbeaten and unscored upon, having disposed of Clemson 5-0, Nashville University 10-0, and Georgia Tech 12-0. Alabama was 4-1-0, with victories over Florida 29-0, Mississippi State 6-0, Nashville 17-0 and Georgia 16-5. The team's only loss had been to Clemson, 18-0, in the second game of the season.

Auburn kicked off to open the series' ninth game, played at Birmingham's West End Park on Saturday, November 12. Auburn quickly recovered a fumble at Alabama's 15-yard line. "After holding Auburn twice for downs, Alabama gave way before the terrific onslaught and the initial touchdown," reported the *News.*

G. W. Streit got the score, Randolph Reynolds converted and the Orange and Blue was off and running.

The *Birmingham News*

A *News* reporter wrote, "For the rest of the half, Auburn made touchdowns almost at will, going around end, through center or any other old way that seemed to suit their fancy."

Humphrey Foy scored two touchdowns, Streit added another and Reynolds converted twice. At intermission, Auburn led 23-0.

Alabama got on the scoreboard in the second half and the *News* had this to say about the Crimsons' only score of the game: "Alabama then with the ball made a heroic and finally successful effort to touch the hitherto virgin goal line of the warriors from Auburn."

Harvey Sartain did it. The *Birmingham News* quoted the final score of the game as 29-6, stating that Auxford Burks' conversion was good. In a special dispatch that was sent to the *Atlanta Journal*, Burks was also given credit for a successful point-after, ". . . and Burks kicked a pretty goal," said the *Journal*.

Records at Alabama and Auburn, plus today's Southeastern Conference Football guide, all carry the 29-5 score.

The reporters were at the game and it seems reasonable to accept their eyewitness account as official—Auburn 29, Alabama 6.

Reynolds scored Auburn's last touchdown and also added the conversion as Auburn took a 7-2-0 series lead. In total points, Auburn was way out front, 242-82.

Two weeks later, Alabama lost to Tennessee 5-0, before undertaking a schedule of three games in three days during the first weekend in December. On Friday, they blanked LSU 11-0 in Baton Rouge. It was on to New Orleans the next day for a 6-0 shutout of Tulane. Then on Sunday, an Alabama football team made its first journey into the State of Florida and dropped the Pensacola Athletic Club 10-5. The Crimsons completed their first 10-game schedule with a 7-3-0 record.

Auburn capped its perfect 1904 season with a 17-6 victory over Georgia and finished 5-0-0.

1905
Game 10

Mass Muscle and Chain Lightning

Rough times set in at Auburn in 1905 following the perfect season of the year before. When the time rolled around to play Alabama, the Orange and Blue had only one win, an 18-0 blank of Mississippi State. There were 6-0 losses to Davidson and Clemson, plus a 54-0 embarrassment at the hands of powerful Vanderbilt.

The football scene at Tuscaloosa was somewhat brighter, but not considerably so. The Crimsons had suffered defeats to Vanderbilt, Georgia Tech and Clemson by a combined score of 71-5. However, on the other side of the ledger were victories over Maryville, Mississippi State, Georgia and Central Kentucky by an aggregate count of 108-0.

The disappointments suffered throughout the season by both teams meant absolutely nothing to their rooters that November 18, as they made their way towards Birmingham's West End Park, site of the contest.

After all, it was Alabama vs. Auburn. The biggie. The only one that really mattered.

"Long before the time of the game," reported the *Birmingham News,* "crowds began streaming through the gates of the park and when the whistle blew, it was estimated that 4,600 spectators were

CRIMSON AND WHITE WAVES IN VICTORY OVER AUBURN

University of Alabama Wins Football Game 30 to 0.

EVERY INCH HOTLY CONTESTED

Orange and Blue Players Fight Gamely, but Are Unable to Withstand Fierce Onslaughts of Tuskaloosa Team With Its Lightning Formations.

THOUSANDS PACK THE STANDS

The Birmingham News

around the field. The grandstand and bleachers was packed, and on the far side of the field, coaches and buggies gaily decked out in the colors of the favorite university completed a solid mass of enthusiastic onlookers. The crowd was the largest in the history of football in Alabama, and the scene was the most animated ever witnessed around an Alabama gridiron."

A student reporter for the *Glomerata,* Auburn's year book, saw it this way back in 1905: "Under clear sky and full sail the contest was begun, and for fully fifty minutes waged the battle fierce and raging, but the fellows from the 'city of oaks' proved stronger, and for the third time in 10 contests, Auburn was defeated by the U. of A. And Auburn's disappointment was never so keen as now."

Final score: Alabama 30, Auburn 0.

It wasn't too surprising that Alabama won the game, but the margin of victory caught everyone unprepared, including a reporter for the *News,* who wrote, "The team that it was believed would give Alabama a tough fight and play the Crimson and White to a standstill, was crushed and battered by a mass of muscle and educated chain lightning."

Auburn won the toss and elected to receive. A punt quickly followed and Alabama immediately scored. Steady gains by Harvey Sartain, Auxford Burks, Lafayette Ward and T. S. Sims got the ball down close for Sims' touchdown run. Truman Smith's kick was good and the Tuscaloosa lads led 6-0 after seven minutes of play.

Reported the *News,* "the mass of Crimson and White students and sympathizers went wild. Hats and canes were thrown in the air, and the regular college yell lost in the uncontrolled burst of enthusiasm."

Raymond Sturdivant registered the second Alabama tally, and once again, Smith converted for a 12-0 lead.

Auburn's only scoring chance came just before intermission, but the Orange and Blue had to settle for nothing. Alabama's Smith was standing in punt formation at his own 20-yard line. The snap sailed over his head and as he ran the ball down and frantically tried to kick it, in stormed J. Haygood Patterson, who blocked the punt. Auburn got the ball at the three-yard line; they ended up on the five.

W. P. Moon, an Auburn guard, apparently saw more "red" in Alabama's crimson jerseys than he could personally control. Two years before, he had been thrown out of the game for kicking and slugging Alabama's William Oates. During the second-half of the 1905 game, he was ejected again. "He kicked Sims in the head and landed a couple of good wallops on the player's body," wrote the *News.* "Things appeared bright for a general mix-up for a time, but cooler heads prevailed.... Moon states the reason he kicked and hit Sims was because the latter applied a vile epithet to him, which no gentleman could or would tolerate.... Sims met Moon after the game and apologized to the Auburn player, saying that he regretted his hasty language and that he meant nothing by it, as he was excited in the heat of play."

Meanwhile, Alabama was recording second-half touchdowns by Sims (his second of the game), Burks and Ward. Smith's conversions were perfect each time for the final 30-point total. It was Alabama's third series win against seven setbacks.

Throughout the lopsided defeat, though, the "old Auburn spirit", a spirit for which that college is noted today, was ever-present back in 1905. A *News* correspondent wrote, "The Auburn men were not showing their disappointment, for cheer after cheer rang out for the Orange and Blue, even while their team was losing ground."

However, the big sports news of the day wasn't Alabama beating Auburn, or W. P. Moon, or Auburn's spirit. The big news was football fatalities. In 1905, there were 14 gridiron deaths. In the past five years, a staggering total of 71 boys had been killed playing high school and college football.

The general public, the press, the college officials, the Congress and even President Teddy Roosevelt were up in arms and demanding that either sweeping rule changes be made to modify the brutal feature of the game or the sport be abolished.

Changes were made, many of them prescribed by John Heisman, who had coached at Auburn from 1895 to 1899.

Football once again had a future.

1906
Game 11

Axed by Auxford

Alabama played a six-game schedule in 1906. Discard one of those games and the Crimsons' defense did not allow a touchdown. But that one game is there, and it represents the University of Alabama's all-time worst gridiron defeat—a 78-0 licking by Southern football's biggest bully of the era—Vanderbilt. In six seasons, the Nashville terrors had lost only five of their 50 games, and had outscored opponents by a margin of 1,711-130.

J. W. Pollard, Alabama's 10th head coach in its 15-year football history, was preparing his troops for Auburn with wins over Maryville, Howard and Mississippi State, plus the Vanderbilt nightmare. Tennessee would come later.

Over at the "Loveliest Village Of The Plains," the football picture was anything but lovely. Auburn, under coach Mike Donahue, was winless against Sewanee, Georgia Tech and Clemson. Donahue's only encouragement lay in the fact that his team had surrendered only 27 points.

November 17 dawned, and once again Alabama and Auburn packed their game gear and headed for Birmingham for the 11th renewal of the intrastate gridiron conflict.

Over 4,000 fans jammed the stands at the Fair Grounds and watched as Alabama's Auxford Burks axed Auburn by scoring all the game's points in a tough 10-0 victory.

Auburn played the game under protest, maintaining that T.S.

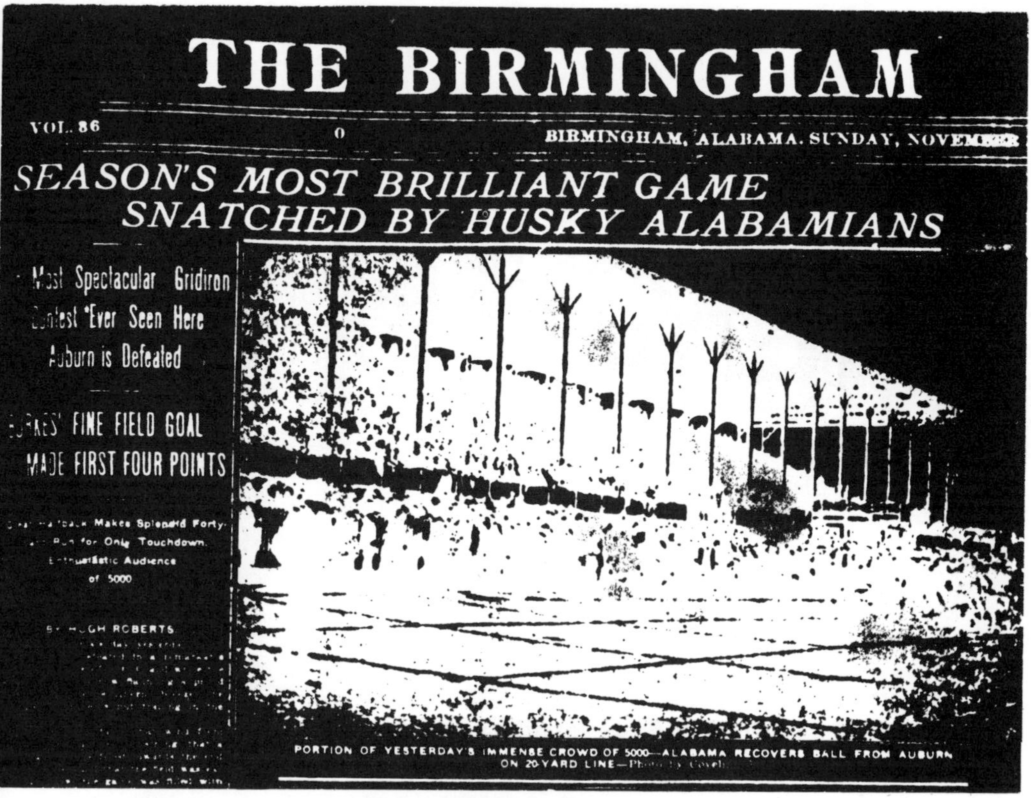

THE BIRMINGHAM

VOL. 86 — BIRMINGHAM, ALABAMA, SUNDAY, NOVEMBER

SEASON'S MOST BRILLIANT GAME SNATCHED BY HUSKY ALABAMIANS

Most Spectacular Gridiron Contest Ever Seen Here

Auburn is Defeated

BURKES' FINE FIELD GOAL MADE FIRST FOUR POINTS

Makes Splendid Forty- Run for Only Touchdown. Enthusiastic Audience of 5000

BY HUGH ROBERTS

PORTION OF YESTERDAY'S IMMENSE CROWD OF 5000—ALABAMA RECOVERS BALL FROM AUBURN ON 20-YARD LINE

Birmingham Age-Herald

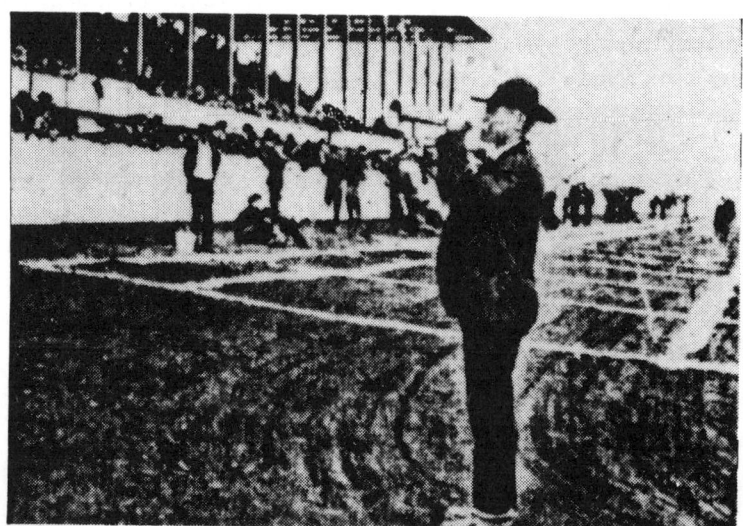

A bugler entertaining the big crowd of 5,000 in attendance for the 1906 game that was played at the Fair Grounds in Birmingham.

Auburn's old football field was not being used for football on this particular afternoon back in the early 1900's. Whatever the dust-raising event was (was it goat-roping?), it attracted a good crowd of the local gents, some API students (in uniforms) and a group of young school boys. The picture below shows that the dusty playground has been replaced by, well, progress. (Top photo courtesy of Auburn University Archives)

The Birmingham Age-Herald of Sunday, November 18, 1906, carried among its "Pictorial Comment On Events Of The Week" this cartoon of Auburn's loss to Alabama. The score was 10-0, so why a "23" on the placard? Only the artist (Blackman) knows for sure.

Sims, Alabama's left guard, was an illegal player. The protest was made before the game and would later be heard by the Southern Inter-Collegiate Athletic Association (SIAA).

Even though Auburn threatened Alabama's goal several times early in the game, the first half was scoreless. The game wore on, and midway through the second half, the score was still 0-0. Alabama then bucked down to Auburn's 10-yard line, where it was the Crimson's last down.

Something had to be done, and a reporter for the *Birmingham News* described in detail what was done. "Burks, assisted by (Chick) Hannon, began piling up a little hill of earth. The Auburn team, of course, saw this preliminary but satisfied themselves that the work was too deliberate, but they were mistaken. The whistle blew. Hannon (took the snap from center and) placed the ball on the prearranged mound. While every breath was hushed and every heartbeat was coming fast, Burks kicked. . . . the kick had gone true and caused a thousand throats to become hoarse and another thousand hearts to break."

The first field goal of the Alabama-Auburn series had been recorded and the Crimsons led, 4-0.

Late in the game, Burks struck again. He fielded a punt on Auburn's 40-yard line. "With the determination of a bulldog," said the *News,* "Burks started on his mad run for a touchdown. Nothing short of a steam engine could have stopped him. He charged down the field with his head bowed low and when he landed on the other side of the Auburn goal, Alabama rooters went wild."

The point-after was also left in Burks' care and he sailed it right through the uprights and Alabama had won its second straight game from Auburn.

Alabama closed its season two weeks later with a 51-0 thrashing of Tennessee for a final record of 5-1-0.

Auburn later won its only game, a 15-0 encounter with Gordon Military Academy, and concluded its worst season up to that time (1-5-0) with a 4-0 loss to Georgia.

As for Auburn's protest, it was lost, too. And the final result of the 1906 game would forever be in the record books as a 10-0 Alabama victory.

But the Orange and Blue still had a 7-4-0 series lead over Alabama and had almost doubled them in points 242-122.

1907
GAME 12

They Tied Up And Called It Quits

Once again it was Alabama vs. Auburn. And Birmingham was bursting out all over with football fans and their enthusiastic exuberance.

Reporters from the *Birmingham News* and the *Montgomery Daily Advertiser* were there, and these were some of the thoughts they filed for their Sunday morning readers: "Both teams arrived in the city Friday night, the Auburn team quartering at the Hillman Hotel and the Alabama squad stopping at the Florence. The rotundas of both hostelries were well crowded up to the wee small hours of the morning and the college yells rang loud and clear long after midnight.

"At last, the day of all days to football enthusiasts of the state of Alabama had arrived, and now only a few hours remain before the championship for state football honors will be decided for the year.

"During the morning, the streets were filled to overflowing. Just before the game, a desertion of the thoroughfares was very noticeable as hundreds were swinging on the ends of streetcars enroute to the Fair Grounds.

"The colors have been purchased by most every one. Flags are waving from most every location.

ALA-6 AUBURN-6

There was a hot time in the old town back in 1907. (Photo courtesy of University of Alabama Archives)

Auburn-Alabama Game Ends in a Tie

Tuscaloosa Squad, With Coach Pollard's Trick Plays, Had Best of Argument, But Score Was 6 to 6.

The *Montgomery Advertiser*

"When the special trains arrived from Auburn and Tuscaloosa during the morning, a stranger would have thought that President (Teddy) Roosevelt was about to be entertained in royal fashion.

"At 1 o'clock the gates were open and about 1:30, people began pouring through in order to secure choice seats for the great game. The crowd at the game was one of the features of the day and the grandstand and sidelines presented an inspiring sight. There were upward of 5,000 people present."

However, "the day of all days" turned out to be the saddest day in athletic history for both the University of Alabama and the Alabama Polytechnic Institute.

Nobody realized it at the time, but when the sun set on Birmingham that November 16, 1907, it would be 41 years before the two state rivals would again meet on the football field.

It seems appropriate that neither team should win, nor lose, this particular game. And neither team did. It ended all even — Alabama 6, Auburn 6.

Even so, Alabama considered the tie a victory. "The result of the game is most pleasant to the supporters of the Alabama team, as this team was touted as a loser from the start," said the *Daily Advertiser*. "The Auburn players went on the field confident of winning, but after a few minutes of play it was plainly seen that Alabama was a factor and a hard team to down."

The *News* observed, "Odds of 3 to 1 were freely made, and 'even' money was put up that the Crimson and White would not score. Auburn is greatly disappointed, their expectation being that Alabama would be defeated by at least three touchdowns."

As far as the Crimsons were concerned, there was only one setback all afternoon. It came when "the Alabama sponsors were late arriving, the tallyho having broken down enroute to the Fair Grounds."

When time came for their 12th meeting, Auburn and Alabama had played six and five games, respectively, and only one opponent had been able to score on either team. That opponent was Sewanee. The boys from the small Tennessee college edged Auburn, 12-8, and slaughtered Alabama, 54-4.

The "odds makers" had ruled Auburn the big favorite on the strength of its 141 points, to only 53 for Alabama, plus the huge difference in the scores of their games with Sewanee.

Auburn kicked off to open the game and, according to the *Daily Advertiser*, "Alabama returned the kick for a good gain and continued up the field at a rapid pace while the crowd stood watching in amazement."

The Crimsons reached the 12-yard line and Chick Hannon missed a drop-kick field goal attempt. "There was ease in the Auburn camp at this point," the reporter wrote.

With just seconds remaining in the first half, Auburn broke the scoreless tie. The Orange and Blue drove down to the one-yard line, but were hit with a penalty. "The penalty of five yards threw the Auburn boys back, but with a grim determination, a line buck through right tackle carried G.G. Hughes over the line with the ball. Tom McLure kicked goal and the score was 6-0," reported the *Advertiser*.

At this point, Alabama coach J. W. Pollard, protested the touchdown, claiming that Auburn had been given an extra down. "Referee Tufts paid little attention to the protest, stating that he knows positively that the downs were correctly recorded," the *Advertiser* said.

The story continued, "In the second half, Alabama got busy with trick plays that astounded and puzzled the Auburn players. The 'German Play' proved one of the prettiest plays yet seen in this city." It was also reported that the Crimsons successfully ran the "military formation" and "dance-trick" plays.

Alabama received the second-half kickoff, and with the benefit of these puzzling plays, marched 85 yards for the tying score. Left halfback Brice Sidney Jones not only scored the touchdown, but also added the conversion to knot the count, 6-6.

The scorekeeper was through for the day, but the teams on the field were not.

Later in the game, Alabama drilled down to Auburn's 12-yard line, and from the same point as earlier in the game, Hannon again missed a field goal try.

"It was now Auburn's turn to rush the ball," wrote the *News,* "and cheered on by the Orange and Blue supporters, the pigskin was shoved foot by foot down the field until it seemed certain a score would result. It was a race against time, however, and when Alabama held for downs on the 10-yard line and a moment later kicked out of danger, the game was over."

Thus, the Auburn-Alabama series was put into mothballs. With the Orange and Blue ahead in games, 7-4-1, and in points scored, 254 to 131.

Auburn went on to defeat Georgia Tech, but lost to Georgia, ending the 1907 season with a 6-2-1 record. In the next two weeks, Alabama topped LSU and Tennessee for a final 5-1-2 showing.

It is interesting to note that in this particular period of football history, the sports pages of Southern newspapers granted Yale almost as much coverage as the local teams. Of course, it could have been the awesome record that the Elis were building during those years. Yale was in its 26th year of football and had already posted an incredible 304 victories. Since 1900, Yale had lost only three of 90 games.

As Auburn and Alabama interrupted their series for awhile, both teams had completed 16 years of football. Auburn's 80-game history showed a 44-29-7 (.594) record. Alabama had played 83 games, and its record stood 45-34-4 (.566).

Saturday, November 16, 1907. A sad day, indeed, for citizens of the State of Alabama who had developed a consuming passion for the pastime of football. They were to be deprived of 41 years of what had been, and later would become again, one of the most spirited and colorful college football rivalries in the nation.

In reviewing the "last" game of the series, a *Daily Advertiser* reporter wrote, "The game was filled with rough play and when the whistle was blown for the end of the battle, two players got together in a fisticuff. The cause of the trouble between the belligerents not being learned. An Auburn man and an Alabama man were striking at each other."

Who knows? Maybe that's the way it should have ended.

1908-1947

A 41-Year Time Out Over $34.00

Legends die hard, if ever. For example, in the State of Alabama and around the South, even today legends having to do with why Alabama and Auburn stopped their football series after 1907 are alive and well.

Stories of violence abound as the contributing factor that led to the severing of athletic relations between the two rivals. "Somebody was shot," or was "knifed," or because of "dirty play," or "uncontrolled fighting after the game" are among the legends of what took place over seven decades ago.

They are more than legends. They are myths.

Rather, insofar as the 1908 game is concerned, the No. 1 stumbling block was a pure and simple disagreement over dollars and cents. A secondary issue was officiating, and specifically the geographical origin of the person who would be designated as "umpire" of the Auburn-Alabama football game.

In later years, as repeated efforts to resume the series were made, even the issues of money and officiating disappeared from the picture.

But back to 1908. Among the stipulations of the contract that governed the 1907 Alabama-Auburn football game was a provision for a hotel allowance for 17 men from each team at a cost of $2.00 per man, per day, including lodging and meals.

On January 23, 1908, Alabama coach J. W. Pollard received a proposed contract from Auburn football manager Thomas Bragg, calling for expenses for 22 men per team at $3.50 per day (total cost, $154.00 for two nights), and that the game should be played on November 14 at the Birmingham Fair Grounds.

After reviewing the proposal, Alabama officials offered a substitute contract that called for the expenses for 20 men at $3.00 per day, a rate they said would easily secure good accommodations in Birmingham—total cost for two nights, $120.00. The Alabama contract was sent to Bragg on February 24 and was promptly returned with a statement that Auburn would not agree to any reduction in the number of men or per diem rate as contained in the first proposal.

In this letter to Pollard, Bragg also indicated that Auburn was not entirely satisfied with Alabama's suggestions with respect to the selection of officials for the 1908 game. In addition to flatly rejecting the financial terms proposed by Alabama, he said that Auburn would come to a decision on arrangements for officials by April 1.

The *Tuscaloosa Times-Gazette* reported, "Pending Auburn's decision of officials, the question of contracts was allowed to remain quiescent until April 6, when Mr. Bragg was approached again by letter asking if a decision in regard to officials had been reached."

Bragg's reply to this letter was that the question of officials would be decided as soon as Alabama signed and returned "on to Auburn" the contract for the game. Although the newspaper account is not specific on this point, it is obvious that the contract referred to was the one Auburn had sent in January, calling for expenses for 22 men at $3.50 per day.

On Friday, April 24, the Alabama Executive Committee on Athletics held a meeting and drew up a contract that called for 20 men on each team, hotel expenses at a rate of $3.00 per day, and Southern men to act as game officials. The committee also instructed Pollard that should Auburn refuse this contract, that he (Pollard) was to open negotiations with other colleges for a game to be played in Birmingham on the date (November 14) that had been set aside for the Alabama-Auburn contest.

The difference between Auburn's proposed contract and Alabama's was $34.00.

The next day, April 25, Auburn's football coach, Mike Donahue, accompanied the baseball team to Tuscaloosa. A meeting with Alabama officials on the football game was planned. Prior to the meeting, in an interview, Donahue disclosed that Auburn would insist "on a Northern man" as umpire in the game.

Later the *Times-Gazette* reported, "At a meeting which took place between Mr. Bragg and Mr. Donahue of Auburn, and Mr. Pritchard and Dr. Pollard of Alabama, held in the parlors of the McLester Hotel, the question of officials was thoroughly thrashed out. Auburn advanced as her reason for insisting on a Northern umpire that there was not a man in the South of sufficient ability to act as umpire in intercollegiate contests."

Alabama disagreed. Alabama also countered that it would cost approximately $250.00 to bring an umpire from the North and that such an expenditure was totally unnecessary.

The *Times-Gazette* story continued, "Furthermore, Alabama could not appreciate the necessity of going so far away from home to procure officials for this particular contest, when Mr. Bragg had stated but a few minutes before that while Alabama considered the Auburn-Alabama game the most important on its schedule, there were at least four other games on the Auburn schedule which he considered fully as important as that with Alabama, and followed up his declaration with the statement that he had accepted, or was to accept, Southern men as officials in all these other contests."

Alabama's suggestion of officials who had formerly handled the Auburn-Alabama games was flatly rejected by Bragg and Donahue. Auburn also turned down any suggestion to reduce the number of players and the expenses as called for in its original contract.

"Auburn's refusal to entertain any of Alabama's suggestions made it evident that a compromise was impossible, so the discussion was closed," wrote the *Times-Gazette* reporter.

On April 28, three days after the meeting with Auburn officials in Tuscaloosa, Pollard sent Bragg the contract the Alabama committee had decided upon four days earlier. Also included in the correspondence were the minutes of the committee meeting and a letter that stated, "I would greatly appreciate an answer from you as to whether or not you are willing to sign up a contract which I enclosed with this letter, within ten days, by May 11."

"AUBURN SIDE IS PRESENTED," read a headline in the May 17, 1908, edition of the *Montgomery Advertiser*. The story followed: "The athletic authorities of the Alabama Polytechnic Institute are out today with a statement answering the Alabama version of the much-talked of disagreement between Auburn and Alabama regarding the annual football game between the two colleges this coming fall. The Auburn version of the efforts of the colleges to come to an agreement differs materially from the accounts that have been published from Tuscaloosa in the last few days."

Then, quoting directly from the statement, attributed to Bragg, the story continued: "The Auburn athletic authorities have heretofore refrained from giving anything to the press with regard to the Alabama-Auburn disagreement, as they are opposed to airing these controversies in print, but the communication from Messrs. Pollard, Pritchard and Turnipseed, which recently appeared in the *Birmingham Age-Herald*, is such an ex parte statement, and is so inaccurate, that it cannot be allowed to pass unanswered."

As for the 1907 contract and the $2.00 expenses, Bragg said he reluctantly accepted the contract rather than engage in a controversy, because he had not anticipated the increased expenses. He said this was pointed out to Pollard at the time and Pollard said, "We can make this up in our next year's (1908) contract." Bragg went on to say that he thought he could secure a special low hotel rate in Birmingham as he had in Atlanta for several years.

"I was sadly mistaken, and although I made efforts to make special rates at some of the leading Birmingham hotels, and was unable to do so, our hotel ranged from $3.50 to $3.75 per day, the meals on the 'A La Carte' being particularly high. . . . the 1907 contract occasioned a loss of from $1.50 to $1.75 per man for two days, and while this was an absolute necessary and legitimate expense, it had to be paid for out of Auburn's share of the proceeds of the game," Bragg's statement continued.

Bragg said that he told Pollard verbally and by letter that he would be willing to take $3.50 as the maximum rate, and if the team's actual expenses came to a lesser figure, that Auburn would agree to charge only the amount of the bill actually incurred.

Quoting from Bragg's statement again: "With regard to the committee's assertion that Mr. Donahue and myself stated that there was no man in the South capable of umpiring an intercollegiate contest, I would emphatically deny that we made any such statement. We simply stated that we did not know of a satisfactory available man to officiate as umpire in the Alabama-Auburn game, and we asked Dr. Pollard to suggest some men for our consideration, though he failed to do so. . . . Moreover, we did not ask that an Eastern man be selected as umpire until after we had failed to agree upon some available Southern man.

"The resolutions sent to the Auburn management were in the nature of an ultimatum, dicating the only terms upon which the Alabama authorities would sign a contract for next season, and using as a threat the statement that negotiations were being opened with other colleges for a game on November 14, before the

Auburn authorities had had the opportunity to finally pass upon the matter."

Two days later, May 19, the *Age-Herald* reported, "Auburn's action in this matter is indicative of a desire to evade its annual game with Alabama.... Alumni of both institutions in Birmingham think that the talk of an Eastern umpire is ridiculous.... The elimination of the Alabama-Auburn game from the season's schedule is a blow to football lovers of this state. The affair, heretofore, has been the game of all games, the only one, in fact, in which everybody in this state was interested.... The people regret that Alabama and Auburn will not meet this year. They care very little for the reasons."

Each school's "Class of 1908" graduated, the long summer months came and went, and it was time for another school year — and also time for the controversy to open up again — like an old wound.

On September 20, 1908, the *Montgomery Advertiser* carried a story headlined, "BOTH MAKE CONCESSIONS ... ALABAMA AND AUBURN WILL PLAY ... THE CONTROVERSY IS ENDED." Auburn conceded its demand for an Eastern umpire; Alabama agreed to Auburn's original terms of 22 men and $3.50 per man, per day hotel allowance. Auburn offered Alabama a choice of four dates on which the contest could be held. Alabama said there would be no scheduling problem. There would, after all, be an Alabama-Auburn football game in 1908.

That was in September.

In a letter of September 19 from Bragg to Hubert Drennon, Chairman of the Alabama alumni committee, Bragg had offered Alabama four Saturdays — October 10, 17, 31 and November 14 — as possible dates for a game. Except for the latter date, Auburn already had games scheduled on the three other dates. However, Bragg said that if Alabama was unable to play on November 14, Auburn would cancel or transfer any of the other three dates in order to meet Alabama. Bragg also stated that if Alabama had to cancel any one of its games, the Auburn management would pay one-half of the forfeiture cost; and that Auburn was more than willing to have Southern men officiate the game. It was now up to Alabama.

Nothing happened for three weeks.

Bragg's letter had been turned over to two of Alabama's alumni representatives on the joint arbitration committee — Hill Ferguson and Jelks Cabiness.

Ferguson and Cabiness answered Bragg's letter on October 13. Their response included the following language to which Bragg apparently took exception:

We feel that you have never made any concession from the stand originally taken by you, and have never made a pretense of meeting Alabama half way in this matter, but as the question seems to have been reduced to that point where the game must be played your way or not at all, and as we believe that the welfare of the sport in this section would be injured by a failure to play, we have decided to accede to all of your demands. If you have any other further ones to make kindly forward them at once, and we will give them our consideration also. . . . We trust that inasmuch as Alabama has acceded to every one of your demands, although feeling them to be unjust and unfair, that you will not allow the question of a date to stand in the way but will at least do that much toward the securing of a game.

Four days later, October 17, Bragg, in a sharply-worded letter, answered the charges that had been leveled by Ferguson and Cabiness. Bragg's reply expressed his skepticism "as to your eagerness to meet our team this season," and chastized the Alabama representatives for waiting four weeks to reply. During those four weeks, two of the dates Auburn had offered to clear for Alabama had passed.

The schedule options for 1908 were running out rapidly. Georgia Tech would not permit Auburn to cancel or postpone their game in Atlanta on November 7; Georgia would not let Alabama out of a November 14 game in Birmingham. That left November 21 as the only remaining available date. Auburn did not have a game booked for that day, but Alabama did—against Haskell Institute, an Indian school. "Even though they are Indians," wrote Ferguson and Cabiness, "we feel that their contract should be protected, unless they are willing to release us, which is not the case."

Alabama agreed to play Auburn on November 28. However, the Auburn Board of Trustees had a longstanding rule prohibiting a game after Thanksgiving.

That meant no available dates were left.

On October 31, 1908, Ferguson and Cabiness answered Bragg's letter of October 17, and the correspondence concluded, ". . . .and the matter is closed as far as we are concerned."

The Alabama-Auburn football series was dead.

AUBURN SIDE IS PRESENTED

Answer to Statements About Football Game

ALABAMA AND AUBURN AT OUTS

Reasons Why Auburn Turned Down the Contract.

Mr. Bragg Declares That The Terms of Orange And Blue Were Reasonable In Every Respect—Correspondence Given.

The *Montgomery Advertiser*, May 17, 1908.

Petty Differences Of Two Athletic Rivals

REVIEW OF ACTION OF ALABAMA AND AUBURN IN ELIMINATING THEIR ANNUAL GAME—UNJUST CRITICISM FROM UNINFORMED.

Birmingham Age-Herald, May 19, 1908

BOTH MAKE CONCESSIONS

Adv. Sept. 20, 1908

Alabama and Auburn Will Play.

THE CONTROVERSY IS ENDED

Auburn Offers Any One of Four Dates.

Alabama Was Generous in Conceding Two of the Three Disputed Points—Auburn Going Half Way Makes Other Concessions.

Montgomery Advertiser, Sept. 20, 1908

Alabama Grants Every Demand of Auburn Team

Birmingham Age-Herald, Oct. 13, 1908

THOSE TWO TEAMS STILL FAR APART

Bragg Answers Letter of Ferguson and Cabaniss

OFFERS ANOTHER DATE

Reviews in Detail the Lengthy Controversy—Says Auburn Has Been Very Generous. His Statement.

Birmingham Age-Herald, Oct. 19, 1908

From Alumni Agreement Bragg Receded The Charge

Alumni Contend That Alabama Yielded to Every Auburn Demand

STILL WILLING TO PLAY THAT POST-SEASON GAME

Messrs. Ferguson and Cabaniss State That Alabama's Endeavor to Break Georgia and Haskel Dates Has Failed.

Birmingham Age-Herald, Nov. 1, 1908

"Tommyrot" and "Bullyrag."

Three years later they tried again. Hugh Roberts of the *Birmingham Age-Herald* wrote on January 12, 1911, "A matter of statewide interest and importance is the fact that Auburn and the University of Alabama, after a long period of athletic differences, have agreed to agree. . . . a series of baseball games may occur this spring. The football teams of the two institutions may meet in the fall."

It was reported that a conference had been held several days earlier between Dr. Eugene A. Smith of Alabama and Prof. Thomas Bragg of Auburn. "It is further understood," wrote Roberts, "that Alabama met the advances with arms outstretched. Perhaps the two gentlemen then embraced, although no minutes are at hand to confirm this rumor . . . there is no doubt in the world that athletic relations will be resumed."

Roberts was correct in his prediction back in 1911. But he didn't have in mind that it would be 37 more years before it actually happened.

The on-again, off-again meetings between representatives of the two colleges were scattered throughout the next 11 months, but nothing concrete resulted from the gatherings. On December 15, Hugo Friedman, graduate manager of athletics at Alabama, wrote a letter to Birmingham newspapers stating that Alabama had offered Auburn three dates in 1912 that should be considered for a game.

"It shows convincingly to the alumni and people of the State that Alabama wants to play Auburn," the letter said, "and 'puts it up' to the latter school to play the game or back down . . . The Athletic management of the University begs to state that it is not our intention to start anew an athletic argument. We hold not the slightest ill will towards Auburn, and all the old scores are forgotten."

The *Birmingham Ledger* reported the same day that alumni representatives from both schools would meet in the very near future.

"J. Q. Smith of Alabama and M. S. Sloan of Auburn, alumni presidents, both declare in strong terms that they favor a renewal of relationships between both institutions and it is stated that alumni of both institutions are very desirous of bringing about a cessation of hostilities."

Auburn refused to play.

Cliff Hare (for whom Auburn's football stadium was named before the "Jordan" was added in 1973), as secretary of the Auburn Athletic Committee, wrote on December 19, "We beg to inform you that final action has been taken by athletic authorities at Auburn to the effect that it is best that athletic relations between the two institutions not be resumed. In reaching this conclusion, the athletic authorities are guided by what they regard as the best interest of true sport."

On Christmas Eve, 1911, the *Birmingham Ledger's* B. H. Mooney wrote, "The excuse offered by Auburn was to the effect that the rivalry would be taken so keen in such a game that unsportsmanlike conduct would result . . . Is it to be inferred that Auburn's attitude means that because she favors clean athletics she cannot meet Alabama?"

The story continued, "The tommyrot dished out by Auburn supporters that Auburn outclassed Alabama is ridiculous." Mooney went on to say that the last three games played between the two teams resulted in no Auburn wins (one tie). "This doesn't look like the records bear out the contention that Auburn has so much over Alabama . . . This outclass stuff won't go very far . . . Many Auburn alumni regret the stand taken by Auburn . . . Auburn authorities should reconsider their action and join Alabama in a magnanimous spirit and bury the hatchet."

Auburn fired back.

A letter to the *Ledger* written by Atticus Mullen said, "The facts are that the Auburn athletic authorities would be the 'goat' in every sense of the word if they allowed the partisan writers and a few Alabama alumni to bullyrag them into playing a football game with Alabama after their refusal. The Auburn authorities have taken a stand for pure athletics. . . The athletic authorities do not propose to be bluffed into doing something that would cause bitterness and hard feelings and result in more annual scandals . . . It is a well known fact that for years the University of Alabama football schedule was made out strictly on the idea of the least hazard of loss . . . Let the Tuscaloosa institution seek games with Vanderbilt and the University of Mississippi. Let them get busy with larger colleges and get their standing without having to get it possibly by a victory or tie game over Auburn."

So much for an Alabama-Auburn football game in 1912.

It was 1923 before the two schools made another attempt to get back together on the football field. It, too, was futile. Dr. Spright Dowell, president of Auburn, spiked the idea. Among Dr. Dowell's reasons for not resuming the series was this statement: "It is our calm conviction that if relations in football were renewed, although it might not return to the old bitterness and practices, we would encounter an equally damaging situation in that football would tend to become the all-the-topic of both institutions and other games, contests and activities would be made subservient to the one supreme event of the year."

Nine years later the series again tried to escape the graveyard. This time, Auburn initiated the effort. On September 16, 1932, the *Associated Press* reported that Dr. J. V. Brown, the Auburn alumni secretary who had captained the Orange and Blue football team in 1894, voiced a strong appeal for the resumption of the game. Brown said, "With the passing of 25 years, much of the old feeling has disappeared. Alumni no longer refer to games in which brass knucks and horse pistols are used. Just between us, we have never believed these tales anyway . . . We believe that the series would not result in mayhem, murder, riot and sudden death, as some of our older alumni insist. We believe more sportsmanship would be shown at this game than any other contests played with rivals by either school."

Dr. Brown's appeal fell on deaf ears.

The politicians could stand it no longer. Five weeks later and they had gotten into the act. On October 21, a headline appeared in the *Montgomery Advertiser* that read, "LEGISLATORS MOVE FOR TILT BETWEEN 'BAMA AND AUBURN."

"By unanimous vote," reported the *Advertiser,* "the Senate Friday morning adopted a joint resolution by Sen. Russell Brown, paving the way for resumption of the athletic relations between the University of Alabama and Auburn . . . Senator Brown's resolution calls for a joint legislative committee comprised of five members of the House and three of the Senate to confer with heads of the two schools."

Sen. Brown was quoted as saying, "I am sure that it will be a matter of a short time before this will have the official approval of the authorities at Alabama and Auburn. . . . The people of this state have long looked forward to the time when the two colleges will be in harmony again. I am sure the time is close at hand."

But the time was not close at hand.

The next group to try at mending the breach was the American Legion. The Legion didn't request that the series be resumed, but used stronger language. A headline in the *Birmingham News* on

AUBURN'S CHARGES

DECLARES EVERY STATE HAS COLLEGES GUILTY OF QUESTIONABLE PRACTICES IN FOOTBALL.

Tuscaloosa Times Gazette, Dec. 10, 1911

AUBURN ALUMNI FAVOR ALABAMA-AUBURN CONTEST

Committees From Auburn and Alabama Alumni to Confer

Will Invite Faculty Members of Auburn to Be Present

Birmingham Ledger, Dec. 18, 1911

AUBURN DECLINES TO MEET ALABAMA

Tuscaloosa News-Gazette, Dec. 19, 1911

FRIEDMAN WRITES TO NEWSPAPERS ABOUT THAT GAME

Graduate Manager Sends Letter to the Sporting Writers.

ALABAMA OFFERS AUBURN THREE DATES FOR GAME

University Bears No Ill Feeling and Does Not Care to Renew Controversy

Birmingham News, Dec. 18, 1911

ALABAMA ANSWERS

BIRMINGHAM COMMITTEE OF ALUMNI CORRESPOND WITH BRAGG

Tuscaloosa Times-Gazette, Dec. 24, 1911

A VIEWPOINT OF FAIRNESS AND NEITHER AN ALABAMA NOR AUBURN VIEWPOINT

BY B. H. MOONEY.

Birmingham Ledger, Dec. 24, 1911

AUBURN-'BAMA GAME CAUSE PLEADED HERE
Dr. J. V. Brown Urges Resumption Of Play Between Educational Institutions

Birmingham News, Sept. 16, 1932

LEGISLATORS MOVE FOR TILT BETWEEN 'BAMA AND AUBURN

Montgomery Advertiser, Oct. 21, 1932

LEGION DEMANDS ALABAMA-AUBURN FOOTBALL BATTLE
Calls On Teams To Meet For Raising Scholarships; Would Use Force

Birmingham News, July 26, 1933

University Trustees Frown On Auburn-Alabama Grid Contest
Board Flatly Declines To Support State Legion Movement

Montgomery Advertiser, Nov. 11, 1934

July 23, 1933 read, "LEGION DEMANDS ALABAMA-AUBURN FOOTBALL BATTLE . . . CALLS ON TEAMS TO MEET FOR RAISING SCHOLARSHIPS; WOULD USE FORCE."

The resolution by the Alabama Legion offered the use of Legion Field in Birmingham free of charge if the two teams would agree to play on Thanksgiving Day for five consecutive years, with the proceeds going to a scholarship fund to educate children of deceased ex-soldiers. The two institutions would share equally in the fund and it was estimated that $250,000 could be raised during the five-year period. The Legion threatened to employ legislative force should it meet refusal in its proposal.

No luck for the Legionnaires, either. But they kept trying.

In November, 1934, Dr. L. N. Duncan, president of Auburn, agreed to a game "any time, any where." Gov. Bibb Graves also encouraged a game between the two schools. However, on November 10, the University of Alabama Trustees flatly declined to support the Legion movement. The resolution adopted by the trustees said: "Alabama approves of the established policy of the colleges of the country in declining to use athletic teams for promotion of extra-mural enterprises. If there is to be a resumption of athletic relations between the two State institutions, the constituted authorities should, after full and free consideration of all the factors involved, initiate and perfect the arrangements.

"That is the proper and usual procedure in American colleges and indeed in the world of amateur sports generally. There can be little semblance of sportsmanship in attempting to use force or duress in the scheduling of amateur athletic games."

Auburn-Alabama football was still another 14 years away.

Montgomery Advertiser, Dec. 1, 1934

In February, 1944, Gov. Chauncey Sparks urged that the series be resumed. Alabama said no. From the minutes of a meeting of the Alabama Board of Trustees on June 3, 1944, the Board's reasons included: "It would result in an accelerated over-emphasis of football in the state . . . The quest for players would be intensified, and already entirely enough is being put on high school athletics . . . Almost inevitably unwholesome rumors would be retailed about how one or the other institutions signed this player or that player in the State. This would lead to suspicion and rancor. . . The intense rivalry that would develop between the two institutions if the game is scheduled and the importance that will be attached to winning this game will make it exceedingly difficult for either institution to attract coaches of high character and proven ability. Such men will see a situation where a demand is likely to be made for the removal of the coach should he chance to lose several games to the other."

It is significant that the reasons the Alabama Board of Trustees gave in 1944 as to why the two schools should not renew athletic relations coincided with those Auburn president Dr. Spright Dowell had presented in 1923. In fact, the minutes of the 1944 University meeting quoted Dr. Dowell and some of his reasons—and in an expanded version, made up a large part of the Alabama resolution.

In the 1945 session of the State Legislature, a bill was introduced to require the two schools to resume the series but the measure was defeated. There was an attempt in the State Senate to tack an amendment to the general education bill that would have held up funds for the two colleges until they agreed to play. That, too, was killed.

On August 15, 1947, the Alabama House of Representatives approved a House Joint Resolution (H. J. R. 77; Act. No. 325) introduced by Sen. Stone. The resolution read:

> *WHEREAS, for many years there has been a lapse in athletic relations between the University of Alabama and Alabama Polytechnical Institute; and Whereas, in the opinion of the majority of the members of the Alabama State Legislature it is to the best interest of the two schools and of the people of Alabama that such athletic relations be resumed; Now, Therefore, be it resolved by the House of Representatives, the Senate concurring, the respective Boards of Trustees of the University of Alabama and Alabama Polytechnic Institute are hereby respectfully requested to make possible the inauguration of a full athletic program between the two schools, and Be It Further resolved that such action be*

taken by the said Boards of Trustees at the earliest practicable date, and not later than May 1949.

Approved August 15, 1947.

On April 20, 1948, Dr. John M. Gallalee, president of the University, phoned Auburn president Dr. Ralph Draughon and suggested a meeting of school officials for discussion of resumption of the series. Two days later they met at the Ann Jordan Farm, located near Alexander City. The farm was owned by the University.

Great headway was made.

Another meeting was held on May 2 at the Jefferson Davis Hotel in Montgomery. Final approval on an agreement was reached. They agreed on a football game to be played in seven months—December 4, 1948, at Birmingham's Legion Field.

On Saturday, May 8, the big news was released to the press. There would, after a 41-year time-out, be an Alabama Crimson Tide—Auburn Tiger football game.

There was rejoicing in the State of Alabama.

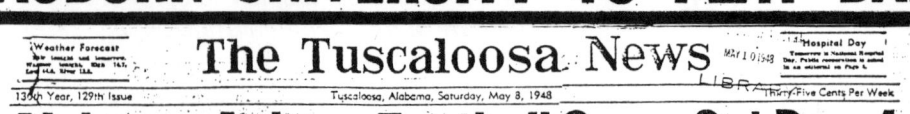

1948
GAME 13

Unwrap the Bandages, Boys

They'll take the bandages off a 41-year old football wound tomorrow to see if the scar is healed.

Sterling Slappey
The Montgomery Advertiser
Friday, Dec. 3, 1948

Destination: Birmingham, Alabama.

Auburn and Alabama sent their fans, bands, pep squads, campus beauties and all of the noise-making power they could muster. Bonfires and huge pep rallies got the Tiger-Tide festivities off to a roaring start on Friday and the excitement continued throughout the night and into the next day.

Birmingham had never seen anything like it. But Birmingham was just the focal point. The whole State was in an absolute frenzy over the first Alabama-Auburn football clash since 1907. And the tempo built as the hands of the clock slowly inched towards zero hour.

The *Birmingham News* reported, "For months, committees from both student bodies had been working out every detail to avoid any trouble. They flipped coins to see who would lead the downtown parade and which band would take the field first—before the game and after."

TIDE, TIGER TO PATCH UP 41-YEAR OLD SPAT SATURDAY

ALABAMA - AUBURN MEND 41 - YEAR GRID BREACH TODAY

War Eagle, Tide Take Over City

Town's Teeming, Mobs Throng Parade Route

Half Century Wait For Alabama-Auburn Game Reaches Climax

rmingham News

Bonfires, Pep Rallies Start Off Tide, Tiger Festivities

Bands, Beauties To Join Parade Here Tomorrow

ALABAMA'S CRIMSON TIDE FLOWS OVER AUBURN, 55-0

Just before the colorful parade through downtown Birmingham on game day, school officials, students, alumni and curious onlookers gathered at Woodrow Wilson Park for an official ceremony—an official "Bury The Hatchet" ceremony.

In the solemn event, the presidents of both student bodies, Alabama's Gillis Cammack and Auburn's Willie Johns together held the hatchet, and after a brief speech by each of the campus leaders, they lowered the hatchet into the ground. The symbol was covered up and as the last shovelful of earth was placed on the grave and given one final whack, the crowd broke into cheers and it was back to the cries of "WAR EAGLE!" and "ROLL TIDE!".

The hatchet had been buried.

No conference championship or national ranking or bowl bid was at stake as the two teams prepared for the big battle. Even so, the entire nation had an ear tuned towards Birmingham. The National Broadcasting Company (NBC) thought enough of the rivalry's official rebirth to air the game on nationwide radio. The play-by-play announcer was Bill Stern, who was perhaps the biggest name in his profession at the time.

Nobody outside the Auburn camp gave the Tigers the slightest chance of winning. The Plainsmen, under first-year coach Earl Brown, opened their season with a close 20-14 win over Mississippi Southern and followed up with a 13-13 tie against lightweight Louisiana Tech. Auburn managed only five touchdowns the rest of the season and lost to Florida, Georgia Tech, Tulane, Vanderbilt, Mississippi State, Georgia and Clemson by an aggregate score of 180-35.

Auburn was 1-7-1.

It wasn't exactly Alabama's year, either. Coach Red Drew's Tide had wins over Duquesne 48-0, Mississippi State 10-7, Mississippi Southern 27-0, Georgia Tech 14-2 and Florida 34-28. Included in its four losses was a 35-0 setback to Georgia, the team's worst defeat since 1910. Other 1948 losses were to Tulane, Tennessee and LSU, plus a tie with Vanderbilt.

Alabama was 5-4-1.

Yes, the hatchet had been buried. After a time-out that lasted 41 years and 18 days, it was finally time to play ball!

As the events of that December 4 unfolded, the hatchet wasn't the only thing that was buried. So was Auburn. The score was 55-0, and one had to flip the pages of Auburn's record book all the way back to 1917 to find a worse defeat.

To add further insult, Alabama sprang a sophomore quarterback on Auburn that day and the young lad turned the Tigers head over tea kettle. His name was Ed Salem, and Ed Salem passed for 159

Ed Salem, Alabama quarterback in the 1948 renewal of the series.

yards and three touchdowns, scored once himself on a 17-yard run and kicked seven conversions.

Alabama won the toss of the coin and elected to receive. Bill Cadenhead returned the kick from the 10 to the 34.

The series was finally and officially resumed.

Gordon Pettus carried three straight times for eight yards, but on the third try Alabama drew a 15-yard holding penalty that took the Tide back to the 23. After a short gain, Jack Brown came on and boomed a long 57-yard punt that Travis Tidwell returned four yards.

CRIMSON TIDE SMOTHERS AUBURN, 55-0

Convict Flogged After Blow That Cost Eye, Report

Salem Throws Three T. D. Passes, Scores Once, Converts Seven

Auburn started at its own 24. On first down, Russell Inman fumbled and Herb "Truck" Hannah recovered for Alabama at the 23. Pettus went for five yards before Salem tried for a quick score, but his pass was broken up in the end zone. Pettus then connected with Rebel Steiner with a pass and a first down at the Tiger 10. Pettus picked up two and on the next play tossed one to Butch Avinger who caught it at the six and scored. Salem's kick was good and four minutes and 50 seconds into the game, Alabama led 7-0.

On Auburn's next series, Cadenhead intercepted a long Tidwell pass but the mistake led to no damage. The two teams then played kick-back. Alabama punted; Auburn punted; Alabama punted; Auburn punted. And, by that time, the first quarter was over.

Fifty-five to zero? At this point in the game, nobody dreamed of such a score.

After still another exchange of punts, and with the aid of a 15-yard clipping penalty, Auburn had Alabama backed up to its own 11-yard line. But out came the Tide. Clem Welsh shot for 23 yards. Salem gained 10 in two carries to Auburn's 44. Salem threw to Jim Cain for six, and a Salem run of four gave Bama a first down at the Tigers' 46. Tom Calvin was on the receiving end of a Salem pass that was good for 13 yards. Calvin blasted for eight and five yards, and the Crimsons were resting at the 20 with another first down. After an incomplete pass, Salem was on target to Welsh for a touchdown. Salem converted for a 14-0 lead.

Just before the half, Welsh went seven yards for another score, Salem kicked good and the Tide was rolling, 21-0.

Auburn fumbled the second-half kickoff and Steiner found it for Alabama at the 19. Two plays later, Salem scooted 17 yards for a touchdown, converted, and suddenly it was 28-0. The rout began to take shape.

Alabama kicked off and immediately forced a punt. One play, and it was 35-0, as Salem and Steiner teamed up for a 53-yard scoring bomb.

Late in the third quarter, Alabama's Larry Laver intercepted a pass at the Auburn 23 but the Tigers held. Midway through the final period, Salem passed 30 yards to Howard Pierson for another score. Salem's point-after made it 49-0.

Five plays later and the Tide had another six. Don Spurrell picked off a Bill Ball pass and waltzed in for the score. Salem made the closest thing to a mistake in the entire game when he missed the conversion, and Alabama had to settle for its 55 points.

The Tigers mustered only five first downs, three net yards rushing, and 45 passing. Meanwhile, Alabama got 18 first downs and 404 total yards. The Tide was penalized 105 yards, Auburn 45.

Alabama had notched its fifth series win; Auburn had seven victories, and one had ended even. In points scored, the Tigers were also on top, 254-186.

"Next year? There will be another Alabama-Auburn football game," reported Alyce Billings Walker of the *News*. "That's what's important to the defeated but spirited Auburnites and to the proud University winner and to all football fans in the State of Alabama."

Yes, there would be another game next year. And what a game it would be.

1949
GAME 14

14-13

Webster's defines the word *upset* as: *To defeat unexpectedly . . . to perturb . . . to tip over . . . to disturb the functioning of.*

When the 1949 game was over, Auburn had unexpectedly defeated; perturbed; tipped over; and disturbed the functioning of— Alabama. It was college football's biggest surprise of the season.

The score was 14-13 but the game was closer than that.

As the 14th renewal of the series approached, Auburn's toothless Tigers had managed a paltry 1-4-3 record, their lone success coming at the expense of a winless Mississippi State (0-8-1) team. Making the upset even more unbelievable was that Auburn had posted only five wins in its last 34 games, while being outscored by almost 500 points.

Meanwhile, Alabama had not lost in the last seven weeks after dropping the first two games of the season to Tulane, who went on to become Southeastern Conference champions that year, and to Vanderbilt.

The professional odds-makers had placed the Alabama Crimson Tide on the "big board" as a whopping 19-point favorite. Auburn boosters, however, are not given to being disturbed by being a three-touchdown underdog. But 1949 might have been a rare exception. It was reported that the decibel level of the "War Eagle" battle cry was measurably less than normal.

The *Birmingham News* reported, "Dr. John M. Gallalee, president

Program cover, 1949.

of the University, warmed alumni hearts with a bold prediction that the Tide will win by a 21-7 score. There was nobody from the Plains that would flatly challenge him. They just kept quiet and decided to wait and see."

Plus, the humiliation that Auburn had had to endure exactly one year earlier was still fresh, and painfully, in memory. It is not easy to forget a 0-55 thrashing.

The Alabama team bused over to Birmingham on the morning of the game. Auburn was already there, having arrived the day before. However, the team was hidden out until just before game time when they went to the stadium under a heavy police escort with flashing red lights and wailing sirens.

Bright sunshine and mild temperatures greeted the 44,000 bug-eyed fans that packed Legion Field that December 3. Suddenly, the place became teeming with excitement. The "second game" of the series was about to start.

Alabama won the toss and received. Neither team put up a big threat and the game turned into one of punt-trading. On the first play of the second period, from the Alabama 43, Jim McGowen punted to Ed Salem who returned 13 yards to the 18. On second down, quarterback Salem retreated to throw, and fired a short one intended for Al Lary. The ball sailed high and was intercepted by Johnny Wallis, who shot 19 yards into the end zone for a touchdown. Bill Tucker kicked the conversion and Auburn had a 7-0 lead.

After the kickoff and another exchange of punts, the Crimson Tide started at their own 37. Sparked by James "Bimbo" Melton's run of 15 yards, Lary's gain of 18 and a 15-yard penalty, Alabama reached the Tigers' 13-yard line, first and 10.

But this was Auburn's day.

The astonishing 14-13 victory over Alabama seems to be the topic of celebration in the post-season banquet of that year. Shown here are (L-R): Wilbur Hutsell, Athletic Director, R.B. Draughon, President, Earl Brown, Head Coach, and Al Biggio, alumnus.

Tom Calvin rammed to the 11. Auburn's Jeep Hayes trapped Melton for a five-yard loss at the 16. Salem completed a short pass, and on fourth-and-10, he threw incomplete.

Just before the half, Salem returned a McGowen punt 28 yards to Auburn's 33. In just two plays, the Tide tied the score. Ed White streaked around right end to the 13, and Salem followed a wall of interference to the right and across the double-stripes. Salem also added the point.

Fifteen seconds later it was intermission and the score was all even at 7-7.

Deep into the third quarter, Alabama reached the enemy's 32, but Salem threw his second interception of the game. As did his first, this one led to trouble. Dickie Flournoy picked it off and was grounded at his own 28. Auburn responded with a relentless 12-play, 72-yard march to victory.

Quarterback Travis Tidwell, who later was to be named the SEC Back of the Year, and was the first All-American to play in the series, kept for five yards. Jeffers got three and George Davis' 10-yard gain resulted in a Tiger first down exactly at midfield. McGowen went to the 42 and Davis to the 39 for another first down. McGowen and Davis each picked up three as the period came to a close with the ball on Alabama's 33.

After play resumed, McGowen broke through for nine yards. Jeffers made it a first down at the 21. The roar of approval was coming across loud and clear from Auburn's side of the stadium. McGowen hit for three yards, and Tidwell advanced seven more before he fumbled. Forty-four thousand hearts instantly missed a thump. Max Autrey recovered the bouncing ball and Max Autrey was on Auburn's side. It was now first down at the 11, but the Tigers needed only one play. Davis blasted off right tackle and dashed into the end zone. Tucker tacked on the all-important point-after and with 12:49 left to play, Auburn led, 14-7.

As the clock ticked down to 3:48, desperate Alabama found itself on Auburn's 18 and with a fourth-and-two situation. Auburn held. And the Auburn people went absolutely crazy.

But Alabama wasn't through. After a punt that went out of bounds at its own 47, Alabama had one more shot. Melvin went to the 50, Salem to the 44 and Calvin to the 34. However, on the next play, Salem was sacked for a big 10-yard loss. He came right back and completed a long pass to Melvin who was tackled by Wallis at Auburn's three-yard line.

Pandemonium!

Travis Tidwell, the first All-American to play in the series, quarterbacked Auburn's 14-13 upset of Alabama in 1949.

Salem went to the one, and with 1:13 remaining in the game, Calvin crashed over for what everybody thought surely was the tying touchdown.

"And the most tense moment in all collegiate football came when Jack Brown took the ball from center and placed it down on the ground," wrote Zipp Newman of the *News*. "Salem's foot came through. The ball never was on line, going plenty high but wide to the right.

"The West stands rocked with joy. Generations of Auburn supporters became delirious in seeing Auburn win from Alabama for the first time since 1904."

The Tide tried an on-side kick but Auburn recovered and was able to control the ball as the final seconds ticked into history.

The statistics were about as close as the game. Auburn led in first downs 11-10, while Alabama's 205 total yards were only 21 more than the Tigers recorded. Auburn was clipped for 20 yards in penalties and Alabama five. Auburn's McGowen was the game's leading ground gainer with 48 yards in 10 carries. Salem accounted for 89 yards rushing and passing. Tidwell completed the only two passes he threw in the game.

The Plainsmen now held an 8-5-1 series lead and were ahead in points, 268-198.

From 0-55 to 14-13 in just one year. It was Auburn's 241st all-time victory on the gridiron, and at that time, the sweetest, by far.

1950
GAME 15

The Red Elephants Remembered

Three-hundred and sixty-five days had passed and Auburn was still celebrating its big upset of Alabama of the previous year. Of course, it could have been that Tiger fans had had nothing else to celebrate. Their team hadn't won a game since.

"A wise investment Saturday before game time would have been a pair of tight earmuffs to ward off the scream of 'War Eagle'—a yell so famous that it was scratched on the sands of the desert and etched into the tundra of the Aleutians during World War II," wrote Dan Cobb of the *Birmingham News*.

Yes, Auburn remembered last year's 14-13 thriller. But Alabama remembered, too, and the Crimson Tide came out rolling with a 76-yard scoring drive on their first series, setting the tone for an easy 34-0 revenge victory before a capacity crowd at Legion Field on December 2.

Auburn, under Coach Earl Brown, was suffering in 1950. The winless War Eagles were beaten by the likes of Wofford and Southeastern Louisiana, and were walloped by most of their other opponents. When the task arose to face the strong Tide, Auburn had scored only 31 points and surrendered 221. In the team's last 44 games, they had won only six, and during that period had been outscored by a staggering total of 1,094-377.

Harold "Red" Drew, in his fourth year as head coach at Alabama, had seen his team lose two games by narrow five-point margins. On October 1 at Mobile, Alabama lost to a good Vanderbilt team that won seven games that year, 27-22. Two weeks later in Knoxville, powerful Tennessee won, 14-9. The Vols went on to an 11-1-0 record and an ultimate No. 2 national ranking behind Oklahoma. That was the year the Sooners lost to Kentucky in the Sugar Bowl, 13-7. Coaching at Kentucky then was Paul "Bear" Bryant.

Despite their 9-2-0 record, Drew's Bama boys were not included in the Top Ten of either the AP or UPI end-of-season final rankings. Princeton, while playing a schedule that included Williams, Brown, Cornell and Colgate, finished No. 6. The UPI, in its first year of playing the poll game, saw fit to count Michigan and Ohio State among its Top Ten despite the fact that both teams won only six games and lost three.

Auburn's Bill McMurray kicked off to Bimbo Melton, who brought it from his end zone out to the 24 and the 15th Tide-Tiger tangle was on.

Alabama was decisive on its first possession. Al Lacy ran for eight, Tom Calvin and Ed Salem for five each, and Bobby Marlow ripped off 15 more to Auburn's 43. After a loss of two by Calvin, Marlow went for seven, Salem for four, Marlow for two, then four, and Calvin's gain of two put the ball on the 26, where it was third-and-four. Salem then lofted a pass that Marlow caught on the run at the five and scored. The conversion by Harold Lutz was missed but Alabama had a quick 6-0 lead.

Auburn took the ensuing kickoff and stormed to the Tide 16. After a loss of nine, quarterback Bill Tucker threw a long pass that was just off the fingertips of Bill Davis. Auburn missed a touchdown by a fraction and, as things turned out, that would be their only scoring threat of the day.

Following an Alabama punt, an Auburn quick-kick, and another exchange of punts, Bama took the ball at its 41 and scored in seven plays. Larry Chiodetti gained seven, Melton 22, Chiodetti three and Calvin one and the Tide was at Auburn's 26. A pass from Butch Avinger to Chiodetti was good for 17 yards to the nine. After no gain, Marlow scored. Lutz kicked good and Alabama was out front, 13-0.

At the half, the Crimsons had rolled up 182 yards to Auburn's 66.

Auburn received the second-half kickoff and drove to midfield where Davis fumbled and Jesse Richardson recovered for Alabama. Eleven snaps later and the Tide had a 20-0 advantage. The big plays were runs of 19 and 12 yards by Calvin. From the two, Marlow scored

Tide takes scrapping Tigers, 34 to 0

Tide can dish it—Tigers can take it!

So, shed no tears, gentle folk, for dear old Auburn

his third touchdown of the game, and Lutz converted.

Opening the fourth period Alabama received a punt and unleashed a time-consuming drive that took almost nine minutes and covered 86 yards and 16 plays. Jim Burkette punched it over from the three. Lutz kicked his fourth extra point of the game for Alabama's final point of the season.

Marlow joins Auburn's R. T. Dorsey (1893) and F. R. Yarbrough (1900) as the only players in the history of the series to score three touchdowns in one game.

Alabama gouged out 23 first downs and cracked Auburn's porous defense for 377 total yards. Auburn got nine first downs and its offense generated only 164 yards. The Tigers lost 20 yards in penalties, twice as many as Alabama.

Marlow's 113 yards in 24 carries was the top individual effort of the afternoon. Calvin gained 87 yards and Auburn's Charley Langler followed with 61.

Following the game, Cobb of the *News* wrote, "Shed no tears, gentle hearts, for old Auburn. She doesn't need them, thank you." If Auburn people didn't cry, then no tears were shed for them. It's for certain that Alabama partisans didn't.

The 1950 Orange and Blue edition has the dubious distinction of being the only team in Auburn football history to lose all its games in a season. Their 1927 brothers came close, but ties against Tulane and Howard got them off the hook.

During the six seasons (1945-1950) since World War II, Alabama had won more regular season games than any other Southeastern Conference team, 45. Georgia had 44 victories, Tennessee 43, and Kentucky and Georgia Tech 40 each. Auburn had become the league's perennial doormat with a mere 14 wins, by far the worst of the Dixie Dozen.

Auburn people were weary, and a change was indicated. A long distance call to Athens, Georgia was to trigger a chain of events leading to a new era of glory by Auburn football.

Ralph "Shug" Jordan was on his way to the Loveliest Village.

Jeff Beard (R) became Athletic Director at Auburn on February 15, 1951, and in less than two weeks hired "his man" — Shug Jordan — as head coach. Jordan (L), Dr. Ralph Draughon (Auburn President) and Beard are shown finalizing Shug's return to the Plains on February 26, 1951.

1951
Game 16

A Return To Auburn, Forever

James Ralph Jordan, better known as "Shug" because of his love for sugar cane during his boyhood days in Selma, Alabama, had returned to Auburn. Jordan, who played center on Auburn's 1929-30-31 football teams and also lettered in basketball and baseball, was named the school's outstanding athlete in his senior year.

Upon graduation in 1932, Jordan began his coaching career as an assistant at Auburn where he remained until 1941 when his coaching togs were temporarily swapped for the uniform of an officer in the U.S. Army. Included among Jordan's numerous battlefield decorations was the Purple Heart for a wound suffered at Normandy. He returned to Auburn in 1945.

A year later, Shug joined the coaching staff of the Miami Seahawks, a professional team of the old All-American Conference—a league that produced today's Cleveland Browns, Baltimore Colts, Los Angeles Rams and San Francisco 49ers of the National Football League. In 1947, Jordan moved to the University of Georgia, where he was a football assistant to Wally Butts, and also the head basketball coach.

Because of Georgia's wretched basketball history, perhaps one of Jordan's all-time great coaching feats was his .623 winning

Shug Jordan, Auburn graduate (1931) and student athlete. Lettered in baseball, basketball and football.

percentage (48-29 record) while in Athens. Even today, it's the highest of any Bulldog cage coach since the Southeastern Conference was formed in 1933. Jordan's 1947-48 Bulldog five won 18 games—still a UGA record for most wins in one season.

On February 26, 1951, Shug Jordan officially became Auburn's head football coach. A lifetime honeymoon between the man and the school had begun.

Both Auburn and Alabama experienced zany football seasons in 1951.

In Jordan's first game, his alma mater broke a 10-game losing streak with a tough 24-14 victory over Vanderbilt on September 29 at Auburn. An easy 30-14 success against Wofford followed. The third game saw the "new" Tigers rally to edge Florida, 14-13.

But the Georgia Tech Yellow Jackets, who went on to finish with a 10-0-1 record in 1951, brought the high-flying War Eagles back to earth with a 27-7 defeat. Then came shut-out wins over Tulane (21-0) and Louisiana College (49-0) and suddenly Auburn was 5-1-0, the team's best start in 19 years.

Crash!

There were consecutive lopsided setbacks at the hands of Ole Miss, Georgia and Clemson that added up to a total score of 119-28, and Auburn was 5-4-0 as the Alabama game approached.

The Crimson Tide opened their season by scoring the most points in one game since 1922—89. Delta State, the opposition that day, got none. LSU, Vanderbilt, Villanova and Tennessee followed on Alabama's schedule and none of those four teams in 1951 was a Delta State. All four tagged the Tide with losses and Alabama had suffered four straight defeats for the first time since 1910.

Coach Red Drew's boys came to life and rebounded with victories over Mississippi State, Georgia and Mississippi Southern, before Tech snapped the mini-streak with a 27-7 defeat—precisely the score the Yellow Jackets had posted against Auburn earlier in the season.

The Tide's record was now 4-5-0 and a November 24, encounter with Florida at Tuscaloosa approached. In a historic game, the Gators won 30-21. It was historic because it was Alabama's last chance to prevent the Crimson Tide's first losing season since 1903.

Also, the 1951 team had amassed another unwanted record during the game leading up to Auburn. The defense had surrendered 181 points, the most of any Crimson team up to that time.

But the season's weird background for both teams was history. A combined record of 9-10-0, 368 points scored by the opposition, a sixth place SEC standing for Auburn, and seventh for Alabama, meant little or nothing to the 42,000 noisy fans who filled Legion Field that heavy, hazy December 1 afternoon.

As the game progressed, Alabama seemed to have only one edge. But that edge turned out to be a decided advantage as the afternoon wore on. The difference between the two teams that day was Bobby Marlow. And it was Marlow who, for the second year in a row, led a rout of the Tigers, this time by a score of 25-7.

The powerful junior running back scored on runs of seven, 39 and 22 yards and whacked the Auburn line 25 times for 232 yards, almost 100 yards more than the entire Tiger team gained on the ground.

Auburn won the coin flip, received, and came out steaming. Bobby Freeman returned Harold Lutz' kickoff from the three to the

24. After a roughing-the-punter penalty gave the Tigers new life at their 38, Homer Williams split left guard for 27 yards to Alabama's 35. Robert Duke hit for eight yards in two tries and Auburn was in good shape at the Tide's 27 with a third-and-two. But on the next play, Williams fumbed and Alabama's Bob Wilga recovered to prevent early trouble for the Tide.

Alabama then worked the ball to Auburn's 31 but stalled and had to kick. After an exchange of punts, the War Eagles started something at their own 38 that ended in heartbreak. After a gain of seven, Williams was off and running again. He went left, got outside and streaked 48 yards before being brought down from behind on a touchdown-saving tackle by Jack Brown, but not before he had reached the Alabama seven-yard line.

Williams was given the ball again and he hammered for seven yards; or almost seven. He was stopped inches short of the goal. Alabama dug in. On second down, Duke plowed into the line but was smashed head-on by Travis Hunt and Jug Jenkins for a big two-yard loss. It was Williams again and this time he was met by Jesse Richardson at the one. It was fourth down and Auburn tried to go "over" the suddenly tough Tide defense. Joe Davis was called upon for a field goal, but his kick sailed wide to the right and a great Alabama goal line stand had been successful.

It was the turning point of the game.

Alabama took over at the 20-yard line and in 10 plays marched for a touchdown. Marlow ripped off a 27-yarder. Tommy Lewis rambled 18 more and suddenly the Tide was at Auburn's 35. Bimbo Melton advanced to the 30 and Bobby Wilson to the 22 for a first down. After an incomplete pass, Lewis managed two. On third down, some Tide trickery caught Auburn off-guard. Alabama lined up for an apparent field goal by Lutz. As holder Wilson took the snap, he stood up and flipped a short pass in the flats to Brown. It was good for a 14-yard gain to the Tigers' six. A holding penalty shoved Bama back to the 21, but they again got close on a pass from Melton to Clell Hobson that clicked for 14 yards. On fourth down from the seven, freshman Jimmy Long threw a devastating block that wiped out two Auburn defenders and enabled Marlow to score. Lutz kicked his only conversion of the day, and as the first quarter came to a close, the Crimson and White had taken a 7-0 lead.

Midway in the second period, Auburn quarterback Vince Dooley fired a pass that was batted into the air by a charging Alabama lineman. Before it could hit the ground, Richardson intercepted at the Tiger 36. This turnover led to Alabama's second touchdown. It

The Tuscaloosa News

ALABAMA CRUSHES AUBURN 25 TO 7

got to third-and-nine and Marlow broke through for 18 yards. Melton gained three, and here came Marlow again as he went for 11 yards before being stopped at the three by Dooley. In two cracks at the line, Melton scored to put the Tide on top by a 13-0 margin.

Marlow returned the second-half kickoff 18 yards to the 34, and in only six plays the score was 19-0. Marlow went for 11 yards, plus the final 39 to cap the quick drive.

Auburn took the ensuing kickoff and, keyed by a successful screen pass from Allen Parks to Lee Hayley that resulted in a 32-yard gain, the Tigers reached Alabama's 19-yard line. Once again, however, Alabama was to allow no trespassing across its goal and took over on downs.

But Auburn was destined to get the next score in the game. Following a 21-yard punt return by Dooley to his own 36, Auburn began a drive that was helped by a roughing-the-punter infraction, and later another roughing penalty to put the ball at the Alabama 30. Bob Jordan lost eight yards and Reges Coptisias got one back, before Dooley's run of 12 yards brought up a fourth-and-five situation at the 25. Dooley threw complete to Hayley for another 12-yard pickup. A penalty cost Auburn five back to the 18, but Dooley passed to Coptisias for a 10-yard advance down to the eight-yard line. Williams, like a madman, crashed through the line, shook off three defenders and scored. Davis converted, and with 2:18 remaining in the third quarter, Auburn now trailed, 19-7.

It took Alabama only seven plays to get another score. Marlow covered the final 22 yards for his third touchdown of the game and sixth TD against Auburn in the last two years. Marlow finished the 1951 season with 728 yards rushing.

The game statistics were all in Alabama's favor—22 first downs to Auburn's 16, and 488 total offensive yards to 255 for the losers. Alabama was taxed for 105 yards in penalties to Auburn's 40. Since the renewal of the series in the 1948, the Tide had been hit with 225 penalty yards; Auburn 125.

James "Bimbo" Melton rushed for 109 yards in 18 carries against Auburn in the 1951 game.

Next to Marlow's 232 yards, Melton gained 109 in 18 carries. Williams was Auburn's leading runner with 107 yards in 15 attempts. Dooley and Parks combined for 11 pass completions for 121 yards.

Auburn still led the series, 8-7-1, and in points scored, 275-257. But Alabama, in just two seasons, had dramatically closed the gap.

Even though the 1951 Crimson and White had a 25-7 victory over Auburn to celebrate, the jubilation, to many fans, had a slightly hollow quality. There was that nagging recollection of Alabama's first losing season since 1903.

1952

Game 17

Alabama-Auburn All Even

The Alabama-Auburn football series was getting close. After 17 games spread over a 59-year period, the record of battles between the two rivals had become all even. Alabama's win in 1952 brought the intrastate standings to 8-8-1. In points scored, it was almost as close—278-275, in favor of the Crimsons.

In 1952, Alabama won 10 games, were the Orange Bowl champions and finished with a No. 9 national ranking. However, even with that performance, the Crimson Tide got no better than a fourth place finish in the Southeastern Conference.

Alabama had to settle behind SEC members Georgia Tech, Tennessee and Ole Miss in what turned out to be a banner autumn for the Dixie Dozen—with four teams rated in the nation's Top Ten.

Meanwhile, at the bottom of the Conference standings were Kentucky, LSU, Vanderbilt . . . . and 12th place Auburn. The Plainsmen had entered another dreaded losing period after seemingly coming alive at the start of the 1951 season, when they reeled off a quick 5-1-0 record.

Coach Shug Jordan, in his second year at the Plains, had a doublebarreled problem aimed at him. First, there was a talent shortage, and next a murderous schedule. Auburn opened the

Alabama's Bobby Marlow scored 36 points and rushed for 477 yards (77 carries) in the 1950-51-52 games. His "36" and "477" would stand as series records until the mid-eighties.

season against Maryland, the defending Sugar Bowl champs and the nation's fourth-ranked team the previous year. The Terps won, 13-7. The next week it was a 20-7 setback to Ole Miss, who finished with an 8-1-2 record, losing only to undefeated Georgia Tech in the Sugar Bowl. The Rebels were voted eighth best in the land that year.

After a 54-7 breather against Wofford, Auburn was back among the region's bullies when they made their annual trip to Atlanta for a date with the 1952 SEC champions, Georgia Tech. The Yellow Jackets won 33-0 enroute to a perfect 12-0-0 record and a No. 2 national ranking.

Next was a 21-0 loss to Tulane, and a wild 49-34 defeat at the hands of Mississippi State. Then Georgia handled the Plainsmen 13-7. Against Clemson, Auburn squeaked to a 3-0 victory and the season's record stood at 2-7-0.

Seven of the Tigers' 1952 opponents combined for a regular season record of 54-15-2 and a .774 winning percentage. Four went bowling, and remember, this was in the days when, excluding the Rose Bowl, the bowl committees picked only eight major teams to attend their post-season parties.

Alabama, suffering its first losing season in 48 years in 1951, rebounded by recording four straight victories to open the fall of '52, winning over Mississippi Southern, LSU, Miami and VPI. Then it was on to Knoxville, where the Crimsons hadn't won since 1941. The Vols kept the streak intact with a 20-0 triumph.

In the next three outings, Mississippi State, Georgia and Chattanooga scored 66 points against Alabama, but the Tide retaliated with 118, and won all three games handily. Appearing on television for the first time, Alabama lost a close 7-3 decision to Georgia Tech in Atlanta as the Nation looked on. A 27-7 win over tough Maryland followed and Alabama was 8-2-0.

November 29 dawned windy, wet and cold, and the miserable weather conditions kept the Legion Field crowd down to about 40,000. Only the Alabama partisans had anything to cheer about as their Tide struck early and easily took care of the weary Tigers, 21-0.

Auburn boosters who braved the dreary day not only had to suffer through the Tigers' fourth loss to Alabama in five years, but they also witnessed the school's 200th all-time gridiron defeat.

It just wasn't Auburn's day.

The Tigers did call the coin correctly and chose to have the football first. After three scrimmage plays they were bogged down at their own nine-yard line and Dudley Spence's long punt went out of bounds at Alabama's 40. The Bama boys went right in for a touchdown. Two running plays gained seven yards before Tommy

Lewis bolted for 22. Bobby Marlow got 15 more to the Auburn 16. One play later, Lewis scored from 13 yards out, Bobby Luna converted and after just four minutes of play, it was 7-0.

On Auburn's next series, a 42-yard run by Fob James led the Tigers to Alabama's 27-yard line, but Cecil "Hooty" Ingram intercepted a Spence pass at the 16. From there, Alabama crunched out a 14-play drive that ended in another score. Marlow lost two, but Luna gained 16. Marlow ran for four, and Lewis for 16 to advance the chains to midfield. Luna carried to the 46, Marlow to the 42, Marlow to the 38 and Luna to the 28. After runs by Lewis and Clell Hobson added seven more yards, Marlow cracked for seven, then four, to Auburn's 10-yard line. Luna managed two and Lewis rushed the final eight yards for his second touchdown of the game. Luna's kick made it 14-0.

Early in the second quarter, Alabama scored its final touchdown of the day. Taking a punt at their own 40, they covered the distance in only seven plays. Marlow carried four times for 43 yards and Luna went over from the four. Luna also added another PAT. In the second half, Auburn got only as close as 30 yards to the Alabama goal and the Tigers had suffered their 12th loss in the last 14 games.

The winners led in first downs 17-9, total yards 357-150, and penalty yards 60-50.

Auburn had seen the last and enough of Bobby Marlow. With 132 yards (950 for the year) he was the leading ground gainer in the series for the third straight year. In three games against Auburn, Marlow scored six touchdowns, rushed for 477 yards in 77 carries for a 6.2 average. Actually, Marlow's rushing total was 80 yards more than all of Auburn's backs gained in those games. In his career at Alabama, Marlow scored 30 touchdowns.

Among the spectators at Legion Field that dark day was Syracuse coach Ben Schwartzwalder and the rest of his staff. They were there to scout Alabama, who would be the Orangemen's opponent in the upcoming Orange Bowl game.

Their observations? They would be interesting, considering the final score: Alabama 61, Syracuse 6.

1953

Game 18

Second Field Goal Puts Alabama First

For the first time in history, Alabama and Auburn met with something more at stake than a State Championship.

In perhaps the most intriguing race in Southeastern Conference history, a total of five teams—Alabama, Auburn, Georgia Tech, Ole Miss and Kentucky—went into action on the season's final Saturday with a chance to claim the league title.

By late afternoon when the final results had been posted and the combinations of wins and losses and ties had been figured out, the winner of the Alabama-Auburn game picked up the SEC trophy, plus a Cotton Bowl bid.

And in a thrilling game that could have easily gone either way, Alabama pulled it out with a late field goal and a 10-7 triumph.

The first few weeks of the season did not produce even the slightest hint that this game would be for any kind of Conference honors. Alabama opened its season against Mississippi Southern on a Friday night in Montgomery and the boys from Hattiesburg left the Crimson Tide and their followers in a complete state of shock with a 25-19 bombshell victory. Eight nights later, September 26, the still-dazed Crimsons played the school's 500th all-time football game in Mobile and were tied by LSU, 7-7.

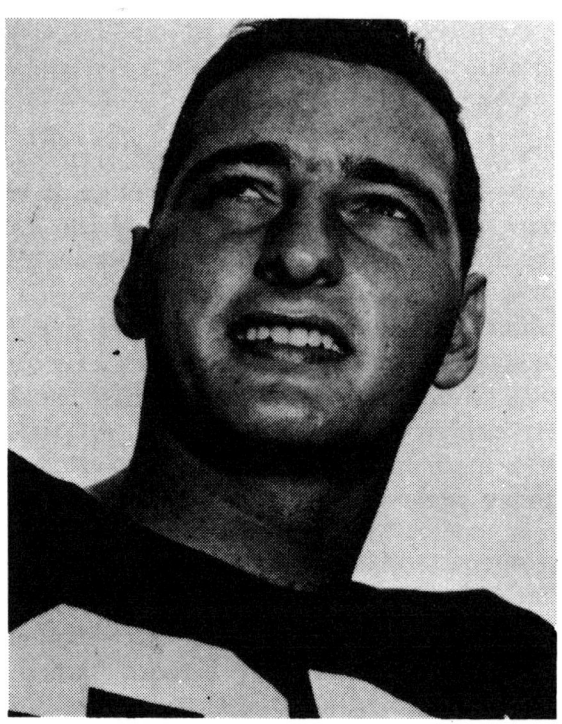

Vince Dooley, Auburn quarterback in the 1951 and 1953 games and later Head Coach at Georgia.

Coach Red Drew's troops momentarily got back on track with wins over Vanderbilt (21-12) and Tulsa (41-13). Then came back-to-back ties—0-0 with Tennessee, and 7-7 versus Mississippi State.

Six games played and a 2-1-3 record. Eventual SEC champs? The odds seemed greatly against it at this point in the season.

During the same six-week period, Auburn had wins over Stetson, Ole Miss, Tulane and Florida by an aggregate score of 100-14. But there was a 21-21 tie with Mississippi State and a one-sided 36-6 defeat at the hands of Georgia Tech.

Alabama came back with victories over Georgia, Chattanooga and Tech before losing to Maryland, the 1953 National Champions, by three touchdowns. Auburn went on to drill Miami, Georgia and Clemson, which gave the surging Tigers a five-game win streak—their longest since 1935. In just three years, Shug Jordan had put a contending football team on the field.

The Tigers were 7-1-1; the Crimson Tide 5-2-3.

A crowd of 43,000 filed into Legion Field on November 28 for the 18th game of the series and excitement ran rampant.

Auburn's opening kickoff went into the end zone and Alabama started offensive action at the 20-yard line. On the game's first play, Tommy Lewis hit the line, was separated from the ball and the Tigers' M. L. Brackett cradled the prize at the 18.

Charles Hataway gained two. On the next play, quarterback Vince Dooley rambled for a big 13-yard pickup to Alabama's three, but Auburn was slapped with a devastating five-yard motion penalty. Two passes fell incomplete, and Joe Davis' field goal try fell unsuccessful. Auburn's golden opportunity had slipped away.

Alabama couldn't move and punted dead at the Auburn 45. Coach Jordan had two different offensive teams in 1953, known simply as "X" and "Y". And here came the X's. An off-side penalty cost five yards, but Dooley, on an option play optioned to keep the ball himself and reeled off a 27-yard gain to the Crimsons' 33. Fob James got five, Davis three, and James 14 and a first down at the 11. James crashed for nine more, and Hataway's gain of one got another Auburn first down at the one. Alabama then stopped a Dooley

sneak and a Hataway buck. But on third down, Hataway blasted off right guard for a touchdown and Auburn had its first lead over Alabama in four years. With 6:51 showing on the clock, Davis converted and the War Eagle fans went wild over their 7-0 lead.

Early in the second quarter, Alabama took over at its own 32 after a punt, and quickly went the distance to tie the score. Bill Stone got four, and on the next five plays, ground was eaten up in big chunks. Hooty Ingram scooted for 11; Stone for 14; Ingram for 14; Stone for 10, and Stone for 15. Touchdown. "Bobby Luna converted and the score was deadlocked 7-7 with 43,000 shaking from the great drama," wrote Zipp Newman of the *Birmingham News.*

Dooley fielded the ensuing kickoff at the 13-yard line and raced 44 yards to Alabama's 43. Dooley then hit James Long with a pass that was good for 19 yards. Fob James rammed for four, Charles Little for three, and Hataway for three to give the Plainsmen a first down at the 14. James went to the 10, Hataway to the nine, and James to the six. That brought up a fourth-and-two situation. On the big play, Dooley went over right guard but the ball popped free and Alabama's Ralph Carrigan recovered it at the five.

An untimely turnover had foiled Auburn again and the half ended, 7-7.

The third quarter was scoreless and neither team gave the other much trouble—except on defense. The scoreboard clock kept blinking the time away and the tense, tight struggle moved midway into the final period. Auburn got something started but once again a fumble doomed the Tigers' victory bid. Taking a punt at midfield, Auburn worked it to Alabama's 37. Bobby Freeman, Y-team quarterback, then completed a 17-yard pass to Jim Pyburn, but a fumble resulted and Bart Starr recovered for Alabama at the 20.

Two Starr completions to Hill Oliver for 13 and 44 yards keyed a six-play drive to Auburn's 11-yard line. On fourth down, Fred Sington missed a field goal attempt.

Auburn couldn't move and punted to Alabama's 42. Helped by a huge break in their favor, the Crimson Tide set the winning drive in motion. Oliver rammed for 10 yards before Stone gained three to Auburn's 45. Then came the fateful play. Auburn's defense trapped Stone and threw him for a four-yard loss. However, Frank D'Agontino was called for piling-on and the 15-yard penalty gave Alabama a first down at the Tigers' 34. Albert Elmore gained two and Stone went for eight and another first down at the 24. Two short gains and an incomplete pass brought up a fourth-and-seven at the 20. Coach Drew then sent Luna into the lineup with instructions to kick a field goal. Elmore knelt at the 28-yard line, took the snap from center, placed it down, and Luna boomed it through.

With just over a minute to play, the first field goal in the series since 1906 had been recorded by Luna, a senior from Huntsville, Alabama. His kick not only won the game, but the Southeastern Conference championship and a Cotton Bowl bid. Furthermore, it was only the second field goal Luna had attempted in his college career. His other effort, against Tech the year before, had also been good.

At the game that day was Sandy Sanford, who was attending his first Alabama game in 13 years. Sanford was a Crimson Tide legend because of his last-minute field goal in 1937 to beat Vanderbilt in Nashville, 9-7, and send Alabama to the Rose Bowl.

Sanford's kick had been called the "$100,000 Field Goal." It was reported that Luna's successful boot was worth $150,000—the Cotton Bowl's payoff that year.

Auburn outgained Alabama 256 yards to 200 in the 1953 game and was also penalized more yards, 45-35.

In the New Year's Day game at Dallas, the Tide was no match for Rice and a fellow by the name of Dicky Maegle. The Owls hooted, 28-6, in a game highlighted by an incident that caught the whole nation's fancy—Tommy Lewis' off-the-bench tackle of Maegle. The famous play occurred in the second quarter with Rice leading 14-6

Bobby Luna kicked the winning field goal in the fourth quarter of the 1953 SEC Championship showdown. The Tide beat the Tigers 10-7.

and backed up to its own five-yard line. Meagle got free and was heading for an apparent touchdown when Lewis without a helmet, leaped from his seat on the bench and brought Maegle to earth at the Alabama 40. The officials, however, awarded Maegle a 95-yard touchdown run. Maegle also had scoring runs of 79 and 34 yards that day and gained 265 yards in only 11 carries.

Ironically, Alabama's lone touchdown was scored by Tommy Lewis.

1954
Game 19

Turnabout's Fair Play

Since the official rebirth of the series in 1948, Alabama had taken Auburn behind the woodshed and administered what amounted to an old-fashioned country whipping. The kind Mamas and Papas and big brothers dished out back in the days when woodsheds were in style.

Not only had the Tide won five of the six games, but they held a commanding lead in points scored 158-28; first downs 102-63, and in total yards 2,031-1,057.

But the time had come for a change. A drastic change.

Shug Jordan had been at Auburn for only four years and his dedication and untold hours of hard work had begun to pay dividends for happy War Eagle fans. However, the opening weeks of the 1954 season offered absolutely nothing for Auburn to get excited about. After an easy 45-0 rout of Chattanooga in the opener, the Tigers dropped three straight games—19-13 to Florida, 21-14 to Kentucky and 14-7 to Georgia Tech.

But that was it.

The surging Tigers rebounded with shutout wins over FSU (33-0) and Tulane (27-0). Next came a come-from-behind 14-13 decision over Miami in Auburn's 500th all-time football game. Georgia and Clemson were no trouble as the Bulldogs fell 35-0 and Clemson 27-6. Auburn was 6-3-0 with Alabama coming up.

For the second year in a row, Alabama and Southern Mississippi

Bobby Freeman, Auburn quarterback, scored 3 touchdowns, rushed for 102 yards and passed for 64 in the 1954 game.

met in Montgomery for a Friday night season opener; and for the second year in a row the Southerners shocked the Crimson Tide, this time by a score of 7-2. Alabama came to life and defeated LSU 12-0, Vanderbilt 28-14 and Tulsa 40-0. That brought the season to October 16 and a date with Tennessee in Knoxville. In a game that Alabama fans would look back on as historic, the Tide won 27-0. The game, however, would not be remembered as the Crimsons' first win in Knoxville in 13 years, but instead as Alabama's last win anywhere for the next two years!

Following the victory over the Vols, Alabama's scoring punch became virtually non-existent against Mississippi State, Georgia, Tulane, Georgia Tech and Miami. There were, however, back-to-back scoreless ties with the Bulldogs and Green Wave. The Tide's record was 4-4-2.

Auburn was pegged as a solid two-touchdown favorite because of developments during the past five weeks. Alabama was winless and had scored only two touchdowns; Auburn was unbeaten and had surrendered just three touchdowns.

On November 27, the normal capacity crowd showed up at Legion Field and watched Bobby Freeman, Auburn quarterback, score three touchdowns, set up the other, and run and pass for 166 yards to lead a 28-0 War Eagle victory.

It was reported that Auburn's delirious fans celebrated all night — and then some.

The 19th game of the series got underway as Alabama won the toss and received. The Tide soon punted, Auburn did likewise, and Alabama kicked back again. The Tigers then moved 60 yards in 13 plays for a score. Joe Childress ran for two and Dave Middleton's gain of eight got a first down at the 50. Sticking to straight ahead, power football, Childress went to the Alabama 45; Fob James to the 34; James to the 32; Childress to the 29; Freeman to the 20; James to the 14; James to the 12; Middleton to the nine; Childress to the three, and Childress to the one. From there, Freeman dived across for the touchdown. Childress converted and with 12 seconds remaining in the first quarter, Auburn had taken a 7-0 lead.

Just before the half, Auburn got down to Alabama's nine, but Tommy Tillman crashed through to block a field goal try by Childress.

Taking the second-half kickoff, the Tigers swiftly moved to a 14-0 advantage. Freeman returned the kick 11 yards to the 36. On the first down, Childress rumbled for 19 yards to Alabama's 45. After a gain of four by Middleton, Freeman smacked through right guard on an option and sped 41 yards for a touchdown. Childress converted.

Auburn's next series resulted in a drive that was stopped at Alabama's nine-yard line. Unable to move, the Tide punted out of bounds at the Auburn 46, where the Tigers started another scoring march. James got 11 yards and Childress three. A Freeman-to-James pass added 13 more to Alabama's 27. Freeman got free and wasn't stopped until he had reached the Tide two. On the first play of the fourth quarter, Childress smashed over for the touchdown, and his conversion made it 21-0.

Late in the game, Auburn scored again. Taking a punt at its own 40, the distance was covered in 10 plays. James gained 16 yards in two tries. On a Freeman-to-Childress pass completion, a clipping penalty pushed the scrimmage line back to midfield. On third down, Jim Pyburn made a fabulous grab of a Freeman pass for a 13-yard gain and a first down at the 34. Freeman went to Childress again and this time it was good for 14 yards. Alton Shell ripped off a 15-yarder to the Tide five. Two plays later, Freeman sneaked over to become the fifth player in series history to score three touchdowns in one game. Childress added his fourth point-after for the final 28-point victory margin.

The series was tied—9-9-1.

Freeman led all rushers with 102 yards. Childress and James followed with 97 and 85 yards respectively, as this Auburn trio carried the ball an even 50 times during a busy afternoon. The game statistics weighed heavily in Auburn's favor—first downs 22-9, and total yards 418-126. The winners were also penalized more yards, 50-35.

After the game, the Auburn coaching staff and other school officials sat around nervously awaiting phone calls from bowl committees in Dallas and New Orleans. Just after five o'clock a Sugar Bowl official rang Coach Jordan to inform him they had chosen SEC champ Ole Miss and Navy. At 7:30 p.m., the Cotton Bowl called to report that Georgia Tech (7-3-0) had been selected to play the Southwest Conference representative, Arkansas.

"I think they passed up the best team east of the Mississippi (River). But it's their show and there is nothing we can do about it," said Jeff Beard, Auburn athletic director, to Sam Davis, a reporter for the *Montgomery Advertiser.*

Jordan told the same reporter, "We definitely proved we had the best team in the SEC going down the stretch. My only regret is that our boys did not get the honor they justly deserved. We have a great football team and it would have put on a great show in any bowl."

Obviously, Auburn's sixth place finish in the SEC destroyed its chances for a berth in the Sugar or Cotton. There was never a chance for the Orange Bowl to pick the Tigers. Because of Alabama's 61-6 slaughter of Syracuse two years earlier, the Orange people went scurrying for conference tie-ups to prevent the recurrence of such a disaster. At the time, the Orange Bowl was committed to contests between Atlantic Coast Conference and Big Eight teams.

Jordan was right about one thing, though, when he said that his

team would put on a great show in any bowl. The Gator Bowl took heed, invited Auburn, and the Tigers proceeded to drill Baylor 33-13 to finish the season with eight wins against three early-season setbacks.

The 1954 Alabama-Auburn game marked the end of Harold (Red) Drew's coaching career at Alabama. He had coached there for eight years (1947-54) and recorded a fine 54-28-7 record, including one Southeastern Conference championship, two trips to the Cotton Bowl and one to the Orange Bowl.

1955

Game 20

"Yiiieeee!"

In 1950 when Auburn had gone 0-10-0 for the season, Alabama fans laughed, poked fun at and cracked jokes about Auburn.

In 1955, Alabama was winless after its first nine games. Auburn was more than hell-bent on making it one more. The Tigers did. The score was 26-0, and five years "later," Alabama was 0-10-0. Auburn wallowed in it. It was their turn with the jokes. As one die-hard War Eagle put it, "This is one of the greatest happenings in American history. Alabama . . . . 0-10-0 . . . . YIIIEEEE!"

Yes sir, the War Eagles loved it.

Still, though, Auburn was beginning to develop a Rodney Dangerfield complex. They were getting "no respect." Mississippi's 5-1-0 Southeastern Conference record nosed out Auburn's 5-1-1 finish for the league championship. The Tigers were, in turn, one-half game better than Georgia Tech's 4-1-1.

Overall, Ole Miss was 9-1-1; Auburn and Tech, 8-1-1. The Rebels' only loss of the year was to Kentucky. Auburn's lone defeat was to Tulane, and Tech's one setback was to Auburn.

However, for the second year in a row, the Cotton and Sugar Bowls bypassed Auburn in favor of Ole Miss and Georgia Tech, which left the War Eagles again with a Gator Bowl bid. The Gator was only 10 years old at the time and had not gained the status and prestige that it enjoys today. Auburn's appearances in the early, struggling days of the Gator Bowl has prompted the Jacksonville people to credit the Tigers with "saving" their bowl.

When the time came to play Alabama, the Crimson Tide, under new head coach J. B. (Ears) Whitworth, had lost to Rice, Vanderbilt, TCU, Tennessee, Mississippi State, Georgia, Tulane, Tech and Miami by an overwhelming score margin of 230-48.

Also, when it came time to play Alabama, there were strong

Fob James, Auburn halfback, gained 253 yards in 50 carries against Alabama in the 1952-53-54-55 games. He would later become the Governor of Alabama in 1978.

rumors floating about that Coach Shug Jordan was about to leave Auburn for Florida. It was reported that Jordan had been offered a longtime contract by the Gators at $21,000 a year, about $5,000 more than his Auburn salary at that time.

Forty-five thousand ticket-holders showed up at Legion Field on November 26 and the 20th scrap of the series was on. Auburn, a three-touchdown favorite, got its choice and received the opening kickoff. However, it was late in the first quarter before the Tigers could get their offense in gear.

After a Bart Starr punt went over the goal line, Auburn started at the 20-yard line and marched away for a score. On a third-and-nine at the 21, Alton Shell got things rolling with a 14-yard gain. Quarterback Howell Tubbs threw complete to Jimmy Phillips for 20 more to Alabama's 45. Three plays later, it was fourth down and a yard to go for a first down. Fob James got it with a three-yard rush as the first quarter came to a close.

Bobby Hoppe went for 11 yards when play resumed, and then two more to the 23. Tubbs then rifled a scoring strike to end Jerry Elliott. Childress' converson was blocked by Knute Rockne Christian. Auburn still 6-0.

Joe Childress, Auburn back, scored 2 touchdowns, kicked 6 conversions and rushed for 165 yards in 28 carries in the 1954-55 games.

After the ensuing kickoff, Alabama worked the ball to just inside Tiger territory. Starr punted and Auburn went on the attack again from their own 10. Twelve plays later and the 90 yards had been taken care of. The big plays in the long drive were Tubbs' run of 25 yards and a Tubbs-to-James pass for 14. The final nine came when Tubbs passed to Elliott for his second touchdown catch of the game. This time Childress made the point-after and the score was 13-0 when the first half ended a few plays later.

Early in the third quarter, Alabama reached Auburn's seven-yard line, but a clipping penalty ended the Tide's threat to get back into the ball game. Taking over at the 16, the War Eagles moved to Alabama's 37 but wound up punting into the end zone.

On first down from the 20, Alabama's Clay Walls fumbled and Tim Baker recovered for Auburn at the 24. The Tigers were close again but it was tough. On a third-and-11 situation, James caught a Tubbs' pass for 12 yards. Three straight carries by Childress resulted in the touchdown. Tubbs tried the conversion this time and he too missed, but Auburn had built up a 19-0 lead.

On its next series, Alabama had to punt and Janes returned the kick 32 yards to the Tiger 47. Tubbs, on a beautiful run, broke away for 36 yards to the Crimsons' 17. Childress popped through for 14, and Tubbs got the final three yards and the final TD. Childress kicked true and that was the ball game.

The series was now back in Auburn's favor, 10-9-1.

In the game, Auburn led in first downs 21-8 and in total offensive yards 356-171. Alabama was caught for 50 yards worth of penalties

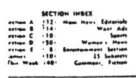

Last words from Auburn and Tuscaloosa—

'We're fine'—Shug; 'We're ready'—Whit

The Birmingham News

AUBURN WINS; TECH, REBS INVITED

The Birmingham News BUSINESS NEWS, WANT ADS SECTION B

An old Auburn remembers lean years—

War Eagles yelled early, late and loud

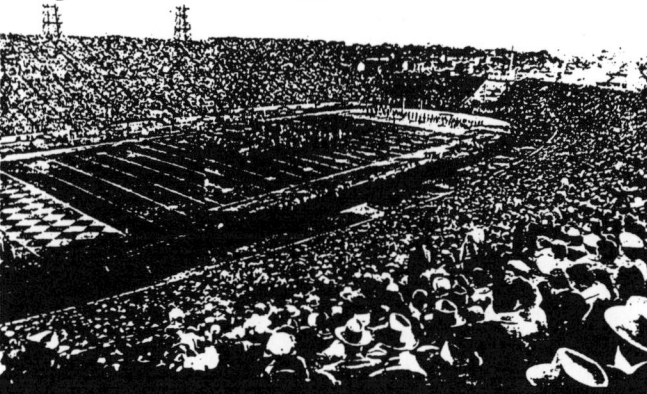

as opposed to 30 for Auburn. Childress' 68 yards in eight carries and James' 54 yards in 13 attempts led the ground gainers for the day.

Vanderbilt, with losses to Georgia, Ole Miss and Tennessee, was selected as Auburn's opponent in the Gator Bowl and the Commodores surprised the favored Tigers, 25-13. Tech topped Pittsburgh 7-0 in the Sugar Bowl while Ole Miss edged TCU 14-13 in the Cotton Bowl.

Even though the Gator Bowl loss left a bad taste to an otherwise excellent season, Auburn still had its second straight win over Alabama to celebrate in 1955, along with a No. 8 national ranking in the final polls.

As for Shug going to Gatorland, he later said, "I love Auburn." And Auburn loved Shug. Undoubtedly that love, and perhaps other inducements, were enough to make him stay and to put the rumors to rest.

1956

Game 21

"Nobody Asked For A Refund"

Alabama picked up in 1956 where it had left off in 1955—losing. First Rice, then Vanderbilt, TCU and Tennessee beat up on the Tide and pushed the team's winless skein to 20 games. In those games, victorious opponents had racked up 438 points and Alabama only 88.

It was October 27 at Tuscaloosa that the horrendous and humiliating streak was broken—with a squeaking 13-12 victory over Mississippi State. It was the Crimsons' first triumph in two years and two weeks.

The following Saturday, things returned to normal as Georgia came out on top. Six weeks into the season, Alabama owned a dismal 1-5-0 record—better than at the same stage of the season a year ago, but still dismal.

Auburn was struggling, too. The Tigers had only a split in their first six games. There were wins over Furman, Kentucky and Houston by a combined score of 66-0. However, losses to Tennessee, Georgia Tech and Florida added up to an 83-14 debit.

The grid scene brightened considerably at the Plains during the next three weeks as the War Eagles walloped Mississippi State, Georgia and FSU. During the same time, Alabama went 1-1-1 by whipping Tulane, losing to Tech and tying Mississippi Southern. The Tigers were 6-3-0, the Tide 2-6-1, and it was time for the 21st meeting between the two rivals.

"The afternoon was perfect for football, or hitching the horse up and taking a buggy ride, for hunting scalybarks, or just sitting and clapping for Mother Nature in the hope that she would oblige with an encore. Forty-five thousand had paid their money to see something spectacular, and nobody asked for a refund," wrote Henry Vance of the *Birmingham News*, about that December 1 day.

Certainly Auburn didn't ask for a refund. The War Eagles scored 27 points in the second quarter and pranced through an afternoon of fun in the sun by a score of 34-7, for their third straight victory over Alabama.

Early in the game, Alabama moved to the Auburn 18, and later to the 24, but couldn't cash any points either time and the hope of an upset vanished.

On the first play of the second quarter, Auburn's Tommy Lorino called for a fair-catch of a punt on his own 46, and the Tigers started to roar. On second down, quarterback Howell Tubbs and end Jimmy Phillips combined for a 40-yard pass play that carried to Alabama's 14. On fourth down from the six, end Jerry Elliott made a diving catch in the end zone on a pass from Tubbs, Tubbs' kick made it 7-0 and the second period scoring orgy had begun.

Auburn's next series started at their own 49. Tubbs went to Lorino for 27 yards, then to Phillips for 12 more at the Tide 12. On third down from the 11, Tubbs started wide, cut inside and scored. His conversion was no good and the score was 13-0.

Alabama's Don Kinderknecht fumbled the ensuing kickoff and Cleve Wester recovered for Auburn on the Tide 12. James Cook swept left end and went to the one. On the next play, Cook fumbled at the goal, but as if to prove the rule that "when things are going right, they are going right," the ball bounced over the goal and Billy Kitchens fell on it for a touchdown. Billy Atkins converted to make it 20-0.

A few plays later, Auburn had another TD. Atkins intercepted a Bobby Smith pass at the Alabama 38. Three plays got it to the 21 and Cook passed to Elliott, who once again made a great diving catch for a touchdown. That was it for the first half and as the athletes turned the field over to the musicians, the score was Auburn 27, Alabama 0.

To begin the third quarter, Auburn received the kickoff and started moving right away. A Bobby Hoppe run for 20 yards and a Tubbs-to-Phillips pass for 15 featured a snappy drive that brought Auburn to

The Birmingham News — COMPLETE SPORTS
SECTION C, SUNDAY, DECEMBER 2, 1956

Pitt to meet Jackets; Syracuse in Cotton—

Vols to play Baylor in Sugar; Tech in Gator

Auburn smacks down Tide, 34-7

Best we've met, says Tide's Whit
BY BENNY MARSHALL

Tigers get 27 in hot 2nd qtr.
BY ZIPP NEWMAN

THIS HOWELL TUBBS-TO-JERRY ELLIOTT BEAUTY GOT FIRST OF AUBURN SCORES
...Elliott eluded Alabama Halfback Jim Bowdoin (31) to make catch

BOWL BID, SEC TITLE, PERFECT YEAR—

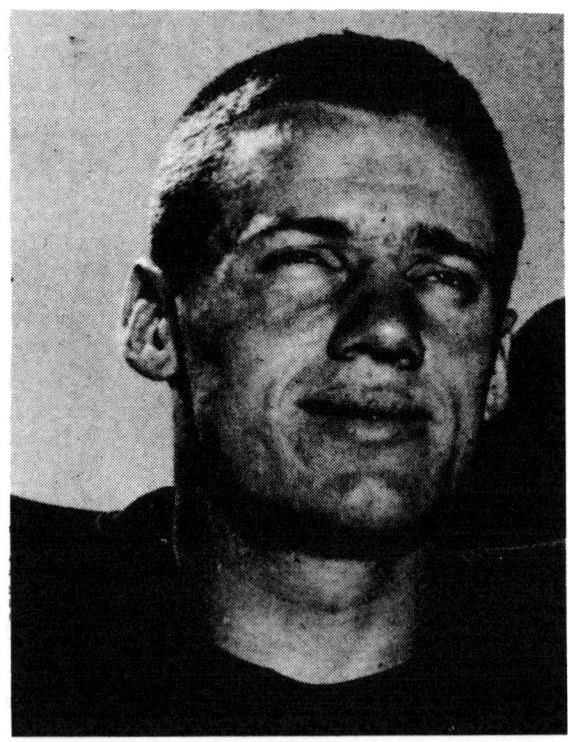

Jerry Elliott, Auburn end, holds series record of 4 touchdown receptions.

Bobby Hoppe, Auburn back, riddled Alabama for 112 yards in only 8 carries in the 1956 game.

the Alabama 17-yard line. On the next play, Lorino took a pitchout, broke a tackle at the line of scrimmage, and then dashed across for a score. Tubbs added the point-after.

Alabama, anxious to prevent a whitewash from going into the record books, came back with a 75-yard touchdown drive on their next possession. Don Comstock got it started with an 11-yard run to the Tide 36. After an incomplete pass, Comstock came back for seven more. Then Charles Nelson passed complete to Ed Pharo for a 13-yard gain to Auburn's 44. Nelson got seven, and James Loftin shot for 27 yards down to the Tigers' 10. Comstock went to the eight and Loftin covered the balance on the next play. Baxter Booth kicked the conversion.

Although Auburn's scoring was over for the day and the season, it didn't appear that way when the Tigers got the ball back. Highlighted by a 43-yard scamper by Hoppe, Auburn's drive reached the Tide one-yard line. There, as James Walsh attempted to plunge for the TD, Alabama defenders separated him from the ball, recovered the fumble and took over again.

Very late in the game, Alabama "scored" on a 61-yard pass from Smith to Bobby Jackson, but off-setting personal fouls nullified the play.

Auburn's 489 total offensive yards (333 rushing and 156 passing) set a modern (since 1948) series record, bettering the previous mark by one scant yard, set by Alabama in the 1951 game.

Hoppe led all rushers with 112 yards, while teammate Tubbs ran for 45 yards and passed for 103. In two games against Alabama, Elliott had caught four touchdown passes.

The Tigers took a two-game series lead, 11-9-1, and had scored 370 points—75 more than Alabama.

Auburn finished fifth in the final Southeast Conference standings, but the War Eagles were on the verge of better days. Much better.

1957

GAME 22

"We're No. 1"

In the 1957 pre-season polls the best Auburn could do was a No. 15 ranking. The Tigers were coming off a fifth-place standing in the Southeastern Conference the previous year, and the team would be serving the second year of a probationary period set down by the NCAA. Furthermore, a glance at Auburn's early schedule offered little encouragement for even the most loyal War Eagle fan.

In the first 20 days of the season, Auburn had to face the previous year's No. 2 and No. 4 nationally-ranked teams—both on the road.

Thus, Auburn's historic 1957 season unfolded. . . .

GAME 1 (Sept. 29 at Knoxville)—In what was considered a huge upset at the time, the Tigers topped Tennessee 7-0. The Vols were defending SEC champs and had finished 1956 as the Nation's second best team with a 10-1-0 record. Billy Atkins' short touchdown run in the second quarter capped a 57-yard drive. Atkins also added the point-after. The big win pushed Auburn all the way to seventh place.

GAME 2 (Oct. 5 at Auburn)—Chattanooga fell 40-7 and the Tigers fell back to ninth in the polls.

GAME 3 (Oct. 12 at Auburn)—In a real "cat scrap," Kentucky's Wildcats gave the host Tigers all they could handle. Atkins' six-yard run in the third quarter gave Auburn a 6-0 margin of victory, just enough to preserve the No. 9 ranking.

GAME 4 (Oct. 19 at Atlanta)—It was Atkins again. His 31-yard

The Birmingham News — COMPLETE SPORTS
SECTION C — SUNDAY, DECEMBER 1, 1957

WITH TREMENDOUS FIRST HALF—

Auburn swamps Alabama, 40-0

Tiders agree: No. 1!  Lorino sparks victory

---

The Mobile Press Register
SUNDAY MORNING, DECEMBER 1, 1957

From The Bench — By Vincent Johnson
Out 'O' Doors — By Bill Ziebach
The Sports Whirl — By Dennis Smitherman

Auburn Flails Tide, 40-0, To Finish Unbeaten

Tigers Take 1st SEC Title
By DENNIS SMITHERMAN

Rebs Tie Maroons, Win Sugar Bowl Bid

Advertiser-JOURNAL
Montgomery, Ala., Sunday, Dec. 1, 1957

SPORTS. NEWS. MARKETS C

Auburn Mauls Hapless Alabama, 40-0
To Finish Unbeaten, Untied, Uninvited

Auburn Number One Team In Nation

the Grandstand
by Max Moseley

Central Alabama Conference

The Birmingham News — COMPLETE SPORTS
PAGE 25 — TUESDAY, DECEMBER 3, 1957

500 points ahead of Ohio State—

Dusting 'Em Off—
Shug all but wept with joy

Auburn No. 1 by a landslide
BY THE ASSOCIATED PRESS

138

field goal in the second quarter beat Georgia Tech 3-0. The Yellow Jackets had finished 10-1-0 in 1956 and were ranked No. 4. Auburn's defense, fast becoming the best in the land, saved the day by stopping Tech once on the four-yard line and later on the five. The Tigers leaped to fourth.

GAME 5 (Oct. 26 at Houston)—No trouble with the Cougars as Lloyd Nix hit Phillips with a 71-yard scoring bomb on the game's first play and Auburn went on to post an easy 48-7 win. Still No. 4.

GAME 6 (Nov. 2 at Auburn)—Florida, a team that didn't lose but one other game in 1957, was completely shut down by Auburn's devastating defense. The Gators managed only 83 total yards on offense. A 13-0 score sent Auburn's Homecoming crowd home happy. Rankwise, the War Eagles moved up again—to No. 3.

GAME 7 (Nov. 9 at Birmingham)—For the second week in a row, Auburn faced a team that was to lose only one other game in '57—Mississippi State. State held a 7-0 halftime lead but the Tigers came back for a 15-7 victory, and remained in the No. 3 spot in the polls.

GAME 8 (Nov. 16 at Columbus)—The Nation's No. 1 defense sent Auburn to a No. 2 ranking. A 52-yard drive in the second quarter ended with Nix's four-yard toss to Jimmy Phillips—enough for a slim 6-0 victory over Georgia. In the final period, the Bulldogs had the ball and a first down at Auburn's four, but fumbled it away.

GAME 9 (Nov. 23 at Tallahassee)—Over piercing screams from Ohio State's Woody Hayes and the rest of the Big Ten, Auburn replaced the once-beaten Buckeyes as the No. 1 team with a 29-7 win over Florida State.

GAME 10 (Nov. 30 at Birmingham)—vs. Alabama.

While Auburn was enjoying its fabulous football autumn, the grid situation at the University of Alabama was dreary, dreary, dreary. The Tide had won only two games-14-13 over Georgia and 29-2 over Mississippi Southern. There was also a 6-6 tie with Vanderbilt. Losses were to LSU, TCU, Tennessee, Mississippi State, Tulane and Georgia Tech. Alabama had won only four of its last 35 games.

The last day of November approached and 45,000 people went to frigid Legion Field to see if Auburn could defend college football's most prestigious status. Temperatures were at the freezing mark and the bitter cold afternoon was punctuated by icy 25 mile-per-hour winds.

It was the coldest day on which any game had been played in the history of the series, but it didn't affect the red-hot Auburn Tigers as they built an early lead and routed the hapless Crimson Tide, 40-0.

At the conclusion of the game, Auburn had won its first Southeastern Conference Championship, completed its first perfect sea-

Billy Atkins scored 18 points against Alabama in the 1956 and 1957 games.

son since 1913 and, for the frosting supreme, captured the title of National Champions.

As for the game, the outcome was never in doubt. Auburn had a 14-0 lead seven minutes after the opening kickoff and by intermission the score was 34-0.

Auburn kicked off. On second down, Gary O'Steen fumbled and the Tigers' Zeke Smith recovered at the Tide 26. Tommy Lorino, on first down, shot to the one. One play later Atkins bulled through left tackle for a touchdown. Atkins also converted and it was 7-0, quickly.

On the next series, Alabama punted to Auburn's 35. Bobby Hoppe gained four and Lorino zipped around left end for 28. Nix passed complete to Lorino for 21 more yards to the Alabama 12. Hoppe gained three, Nix three, and Atkins then scored his second touchdown from the six. After Atkins' conversion, it was Atkins 14, Alabama 0.

Late in the quarter, a short 19-yard Alabama punt set up the Tigers' third score from their own 46. After a one-yard gain by Pat Meagher, Bryant Harvard broke loose for 20 to Alabama's 33. Robbie Robbs went to the 29; Lamar Rawson to the 18, and Harvard to the 11 as the first period ended. When play resumed, Hoppe carried to the nine, an off-sides penalty pushed it to the four, Hoppe went to the two, and Nix blasted over. Atkins' toe made it 21-0.

O'Steen took the ensuing kickoff at the seven and would have gone all the way had it not been for Zeke Smith's saving tackle at Alabama's 43. The Tide reached Auburn's 32 where Bobby Smith's pass was deflected by Jackie Burkett into the hands of a speedy Lorino who grabbed it, cut down the West sidelines, and raced 79 yards for a touchdown. Atkins once again kicked good but a five-yard penalty cancelled the play and his next try failed. Still, Auburn led 27-0.

Later in the game, Burkett intercepted a pass and rambled 66 yards for another score. Atkins made it 34-0. On the next possession, Auburn drove 71 yards to Alabama's three. Harvard's pass to Bobby Wasden was dropped in the end zone as the first half ended.

By now, many in Alabama's portion of Legion Field had headed home. The miserable weather, the 34-0 score, the repeated roars of "WE'RE NUMBER ONE!" and "WARRR EEAGLE!" proved too much to endure.

In the 1957 era, the final national rankings were determined at the end of the regular season instead of after the bowls. Auburn, realizing they had locks on the National Championships, were having the

Tommy Lorino returned an interception 79 yards for a touchdown in the 1957 game.

time of their lives, practically all by themselves. But why not?

The Tigers, fired sky-high, took the second-half kickoff and went 62 yards for another touchdown. Starting at their 38, Hoppe gained three, Lorino four, Nix 15, Atkins four and Hoppe nine to Alabama's 27. From there, Nix rolled right and fired a pass to Phillips in the end zone. It really didn't matter that Atkins' conversion was no good.

Late in the game, Nix ran 77 yards to Alabama's two but a penalty nullified the play. With just minutes remaining to be played, the Tide got down to the Auburn eight but the Tigers' savage defense said "no".

"November 30, 1957, from here to eternity will be a national holiday for Auburn," wrote Zipp Newman of the *Birmingham News*.

Auburn gained 343 yards that day to Alabama's 197. The Tigers also led in first downs 11-10 and penalty yards 75-30.

The final Associated Press (AP) poll showed Auburn as a landslide winner. The SEC Champs received 3,123 points to 2,646 for runner-up Ohio State. Michigan State, Oklahoma and Navy rounded out the top five teams in 1957.

Auburn's defense, featuring Zeke Smith, Jackie Burkett, Ed Baker, Gerald Wilson, Cleve Wester, Jimmy Ricketts, Jimmy Phillips, Ben Preston, John Whatley and James Warren, was also overwhelmingly No. 1. The Tigers surrendered only 28 points (four touchdowns) all season and an average of 133 yards per game (67 rushing and 66 passing).

It didn't seem to matter to the United Press International that Auburn was the only unbeaten college team in the country in 1957. The UPI still voted Ohio State as its No. 1 team, even though the Bucks lost to TCU 18-14 and had 85 points scored against them. The UPI had Auburn second.

The press releases and newspaper stories came flooding out of Columbus (Ohio) and other Midwest cities asserting that the Buckeyes' Big Ten schedule was much tougher than Auburn's Southeastern Conference opposition.

In 1957, Auburn met as many teams that finished in the top 15 as Ohio State did—one. (The Tigers edged No. 12 Tennessee 7-0; the Bucks nosed No. 7 Iowa 17-13). And the fact remains, since the SEC had been formed in 1933, the league, through 1957, held an 11-9-1 advantage over Big Ten teams, and had outscored those teams 227-189.

But, the UPI board of coaches swallowed the Big Ten's propaganda and voted Woody's team No. 1.

The story of Auburn's National Championship, however, wasn't the only big football news in the State of Alabama that November 30. The state's newspapers were also crammed with stories about Paul (Bear) Bryant's pending return to the University of Alabama from Texas A&M.

Bryant's Aggies had lost to Texas on Thanksgiving two days before and the hot rumors were circulating—rumors that had Bryant in Tuscaloosa, in Birmingham, at Legion Field—practically everywhere. On Friday, Bryant was actually in Falfurras, Texas, deer hunting. Saturday he was in Houston and announced that his A&M team would play in the Gator Bowl against Tennessee.

On Monday, December 2, it became official: the Bear was "coming home".

FINAL ASSOCIATED PRESS RANKINGS, 1957

	TEAM	RECORD	LOST TO
1	Auburn	10-0-0	----
2	Ohio State	8-1-1	TCU
3	Michigan State	8-1-0	Purdue
4	Oklahoma	9-1-0	Notre Dame
5	Navy	8-1-1	North Carolina
6	Iowa	7-1-1	Ohio State
7	Mississippi	8-1-1	Arkansas
8	Rice	7-3-0	Duke, Texas, Clemson
9	Texas A&M	8-2-0	Rice, Texas
10	Notre Dame	6-3-0	Navy, Iowa, Michigan State
11	Texas	6-3-1	South Carolina, Oklahoma, SMU
12	Arizona State	10-0-0	----
13	Tennessee	7-3-0	Auburn, Mississippi, Kentucky
14	Mississippi State	6-2-1	Auburn, Tennessee
15	N.C. State	7-1-2	William & Mary
16	Duke	6-2-2	Georgia Tech, North Carolina
17	Florida	6-2-1	Auburn, Mississippi State
18	Army	7-2-0	Notre Dame, Navy
19	Wisconsin	6-3-0	Iowa, Ohio State, Michigan St.
20	VMI	9-0-1	----

A total 360 writers/broadcasters cast votes in the final poll. Auburn received 210 first place votes, Ohio State 71, Michigan State 30, Oklahoma 22, Arizona State 10, Iowa 7, Navy 6, Mississippi 3, and VMI 1.

Auburn's margin over Ohio State was by 477 points [3123-2646]. This was the 22nd year of the AP poll and it represented the second biggest difference between the two top teams. In 1950, Oklahoma had topped Army by 583 points.

A RECAP OF AUBURN'S RISE TO THE TOP....

Pre-season....15th
Sep. 23.......Unranked
Sep. 30.......7th
Oct. 7.......9th
Oct. 14.......9th
Oct. 21.......4th
Oct. 28.......4th
Nov. 4.......3rd
Nov. 11.......3rd
Nov. 18.......2nd
Nov. 25.......1st
Dec. 2.......1st

Bear Bryant Quits Ags; Alabama Bound

Good news/bad news: good for UA, bad for A&M and AU.

The day Auburn wrapped up the 1957 National Championship, a Russian Sputnik was swirling around the earth every hour and a half and President Eisenhower was recovering from a cerebral blood clot suffered just three days earlier. Playing at the local theaters in Birmingham were *April Love,* starring Pat Boone and Shirley Jones; *Les Girls,* with Gene Kelley and Mitzi Gaynor; *Jet Pilot,* featuring John Wayne and Janet Leigh, and *Jailhouse Rock,* with, who else, but Elvis himself. In the comic strips, Blondie was, even then, freaking out Dagwood, and Dick Tracy had just captured "The Mad Murderess" Elsa.

Auburn fans have probably forgotten that year's Sputniks and movies and Elsa. But never, no never, will loyal War Eagles forget their 1957 football team.

1958
GAME 23

The Shug & Bear Show

The 1958 Auburn-Alabama game pitted Shug Jordan and Bear Bryant against each for the first time as head coaches. There would be 17 more such personal duels.

Auburn's pre-season football fever had never run so red-hot. Not ever. The Tigers were defending their National Championship honors and a majority of the team, especially the defensive unit, was returning to the Plains confident of a repeat performance.

The Alabama camp was heating up, too. After all, Bryant had returned as head coach and uplifter of the rockbottom Tide football fortunes. He was fully expected to begin immediately performing miracles.

Auburn started the 1958 season with a bang. Appearing on television for the first time, the Tigers' awesome defense did not allow Tennessee a first down and slammed the Vols with a minus 13 yards rushing, enroute to a 13-0 victory.

A 30-8 cracking of Chattanooga and an 8-0 blank of Kentucky followed. Auburn's next game cost another Southeastern Conference championship and very possibly a second straight national title. It was the annual journey to Atlanta to face Georgia Tech, an old nemesis indeed to Auburn. It was just an ordinary Yellow Jacket team in 1958 (5-4-1) but Bobby Dodd's troops pulled out an upset 7-7 tie. Still, Auburn had not lost in its last 18 games.

The Tigers bounced back with a 20-7 win over Maryland and

A young Ralph Jordan and Paul Bryant during their college playing days at where else?—but Auburn and Alabama.

survived a weird 6-5 squeaker over Florida. Easy wins over Mississippi State (33-14), Georgia (21-6) and Wake Forest (21-7) brought Auburn's record to 8-0-1 and a No. 2 national ranking.

Bryant's first game as coach at Alabama was at Mobile on Saturday night, September 27. The opposition was LSU, which at the time was in a slump of its own, having had a 5-5-0 record the year before. But as fate would have it, Bear drew as his first assignment the team that would become National Champions that year. It was a team that featured Billy Cannon, who went on to win the Heisman Trophy, and the famed Chinese Bandits. Alabama played LSU tough, but lost 13-3.

A scoreless tie with Vanderbilt went into the record book before Bryant's first Alabama win came against Furman at Tuscaloosa on October 11 by a score of 29-6. After a 14-7 loss to Tennessee, the Tide put victories back-to-back for the first time in four years, dropping Mississippi State 9-7 and Georgia 12-0.

After only five games, it was becoming quite obvious that Bryant's strategy for rebuilding the stagnant situation he had inherited was DEE-fense.

Next was a 13-7 loss to Tulane, then a 17-8 win over Tech, plus a 14-0 victory over Memphis State. Alabama would face Auburn with a 5-3-1 record.

Considering Alabama's previous three-and-a-half seasons and a disastrous 4-28-4 record (by a 720-216 score), Bryant, in only nine games, had already performed what was expected of him—a miracle.

Auburn's rugged defense had almost been matched by Alabama. In fact, the Tigers had surrendered 61 points—just seven less than the Tide had given up. Neither team had kept the scorekeepers busy

Cleve Wester of Albany, Ga., lettered at defensive tackle for Auburn in 1956-57-58 (All-SEC as a senior). The Tiger "D" allowed their opponents a paltry 4.9 points per game during this period while posting a 26-3-1 record.

The Birmingham News   SPORTS and NEWS   SECTION C
SUNDAY,
NOVEMBER 30, 1958

In Legion Field donnybrook—

Tigers beat back Tide, 14 to 8

'Bama closes with a rush

as Auburn was averaging 18 points per game; Alabama 11. Thus, it was generally expected that the 23rd series meeting would be a defense-oriented, low-scoring affair—and it was. Auburn won, 14-8. The game, for the second straight year, was played on a bitter cold day but that mattered little to the 45,000 bundled-up fans who streamed into Legion Field that November 29. A contest was expected.

Auburn broke on top on its second possession. Alabama's Gary O'Steen quick-kicked 43 yards to the Tigers' 47-yard line but the tactic backfired. Auburn turned it into a touchdown. On third-and-six, Frank Nix was back to pass but was forced to run. He turned the play into an eight-yard gain and clutch first down at Alabama's 41. Jimmy Pettus burst through the middle for 16 yards. Bobby Lauder gained three and Dick Wood hit with a nine-yard pass to Leo Sexton for another first down at the 13. Wood went to the eight and Ed Dyas to the seven. Wood then discovered Pettus all alone in the end zone and shot one his way. Touchdown! With 7:54 remaining in the first quarter, Dyas tacked on the point-after and Auburn led 7-0.

Late in the second quarter, Nix fumbled and Dave Sington's recovery gave the Tide a shot in the arm at Auburn's 37. Bobby Jackson drilled a pass to Duff Morrison for a 16-yard advance at the 21. O'Steen went for seven and Bama was in great shape with second-and-three at the 14. However, a wild Jackson pitchout lost six, and then Auburn's Gerald Wilson chased down Jackson and sacked the scrambling quarterback back at the 32. Alabama punted and in a few moments the half ended with Auburn nursing a 7-0 lead.

Early in the third period, Auburn marched to the Alabama 32 and stalled. Tommy Lorino punted to the one-yard line to keep the pressure on the Tide.

Alabama couldn't get going and Laurien Stapp kicked out to his 42. Auburn came surging back. Sparked by a Pettus run of 17 and a tremendous catch by Lauder of a Wood pass, Auburn was knocking on the door with a first down at the Alabama two. The Tide put on a classic goalline stand and held for four straight downs. It was an inspired performance, and Alabama fans were delirious in their appreciation.

A 14-8 Auburn victory in 1958 is reflected on the face of Alabama's Bobby Jackson.

Lloyd Nix played defense for Auburn in 1956 before taking over at quarterback in 1957-58. At the QB position, he never lost a game—19-0-1.

Stapp again punted from the end zone but this time only to his 39. Auburn was not to be denied again. Lauder got two. Wood's aerial to Joe Leichtnam was good for 24 yards to the 13. Pettus swung right and picked up six. Nix blasted for six more and a first down at the one. On the first play of the fourth quarter, James Reynolds rammed in for the touchdown. Wilson's kick was perfect and Auburn stretched the lead to 14-0.

Marlin Dyess' 36-yard kickoff return, Walter Sansing's 16-yard run, and a Jackson-to-Dyess pass for 12, highlighted a Tide drive to the Auburn 17, but a holding penalty snuffed the drive and Auburn took over.

Failing to get a first down, Lorino punted out to his own 45 and the Crimson Tide started again. Ravis (Red) Stickney managed one, O'Steen six and Stickney seven for a first down at the 31. Jackson went to Dyess again on a pass that was good for 16 yards. Stickney struck for six and the ball was at the nine. Dyess then took a pitchout from Jackson, headed wide, turned the corner and scored. Foregoing a possible tie and thinking only of winning, Alabama went for a two-point conversion and got it when Jackson flipped a pass to O'Steen. Auburn 14, Alabama 8.

Suddenly, Legion Field had a ball game.

Alabama attempted an on-sides kick but Auburn's Cleve Wester claimed the squiggler at his 44. Auburn got a drive working for a few plays but a Lorino fumble and a recovery by Don Cochran gave the ball to Alabama at the Tide 27.

There was 3:56 left to play and Legion Field exploded. The shadows had crept across the field and the early afternoon chill had now grown icy cold. For the first time in five long years, the victory-starved Crimson Tide rooters could smell an upset of Auburn and they screamed uncontrollably for their warriors to take it in for a touchdown.

Stickney bulled for three and fumbled; but he recovered. Once more Jackson found Dyess as a target and hit him for a 17 yard gainer. The same play clicked for four more to Auburn's 49 as the clock showed 2:53. Jackson then threw to Jack Wise at the 42 for another first down. On the next play, Jackson was trapped trying to throw but wiggled free and gained one. He then threw incomplete.

The next play resulted in near heart failure for partisans of both teams. Jackson quickly retreated to pass and spotted Jerry Spruiell deep and open. Jackson fired away. On a great defensive play, Rawson streaked into the play and tipped the ball away at the last split second. It saved a touchdown and the ball game for Auburn. But Alabama had yet another shot. It became fourth-and-nine and the ball was still on the Auburn 41. Jackson coolly completed a pass to Wise good for 13 yards and a first down at the Tiger 28. By now the clock had blinked down to 1:26.

Auburn's hard-nosed defense then reared its head and thwarted the Tide's threat. A rushed Jackson had to settle for no gain. Alabama was then hit with a five-yard delay penalty back to the 33. A short completion gained only three. On the next play, the Tigers' rushing linemen were clawing all over Jackson and he threw wildly. It cost Alabama a five-yard penalty but more importantly a down, as the officials ruled intentional grounding of the ball. That brought up fourth down and game-to-go. A harrassed Jackson threw incomplete and War Eagle fans let go a mighty roar of jubilation and relief.

After the Tigers ran two plays, the game ended and the 1956-57-58 Auburn teams had set a new all-time school record — 24 straight games without a defeat, breaking the old mark by one game, set by Coach Mike Donahue's 1913-14-15 teams. Furthermore, Auburn took a 13-9-1 series lead over Alabama and was well out front in scoring, 425-303.

The statistics were about as close as the game. Auburn led in first downs 13-12 and total yards 260-224. Jackson completed 13

The Birmingham News — CLASSIFIED–WANT ADS — SECTION B
SUNDAY, NOVEMBER 30, 1958

43,067 watch thrilling windup; Tigers win, 14-8—

'Glory, glory to Ole Auburn': And to gallant Tide, too

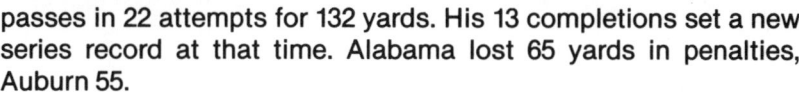

passes in 22 attempts for 132 yards. His 13 completions set a new series record at that time. Alabama lost 65 yards in penalties, Auburn 55.

As unbelievable as this may seem, it actually happened. In the 11 meetings since the series had been resumed in 1948, the total offensive yards were exactly the same for both teams—2,923 for Auburn and 2,923 for Alabama. The Tigers' figures were 2,106 rushings and 817 passing. Alabama's totals were 2,165-758.

Other statistics were amazingly close during the same period. For example, in first downs, Auburn led 152-149; in passes attempted, Auburn led 152-147; in passes completed, Auburn led 62-60; in passing percentage, Alabama led .408-.407; in points scored, Alabama led 173-170; in wins, Auburn led 6-5.

Because of the NCAA probation, for the second straight year a great Auburn team was denied a bowl appearance. Jordan's 1958 club ended with a 9-0-1 record and a final AP and UPI ranking of fourth, finishing behind LSU, Iowa and Army.

Not bad. Not bad at all when one considers the condition of Auburn football when Jordan had taken it over just eight years earlier.

As for Bear Bryant's football future with Alabama's Crimson Tide, well. . . .

Roger Duane Smith—better known as Zeke—anchored Auburn's great defensive teams in 1957-58-59. He made All-America in 1958-59 and was awarded the Outland Trophy as college football's most outstanding lineman his senior year.

1959
GAME 24

Some Changes

In the past five games of the series, 1954-58, inclusive, Auburn had hammered obedient Alabama into submission. Besides winning all five, the Tigers had outscored the Crimsons 142-15 (21 touchdowns to two), and almost doubled the Tide's total offensive yards, 1,866-992. But, just as in 1954, there would be a changing of the gridiron guard and the intrastate dominance was about to switch over to the side of the Crimson Tide.

Bear Bryant had taken over and, in just one year's time, transformed the Tide into one of the toughest defensive units in the Nation. However, when his boys tried their talents at offensive football, they were a little lacking. But Bryant was just "borrowing time" until HIS recruits would arrive.

In 1959, the most points Alabama scored in one game was 19, and the team averaged only nine points per game; yet, they lost only one regular season game, and that was the opener to that year's Southeastern Conference champion, Georgia and Fran Tarkenton, 17-3. No other team would score more than seven points on the Tide the rest of the way.

Following the Georgia game came a 3-0 win over Houston; a 7-7 tie with Vanderbilt; a 13-0 win over Chattanooga; a 7-7 tie with Tennessee, and wins over Mississippi State 10-0; Tulane 19-7; Georgia Tech 9-7, and Memphis State 14-0.

In the 1959 opener Auburn lost its first game since November 3,

1956—after 23 wins and one tie—3-0 to Tennessee. Hardin-Simmons and Kentucky then fell with ease. The Tigers' 300th all-time football victory came the next week, a thrilling 7-6 notch over Georgia Tech in a downpour in Atlanta. Then Florida, Miami and Mississippi State were put away. That brought the season to November 14 and an SEC title showdown with Georgia. The Bulldogs won 14-13 when Tarkenton threw a fourth-down, 13-yard touchdown pass with only 30 seconds left in the game. After the heartbreaker in Athens, Auburn regrouped and thumped Mississippi Southern 28-7.

And once again it was Tide-Tiger time.

Even though Alabama had scored a mere 85 points, they owned a 6-1-2 record record because the defense had allowed just 52. Auburn was 7-2-0 and its offense had produced twice as many points as Alabama's, 174. The Tiger defense was solid as usual, surrendering only 54 points.

Auburn was a six-point favorite, but it didn't pan out that way for the gamblers or the Tigers. Alabama broke a five-year series stranglehold by the Plainsmen with a 10-0 victory, in a game played on a slow, muddy track as a result of rains throughout the week.

For the third consecutive year the day of the game was cold and windy. This game was also played on grass as green as grass gets. Sixty gallons of fresh paint was purchased and the drab, frost-bitten grass was sprayed a bright green, just for the big game.

Auburn won the toss of the coin that November 28 and elected to take the wind. Costly penalties hurt both teams in the first few minutes. Alabama received the opening kickoff but couldn't move. Tommy White was back to punt and bobbled the snap, started to run, then kicked a short 18-yarder. But Auburn was hit with a roughing-the-kicker penalty and Alabama retained possession with a first down at its 38. The Tide moved to the Tiger 40 before punting down to the 18. The penalty had cost Auburn 41 yards.

On the Plainsmen's first play, quarterback Bobby Hunt fumbled and Alabama's Pat Trammell recovered at the 24. However, two straight 15-yard penalties pushed Bama all the way back to midfield.

Alabama quick-kicked; Auburn punted; Alabama punted; Auburn punted. By this time the game was into the second quarter and after all the punts and runbacks, Alabama came out with the ball on its own 30-yard line and finally mounted a drive deep enough into Tigerland for a successful field goal. Here's the way it went: Gary O'Steen gained three and Trammell threw complete to W. E. Richardson for 21 yards to the Auburn 46. On the next play, Trammell faded to pass and wiggled out of a trap for a 24-yard advance to the

22. It was Trammel again, this time with a completion to Gary Phillips for eight yards to the 14. Marlin Dyess drove for two and a first down. Richardson got only one, and after two incomplete Trammell passes, place kicker Tommy Brooker came upon the scene.

Standing at the 27-yard line, Brooker calmly booted the ball through the bars and Alabama led 3-0 with 9:01 left to play in the first half. It was only the third field goal in series history and Auburn had yet to kick one.

To start the second half, Alabama had its choice of wind advantage or the ball and decided to take the ball and let Auburn have the breeze. The Tide strategy was to have the wind at their backs in the fourth quarter.

Taking the kickoff, Alabama drove to Auburn's 23 but Lamar Rawson intercepted a Trammell toss at the eight and returned it 15 yards. Joe Doland got off a 52-yard punt to the Tide's 25. From there, Alabama went for its clinching score.

O'Steen rushed for eight and then two yards and a first down. Richardson got nine and Trammell threw incomplete. Richardson rammed for two and another first down at Alabama's 46. Dyess struggled for one and Richardson ripped right up the middle for 14 yards to the Tigers' 39 and another first down. Bobby Shelton, subbing for Trammell at quarterback, hit a racing Dyess at the 35 and the Tide halfback raced over for a touchdown. With 2:56 remaining in the third period, Brooker converted for a big 10-0 Bama advantage.

With seven minutes left in the game, Auburn reached Alabama's 14 but Richardson intercepted a Hunt pass and the old ball game was locked up.

Alabama had finally defeated Auburn.

The Crimsons crunched out 15 first downs to Auburn's nine and 260 total yards, to only 131 for the Tigers. Alabama also led in penalty yards 73-20. But Auburn was still on top in the series, 13-10-1, and in points scored, 424-314.

Bowl bids? Auburn, for the fourth straight year, could not accept a post-season date because of its probation. Alabama turned one down, but later reconsidered. After the game, Bryant was quoted by the *Birmingham News* as saying, "I'm disappointed for our seniors. The bowls all picked fine matches. They all picked fine teams and they look like terrific games . . . We are not going to a bowl, period."

There were still two post-season slots available-one in the Gator Bowl and one in the brand new Liberty Bowl at Philadelphia. It was reported that Bryant wanted the Gator bid but because of some ill feelings that existed between the Jacksonville bowl people and the University, the Gator Bowl refused to extend an invitation. The feelings had been lingering since 1950. The struggling Gator Bowl was only five years old and was desperately trying to land big name teams such as Alabama. The Tide was 9-2-0 in 1950—and bowl-less. The Gator begged; Coach Red Drew and Alabama refused.

The Gator Bowl hadn't forgotten and thus in 1959 invited a Georgia Tech team with a 6-4 record that included losses in three of its last four games. One of the defeats was to Alabama, 9-7.

That left one availability. Alabama got the invitation, accepted, went to frigid Philadelphia to help inaugurate the Liberty Bowl, got beat by Penn State 7-0, and went home.

Bryant's second Alabama team finished 7-2-2.

In one of the most remarkable coaching jobs in Southeastern Conference history, or anywhere for that matter, Bear Bryant took over a team that, in three and a half years had won only four games and surrendered over 700 points, and in just 21 games, had come to be ranked among the nation's Top Ten—No. 10 in the 1959 AP poll. Also, the team was third in the country in defense against scoring.

1960
GAME 25

X vs. Y

Team X has the best defense against scoring in the nation; team Y is fourth best in the same category. QUESTION: If team X plays team Y, which of the following would you choose as the final score?
- (A) 20-14
- (B) 0-0
- (C) 14-13
- (D) 3-0
- (E) 35-21

Alabama, America's No. 1 defensive team against Auburn, America's No. 4 defensive team. That's the way the 25th series game stacked up in 1960. The Tigers were 8-1-0; the Tide 7-1-1. And it was Tennessee, with a 6-2-2 record that year, that handed both teams their lone defeats. In the second week, the Vols beat the Plainsmen 10-3 at Auburn; two weeks later they dropped Alabama 20-7 at Knoxville. Those 20 points scored that October 15th were the most recorded on Alabama since Bear Bryant's return and no opponent would score that many again until four years later.

Besides a 6-6 tie with Tulane, the Tide defeated Georgia, Vanderbilt, Houston, Mississippi State, Georgia Tech and Tampa. Against Tech, Alabama trailed 15-0 but pulled out a 16-15 victory. Meanwhile, Auburn was defeating Kentucky, Chattanooga, Tech, Miami, Florida, Mississippi State, Georgia and FSU.

Alabama's scoring ratio was 178-53; Auburn's was 155-77.

Tommy Brooker's chip-shot field goal was the difference in a 3-0 Tide win over Auburn in 1960.

The correct answer to the quiz is "D". In a brutal defensive confrontation, Alabama (the X team) edged Auburn (the Y team) by a field goal, 3-0, before a screaming, overflow crowd at Legion Field on November 28.

Tommy Brooker did all the damage in the second quarter and the remainder of the afternoon was devoted to vicious defensive play.

Auburn received the opening kickoff but had to punt. Alabama started at its own 36 and drove to the Tiger 23 and Brooker came on for a field goal try which was wide to the right.

The Tigers, going nowhere, punted and Bama staged a drive of 44 yards, once again to Auburn's 23. However, James Price intercepted a Bobby Skelton pass to snuff another threat.

Auburn punted again as the first quarter came to a close. This time Alabama started at its 39 and six minutes and 23 seconds later had won the game.

On a keeper, quarterback Pat Trammell ran for six yards. Mike Fracchia blasted the middle for six more and a first down at the Tiger 49. An illegal procedure penalty cost the Crimsons five. On two straight draw plays, Fracchia went eight and five yards to Auburn's 41, where it was third-and-two. A trapped Trammell got free for eight big yards and another first down at the 33.

After an incomplete pass, Trammell threw to Bill Battle, who made a great catch for 13 yards at the 20 and a first down. Leon Fuller slammed off right guard to the 17, and Trammell ran for nine more yards for a first-and-goal at the eight, where the Tigers got tough. Fracchia got just one. On the next play a poor exchange between Trammell and Fracchia resulted in a four-yard loss back to the 11. Skelton got five to the six.

That brought up a fourth-and-goal situation at the six-yard line and Brooker was called upon to get the job done. Standing at the 12 and with Skelton holding, Brooker booted it through the uprights for three gigantic points. There was 8:37 remaining in the second quarter.

Alabama continued to supply the defensive pressure and bottled up Auburn so effectively that the Tigers did not record a first down until 47 seconds before intermission. By that time, the Tide had racked up 10 first downs.

In the second half, Auburn's defense shut down the Tide with only one first down. However, the Tigers got just four and could never get their offense moving. There were only 313 yards gained all day — 179 by Alabama, 134 by Auburn. The Tigers punted nine times, Alabama seven, and the two teams kicked the ball almost 700 yards during the stand-off afternoon.

Advertiser-JOURNAL
Montgomery, Ala., Sunday, Nov. 27, 1960

SPORTS, MARKETS, NEWS

Bowl-Bound Bama Bumps Auburn

Brooker's Kick Tide Margin In 3-0 Victory

By MAX MOSELEY
Advertiser Sports Editor

LEGION FIELD, BIRMINGHAM — Tommy Brooker, 208-pound injured flankman from Demopolis, came off the bench in the second quarter to kick a 22-yard field goal and Alabama's Crimson Tide took an exacting 3-0 victory over cross-state Auburn in a bitterly fought Southeastern Conference battle played before a capacity crowd of near 45,000 spectators.

Quarterback Pat Trammell started a amassing Alabama's scheme of offense that contained the ball the major part of the contest. The Alabama team out-played the Tide-gers through out the contest and interspersed numerous runs but several were able to crash a wrong Auburn defense led by All American Ken Rice.

Alabama Coach Paul Bryant accepted a bid to the Bluebonnet Bowl in the dressing room immediately after the Tide's 3-0 victory over Auburn Saturday.

ALABAMA QUARTERBACK PAT TRAMMELL (12) BREAKS THROUGH FOR SIX YARD GAIN AS AUBURN TACKLERS CLOSE IN
Plainsmen Tackle Billy Wilson (78), End Dave Edwards (80), Fullback Jon McGeever (36), Guard Jimmy Putman (65) Pursue Fighting Tider

The Tigers led the series now by two games—13-11-1. The 1960 season marked Shug Jordan's 10th at the Plains as head coach and during that time his Auburn teams were 71-29-3 for .704 batting average. Further, after Jordan's recruits arrived, his last eight teams had posted an even more impressive record of 64-16-3 for a .789 winning percentage.

Three weeks after the regular season's final game, Alabama went to Houston to play Texas in the second Bluebonnet Bowl, and for the second straight game, Brooker provided all the Tide's scoring punch. His third quarter field goal gave Bama a 3-0 lead but the Longhorns matched it in the final period and the game ended in a 3-3 tie.

The Crimson Tide finished with a fine 8-1-2 record, a third place Southeastern Conference finish and a No. 9 national ranking. Auburn was 8-2-0, fourth in the SEC and 11th nationwide. The AP and UPI voted once-beaten Minnesota (8-1-0) as National Champions over unbeaten Old Miss (9-0-1). However, the Football Writer's Association of America, casting their ballots after the bowl games, voted Johnny Vaught's Rebels as the best. Minnesota lost in the Rose Bowl; Old Miss won in the Sugar Bowl.

Alabama allowed only 5.1 points per game in 1960—tops in the nation. Old Miss and Arkansas tied for second with 6.4 points, and Auburn's 8.0 was good for fourth.

1961
GAME 26

Tide Rolls To No. 1

It is ironic how the thunderous rebounds of the football programs at Auburn and Alabama were so similar. In 1950 the Tigers lost all 10 of their games, but seven years later a National Championship came to roost at the Plains. The Crimson Tide did not win a game in 1955 and six years after that disastrous season, they too, had captured a National Championship.

The year 1961 belonged to Alabama. Bear Bryant's Crimson TIde streaked to an 11-0-0 finish, the only team in the country to win all its games, and allowed only three touchdowns all season.

SEPT. 23—The Crimson Tide's road to gridiron glory began in Athens where Alabama cracked Georgia 32-6. The Bulldogs got only five first downs and 112 yards. The Crimsons were ranked No. 4 behind Iowa, Ole Miss and Ohio State.

SEPT. 30—In a night game at Mobile, Alabama scored a second quarter touchdown and Tim Davis added a 25-yard field goal in the third period. Meanwhile, the defense held Tulane in check with 111 yards for a 9-0 win. Iowa stayed first in the polls and Ole Miss second. TCU stunned Ohio State with a 7-7 tie and the Buckeyes' third place slot was taken over by Georgia Tech. Alabama stayed No. 4.

OCT. 7—In the third straight road game, Alabama topped Vanderbilt 35-6 at night in Nashville as Pat Trammell scored three touchdowns. The Commodores could accumulate only 77 yards. There

Pat Trammell, rugged Alabama quarterback. He played in three victories over Auburn, 1959-60-61.

was a wholesale shakeup of the top four teams after the results were posted that weekend. Iowa edged Southern Cal 35-34 but fell to second; Ole Miss blanked FSU 33-0 and moved to the top; Tech lost to LSU 10-0 and fell from contention. Alabama moved up to No. 3.

OCT. 14—N.C. State's Roman Gabriel passed for 123 yards but the Wolfpacks' ground game managed only five yards and the Tide came from a 7-0 deficit to win 26-7 at Tuscaloosa. It would be the last touchdown scored on Alabama for the remainder of the year. Somehow though, the victory dropped Bama two notches to No. 5. Michigan State beat Michigan 28-0 and zipped to No. 1; Ole Miss routed Houston 47-7 and fell to second; Texas' 28-0 win over Oklahoma advanced the Longhorns to third place, and Iowa moved to fourth after topping Indiana 27-8.

OCT. 21—Trammell completed 13 of 19 passes for 156 yards to lead a 34-3 trouncing of Tennessee at Birmingham. Alabama's awesome defense allowed the Vols a mere 61 total yards. Michigan State remained atop the polls with a 17-7 win over Notre Dame; Ole Miss beat Tulane 41-0 to stay in second place, and Texas remained No. 3 by axing Arkansas 33-7. Alabama and Iowa swapped positions—the Tide went to fourth, the Hawkeyes to fifth.

OCT. 28—In a night game at Houston, the Cougars gained 196 yards but couldn't score and Bama posted a 17-0 success and stayed No. 4. Michigan State, Ole Miss and Texas won easily and the top four positions remained the same.

NOV. 4—Back at Tuscaloosa, the Tide blanked Mississippi State 24-0. But Michigan State and Mississippi had their apple carts upended by upsets. Minnesota sent the Spartans crashing to sixth with a 13-0 zip job, while LSU zeroed in on the Rebels, 10-0, tumbling them to seventh. Third-place Texas smothered SMU 27-0 and climbed to No. 1 and Alabama went to No. 2. Ohio State and LSU claimed third and fourth place, respectively. Now it was Texas and the Tide waiting for the other to falter. In this era, the National Champion was still crowned at the conclusion of the regular season and each team had three games remaining. Left on Texas' schedule were Baylor, TCU and Texas A&M. Alabama had to play Richmond, Georgia Tech and Auburn.

NOV. 11—Alabama 66, Richmond 0 at Tuscaloosa. Texas bopped Baylor 33-7. Ohio State and LSU also won, but it didn't matter. The race for first place was now between Texas and Alabama—until one or the other stumbled.

NOV. 18—One stumbled. TCU, with a lowly 3-4-1 record and a 26-point underdog, shocked the college football world—and Texas—

with a 6-0 win over the Longhorns. That evening in Birmingham, Alabama took Tech 10-0 in a game marred by the Darwin Holt-Chick Graning incident that eventually led to the severing of athletic relations between the two schools. In the heat of battle, Holt, on a late hit, smashed Graning's face with an elbow. Graning's injury required major surgery. The fuse had been lit and the feud was on. Atlanta and Birmingham had their first real squabble since the old Cracker-Baron baseball days through the 1950's.

Alabama went to No. 1, while Ohio State (7-0-1) moved to second. All the other contenders now had lost at least once and were out of the title picture.

NOV. 25 — Alabama had an open date. Ohio State completed its schedule with an 8-0-1 record by smashing Michigan 50-20 and moved ever so close to No. 1. By not playing, Alabama lost 10 poll points; Ohio State picked up 44 points. The tally was: Bama 459, Bucks 452.

Thus, Alabama's game with Auburn was for a Crimson Tide National Championship. To win it, the Tide had to have a convincing triumph. A close encounter and the AP pollsters would surely spring the 1961 title Ohio State's way.

A point or two here and there, and Auburn could have also been undefeated when the time arrived to meet Alabama. Auburn had one-point losses to Tech (7-6) and Mississippi State (11-10), plus a two-point defeat to Kentucky (14-12). The Tigers' six wins included a couple of close calls — Tennessee 24-21, and Georgia 10-7 — before a 32-15 win over Florida. However, Auburn was 6-3-0 and snorting.

Auburn wanted to knock Alabama out of the National Championship. Ohh, how they wanted to do just that. The War Eagles would gladly have Ohio State win it, if that's what beating Alabama would mean. Well, the Tigers played a big part in settling the duel for No. 1. They were the victims in the convincing triumph the Tide needed. Alabama took them apart. The game was never in doubt as the rugged Crimson Tide smashed the Tigers by a score of 34-0 before a record series crowd of 54,000, jamming an enlarged Legion Field.

Auburn received the opening kickoff and quickly fumbled. McGeever dropped the ball and Holt recovered for the Tide at Auburn's 36. Six plays and it was 7-0. Mike Fracchia burst for six; Bill Richardson got three; Trammell kept for four, and a first down at the 23. Fracchia managed only one before Trammell completed an 11-yarder to Richardson at the 11. On the next play, Richardson got the remaining 11 yards. Tim Davis converted and in just four minutes and 11 seconds, the Tide was making waves.

Later in the first quarter, Auburn put on a 69-yard march to Alabama's 26 but a field goal attempt by Woody Woodall was no good. The Tigers still had a .000 average in field goal kicking in the series.

The ball was placed on the 20-yard line and Bama scored in 12 plays. Five runs by Fracchia adding up to 41 yards, and three by Cotton Clark that totaled 19 yards, led the drive that reached Auburn's 10. From there, Trammell threw complete to Bill Battle at the one. Trammell's sneak got the score. With the game 3:22 into the second quarter, Davis' conversion made it 14-0.

On Alabama's next possession, a drive of 32 yards to the Tigers' 19 stalled, but a field goal by Davis increased the count to 17-0.

With just nine seconds showing on the first half clock, the Crimsons tallied again. Clark returned a punt 14 yards to Auburn's 42. Trammell threw consecutive strikes to Red Wilkins for 12 and nine yards to the 21. After an incomplete pass, Clark cracked for one and a first down. Trammell was off target twice before connecting with Richard Williamson for a touchdown. Davis' kick made the score 24-0.

By now, thunderous roars of "WE'RE NO. 1! WE'RE NO. 1! WE'RE ... !" were coming from Alabama's side.

Alabama took the second-half kickoff and drove 67 yards for its fourth touchdown of the day. Starting at his own 33-yard line, Larry Wall rammed for five and 11 yards. Trammell picked his way for three, and Wall for four before a five-yard penalty against the Tigers resulted in a first down at Auburn's 39. Wall went to the 36, then to the 23. On a third-and-11, Trammell found Battle open for a pass that gained 20 more yards to the four. On second down from the five, Richardson took a pitchout from Trammell and scored his second touchdown of the game. Davis kicked good again and the score mounted to 31-0.

Midway through the fourth quarter, Alabama received a punt at Auburn's 42 and a zany drive ended in another Davis field goal. A delay penalty cost the Tide five, and Trammell lost four more. However, Trammell drilled a 30-yarder to Williamson to the 21, then a 10-yarder to the same receiver. A five-yard penalty set Alabama back to the 16 and after three straight incomplete passes, Davis added a 24-yard three-pointer with 8:42 remaining in the game. The scoring was over for another year.

Even though Auburn blasted out 17 first downs (Alabama got 20) and gained a total of 220 yards, the Tide's defense wouldn't let the frustrated Tigers across the goal. Alabama totaled 315 yards as Trammell paced the way with 10 completions in 21 attempts for 136

Undefeated Alabama Rolls Over Auburn, 34-0

Birmingham Post-Herald

FINAL EDITION

VOL. 91—NO. 229 BIRMINGHAM, TUESDAY, DECEMBER 5, 1961 22 Pages In Two Sections

Tide Rolls—Into 1961 Championship

yards. Alabama led in penalty yards also, 40-5.

The Plainsmen had not scored on Alabama in three years and the Tigers' series lead was now one game—13-12-1. In points, Auburn was ahead 424-351.

On Monday it became official: Alabama was the 1961 National Champion of collegiate football! Both the AP and UPI said so.

It seems only fair, though, that a little piece of the big No. 1 trophy should go to Texas Christian University. The Horned Frogs had tied Ohio State and beat Texas to propel the Tide to the top—even though Alabama by far had the best team in the Nation that year.

Auburn didn't go bowling in 1961, but they could have. The brand new Gotham Bowl, to be played at the old Polo Grounds in New York, invited Shug Jordan and his Tigers up to the big city to play Baylor. Auburn said "thank you, but. . . ."

The Gotham settled for Utah State instead. Baylor won 24-9 before some 45,000 frigid, wind-swept empty seats.

Alabama went to the Sugar Bowl and surrendered its first points in five games in a 10-3 victory over Arkansas.

The 25 points Alabama allowed in 1961 easily gave it the national defensive scoring title for the second straight year. Furthermore, the Crimsons' super defense gave up only 56 yards per game rushing and 77 passing.

Completing the top five teams in the final polls were Ohio State, Texas, LSU and Ole Miss, putting three SEC teams in the Top Five.

Paul William Bryant's football miracle had been completed. He took over an Alabama football program that had won only four of its previous 36 games, and in four short years, brought a National Championship to Tuscaloosa.

1962

Game 27

Joy And Desperation

Alabama beat Auburn again, and in the past four years, the series scoreboard read: Crimson Tide 85, War Eagles 0.

If Auburn hadn't already become desperate in the intrastate feud, they were about to be. The 1962 score was 38-0. The game was played on the first day of December and the usual sellout Legion Field crowd witnessed the longest run in series history to date.

After 27 games, the series was tied again — 13-13-1.

Alabama, all-powerful in 1962, reeled off eight straight wins and had not lost a game in over two years. The Tide topped Georgia, Tulane, Vanderbilt, Houston, Tennessee, Tulsa, Mississippi State and Miami by a total tally of 225-32. However, on November 17 in Atlanta, Georgia Tech (7-3-1) stung the Crimsons 7-6 and the streak was broken. Alabama had not lost since October 15, 1960, a string of 26 games, including one tie.

Thus, Auburn had to face an angry Alabama team, a team that was ranked No. 5 in the nation, and a team that had the second best record against scoring.

Auburn had won its first five games, including a tight 22-21 victory over Tennessee, and back-to-back 17-14 triumphs over Tech and Clemson. Florida then knocked Shug Jordan's team from the unbeaten ranks by a 22-3 score. The Tigers came back with a 9-3 win against Mississippi State before being shocked 30-21 by a weak Georgia team that won only two other games all season. A 14-14 tie

Lee Roy Jordan, Alabama's All-American linebacker, played in three straight shutouts over Auburn. He went on to become a perennial All-Pro with the Dallas Cowboys.

with FSU brought Auburn's record to 6-2-1 with Alabama coming up.

The Tide won the toss, took the football and within a matter of seconds, scored. George (Butch) Wilson fielded the opening kick on the eight-yard line, cut right, picked up some blockers and away Mr. Wilson streaked — 92 yards and a touchdown — the first kickoff return for a score in series history and also the longest touchdown run the series had ever seen. The feat would be surpassed later, but in 1962, it was a record.

While the dazed Tigers stood around wondering what had happened, Tim Davis converted and just like that, it was 7-0. Auburn would not recover for the rest of the afternoon.

Late in the quarter, Auburn's Larry Laster sent a booming 72-yard punt that Benny Nelson returned 12 yards to the 28. On second-and-12, Eddie Versprille broke for 13 yards and a first down. Nelson then swept around end for a big 39-yard gain all the way to Auburn's 22. Two plays later from the 17, quarterback Joe Namath, on a keeper, circled left end and scored. Davis' point-after made it 14-0, one minute into the second period.

Alabama kicked off and immediately forced a punting situation. With the scrimmage line at Auburn's 32, Lee Roy Jordan, Butch Henry and Wilson stormed through and blocked Jon Kilgore's kick. The ball bounced all the way back into the end zone, and after a mad scramble for the stray pigskin, Alabama's Bill Battle came up with the prize and a touchdown. Davis made it 21-0.

The winners almost scored again just before intermission, but Nelson, after completing a 10-yard run to the two, fumbled and George Ross recovered for Auburn in the end zone.

Early in the third period, Auburn had to punt from its own end zone and Alabama started another scoring drive from the Tiger 29. Clark got two yards before Namath threw to Carlton Rankin for a gain of 13 and a first down at the 14. Clark went to the 10, Namath to the three, and Versprille to the two. From there, Namath went over, but a personal foul penalty pushed the ball back to the 15. No problem. Namath immediately hit Clark for a touchdown. After a Davis conversion, the score was 28-0.

It wasn't Auburn's day. Rose took the ensuing kickoff and when he was belted hard, the ball popped free and Alabama's Dick O'Dell plucked it from the air and was downed at the Tiger 28. From the 23, Davis kicked a field goal to make the score 31-0.

On the last play of the third quarter, Clark punted to Billy Edge, who fumbled, and Wilson recovered for Alabama on the Auburn 16. Namath, on first down, shot a bullet to Williamson. Touchdown!

George "Butch" Wilson returned opening kickoff for a touchdown in 1962.

Davis kicked good and in two games against the Tigers, he had scored 18 points on nine conversions and three field goals. Two of his younger brothers would also kick for Alabama in later years.

Alabama led in first downs 14-11, and held Auburn to only 28 yards rushing. However, Jimmy Sidle and Mailon Kent combined for 202 air yards on 12 completions in 30 attempts. Seven turnovers (three intercepted passes and four fumbles) played a big part in keeping Auburn off the scoreboard. The Tide registered 301 total offensive yards, led by Nelson's 62 ground yards and Namath's 62 passing yards. The officials were kept busy walking off a total of 147 yards in penalties—75 against Alabama and 72 against Auburn.

In the past two years against Alabama, even though Auburn had gained 450 yards, the Tigers hadn't scored, mainly because of turnovers—12 in all.

Alabama went on to blank Oklahoma 17-0 in the Orange Bowl, finished with a 10-2-0 record, and surrendered only 39 points (second in the Nation to LSU's 34). Still, the best the Crimson Tide could do in the polls was fifth. Southern Cal (11-0-0), Wisconsin (8-2-0), Ole Miss (10-0-0), and Texas (9-1-1) finished, in that order, ahead of Alabama in 1962.

In Bear Bryant's first five years at Tuscaloosa, he had compiled a 41-8-5 (.805) record.

1963
Game 28

"Tick Clock! Tick! Darn You, Tick!"

Alabama was 7-1-0, ranked No. 6 in the nation and was already headed for the Sugar Bowl. Auburn was 8-1-0, pegged as the ninth best team in the country and a week earlier had accepted an Orange Bowl bid. With those accomplishments neatly tucked away everybody expected a real rock 'em, sock 'em match between the hated rivals as they prepared to meet for the 28th time. And that's what the men on the field produced — an afternoon of skullbusting that had Legion Field's full house roaring from kickoff to close down.

Bear Bryant's charges opened the season with wins over Georgia, Tulane and Vanderbilt by an aggregate 81-13. Then came not only the first defeat of the season, but also Bear Bryant's first loss at Tuscaloosa since his return. Florida broke the streaks by a score of 10-6. Tennessee was whitewashed 35-0 at Birmingham. Houston went to the campus and got beat 21-13. Those 13 points by the Cougars were, however, the first time in 30 games that a team had been able to score more than one touchdown against Alabama. Next came a rugged 20-19 squeaker over Mississippi State and a 27-11 win over Georgia Tech.

The Tide then turned their attention toward Auburn.

Shug Jordan's 1963 crowd could very easily have been tagged with the label — "Cardiac Kids." In the course of the season they had

Howard Simpson's two heads-up defensive plays preserved Auburn's 10-8 win over Alabama in 1963.

beaten Kentucky by one point, Tennessee by four, FSU by six, Houston by seven and Tech by eight. The Tigers' three other wins were shutouts of Chattanooga, Florida and Georgia. Auburn's only setback came in the seventh week of the season, and it was also a close one, 13-10 to a strong Mississippi State team that went on to lose only two games that season.

Don Brown of the *Birmingham News* reported on game day, "The Tigers are loose, confident, relaxed and sincerely dedicated to winning this football game."

And the Tigers did win it—10-8—on the strength of two great defensive plays by Howard Simpson.

Governor George Wallace met the team captains and seniors at midfield and tossed the coin. It fell in Auburn's favor and rather than the ball, the War Eagles chose a strong 25 mile-per-hour wind and kicked off. Benny Nelson returned Mike Fuller's long kick to the Tide 23-yard line and the feud was on. Buddy French shanked a fourth-and-one punt into the wind for only 13 yards to set Auburn up at the Alabama 45. The decision to "take the wind" paid early dividends as the Tigers cashed in on the opportunity for a score.

Tucker Frederickson managed one yard. Quarterback Jimmy Sidle got zero on a sweep, was shaken up and replaced by Mailon Kent, who immediately hit Richard Waid over the middle for 12 yards and a first down on the 32. Frederickson found a hole at center and cracked for seven. Larry Rawson's run of three yards got another first down at the 22. Frederickson hit the middle for four, Kent gained two and Frederickson two. That brought up fourth down at the 14 and brought on Marvin "Woody" Woodall for a field goal try. Standing at the 22, Woodall made history when he kicked Auburn's first field goal in the series. With 8:28 remaining in the quarter the Tigers led 3-0—Auburn's first advantage over Alabama in five years.

On the next Tide series, once again it got to fourth-and-one, and once again French couldn't buck the blustery wind and got off only a 12-yard punt to Alabama's 48. The Tigers couldn't do it this time as Al Lewis' crunching hit separated Sidle from the ball and Charles Stephens recovered for Bama at the 35.

After an exchange of punts, plus a 15-yard clipping penalty against Auburn, the Crimsons had a first down at the Tiger 39. Joe Namath, in his junior year, went for six as the first quarter ended. After exchanging goals, Eddie Versprille broke through for 10, then added four more to Auburn's 19. On the next play Simpson crashed through the line and got a hand on a Namath pitch-out. After a desperate scramble for the bouncing ball, Simpson won the chase for Auburn at the 15.

Bear Bryant salutes Shug Jordan on a victory well earned as the two meet at mid-field immediately after Auburn's 10-8 triumph in 1963. (Photo courtesy of Robert Adams, Birmingham News.)

The rest of the quarter was a punting exhibition and the first half came to a close with the Tigers holding on, 3-0.

Ten minutes into the third quarter found French and Jon Kilgore still punting away. Then came Simpson's second heads-up play, the one that won the game for Auburn. Kilgore was standing at his 35-yard line and got off a low, line-drive kick that hit the ground and darted right past the waiting Nelson. As the ball went by, Nelson touched it and suddenly it was "anybody's ball." Nelson finally chased it down and, as he was about to pick it up, here came that man Howard Simpson. Simpson smashed viciously into Nelson and the ball squirted away. It was recovered by—who else—Simpson. Auburn was in possession at Alabama's seven-yard line.

War Eagle fans roared with delight.

Rawson lost a yard and Sidle threw incomplete into the end zone. On third down, Kent came on again in relief of Sidle, rolled right, and drilled one that Frederickson caught at the two and scored. Woodall was good with the conversion and with 5:17 left in the third quarter, Auburn had a big 10-0 lead.

The next time Alabama got the ball, Namath fumbled and Chuck Hurston recovered for Auburn at the Tide 24. However, two penalties shoved the Tigers back and Kilgore punted into the end zone.

Boom! On first down, Nelson shot straight ahead and was off to the races—80 yards and an Alabama touchdown. Nobody touched him and Benny Nelson had recorded the longest run from scrimmage in the series at that time. Going for the two-point conversion, Namath faked a pass and dived over.

Auburn's lead suddenly was chopped from 10 to two points.

The game moved into the fourth quarter and after an exchange of punts, Billy Piper picked off a Sidle pass and returned it eight yards to Alabama's 45. Runs by Namath, Hudson Harris and Jackie Sherrill netted 17 yards and the Tide had the Tigers sweating down at the 38. But Harris fumbled after being belted by Frederickson and Billy Edge. Auburn's Steve Osburne came up with the big recovery to stop the Tide threat.

With just over four minutes left in the game, Auburn was punting again. On a fourth-and-four at the Tide 31, Namath fired a gambling pass that was broken up by George Rose and the fired-up War Eagles began to smell victory. Auburn couldn't move and Kilgore punted into the end zone. Starting at the 20, Namath connected with Jimmy Dill for a 20-yarder. After two incompletions, Namath found Dill again for 14 yards to Auburn's 46; however, Alabama was caught clipping on the play and the Tide retreated to their own 36.

On the next play, Nelson slipped past the Auburn secondary and was streaking down the sidelines all alone, but the Tigers' frantic pass-rush hurried the Namath bomb and the ball sailed just out of Nelson's reach. That brought up a fourth down and another long pass by Namath was no good.

Auburn's portion of Legion Field went wild.

It was now Auburn's ball and Auburn's ball game. As quarterback Kent was sneaking three straight times to kill the clock, reporter Brown spotted a Tiger player jumping up and down on the sidelines and screaming at the top of his lungs, "Tick clock! Tick! Darn you, tick!" The story continued, "His voice almost drowned by the pandemonium all about, Auburn Tiger center Jerry Popewell was doing a little sincere begging about 4 p.m. Saturday.

"And the Legion Field scoreboard—where bright lights gleamed 'Auburn 10, Alabama 8'—the clock obeyed. Practically all the west stands helped, for that was where Auburn fans were deliriously crazy. They screamed out the final seconds of a historic two hours.

"At the instant time stood still, 0:00, Coach Ralph (Shug) Jordan and the Auburn players literally went into orbit."

As Jordan happily rode atop the shoulders of his victorious players, Benny Marshall of the *News* wrote, "Bryant looked up at

Woody Woodall's 22-yard field goal helped Auburn beat Alabama 10-8 in 1963.

Benny Nelson, Alabama back, scored on an 80-yard run in the 1963 game.

Advertiser-JOURNAL
Montgomery, Ala., Sunday, Dec. 1, 1963

SPORTS, NEWS, MOVIES

Miami, New Orleans Here We Come!
It Happened! Auburn 10, Tide 8

Jordan. Then Bryant stepped back. And then he saluted. Bryant of Alabama hasn't had much practice, but he can lose with grace, like he wins with grace. And if he died a little on the inside, Legion Field at 4 o'clock on Saturday afternoon wasn't the place to show it.

"Four times in a row, he had been a happy winner. Now, it was Jordan's time.

"Paul Bryant actually saluted."

The victory pushed Auburn back into the series lead, 14-13-1, and the Tigers had registered 434 points, Alabama 397.

Alabama got seven first downs, 224 total offensive yards and held the Tigers in check with just five first downs and 131 yards. But, five Tide turnovers—and Howard Simpson—made the difference on the scoreboard. Namath, who completed only four of 17 passes against Auburn, was suspended from the team a few days later and would miss the Tide's two final games of the season. Two weeks after its loss to the Tigers, Alabama defeated Miami 17-12 behind the quarterbacking of Steve Sloan.

The Alabama-Miami game was originally scheduled for November 23. However, that was the day after President John Kennedy was killed and the game was postponed until December 14.

For the first time in a decade, both Alabama and Auburn went bowling the same season. The Crimson Tide met unbeaten SEC Champions Ole Miss (7-0-2) in the Sugar Bowl and used four field goals by Tim Davis to upset the sixth-ranked Rebels 12-7. The victory was saved by a great goal line stand that stopped Mississippi at the two-yard line as the game ended. Auburn went to Miami and lost 13-7 to Nebraska (10-1-0) in the Orange Bowl. Still, though, the War Eagles had their thrilling 10-8 triumph over Alabama to cherish for a year.

Auburn finished with a No. 5 national ranking; Alabama ninth. Both teams recorded 9-2-0 records in 1963. It was the first time since 1915, and only the second time in their football histories, that both ended a season with identical records.

Joe Namath passed for 201 yards and 3 touchdowns against Auburn in 1962- 63- 64.

1964
GAME 29

Back To Tuscaloosa

The National Championship returned to Tuscaloosa in 1964 as the result of an incredible upset that took place on the season's final Saturday.

Alabama's drive towards the title started on September 16 at home in a 31-3 win over Georgia, in Vince Dooley's first game as the Bulldogs' head coach. Senior Joe Namath scored three touchdowns and connected on 16 of 21 passes to turn a 7-3 halftime score into a rout. The pollsters placed the Tide in the No. 4 slot.

The following week was a night game in Mobile and Bear Bryant's charges scored the first six times they had the ball to thump Tulane 36-6, and move up one notch to third. Another night game was on tap a week later in Nashville where Vanderbilt held Bama scoreless in the first half before losing 24-0. Rank: No. 3.

North Carolina State was next. In the second quarter of a scoreless game, Namath sprinted right and planted his foot to cut back. Down he went. His right knee had collapsed. In years to follow Namath's nimble knee would be a subject of continuing intense interest to every football fan in America. It all began on the afternoon of October 10, 1964, in sunny Tuscaloosa. Steve Sloan came out of the bullpen and quarterbacked a 21-0 victory over the Wolfpack. There was no change in the rankings.

The Tide then moved into hostile territory—Knoxville, Tennessee—where they had won only seven of 19 games in the past.

Tucker Frederickson, Auburn's All-American back, gained 117 yards against Alabama in the 1964 game.

Bryant had them ready and the Crimsons left town after bagging the Vols, 19-8. Still, a No. 3 national standing.

On October 24, a snapping squad of Florida Gators went to Tuscaloosa and led 14-7 in the third quarter. Alabama came back to tie the score and, with 3:06 left to play, David Ray kicked a field goal for a 17-14 win to keep Bama third in the polls.

Meanwhile, unbeaten Notre Dame, under new head coach Ara Parseghian, was at the top of the polls, followed by Arkansas, Alabama and Nebraska, all with perfect records as well. By now, all the other major teams had lost at least once.

On the last day of October in a night game at Jackson, Mississippi State took the opening kickoff and drove for a touchdown. Bama, however, bounced back to post a 23-6 win. The Tide moved to No. 2, replacing Arkansas, who had been unimpressive the last two weeks although winning over lightweight Wichita State and Texas A&M, both games by 17-0 scores.

On November 7 at Birmingham, LSU led 9-7 after three quarters before the Tide rallied for a 17-9 victory. That same day, Notre Dame had its only close call up to that point in the season, a 17-15 win over Pittsburgh. Arkansas blanked Rice, and Nebraska clobbered Kansas.

The following week, the Alabama-Georgia Tech series, which began in 1902, came to an end. Namath came off the bench with 1:40 left in a scoreless first half and threw touchdown bombs of 48 and 45 yards as Bama captured the last of the 46 games between the ancient rivals, 24-7. There was definitely no love lost between the University of Alabama and the Georgia Institute of Technology. Notre Dame topped Michigan State 34-7 to remain atop the polls and Alabama stayed a distant second. Arkansas and Nebraska were still ranked third and fourth, respectively.

The Crimson Tide was now 9-0-0 and staring at Auburn.

Meantime, the Tigers were 6-3-0 with wins over Houston 30-0, Tennessee 3-0, Chattanooga 33-12 (Auburn's 600th all-time football game), Southern Mississippi 14-7, Mississippi State 12-3 and Georgia 14-7. There were losses to Kentucky 20-0, Tech 7-3 and Florida 14-0. But Coach Shug Jordan had his Tiger team primed and ready to give Alabama all it could handle, and then some.

The excitement over the 29th meeting was made even livelier because, for the first time, the game would be beamed on nationwide television. Because the TV people said so, one team had to dress in all-white while the other could wear its colored home jerseys. That started a tradition that still exists today—Auburn wears its blue shirts one year; Alabama its crimson tops the next year—TV or no TV.

In 1964, Auburn was dressed in white, and a state record crowd of 68,000 jammed an again-enlarged Legion Field on Thanksgiving Day. The Auburn-Alabama rivalry had the full attention of the turkey-day football fanatics all over America. And America watched a thriller as the Tide won, 21-14.

Auburn won the toss and elected to receive. After an exchange of punts, the Tigers were about to kick again from their own 39-yard line. However, the ball was snapped over punter Jon Kilgore's head and bounded all the way into the end zone. Kilgore rushed back and appeared to have the ball, but it fell from his grasp and Alabama's Steve Bowman stormed in and pounced on it for a Crimson Tide

Alabama's Ray Ogden completes his historic 107-yard kickoff return in the 1964 game.

touchdown. Ray's conversion was no good and with 5:42 left in the first quarter it was 6-0, Alabama.

Keyed by a 15-yard penalty and the pile-driving rushes of Tucker Frederickson, Auburn immediately drove down to Alabama's 29 but was stalled. The Tide retaliated with a 50-yard march to Auburn's 21 and Ray's field goal try was unsuccessful. Auburn knocked out a couple of first downs before Kilgore's long punt was downed by John McAfee at the Tide two.

Alabama could manage only one yard in three cracks and Buddy French's slicing punt went out of bounds at the Tide 29. Frederickson shot for a big 17-yard gain, then five more to Alabama's seven. Jimmy Sidle went to the three, and Frederickson carried several red-shirted people over the goal as he scored for Auburn. Don Lewis kicked the point-after to put the Tigers ahead and that's the way the first half ended: Underdog Auburn 7, undefeated Alabama 6.

What did Coach Bryant say to his team in the locker room? Probably something along the lines of, "... boys, we need a touchdown...!"

And to begin the second half, Alabama got one so quickly that many fans slow in returning to their seats after halftime refreshments missed it.

Ray Ogden fielded the second-half kickoff seven yards deep in his end zone, and remembering what The Coach had just said, gave himself a green light. Ogden went roaring straight up the middle, found an alley that his blocking teammates had provided, and streaked untouched for a touchdown. One-hundred and seven yards! It is still the longest run in series history. Shocked Auburn couldn't re-group in time and Sloan rolled out to run for two more points and a 14-7 Alabama lead.

A bad snap on a punt for one touchdown; a 107-yard kickoff return for another. Alabama was living right that November 26 afternoon.

Midway in the third period Auburn hammered out a tough, 15-play, 79-yard drive. But Auburn needed 80 yards. At Alabama's 18, Frederickson lashed to the five for the Tigers' fifth first down of the march. With the huge noisy crowd going mad, the Tide defense stood up. Sidle got one yard and Tom Bryan managed three to the Tide one-yard line. On third down, Bryan tried again but was shoved back a yard. The ball was given to hard-running Frederickson, but Alabama's charging linemen stopped him cold and the Tide had held.

Alabama worked the ball out to the 24-yard line as the fourth and final period got under way. On fourth down, French punted only 12

Birmingham Post-Herald

BIRMINGHAM: Cloudy, colder. *Alabama's 'Good Morning' Newspaper* ALABAMA: Colder, cloudy.

VOL. 94—NO. 226 BIRMINGHAM, FRIDAY, NOVEMBER 27, 1964 40 Pages In Four Sections

Orange Bowl Next
Tide Sinks Tough Auburn, 21-14

Climaxes A Perfect Season

BY BILL LUMPKIN
Post-Herald Sports Editor

Thanksgiving Day fare for Birmingham and all Alabama—a near-perfect football game, with the Crimson Tide getting up off the floor through a sensational 107-yard kickoff return touchdown by Ray Ogden that led to a 21-14 victory for Alabama.

Thus ended one of the Crimson Tide's greatest seasons, with no defeat to mar the record.

It was Alabama's 10th triumph of the year and the seventh time a Crimson Tide eleven has ended with a perfect record.

Ogden's sensational kickoff return, that put the Tide in front to stay, came as the second half opened.

His feet drummed a steady beat of victory as he went all the way, starting behind his own goal line and ending behind Auburn's.

But for Auburn partisans, it also was a game in which they could take glory. The Tigers fought from the start and their efforts were outstanding.

★ ★ ★
Football City Seen By U. S.

BY JAMES BENNETT

Legion Field was a good-sized city yesterday.

For several hours, its 68,000 people made it the fifth largest in Alabama.

It had a mayor, a police force, a hospital and most of all football. That's what it was all about.

As the population roared, the nation watched Alabama over network television remain unbeaten and untied winning over traditional rival Auburn 21-14.

The Tide, getting into its winning ways in the game with a first quarter score, set the stage and a climactic season's end of football in an afternoon of excitement in Birmingham.

While Alabama scored three times, a defense-minded Auburn team scored twice and paid no deference to the Tide's dreams of an undefeated season and bid for top honors as the nation's number one team.

The crowd loved it.

'We're No. 1.'

FULL HOUSE—This aerial photo by Post-Herald television. The Alabama victory evened up the A[...]

The Birmingham News
LATE FINAL

77th Year—Vol. No. 262   70 Pages—5 Sections   Birmingham, Ala., Tuesday, December 1, 1964

AP poll makes it official
'BAMA BEST IN ALL THE LAND

Birmingham Post-Herald

FINAL EDITION

BIRMINGHAM: Cold and fair. *Alabama's 'Good Morning' Newspaper* ALABAMA: Fair and cold.

PRICE TEN CENTS

VOL. 94—NO. 229   BIRMINGHAM, TUESDAY, DECEMBER 1, 1964   20 Pages In Two Sections

Ranked No. 1 In Nation
Alabama Wins National Football Title

City Votes Today On Rule Choice

'We're No. 1' Rolls Over UA Campus

4500 Students Attend Impromptu Pep Rally To Pay Tribute To Tide, Bryant

BY TIM ROBINSON

yards to Bama's 36 and Auburn had another big break as a result of Alabama's kicking game that day. Bryan burst through for 12 yards and Frederickson's seven-yard rush took it to the 17. Switching to the passing game on second-and-three, Bryan's aerial went awry and John Mosley intercepted at the one-yard line to foil the War Eagles again.

With just over 12 minutes left to play, Alabama punted and Auburn quickly drove back to the Tide 22, but Jim Simmons hit Bryan, caused a fumble, and Alabama's Dan Kearley recovered to snuff out still another Tiger threat.

On first down, Bowman hit a big hole in the dazed and demoralized Auburn line and went 52 yards. One play later, Namath faked beautifully and threw a 23-yard scoring pass to Ray Perkins. Perkins also added the conversion and Alabama, who had been fighting for its football life all afternoon, suddenly discovered they had a 21-7 lead with just under eight minutes remaining in the contest.

Don Brown, a reporter for the *Birmingham News*, wrote this about the Alabama scoring drive, "... Namath's right knee bore heavy taping, and both his shoes were covered with white adhesive tape, for some unexplained reason." In reality, they were taped for additional support. Thus, the white-shoe craze in athletics was born.

Late in the game, Auburn's Lewis recovered a Wayne Trimble fumble at Alabama's 43. Four straight Bryan pass completions, the last one to Sidle for 16 yards, and the Tigers had a touchdown. But it was too late. Only 27 seconds were left in what had been a frustrating afternoon of football for Auburn. Lewis kicked the conversion, but...

The series was again tied, this time at 14-14-1, and Auburn's point total read 448, Alabama's 418.

Statistically, Auburn had the better of the 1964 game. The Tigers led in first downs, 19-10, and in total yards 301-245. In penalty yards, it was 50 against Alabama, 39 against Auburn. Frederickson was the leading rusher with 117 yards in 22 carries. Bryan accounted for 210 yards (114 passing and 96 rushing) while Namath was six-for-nine in passing for 76 yards; Sloan four-for-five, 45 yards.

Because the game had been played on Thanksgiving, Alabama had to wait two days in hopes of a Notre Dame loss to Southern California in the season's finale to take place in Los Angeles Saturday. USC, who had already lost three games, trailed 17-7 at halftime and the Tide's hopes seemed hopeless, at best.

In the third quarter, leading 17-7, the Irish reached the Trojans' nine-yard line but fumbled. Later, a penalty nullified an Irish touchdown. With 4:30 left in the game, Southern Cal scored to cap a long 92-yard march, but ND still led, 17-13. The Trojans got the ball back, and on a fourth-and-10 situation from the Irish 40, quarterback Craig Fertig heaved a desperation pass that Rod Sherman caught for a touchdown with 95 seconds left in the game. Somehow, USC had upset Notre Dame, 20-17.

Alabama had the National Championship again, according to the AP and UPI. However, in Washington, D.C., a group of citizens headed by Jerry Nickerson and Robert Hutchison weren't satisfied. They wanted the championship decided in a new post-season game to be called the Presidential Bowl. To make it worthwhile for the teams, they offered Notre Dame and Alabama $300,000 each (plus expenses) to meet in Washington's D.C. Stadium. The Athletic Departments of both schools flatly rejected the offer and the committee said they had no plans to invite any other teams. The idea was dropped.

In 1964, bowl games still didn't count in the final AP or UPI polls, and for Alabama it was a good thing. In one of the all-time classic bowl games, Texas whipped the Tide 21-17 in the Orange Bowl. In the game, the Longhorns halted Alabama on the six-inch line in the last minute of play. The 21 points Texas got that night in Miami were the most scored against the Tide in any single game since Bear Bryant became the Alabama head coach 76 games ago.

1965

GAME 30

It Stayed In Tuscaloosa

In 1965, Alabama capitalized on the most bizarre finish in college football history to capture its second straight National Championship.

On television for their third straight game, the Crimson Tide opened the season in Athens and lost 18-17 when Georgia scored on a controversial 73-yard "flea flicker" play and a successful two-point conversion in the last two minutes of the game.

The Tide then toppled Tulane 27-0, edged Ole Miss 17-16, beat Vanderbilt 22-7 and was tied by Tennessee 7-7. Thus, at the halfway junction of the season, Alabama was 3-1-1 and just trying to survive in the Southeastern Conference.

During the same five-week period, Auburn had won only twice, 23-18 over Kentucky and 30-7 in its annual scrimmage with Chattanooga. There were losses to Baylor 14-8, and Georgia Tech 23-14, plus a 13-13 tie with Tennessee.

However, six weeks later, Alabama and Auburn found themselves playing for the SEC Championship. Everybody else in the league had been eliminated from the race and the Tigers' 4-0-1 league mark was tops, while the Tide's 5-1-1 record was second best.

On the national scene, Michigan State (No. 1), Arkansas (No. 2), and Nebraska (No. 3) had already concluded perfect 10-0-0 seasons when November 27 rolled around and time for the 30th collision between Auburn and fifth-ranked Alabama was at hand.

Internationally, the news was getting grim. There were 106 Americans killed that week in Viet Nam, the most in any one week up to that time, and raised the total Americans dead to 1,095 since this country's involvement in the war in 1961. Angry protests were springing up all over the nation. Little did anyone know at the time, but the war and the rallies had only begun.

Seventy-thousand fans jammed Legion Field and fully expected a classic SEC championship showdown. However, the game turned out to be, well, not exactly a classic. Alabama won, 30-3.

Auburn received the opening kickoff and acted as though they meant business by quickly marching to Alabama's 27-yard line. The Tigers were stopped, immediately recovered a Tide fumble, but dropped it right back, and Alabama accepted the generosity and scored.

Steve Sloan completed a 13-yard pass to Tommy Tolleson during a snappy, six-play drive that carried to Auburn's 11. From there, Sloan found Tolleson again, this time for a touchdown. David Ray missed the conversion and with 5:05 left in the first quarter, Bama was the early boss, 6-0.

Early in the second quarter, Ray intercepted a Bowden pass at the Tide 36. Sloan made things seem simple. He drilled a nine-yard pass to Dennis Holman, came right back with a 22-yarder to Hal Moore, and then popped Ray Perkins with a 33-yard touchdown toss. Three plays, three passes to three different receivers, and the 64 yards were covered just that quickly. A two-point conversion failed and the score was 12-0.

About five minutes later Alabama added a field goal. Bobby Johns intercepted Bowden and the Tide began at their 37. Leslie Kelly carried three times for 20 yards and Sloan completed a 20-yard pass to Wayne Cook to pace a drive to the Auburn 10. The Tigers kept a touchdown off the books but Ray's field goal made it 15-0.

Auburn took the ensuing kickoff and worked it to Alabama's 27 where Don Lewis pounded a 44-yard field goal—the longest in series history at that time.

The half ended with the Tide on top, 15-3.

Auburn tried desperately to get back in the ball game in the third quarter and moved down to Alabama's 18. However, Bowden threw his third interception of the game, this one to David Bedwell, and that finished any rally thoughts that the Tigers might have had, because on this particular day it was disastrous to let Steve Sloan play with the football.

From his 37, Sloan let a long one fly that Perkins snagged on a diving catch 32 yards downfield at Auburn's 31. Six plays later, Kelly crashed over from the two. Sloan went to Tolleson for the two-point conversion and a 23-3 advantage for the Tide.

One minute and 14 seconds later Alabama scored again. Bowden, back to pass, was hit by Ben McLeod, fumbled, and John Sullivan recovered for Alabama on the Tiger 28. On first down, Sloan threw over the middle to Don Shankles, who caught it at the 20 and raced for a touchdown. Ray converted to conclude the scoring.

Late in the game, a young sophomore quarterback by the name of Kenny Stabler led a 46-yard Tide drive to a first down at Auburn's one-yard line. But the battling Tigers held and kept the final score at 30-3.

Now, after 30 series games spread over a 72-year period, there was a difference of only one game and three points. Alabama led 15-14-1, while Auburn was ahead in scoring, 451-448.

Sloan set a new series record with 226 yards passing as he completed 13 of 18. Alabama not only ripped Auburn on the scoreboard in 1965, but on the statistics sheet as well. The Tide had more first downs 20-13, more yards rushing 175-138, more yards passing 246-93 and more total yards 421-231. In penalty yards, it was Alabama leading there, too, 60-35.

The Crimson Tide, with an 8-1-1 record, was asked to return to the Orange Bowl for the second straight year, this time to meet unbeaten Nebraska. Auburn was invited to Memphis, where the Liberty Bowl was being played for the first time after unsuccessful attempts in Philadelphia and Atlantic City during the past six years. The Tigers would meet Ole Miss.

For the first time, the Associated Press and the Football Writers' Association of America (FWAA) decided to wait until after the bowl games before a final vote to decide which of the three 10-0-0 teams

(Michigan State, Arkansas, Nebraska) should be selected as the nation's best.

That decision was a tremendous break for Alabama.

As the New Year's Day dramatics began to unfold, first it was Arkansas that bit the dust in the Cotton Bowl, losing 14-7 to an LSU team that had gone to Dallas after losing to Florida, Ole Miss and Alabama by a combined score of 68-14.

Next came the Rose Bowl, where Michigan State was just expected to go through the motions to wrap up the National Championship. UCLA was the opposition and UCLA had lost to the Spartans 13-3 during the regular season, and had also been beaten by Tennessee and tied by Missouri. Final score: UCLA 14, Michigan State 12. So much for Michigan State.

That brought up the Orange Bowl that night and Nebraska was now ready to stake undisputed claims on the No. 1 spot as the Nation's only undefeated team. However, the 'Huskers hit a red-hot Alabama team that gouged out 29 first downs, gained 518 yards, built a 24-7 halftime lead and coasted to a 39-28 victory.

In 1942, some stunning developments took place on the final regular season day when the Nos. 1 and 2 ranked teams in the Nation were walloped by a combined score of 89-12. Boston College (No. 1) lost 55-12 to Holy Cross, and Georgia Tech (No. 2) was crushed by Georgia 34-0.

However, the shocking turn of events that concluded the 1965 season were even more electrifying than what had happened in the fall of '42. In one day, LSU, UCLA and Alabama, with a combined 22-6-2 record, beheaded the country's 1-2-3 teams and their perfect 30-0-0 record.

Following these unexpected developments, the AP and FWAA voted Alabama as the 1965 National Champions—the Crimson Tide's third title in the past five years. Michigan State was second, followed by Arkansas, UCLA and Nebraska. Two other SEC teams finished in the Top Ten that year—Tennessee seventh and LSU eighth.

1966
GAME 31

Victories Vs. Votes

In 1966 Alabama was the defending National Champion, the only team in the country to finish with a perfect record, and owned the Nation's longest winning streak. But those glowing credentials got the Tide only a No. 3 national ranking behind Notre Dame and Michigan State. It was the year the Irish and Spartans played to a dull 10-10 tie in a game that was unprecedented in terms of advance media buildup; and which, in the end, neither coach seemed to want to win.

As Auburn approached on Alabama's schedule, the powerful 9-0-0 Crimson Tide had allowed opponents only five touchdowns and were ahead in scoring, 260-37.

Auburn was suffering through its most dismal season in 14 years. The Tigers had defeated only Chattanooga, Wake Forest, TCU and Mississippi State, four teams that combined for just 12 wins that autumn. Coach Shug Jordan's troops had lost to Kentucky, and to 1966 powerhouses Tennessee, Georgia Tech, Florida and Georgia, whose total record was 33-7-0 that year.

Sixty-seven thousand showed up at Legion Field on December 3 while a national television audience tuned in and watched as Alabama bunched its scoring in the second and third quarters and manhandled the struggling Tigers, 31-0.

Auburn fought the heavily-favored Tide on even terms for the first 23 minutes and 42 seconds of the game. Early in the second period,

"Mama said there'd be days like this...." These photos of Coach Bryant and Coach Jordan were not taken at an Alabama-Auburn game.... but they could have been.

mainly on six pass completions by Kenny Stabler, Alabama drove 69 yards to Auburn's 14, but Steve Davis missed a field goal.

The Tigers' Tommy Lunceford punted to Alabama's 35 and here came Stabler again. On second down, he faked a run to the left, stopped and lofted a long pass to Ray Perkins who caught it on the run and scored on a play that covered 63 yards — the longest scoring pass play in series history at the time. Davis' point-after made it 7-0 and there was 6:18 left to play in the first half.

Alabama kicked off, forced a punt and scored again. Taking over at the Auburn 48, Stabler completed a short pass to Perkins, then connected on his eighth straight, a 16-yarder to Dennis Homan to the Tiger 28. After an incompletion that broke the string, David Chatwood rambled for 17 yards on a draw play, and Stabler slipped around end for nine to Auburn's two. Two plays later, Leslie Kelley plunged over, Davis kicked good and with just over a minute left before intermission, the Tide was talking, 14-0.

There was time, though, for three more points. Loran Carter fumbled and Richard Cole recovered for Bama at the Tiger 43. Stabler ran for 16 and then threw for 21 to Homan to Auburn's six-yard line. Following an incomplete pass into the end zone, Davis kicked a field goal only four seconds before the half ended to make it 17-0.

In the third quarter, Lunceford fielded a high snap on punt formation but couldn't get the kick off, and Alabama took over at the War Eagles' 44. Triggered by a Stabler run of 10 yards, a Stabler-to-Perkins pass of 16, a personal foul penalty against Auburn for 15 more yards, and Alabama got it down close for Kelley to take it over for his second touchdown of the game. With just over five minutes left in the period, Davis got his kick to make the score 24-0.

Two minutes and one second later it was 31-0. Wayne Owen intercepted a Carter pass at the Auburn 41. Wayne Trimble came on at quarterback and quickly hit Donnie Sutton with a touchdown pass. Davis converted again.

Stabler's tandem offense showed 221 yards on nine runs for 52 yards and 11 pass completions (16 attempts) for 169 yards. Alabama doubled Auburn in first downs, 22-11, and more than doubled them in total yards, 375-174. In the last two years while getting clobbered in the series by a score of 61-3, Auburn had committed 14 turnovers to Alabama's three.

Alabama used the 31st game of the series to take a 16-14-1 lead — the Tide's first two-game advantage ever over Auburn. The scoring was now also in Alabama's favor, 479-451.

For the second straight year, it was an Alabama-Nebraska matchup in a big bowl, this time the Sugar. The Cornhuskers' only loss was a shocking 10-9 setback at the hands of Oklahoma (a four-time loser that year) in the final regular season game.

Stabler and Alabama stung Nebraska early and went on to record a 34-7 rout, the second most lopsided score in Sugar Bowl history.

Eleven wins, no losses and no ties; 21 consecutive games without a defeat; defending National Champions the past two years. Still, only a No. 3 ranking. Had Notre Dame or Michigan State been riding the same crest in 1966, Alabama couldn't have slipped ahead of them had the Tide whipped Vince Lombardi's Green Bay Packers twice in one day.

The Eastern and Midwest writers and coaches, who have the majority of the voting voice in the polls, were determined for the Southeastern Conference and Alabama not to have a third straight National Championship.

It was a bitter pill for Alabama to have to swallow.

1967
GAME 32

AU Couldn't Believe It. Neither Could UA.

Incredibly, Alabama defeated Auburn in 1967.

"The Tiger dressing room was about the saddest place a fellow could find," reported Jimmy Bryan of the *Birmingham News*. "The muddy, bloody boys-men wept openly and unashamed. This was the one Auburn wanted most of all, and Auburn didn't get it . . . Auburn came close, terribly close."

The final score was 7-3. While final scores are sometimes the only preserved relic of a game, they by no means always reflect a true picture of what happened. Auburn spent an unbelievable afternoon that day in 1967 on the gridiron.

Speaking of irons, there's an old Southern saying that goes thusly: "When the iron is hot, iron!" Auburn had a hot iron throughout the first three quarters of the game, but . . .

Alabama opened the season just as incredibly as it closed it 10 games later. The Tide met a good FSU team in a night game at Birmingham and the final score was a wild, wild 37-37 tie. That was the most points scored against Alabama in 98 games dating back to the 40-0 Auburn win in 1957. The Tide recovered to dump Southern Mississippi, Ole Miss and Vanderbilt by an aggregate 81-31 total, but it became obvious suddenly that Alabama's defense wasn't what it had been for the past eight years.

On October 21 at Birmingham's Legion Field, Tennessee, destined to become the 1967 SEC Champions, handed Alabama its first defeat in 25 games by a 24-13 score. Two ties had marred the otherwise perfect Bama skein.

From then on, though, Bear Bryant got the defense back into its customary rugged shape to allow only two touchdowns in the next four games, as the Tide dropped Clemson, Mississippi State, LSU and South Carolina.

Auburn got its season started with a warm-up 40-0 blanking of Chattanooga before losing to Tennessee 27-13. The Tigers scored 119 points in their next three games in wins over Kentucky, Clemson and Georgia Tech. Then came a 7-0 loss to a strong Miami (Florida) team, victories over Florida and Mississippi State, and a loss to Georgia. Auburn's three defeats in 1967 were to teams whose combined regular season records totaled 23 wins against only seven losses.

On game day, Alabama was 7-1-1, ranked eighth in the country, and favored to win. Auburn was 6-3-0, but had scored 53 more points than its state rival.

Saturday, December 2 dawned dark, wet, windy and altogether miserable. All 70,000 or so tickets had been sold since summer, but many fans decided not to brave the weather conditions, and either stayed at home or in the warmth of their automobiles once they arrived at the stadium.

Even so, the big Legion Field arena appeared filled to capacity. A mass of umbrellas warded off stinging rains that came blowing in on strong gusts of wind. The playing field was a pigsty. The coldest day in series history was in 1957; the wettest in 1967.

Alabama won the coin toss and to nobody's surprise chose not to handle the ball, but to take the strong wind instead. Dudley Kerr kicked off to Auburn's Freddie Hyatt. The footing was already so treacherous that defenders storming down the field could hardly maneuver. As a result, Hyatt almost broke for a touchdown. However, Alabama's Eddie Propst made a saving tackle at the Auburn 39.

The Tigers' unbelievable afternoon of football had begun.

Auburn punted . . . Alabama punted . . . Auburn punted . . . Alabama punted . . . Auburn punted. Auburn was getting the best of the duel and by now the Tide was backed up to their own six-yard line. Alabama punted again and Auburn started from the Tide 41.

Dwight Hurston broke through for 11 yards and came back for three more. Roger Giffin gouged out eight more in two carries for a first down at Alabama's 19. On second-and-nine, Loran Carter com-

Kenny Stabler enroute to his game-winning 47-yard touchdown run in the fourth quarter and a 7-3 Bama win in 1967.

pleted a 13-yard pass to Tim Christian and the War Eagles were screaming with a first down at the five.

On a surprise call, Carter threw incomplete. Carter then gained one yard, then one more. That brought up fourth-and-goal at the three. Forsaking a field goal, the ball was given to Richard Plagge who was met head-on by Bama's Dickey Thompson and Mike Hall and stopped at the two.

Alabama got the ball but had to resort to the punt again. Auburn started the next drive from the Tide 40. A Carter-to-Christian pass was good for 11 yards. On the first play of the second quarter, Carter got free for a 13-yard gain to the 16, first down. Then came another big defensive play. Carter, back to pass, was coralled and in a frantic attempt to get free, was chased down by Bob Childs for a costly momentum-killing 10-yard loss. The next two plays gained only four yards, to the 22, and John Riley came on for a field goal try. It was wide and short.

Alabama took over at its own 20, moved to its initial first down of the game, and eventually punted to Auburn's 22. The Tigers moved the ball again before punting back deep into Tide territory. Alabama kicked right back and the Plainsmen started another drive, this time from the Bama 40.

Mike Currier went for 10, then blasted for 16 more and a first down at the Alabama 14. Giffin went to the 12, Carter to the seven, and Currier to the six. It was fourth-and-two. Once again passing up a field goal try from close in, Auburn went for the TD. They didn't get it. Giffin was stacked up one yard shy of the goal, and Alabama had escaped once more.

After another exchange of punts, the half ended all even — 0-0 — just as it had in 1907, the only other game in which Alabama and Auburn had played a scoreless first half.

Auburn took the wind at the start of the second-half and promptly forced a short 16-yard punt to get good field position at Alabama's 40. On third-and-eight, Carter passed 14 yards to Christian to the Bama 24. Three plays netted only three yards and Riley came on. This time he slammed a successful 38-yard field goal and, with 10:33 left in the third quarter, Auburn had finally taken the lead, 3-0.

Later in the period, Auburn's Don Webb recovered a Pete Jilleba fumble at the Tide 23. The Tigers could move only three yards and on another field goal try from the 38, the snap was fumbled and it was Alabama's ball.

On first down, quarterback Kenny Stabler snaked for 13 yards to Auburn's 49, bringing up Alabama's first possession past midfield and registering only its second first down of the game. Still, they trailed by only three points.

Steve Davis punted to Auburn's nine and for the first time all day, Alabama had the Tigers "backed up." But not for long. Tommy Lunceford punted and Buddy McClinton immediately intercepted a Stabler pass and returned it 22 yards to Alabama's 41 as the third quarter came to a close.

Auburn banged away to get it down to the 27 and Carter hit Christian again, this time for a 12-yard gain. But the Tigers were offside. Instead of a first down at the 15, it was third down at the 32. The play would prove to be Auburn's undoing in 1967.

On fourth down, Lunceford stood in punt formation at the Tide 46. The snap from center was low and Luncefore couldn't handle it. The swarming Crimsons were all over him and Bama took over.

Tommy Wade sloshed for five yards, then two to Auburn's 47. Then it happened. Stabler, on an option sweep, kept the ball, broke through the line and slopped through the mud 47 yards for a touchdown. Davis added the conversion and Auburn, in complete command of the game all day long, trailed 7-3. The clock showed 11:29

left to play.

Shocked Auburn could never get anything going after Stabler's zinger and the Crimson Tide just kept punting away and held on for the victory—a weird one by any standard.

"I don't really know what to say," Coach Shug Jordan told the *News'* Bryan after the game. "I've been around long enough to know the only thing that counts is what you read on the scoreboard lights ... But I don't think the best team won today."

Bryant said, "Yes, we were lucky to win the game, what else do you want me to say."

Auburn's Lunceford punted nine times for a 41-yard average and Davis answered with 13 kicks and a 37-yard average. That's almost half-a-mile of booting a wet, heavy football in one afternoon.

Auburn rammed out 13 first downs; Alabama got only four. The total yardage was 216-176, Auburn. Eighty-four of Alabama's yards came on Stabler's run and a 37-yard drive late in the game. The Tide was penalized 40 yards, Auburn 15. Stabler ran for 88 yards to lead all ground gainers. In three games against Auburn, Stabler had accounted for 341 yards (140 rushing and 201 passing). Carter passed for 117 yards on 10 completions in 19 throws.

The Tide now led the series 17-14-1 and in scoring, 486-454.

The Auburn dressing room was depressing. The players were numb from the unbelievable game just finished. The seniors not only had never beaten Alabama in their four years at the Plains, neither had they scored a touchdown against the Tide. As freshman, Alabama won 17-0. Then came sophomore and junior losses of 31-3 and 31-0. Plus the one Auburn's 1967 players would never, never forget—7-3.

The Cotton Bowl invited Alabama to its New Year's festivities, the Tide's ninth bowl game in nine years. Texas A&M, the opposition, had opened the season with consecutive losses to SMU, Purdue, LSU and FSU but roared back with six straight wins to capture the Southwest Conference title and the host spot in Dallas.

The Aggies were not even listed among the Top 20 teams in the Nation, but they made it seven victories in a row with a thrilling 20-16 upset triumph over the eighth-ranked Tide.

The game concluded Bear Bryant's first decade as head coach at Alabama and his teams had put an 88-14-7 (.839) record in the University's athletic archives. Also included were eight finishes in the Nation's Top Ten, four SEC Championships, three National Championships and nine bowl games that included three wins in the Sugar and two in the Orange.

Bryant's teams had scored 2,208 points in 10 years (109 games)

and surrendered only 719. That comes out to an average score per game of 20-7.

However, by Bear's and Bama's standards, a "dry spell" was around the corner.

1968
GAME 33

A Fifth (Straight) For Bear

For the first time in 12 years Alabama and Auburn met in their annual fuss and neither team was ranked in the Nation's Top Ten. The Tide had been there eight times and the Tigers four.

Ranked 15th, the 7-2-0 Crimsons entered the Auburn game as the Nation's top defensive team against scoring, having surrendered only 88 points. Except for a 31-7 win over Vanderbilt, all of Alabama's 1968 games were close, tight struggles. There were 10-8 and 10-9 losses to Ole Miss and Tennessee, and victories over VPI 14-7, Southern Mississippi 17-14, Clemson 21-14, Mississippi State 21-13, LSU 16-7 and Miami 14-6.

Auburn, 6-3-0, was ranked 18th. The season opened with a 37-28 loss to SMU and marked the first time in 16 years the Plainsmen had dropped three games in a row. Mississippi State, Kentucky and Clemson went down by a 73-17 combined score, before Georgia Tech squeezed out a 21-20 win. Auburn then topped Miami 31-6, Florida 24-13 and Tennessee 28-14. Then Georgia, on the way to the Southeastern Conference Championship, beat Auburn 17-3.

Auburn had scored 207 points, the Tide 150; Alabama had allowed only 88 points, the Tigers 125.

Warr Eagle! Rolll Tide! Nobody seemed to care that neither team was rated among the Top Ten because 71,534 fans, for a new state attendance record, streamed into Legion Field that heavy, overcast November 29 to witness the 33rd game of the series.

And the record crowd saw Alabama win its fifth straight over Auburn, this one by a score of 24-16.

Team captains, Alabama's Mike Hall and Auburn's Loran Carter, met for the coin toss. The Tide won and opted to play defense first. Mr. Hall and Mr. Carter trotted back to their respective sidelines.

The Tigers took the opening kickoff and hurriedly drove to midfield before being stopped by an interception. It was Mr. Hall intercepting Mr. Carter. Starting at their own 43, Alabama came out throwing and scored in only four plays. Scott Hunter, who had succeeded Kenny Stabler as the Alabama quarterback, drilled a nine-yarder to Donnie Sutton. One play later, Hunter came back to the same receiver for 10 more to Auburn's 36. Ed Morgan then smashed through the line, darted left, cut back to the middle and dashed across for a touchdown. Mike Dean's conversion was good and after only one minute and 47 seconds of play, Alabama was on its way, 7-0.

Five minutes later Auburn made a big defensive play but missed a golden opportunity to tie the score. Donald Webb blasted through and blocked a Frank Mann punt that the Tigers recovered at the Alabama 10. Dwight Hurston carried to the eight, Micky Zofko to the six, and a pass gained only one. It was fourth-and-goal at the five, and Auburn brought out John Riley who kicked a field goal for a 7-3 score.

The game rocked along. Late in the second quarter, Auburn's Carter pitched another pass to Alabama that led to a Tide touchdown. Tommy Weigand picked this one off and was grounded at the Tiger 37.

Morgan got two. A pass from Hunter to Pete Moore was good for 14 yards to the 21. Morgan made another yard and the Hunter-Moore combo clicked again, this time for 10 yards and a first down at the 10. On fourth down from the six, Morgan rammed over for a touchdown with just 1:27 before intermission. Dean's kick made it 14-3.

As the first half ended, Auburn's series touchdown drought had now reached 14 quarters.

The Tide received the second-half kickoff and had to punt to Auburn's 26. Weigand intercepted another Carter pass to lead to Alabama's third touchdown. Starting from the Tiger 33, six quick bursts through the line got the ball down to the three. Hunter passed complete to Hall for the touchdown. Dean's kick was good and Bama had built a 21-3 bulge.

With two minutes and 48 seconds remaining in the third period, the Tigers finally scored a touchdown against Alabama.

After a punt, Auburn struck quickly for 70 yards and its first series six-pointer since 1964. On third-and-nine, Carter got away for 14 yards to the 45. Then, Carter shot a pass to Mike Currier, who caught it at the Alabama 40 and literally outran everybody on his way to the end zone. Riley kicked good to bring the Tigers to within 11, at 21-10.

"Hey! Scoring a touchdown against Alabama isn't all that hard," was Auburn's sudden attitude. "And it's a helluva lot of fun!" They enjoyed it so much, they promptly did it again.

The Tigers kicked off, forced a punt, took over at their own 30, and launched a scoring drive. Carter passed 32 yards to Connie Frederick to the Tide 38. On the first play of the last quarter, Currier crunched to the 32. On the next play, Carter rifled one toward Tim Christian at the Tide three-yard line. Interference was called and Auburn was first-and-goal. On second down, Carter went to the air and to Christian again. Touchdown! Although a two-point conversion attempt failed, it didn't seem to matter. War Eagle fans shrieked loud and long. It was 21-16, and another touchdown could win the game.

The Tigers were snarling. They kicked off and made Alabama punt again. Mann got off a boomer to be fielded by Buddy McClinton at the Tiger 32. But McClinton fumbled and Bobby Swafford recovered for Alabama.

Auburn had been stabbed by a jagged bolt of lightning.

Heartbroken, the spirited Tiger fans screamed for their team to hold and get the ball back. The Tigers held, but not enough to prevent a 30-yard field goal by Dean to up Bama's lead to 24-16.

There were 10 minutes left to play, and the Orange and Blue was very much in the game. A touchdown and two-point conversion would at least knot the score at 24-all.

The fighting Auburn team never gave in. With two minutes to play, Alabama's relentless Tide was down at Auburn's five-yard line but couldn't score. A field goal would have put the game completely out of reach, and Dean stood at the 12-yard line to do just that. But Auburn's Ron Yarbrough fired through the line and blocked the attempt.

As the game wound down to the final seconds, quarterback Carter was desperately pegging away, trying for a miracle that might produce a touchdown, a two-point conversion and a 24-24 Auburn "victory."

But it didn't happen. Two Auburn miracles in a week's time were perhaps too much to expect anyway. The Auburn freshmen and the Alabama freshmen had met a week earlier in Tuscaloosa. In the first half, the Crimson Tide yearlings handled Auburn's Tiger Cubs easily and led by a score of 27-0. But quarterbacking the Auburn team was a young man named Pat Sullivan. Sullivan, in a prophetic performance, completed 13 passes for 245 yards and four touchdowns. In a miracle finish, Auburn won 36-27. Four of Sullivan's tosses were caught by a lad named Terry Beasley. Sullivan and Beasley would become legends before their careers at Auburn were ended.

In winning the fifth straight game from Auburn, to take an 18-14-1 series lead, the Tide got 19 first downs to Auburn's 10, and outgained the Tigers 369-257. Morgan led all rushers with 92 yards in 21 carries. In passing, Hunter was 18-for-37 for 173 yards; Carter 11-for-25 for 186 yards. Auburn was penalized 83 yards, Alabama 34. Seven Tiger turnovers once again shattered any hopes of winning the game. In the last 11 series games, Auburn had turned the ball over to Alabama a staggering total of 51 times. Alabama reciprocated only 19 times as the Tide won nine of the 11 games.

Auburn went to El Paso for a Sun Bowl date with Arizona, and won easily, 34-10 to conclude a 7-4-0 season.

Alabama finally made its first appearance in the Gator Bowl against Missouri. Behind by only 14-10 early in the fourth quarter, the Tide saw the Tigers explode for three touchdowns and a final verdict of 35-10, Alabama's worst defeat in 11 years. The Tide's finishing record of 8-3-0 marked the first time in 10 years that that many games had been lost in one season.

Historically, the most dominant factor in Alabama's string of five consecutive victories over Auburn in the 1960's had to be the great quarterbacks Coach Bryant brought to Tuscaloosa. Namath, Sloan, Stabler, Hunter. All of them figured prominently in Alabama defeats of the Tigers, and all of them led Tide teams in a "Golden Era" of championships, bowl games and national prominence. All of them also became pro quarterbacks and two—Namath and Stabler—would later lead their teams to Super Bowl triumphs.

As had happened so often in the Alabama-Auburn series, the pendulum was set to swing the other way. Ironically, a quarterback would play the key role in the drama.

1969

Game 34

Bear's Longest Football Day—Ever

The Pat Sullivan-Terry Beasley era of Auburn football burst upon the varsity scene on September 20, 1969 at Cliff Hare Stadium on the home campus. The duo's personal statistics were good for the coming-out party but the team's performance was even better. The War Eagles wrecked Wake Forest by a score of 57-0.

Sullivan threw only nine passes, but completed seven for 98 yards and one touchdown. He rushed for two other scores and gained 52 yards in just four carries. Beasley caught four passes for 72 yards.

The following week, Tennessee intercepted five Sullivan throws that led to a 45-19 Vols' victory enroute to the Southeastern Conference Championship. Auburn retaliated with bomb jobs on Kentucky (44-3) and Clemson (51-0). Then came two close decisions, a 17-14 win over Georgia Tech and a 21-20 loss to LSU. Florida, Mississippi State and Georgia were crumbled by a total score of 106-28 and the Sullivan-led Tigers were 7-2-0, ranked 12th in the nation, averaging 35 points per game and eyeing Alabama with much anticipation.

Alabama had suddenly fallen on "hard times." There were three losses—14-10 to Vanderbilt, 41-14 to Tennessee, and 20-15 to LSU.

Wallace Clark scored three touchdowns in Auburn's 49-26 win in the 1969 game.

One of the six wins included an incredible 33-32 edge of Ole Miss in a nationally televised night game from Birmingham, as quarterbacks Archie Manning and Scott Hunter locked horns in what turned out to be one of the SEC's all-time classic duels.

Offensively, Auburn was ranked third in the SEC with 407 yards per game and 38 touchdowns. Alabama was one notch behind with 395 yards per game and 35 touchdowns. On defense, Auburn was No. 1 in the league; Alabama was next to last, having allowed 172 points. Both teams had already signed up for post-season bowl dates.

The week of the 34th game of the series, America's newest space heroes, the Apollo 12 moon explorers, Charles Conrad, Richard Gordon and Alan Bean, returned home from a 10-day mission. On the darker side of the news were Lt. William Calley's My Lai massacre trial and tremendous U.S. casualties in Viet Nam and Cambodia. The massive anti-war rallies were hardly news any more.

Cool, bright skies greeted another record crowd jamming Legion Field anxious to see if Auburn, a touchdown favorite, could break a five-game losing streak to Alabama. What the 72,303 fans saw left them limp—51 first downs, 81 passes, 43 completions, 1,074 total offensive yards, the longest run from scrimmage in series history, a 102-yard kickoff return, a phenomenal individual passing exhibition, and 75 points scored—49 of which belonged to aroused Auburn and the remaining 26 to Alabama.

Auburn was ecstatic. The War Eagles reveled in the fact that those 49 points were the most any team had scored against an Alabama football team since way back in 1907.

That November 29, 1969 afternoon was a long one for Paul (Bear) Bryant. He had just witnessed his 353rd college football game as a player, assistant coach and head coach over a 36-year period and never before had he seen an opponent run up so many points against his team.

But when Sullivan, Micky Zofko, Wallace Clark, Connie Frederick and the rest of the Auburn Tigers got through chewing on the Tide's hide that day, War Eagles all over the world were howling with delight. It was a decisive victory but not as easy as the final score might suggest. The Tide won the toss, and naturally, wanted the football. In the early minutes, there were signs that Bama would blow Auburn all the way back to the Loveliest Village with its sixth straight series setback.

The opening kickoff went into the end zone and Alabama started at the 20-yard line. On first down, the Tide unleashed sophomore Johnny Musso for 17 yards and the offensive orgy was on. Hunter

Connie Frederick streaked 84 yards with a faked punt for an Auburn touchdown in the 1969 game.

then completed his first of 30 passes for the afternoon—an 18-yarder to Musso. From the Auburn 43, Musso gained 11, then six, then lost four. On third-and-eight, Hunter hit David Bailey for a 12-yard gain to the Tigers' 18. Musso could only get two and after two Hunter misfires, Oran Buck kicked a 32-yard field goal to put Bama up, 3-0.

Auburn got the ball and started a drive, but stalled and the Tigers punted Alabama back to the 13-yard line. The Tide thundered down the field again. A Hunter-to-Musso pass netted 32 yards; Musso ran for 10; Musso caught another Hunter pass for 24 yards; Hunter completed one to Hunter Husband for nine, and the Crimsons had the Tigers' tongues hanging out and gasping at the 11-yard line. On third down at the six, Hunter threw incomplete, which brought Buck on for another field goal attempt. It was no good. Alabama had already eaten up 145 yards in just 16 plays but had only three points to show for it.

After an exchange of punts, Auburn started at its own 43 and, led by a Sullivan-to-Clark pass of 23 yards, got down to the Alabama 18. A field goal try was missed as the first quarter came to a close.

Following another exchange of kicks, also came an exchange of interceptions. Ken James picked off a Sullivan aerial and Don Webb stole a long one by Hunter at the Tiger 10 and returned it to the 34. From there, Auburn finally got its potent offense cranked up and drove for a touchdown in nine plays. Zofko zipped for seven, but was stopped cold on the next play. On third down, Clark converted with a six yard thrust to the 47. Clark came back for four more and Zofko dashed 18 to Alabama's 31. Sullivan then found his favorite target—Beasley—for 21 yards to the Tide 10. Clark crunched to the three, to the two, then in for the touchdown. John Riley's conversion made it 7-3 with "only" five minutes left before intermission—time for both teams to score again. It was that kind of day.

Alabama returned the ensuing kickoff to their own 31 and started moving. Musso registered 16 yards on two runs. Hunter went to Bubba Sawyer twice in a row for a total of 34 yards. Four snaps and the Tide had rolled to the Auburn 19. On third-and-nine, Hunter completed an 11-yarder to Sawyer for a first down at the seven. Two plunges by Musso got it to the four and a Hunter-to-Husband completion covered the rest. Buck's kick made it 10-7 with "only" 1:23 remaining on the first-half clock.

Starting at the 20, Auburn's Clark ripped loose for a 21 yard gain, then got five more. Two Sullivan completions and a Sullivan run gained 20 more to Alabama's 34. Sullivan then fired a bullet that Frederick took to the Tide three. With just three seconds left, Clark cracked over for the touchdown. Riley's kick made the halftime score 14-10, Auburn.

The action had barely begun.

Alabama kicked off to start the second half and discovered they truly had a Tiger by the tail on this particular day. Clark returned the kick 24 yards to the Auburn 31. Two Zofko runs and two by Clark totaled 15 yards. Sullivan then hit Ronnie Ross with two straight 19-yarders to Bama's 16. Clark tore through the middle for 12, and Sullivan rolled left and sprinted the final four for a touchdown. Riley made the score 21-10.

On Alabama's next series, David Campbell sacked Hunter and caused a fumble that Dick Ingwersen recovered at the Tide 13. After absorbing a holding penalty on first down, Auburn tallied again in five plays, with Zofko going over for the final yard. After Riley converted, Auburn, at 28-10, had its biggest lead over the Tide in 12 years.

The Crimson Tide retaliated with a flair. George Ranager took the

THE OPELIKA-AUBURN NEWS

How Sweet It Is
Auburn Rolls Back The Tide, 49-26
Most Points Ever Scored On Bryant

Auburn celebrates Connie Frederick's 84-yard touchdown run in the Tiger's wild 49-26 win over Alabama in 1969.

ensuing kickoff two yards inside his own end zone. As the Bama blockers floored Tiger after Tiger, Ranager streaked 102 yards for a touchdown and the second longest run in series history. Buck kicked good and Alabama had cut the deficit to 28-17.

Both teams continued to move up and down the field but neither could score as the game moved into the fourth quarter—a quarter that would see 30 more points go on the books and scoreboard.

Receiving a punt, Alabama started at its own 34 and drove for a field goal. Passing on every down, Hunter threw 11 straight times and connected on four—17 yards to Bailey; 14 to Sawyer; 27 back to Bailey, and four to Pete Moore. The chains were at the Auburn four-yard line and Buck kicked a three-pointer on fourth down. It was 28-20, Auburn, and 10:13 remained in the game.

Alabama kicked off, forced a punt and took over at its own 17. On first down, Buddy McClinton intercepted a Hunter pass and returned it 24 yards to the Tide 13. Clark got the first four yards and Zofko the final nine. After a Riley point-after, Auburn had a 35-20 lead.

Webb started Auburn's next scoring drive with a 24-yard punt return to Alabama's 37. Lowry gained two, Sullivan took off around end for 24, Lowry got eight and Clark the final three. Clark became the eighth player in the series to score three touchdowns in one game. Riley converted and the scoreboard highlights were "42-20" and "3:52".

Alabama and Scott Hunter were down but far from finished. From his 29, Hunter completed four consecutive passes for 64 total yards to the Auburn seven. The super effort went for naught when, on the next play, Bobby Strickland circled in and blindsided Hunter, who fumbled, and Maurell Jenkins recovered for the Tigers at the 10.

Auburn could gain only six yards in three tries and Frederick went to punt formation. He fielded the snap cleanly and stunned everyone, including his own coaches and teammates, by deciding not to punt, but to run. And run he did—84 yards for a touchdown—the longest run from scrimmage in the series at that time. The gambling maneuver, also ranked as Auburn's second longest scrimmage run in its football history, surpassed only by Ralph O'Gwynne's 92-yarder in 1936.

As Riley's seventh conversion of the day mounted the score to 49-20, only 37 seconds remained. Still, enough time for another Bama touchdown.

On second down from the 27, Hunter threw a 66-yard bomb to Bailey to Auburn's seven. Hunter went to him again—touchdown. A two-point conversion failed and the wild, wild final of 49-26 was recorded.

The series now stood 18-15-1, Alabama. The Crimsons also were out front in scoring, 536-519.

As for the statistical highlights, Alabama got more first downs, 26-25; Auburn rushed for 349 yards to Alabama's 49; Alabama passed for 484 yards and Auburn threw for 192, and total yards went to Auburn, 541-533. Hunter was 30-for-55 in passing for all of the Tide's 484 air yards. Sullivan was 13-for-26 and 192 yards. Clark led

Scott Hunter, in a losing cause against Auburn, completed 30 passes for 484 yards. In three series games (1968-69-70), Hunter completed 62 passes for a phenomenal 869 yards.

all rushers with 117 yards in 24 carries. Zofko ground out 74 yards in 13 tries while Musso had 79 yards in 22 attempts. Frederick was the second (to Clark) leading ground gainer with his one run of 84 yards.

Hunter's 55 passes, 30 completions and 484 yards are all series records. More than likely, they'll be records for years to come.

Two weeks earlier, on November 15, the day bowl bids were officially extended, Auburn had defeated Georgia and the *Birmingham News* reported, " 'Attention any major bowl — Auburn is available.' Jeff Beard (Auburn Athletic Director) said Saturday after Ralph Jordan's mighty Tigers crushed Georgia 16-3 that he was headed home to listen 'with both ears' for the telephone to ring . . . Auburn deserves a major bowl."

New Orleans didn't call. Neither did Dallas nor Miami nor Jacksonville. The Sugar had picked Ole Miss-Arkansas; the Cotton, Texas-Notre Dame; the Orange, Penn State-Missouri; the Gator, Florida-Tennessee. Auburn, with an 8-2-0 record, was locked out of its much-wanted "major bowl."

But Houston called. The Bluebonnet Bowl people wanted Auburn to come to the Astrodome and play the University of Houston. The Cougars (8-2-0) were second in the Nation in scoring with an average of 38 points per game. It was a team that lost 59-34 to Florida but later mauled Mississippi State 74-0.

The Tigers' trip to Texas was a 36-7 disaster.

Alabama, with only a 2-4-0 SEC record and an eighth place league finish, had agreed to meet rugged Colorado (third in the Big Eight) in the Liberty Bowl. The Crimson Tide trailed 31-13 in the second quarter but amazingly fought back for a 33-31 lead, only to lose finally 47-33. The Buffalos blasted out 29 first downs and 563 total yards. In the last two games, Alabama had been outscored 96-59 and allowed 54 first downs and 1,104 yards.

Auburn finished the 1969 season with an 8-3-0 record. Alabama was 6-5-0 and had surrendered 286 points — the most by any Crimson Tide team ever.

1970
GAME 35

Pat Escapes Panicsville

In the Alabama-Auburn freshman game two years earlier, the Tuscaloosa entry led 27-0 but lost to the Tiger Cubs 36-27. In the varsity game a year later the War Eagles fell behind early and were hanging on the ropes but came back strong for a 49-26 win. During those two years, Alabama boosters had been witnessing and reading about Auburn quarterback Pat Sullivan and the supernatural tricks he could pull once he got on the football field. But most Crimson Tide loyalists were not totally convinced.

Until after the 1970 game.

"I believe! I believe!" Alabama might not have outwardly admitted it, but deep inside, Pat Sullivan had made believers out of even the staunchest Tiger haters.

In the 35th game of the series, Alabama jumped off to a 17-0 first quarter lead but when the long, exciting afternoon of football had gone into the record book, Auburn was a 33-28 winner.

Auburn clobbered its first five opponents in 1970. Southern Mississippi felt a 33-14 sting, Tennessee 36-23, Kentucky 33-15, Clemson 44-0 and Georgia Tech 31-7. LSU broke the streak in the mud at Auburn by a 17-9 score and the Bayou Bengals went on to win the Southeastern Conference Championship. The Plainsmen bounced off the canvas and blasted Florida 63-0—the Gators' worst defeat in 28 years. The next week, the "Awesome Auburn Machine," as it was now being called, buried Mississippi State 56-0.

But then came one of the season's biggest upsets. Georgia, with losses to Tulane, Mississippi State, Ole Miss and Florida, went to

Auburn and shocked the Tigers 31-17. The big surprise also knocked Auburn out of the Sugar Bowl.

On the same day, the Nation was stunned and saddened by the news that the entire Marshall University football team had been killed in a plane crash in Huntington, W. Va., while returning from a game in Greenville, N.C. against East Carolina. All 38 players lost their lives, including four from Druid High School in Tuscaloosa, plus 37 other passengers and crewmen.

The Crimson Tide opened the season against Southern California in a night game at Birmingham and lost 42-21. It was the third consecutive game in which Alabama opponents had scored 40 points or more. It had never happened before. Also, it had been 13 years since the Tide had lost three games in a row.

Bear Bryant regrouped his troops and stomped VPI 51-18 and Florida 46-15 before getting stomped by Ole Miss 48-23. From that point it became a see-saw season. There was a 35-11 win over Vanderbilt. A week later Alabama suffered its first shutout in 115 games by a 24-0 count to Tennessee in Knoxville. After putting together two wins in a row, Houston by 30-21 and Mississippi State by 35-6, the Tide lost to LSU 14-9. Alabama started a new streak by trouncing Miami 32-8 and began the two week countdown for Auburn.

The Tigers led the Nation in passing with an average of 285 yards per game, and were third in total offense with a 448-yard per game average. Auburn was also fifth in scoring with 36 points per game. Sullivan had personally accounted for over 2,500 yards passing and running.

The 7-2-0 Tigers wore the favorite's cloak over Alabama's 6-4-0 Crimson Tide as 71,747 made their way toward Legion Field on a crisp, bright 28th of November.

Auburn lost the toss, kicked off, and 12 minutes and 32 seconds later found themselves behind by 17 points. It could have been Panicsville for Auburn.

The opening kick was brought out to the 25 and in seven plays the score was 7-0. Four runs by Johnny Musso registered 24 yards, David Brungard got free for a 25-yarder, Scott Hunter completed a pass to Musso for 12 and the Tide was at Auburn's 14-yard line. Musso cracked off left tackle for the score. Richard Ciemny converted.

Next, Auburn punted to the Alabama 30 and again the Tide made it look easy. Musso got three before Hunter and David Bailey teamed-up for a 15-yard air gain. On second-and-nine, Musso raced 13 more yards to Auburn's 38. Then Hunter struck. He passed seven yards to Brungard, then 31 to Bailey who was all alone at the 10. Ciemny's kick made it 14-0.

Auburn then muffed a great chance to score. Alabama's Tommy Wade fumbled a punt at the Tide seven. The Tigers got it, but Wade atoned for his fumble by intercepting a Sullivan pass in the end zone.

Starting at the 20, the Tide was at the Tigers' jugular again. Sparked by a Musso run of 15 and a 43-yard bomb from Hunter to George Ranager, Alabama was threatening from Auburn's 13. But the Tigers held and Bama had to settle for three points on a Ciemny field goal. With 3:28 remaining in the first quarter, the score was a shocking 17-0.

The Tigers had not started their game yet, but it was time to get going. Early in the second quarter, Keith Green recovered a Phil Chaffin fumble to bring Auburn's offensive unit onto the field at the Alabama 44. Sullivan went to work. Two completions—13 yards to Harry Unger and 15 yar′s to Dick Schmatz—keyed a quick drive to

Pat Sullivan completed 22 passes (9 to Terry Beasley) for 317 yards in the 1970 game to rally Auburn from a 17-0 deficit to a thrilling 33-28 victory.

A familiar sight to Auburn fans in this particular era — Terry Beasley streaking under a Pat Sullivan bomb.

the Tide one from where Sullivan twisted over for the score. Gardner Jett kicked good and Auburn's comeback capers were underway.

Alabama took the ensuing kickoff and zipped from its own eight to the Auburn 16. But on first down, Hunter threw over the middle into the hands of Auburn's Ronnie Ross at the five. Ross returned 13 yards to give Auburn the ball at the 18. The Sullivan-to-Beasley combination cranked up for completions of 11, 17, 11 and 12 yards. Alvin Bresler threw in a 23-yard run as the Tigers penetrated to Alabama's nine. The Tide prevented a touchdown but Jett's 26-yard field goal brought Auburn to a seven point deficit as the half ended with Alabama ahead, 17-10.

Auburn took the second-half kickoff and went to the Tide 14. A Sullivan fumble recovered by Ed Hines halted the Tiger express. Hunter then took Alabama on a 71-yard excursion to the Auburn 15

Sully & Co. Roar Back, 33-28

Auburn Nabs Photo Finish After Trailing Tide, 17-0

The *Montgomery Advertiser*

before a Crimson turnover gave the hot pigskin back to the Tigers. Dave Beck intercepted a Hunter pass and the grievous mistake more than likely cost Alabama the ball game.

Auburn turned the error into a touchdown. The Plainsmen pounded it out to the Alabama 49 and Beasley, on an end-around, darted 42 yards down to the seven-yard line. Sullivan scored on a keeper on the next play. Jett's conversion tied the score at 17-17 and War Eagle fans were bringing the house down.

Alabama came back on an 85-yard march to the Auburn 10. The Tiger defense stiffened again, and on the second play of what would prove to be an exciting fourth quarter, Ciemny kicked a field goal to give Bama a 20-17 lead.

Auburn struck in eight plays after taking the kickoff. The Tigers swept 74 yards including a 44-yard pass from Sullivan to Beasley. But no touchdown again as Jett booted a 37-yard field goal to knot the score again, at 20-20.

After an Alabama punt to the Auburn 36, it took just five plays for the War Eagles to grab their first lead of the game. Wallace Clark ran for 20 and a Sullivan pass to Zofko netted 22. From the 17, Sullivan shot a scoring strike to Robby Robinett. The point-after by Jett made it 27-20.

It took Alabama only five plays to move back in front. The last of the five was a 54-yard Hunter bomb that Ranager snagged at the 20 and raced across the goal. With the big stadium rocking, Alabama lined up for a two-point conversion. Hunter threw to David Bailey. Two points!

With 5:18 showing on the clock, the score was Alabama 28, Auburn 27. Now it was the Crimson Tide followers who shrieked to the high heavens, while gloom settled over the Auburn side. It was the drama of college football at its exciting best, and the very best was yet to come.

Sullivan, who had proved throughout the past two seasons that he was capable of miracles, quickly went to work. In just four snaps of the ball, Auburn regained the lead. Starting at the 39, Sullivan threw to Bresler for 19. Sullivan then came back to Zofko for a big 36-yard gainer all the way to the Alabama six-yard line. Switching to the running game, Sullivan handed off to Zofko for three, then to Clark for three more and a touchdown. Auburn fans who thought they could scream no more, screamed louder than ever. It was 33-28, and with a two-point conversion, Alabama would need a TD and a two-pointer of their own to win. So Auburn went for it; Sullivan connected with Beasley but Auburn was in motion. The second shot failed.

With three minutes to play, Alabama could win with just a TD.

The Tide tried and moved to their own 44, but Beck intercepted his second pass of the afternoon and Auburn ran out the clock. It had been one of the greatest afternoons of Auburn-Alabama football history.

The series was now 77 years and 35 games old. Alabama was out front 18-16-1 and had registered only 12 more points—564-552.

In the 1970 game, Alabama set a new series record with 31 first downs. The losers gained a total of 513 yards (301 rushing, 212 passing). Auburn had 22 first downs, 140 yards rushing, 317 passing and 457 total yards. Hunter (14-for-21) and Sullivan (22-for-38) accounted for all the aerial fireworks. Auburn was caught with 74 yards in penalties, Alabama only 13. The big difference in the game was turnovers—six for Bama; only two for Auburn. Other individual leaders were Musso, who had 221 yards rushing in 42 cracks and Beasley, who caught nine passes for 131 yards.

Even though Scott Hunter was on the winning side only once in three games against Auburn, he left behind some staggering series passing records that will be enormous challenges to future Tide and Tiger quarterbacks. Hunter completed 62 passes in 113 attempts (55 per cent) for a grand total of 879 yards and four touchdowns. That's 293 yards passing per game.

Auburn went on to the Gator Bowl and Sullivan & Co. put on another fabulous football show. The Tigers' defense now had to switch its attention from Alabama's Hunter to Mississippi's Archie Manning. The Tigers won, 35-28, in a game that produced over 1,000 yards in total offense.

The Alabama players had voted to go to El Paso and the Sun Bowl, but they made it clear that they would not play just any team. The Bluebonnet Bowl got the message and invited Oklahoma, hoping to draw an Oklahoma-Alabama matchup. It worked and the game proved a stunner as well—a 24-24 tie. It was the second time Alabama had played to a tie in the Bluebonnet Bowl.

Auburn finished the season with a 9-2-0 record and a final No. 10 national ranking. Bryant started the season with 193 all-time coaching wins, but his 1970 Tiders went 6-5-1 and left him one short of the 200-victory mark.

1971
GAME 36

The Biggest Game Of All

This was it. Everything, including a possible National Championship, was on the line. It was the most important game the series had ever produced. The real biggie. And to add even more appeal, there would be a Heisman Trophy winner playing in the series for the first time.

Alabama was 10-0-0; Auburn 9-0-0. The Tide was ranked No. 2 in the nation; the Tigers were No. 5. Alabama was on its way to the Orange Bowl; Auburn was heading for the Sugar Bowl.

Both teams had two weeks to prepare for the big battle. The first seven days smouldered. Coaches reached deep into their psychology trick bags to prevent the teams from peaking too soon. Starting on the Monday of game week, the volcano began to rumble. The State's sports pages cranked up. THE GAME began to take on the hysteria of a heavyweight championship fight, the hype of a Super Bowl, and the suspense of a Kentucky Derby.

The entire State was as stirred up as a Friday night rasslin' crowd.

Monday and Tuesday dragged by. Saturday seemed an eternity away. Wednesday came and went. Then it was Thanksgiving Day and one of the biggest days in Auburn football history. If War Eagles everywhere weren't already in enough of a frenzy over the upcoming game, they were completely overwhelmed when Pat Sullivan was named the winner of the 1971 Heisman Trophy.

Friday. By now the suspense had become unbearable. "WHO WILL WIN? WHO WILL WIN? WHO WILL WIN?" Everybody was asking! The press tried to decide. But they couldn't. By game time, "The Line", had Auburn as a four-point underdog. What does "The Line" know? But what does anybody know?

Alabama's side felt they had the best team, at least on paper, and until Saturday that was the only place the game could be played. Auburn was sixth in the nation in scoring with an average of 34 points per game. But Alabama was second best in the country in defense against scoring at 7.7 points per game. Something certainly had to give there.

Tide boosters could also say that their team had played a much tougher schedule in 1971. "We met four real powers; you met only two," was a legitimate argument. They could say that Alabama's 10 opponents had a 61-47-2 record that year, while Auburn's nine foes compiled only a 47-52-0 record. Plus, an independent national publication showed the Crimson Tide's opposition had an average Power Rating of 101.1 to the Tigers' 95.5. Two weeks of playing the game on paper, in offices, taverns, country clubs, churches—everywhere—brought day-to-day activity in the State of Alabama to a virtual standstill.

On the Auburn side of the story was a fellow named Sullivan. And that was Alabama's single doubt. They had seen what Pat could do. A player doesn't win the Heisman Trophy by just standing around, and his heroics in the past three seasons couldn't be discounted.

The Alabama-Auburn collision course had begun on Friday night, September 10 at Los Angeles. Bear Bryant took his team to the West Coast with a brand new offensive concept—the wishbone. The wishbone worked well enough for a 17-10 triumph over Southern Cal and Bryant bagged his 200th all-time coaching victory.

SEPT. 18—Two warmups, both at home. Auburn mutilated Chattanooga 60-7 and Alabama stomped Southern Mississippi 42-8.

SEPT. 25—In a typical rock'em, sock'em, no-love-lost Auburn-Tennessee bash, the Tigers won 10-9 in Knoxville. The Vols would lose only one other game all year—to Alabama. The Tide went to Gainesville and got the Gators' goat 38-0.

OCT. 2—Alabama defeated a fine (10-2-0) Ole Miss team at Birmingham by a score of 40-6. The Tigers clobbered Kentucky 38-6 at Auburn.

OCT. 9—Two easy wins; Alabama over Vanderbilt 42-0 on the road; Auburn over Southern Mississippi 27-14 at home.

No Auburn football player will ever again wear the numbers "7" or "88," belonging to Pat Sullivan and Terry Beasley. In three games against Alabama, Sullivan completed 49 passes for 630 yards. Beasley caught 20 passes for 271 yards. Both are series records.

OCT. 16—The Tigers took Tech 31-14 in Atlanta, while in Birmingham, the Tide topped Tennessee 32-15.

OCT. 23—The University of Houston (9-3-0) went to Tuscaloosa and left a 34-20 loser. Clemson went to Auburn and left on the short end of a 35-13 score.

OCT. 30—The Tigers slapped Florida 40-7 at Cliff Hare Stadium. Alabama journeyed to Jackson for a night game with Mississippi State. Visitors 41, Home 10.

Alabama's Johnny Musso accounted for 569 yards in three series games, 1969-70-71. He rushed for 467 yards (97 carries) and caught eight passes for 102 yards.

NOV. 6—Alabama spent a Saturday night in Baton Rouge and escaped gladly with a 14-7 victory over LSU, a team that won nine games in 1972. In Auburn's third straight home game, Mississippi State fell 30-21.

Meanwhile, another Southeastern Conference team was in the national spotlight. The Georgia Bulldogs were cruising along with a perfect record and had allowed only four touchdowns and 28 points in their last eight games.

NOV. 13—Sanford Stadium, Athens. Between the hedges. Auburn (8-0-0) vs. Georgia (9-0-0). It was the nation's headline game of the day. After Sullivan, Beasley and the rest of the Tiger cast got through bombing the Bulldogs' proud defense, the score was 35-20. Filing from the stadium, happy War Eagle fans each plucked a sprig from Georgia's famous hedge as a souvenir. The shrubbery suffered about as much as Bulldog boosters that day. At Tuscaloosa, the Crimson Tide was making Miami their 23rd straight Denny Stadium victim by a score of 31-3. Bryant's coaching record at the campus stadium now read 38-1-0.

NOV. 27—Legion Field, Birmingham. Seventy-something thousand football fanatics, intoxicated with excitement, jammed every available nook the old steel saucer had to offer. Millions more across the nation were sitting by television sets awaiting 3:05 p.m. CST and the kickoff.

As the teams appeared on the field, the eruption caused Vulcan, Birmingham's great steel statue, to turn his head . . .

Finally, it was 3:05 p.m.

Auburn won the coin toss and obviously wanted the football. At this stage there was no moving the Tide and Dave Beverly came on to stand in punt formation at the 20-yard line. Back went a low snap and before Beverly could get set to kick, Alabama's storm troopers smashed through and buried him in his tracks.

It was a big and early break for Alabama. On first down, quarterback Terry Davis lost two yards. Johnny Musso, the SEC's leading ground gainer, managed four. Davis then got away for a big 10-yard gain to the Auburn eight. David Knapp hit for two to the six and Davis got the rest for the TD. Bill Davis converted and became the third Davis brother to score for Alabama in the series as a kicker. With only 3:17 gone in the game the Crimsons led 7-0. Only a very few, if any, Auburn fans suspected that a pattern had been established.

On their second possession of the afternoon, the Tide started some 60 yards farther way, at their own 20 after an Auburn punt into

Johnny Musso (L) of Alabama and Auburn's Pat Sullivan meet after the 1971 game, won by the Tide, 31-7. In three series games against each other, these two superstars totaled over 1,200 yards rushing and passing.

the end zone. It was wisnbone time as Musso, Joe LaBue, Musso again, Davis and Steve Bisceglia ground out yardage up to the 43. On second-and-nine, Davis hit LaBue with a 17-yard pass to Auburn's 40-yard line and the Tide went back to the ground game. LaBue took it to the 33 and a Tiger penalty got five more to the 28. Musso was stopped once, but then came back for 14 yards to the 14. Bisceglia got two and on the next play, Terry Davis, faking beautifully off the 'bone, pranced over for the touchdown. Bill Davis' kick made it 14-0 with 58 seconds left in the first quarter.

After the kickoff, Auburn got on the track, derailed and got back on again. A Sullivan-to-Beasley pass netted 40 yards to the Alabama 29. But Sullivan fumbled and Terry Rowell recovered for the Tide. Ellis Beck of Alabama fumbled it right back and Danny Sanspree fell on the loose ball at the Tide 31. It took one play for Auburn to get back in the game. Sullivan handed off to Harry Unger who stopped, looked and lofted one to Beasley for a touchdown. Gardner Jett came on for the conversion and the Bama lead had been cut to seven with 13:08 remaining in the first half.

With just five seconds left before intermission, Alabama reached Auburn's seven-yard line but missed a field goal to keep the score at 14-7, Alabama. Still anybody's ball game.

Alabama took the second-half kickoff and after a few plays punted Auburn in deep trouble at the Tiger one-yard line. Sullivan, however, brought them out of danger and for a while the foes sparred in safe territory. Later in the quarter, the Tide took a punt at their 22 and, sparked by the crushing runs of Musso, moved to Auburn's 24. This drive led to a 42-yard field goal by Bill Davis giving Alabama a 17-7 advantage just four plays into the final period. The Davis boys (Terry and Bill) had scored all the Tide points.

It was time for the stars to fall on Auburn.

On a first down play from his own 20, Sullivan was intercepted by Chuck Strickland who returned it to the Tiger seven. Alabama was penalized back to the 12, but Musso scored on the next play. It was 24-7 as Bill Davis converted again.

Auburn got possession again but again had to punt, and Alabama mounted a 61-yard drive to the three. Musso, who had carried the ball over 570 times in his three-year career, fumbled for only the third time. Johnny Simmons recovered for Auburn in the end zone.

Auburn's possession was short-lived. Jeff Rouzie immediately picked off another Sullivan pass and returned it 34 yards to the Auburn five. With a chance to atone, Musso scored on first down. After Bill Davis converted with only 3:33 left to tick away, Alabama contained everything Sullivan and Auburn could throw at them. The big game was over. The Crimson Tide had finally defeated Pat Sullivan. Final score: Alabama (11-0-0) 31, Auburn (9-1-0) 7.

"Before the game there was some doubt in my mind as to which team was better, Alabama or Georgia, but there is no question . . ." Shug Jordan told Clyde Bolton of the *Birmingham News.*

The *News'* Jimmy Bryan went to the Alabama locker room and watched as the Tide players made sure their coach got a fully-clothed shower. "You'll have to excuse me," Bryant told Bryan, "but I've got to get these wet shoes off or die of pneumonia. But I'd rather die now than to have died this morning."

As it turned out, Alabama's super defense was more super than Auburn's super offense. The Tigers got only seven first downs and 26 yards rushing. The passing game resulted in 152 yards with 15 completions on 28 throws. Alabama's wishbone offense whacked out 24 first downs, 278 yards rushing and 122 passing for an even 400 for the day.

Musso had 167 yards in 33 carries. That gave him a three-game series total of 97 rushes and 467 yards gained. However, it left him 10 yards short of the series record held by Bobby Marlow who had gained 477 yards in 77 carries in the 1950-51-52 contests.

Sullivan's three-game series figures included 49 pass completions in 91 attempts for 630 yards. Beasley caught 20 for 271 yards.

Now it was bowl time.

No. 1 Nebraska vs. No. 2 Alabama in the Orange for ALL the marbles—the National Championship. In the Sugar, it was No. 3 Oklahoma, having lost only to Nebraska, against No. 6 Auburn, who lost only to Alabama.

In the afternoon game at New Orleans, the Sooners built a 31-0 halftime lead and went on to win 40-22. That night in Miami, the Cornhuskers led 38-0 at intermission and coasted to a decisive 38-6 victory.

But Auburn will always remember 1971 as the "Year of the Heisman". John Wilhelm Heisman left as Auburn's coach in 1899. Seventy-two years later, the trophy named for him returned to the Loveliest Village of the Plains, courtesy of Pat Sullivan, whose exploits rank at the top in Auburn's rich football tradition.

The Heisman Trophy that Pat Sullivan won in 1971.

1972
GAME 37

"Punt, Bama, Punt!"

This is a true story, and no names have been changed to protect either the innocent or the guilty, if any.

In one of the most incredible football games ever played; no, make that, in the *most* incredible football game ever played, Auburn University defeated the University of Alabama. The score was 17-16.

The game was played in Birmingham on December 2, 1972. Alabama folks would like to forget it. Many have convinced themselves it never happened. Auburn has no intentions of forgetting. It's as though the final score is carved on the face of a giant granite mountain in full daily view of partisans of both camps.

Everybody knows what happened that day, but just for the record. . . .

With 5:30 left in the game, undefeated Alabama, ranked No. 2 in the Nation with a 10-0-0 record, was cozily out front 16-3 and marking time before the final gun. There was no conceivable way for them to lose. But. . . .

Lightning struck. Not once, but twice.

Auburn blocked a punt, picked up the bouncing ball and scored to make it 16-10. A few minutes later, the Tigers blocked another punt, scooped it up and scored again. That tied the game and a conversion won it.

Two blocked punts in a football game has happened before, but when had the same player blocked both kicks, and the same player picked both up to score touchdowns, on two consecutive punts?

Bill Newton blocked 'em; David Langner picked 'em up. Langner wore jersey No. 28 ... Newton wore number 56. Two times 28 equals 56; or 56 divided by two is 28. Given the cosmic impact of the events in the closing moments of the Auburn-Alabama game in 1972, a numerologist someday will undoubtedly unravel and reveal the significance of such an apparently trivial arithmetical coincidence.

While on the subject of blocked kicks, another one took place in that memorable game that must not be overlooked, nor forgotten. Auburn's Roger Mitchell got his hands in the way of Alabama's extra-point attempt following the first touchdown. As things turned out, that effort also became the difference in the final score.

Those two blocked punts and their contribution to the outcome of the game will be remembered and talked about for as long as football is played in the State of Alabama. Although Legion Field seats "only" 72,000 fans, the number who claim "I was there" grows each year.

Alabama was in its second season with the wishbone offense and the new run-oriented attack had pulverized just about everybody in sight. Duke, Kentucky, Vanderbilt, Georgia and Florida were manhandled by an aggregate score of 167-47, an average of 33-9 per game. Then came a close 17-10 win over tough Tennessee, who finished with a 10-2-0 record that year. The Crimson Tide averaged 48 points in each of their next four games while burying Mississippi Southern, Mississippi State, LSU and VPI.

Bear Bryant had his boys ranked in the runner-up slot behind the only other unbeaten team in the country, Southern Cal. Alabama was fourth in the national scoring derby with 37.7 points per outing, and was sixth in being scored against, yielding only 11.6 points per game.

Auburn was next to Alabama's schedule and the Crimson Tide was facing a rambunctious den of Tigers that had an 8-1-0 record, a No. 9 national ranking and was the No. 1 surprise team in America. Pat Sullivan and Terry Beasley had departed the Plains and in view of their absence, the pre-season "guessperts" had Auburn finishing anywhere from fifth to eighth—not in the Nation but in its own Southeastern Conference.

The War Eagles started off with unimpressive wins over two teams with unimpressive records that year—Mississippi State (4-7-0) and Chattanooga (2-9-0). State went down 14-3; the Moccasins fell 14-7. Tennessee, with a 3-0-0 record, was next. The Tigers went to Knoxville and surprised the Vols 10-6. The next week it was on to

BLOCK NO. 1 — A squadron of screaming War Eagles attack in "V" formation. Bill Newton (56) is the first to arrive and slams Greg Gnatt's punt. David Langler (28) scored. Others in the picture are Ken Bernich (53), Roger Mitchell (25), Phil Nichols (94), Danny Sanspree (93) and Bob Newton (76), who is the twin brother of Bill. (Photo courtesy of Joe King)

BLOCK NO. 2—Bill Newton (almost hidden) has already blocked the kick. High in the air is Mitchell (25). Langner (28) seems frozen, not believing that it has happened again. But it had happened again. And he scored again. (Photo courtesy of Joe King)

Jackson to face another undefeated team—Ole Miss. Auburn won 19-13.

Things didn't get any easier. For the third straight week, Auburn had to face another "perfect" team, this time in Baton Rouge on a Saturday night. LSU was 5-0-0 and the host Tigers trounced the visiting Tigers, 35-7.

Finally, back at the Loveliest Village for the first time in a month, the Plainsmen bounced back to defeat Georgia Tech, coming in with a 4-1-0 record, 24-14. In the next three weeks, Auburn downed FSU 27-14, Florida 26-20 and Georgia 27-10.

Auburn had earned its No. 9 national standing no matter who might be surprised.

Alabama was next on Auburn's schedule and the powerful Tide was rated a whopping 16-point favorite. Alabama had already accepted a Cotton Bowl bid to meet Texas. A few days before the Tide-Tiger clash, Coach Bryant jokingly remarked to the Birmingham Quarterback Club, "I'd rather beat that Cow College (Auburn) once than beat Texas 10 times."

Ohh boy! The press hopped on that one.

Another capacity crowd of over 72,000 made their way to Legion Field that sun-drenched day to watch the 37th game of the series. Alabama won the toss and received. Auburn got an early break when Alabama's Greg Gantt, the SEC's leading punter, got off a short 21-yarder to give the Tigers good field position at the Tide 47. But the Tigers could go nowhere and kicked. Bama punted again and Auburn booted it back.

On third down from the Alabama 35, Auburn's Langner intercepted a Terry Davis pitch-out and returned it to the Tide 10, but a clipping penalty took it back to the 25. Hard-running Terry Henley gained four and then three more before breaking free for 14 and a first down at Alabama's four-yard line. Henley rammed to the two and was stopped for no gain on the next play. Quarterback Randy Walls lost three. On a fourth down field goal attempt, the snap sailed over everybody's head all the way back to the Alabama 29.

The Tide promptly went for a score. Steve Bisceglia accounted for almost all the yardage and his three-yard smash capped the 15-play, 71-yard march. Bill Davis' conversion was blocked by Mitchell and the score was 6-0, Alabama, very early in the second quarter.

Later in the same period, Davis added a 24-yard field goal to make it 9-0. Alabama came back again to Auburn's 13-yard line just before the half but this time failed to put points on the board.

The intermission stat sheet showed Auburn with eight net yards total offense; Alabama had 112.

Bill Newton (L) blocked the punts, and David Langer darted in with them.

Thousands of "PUNT BAMA PUNT" stickers were seen throughout the State of Alabama a few days after the 1972 game.

Gardner Jett kicked a 42-yard field goal and 2 conversions in the 1972 game.

Roger Mitchell blocked "the other kick" — Alabama's first conversion attempt in the 17-16 classic.

In the third quarter, Alabama methodically marched 78 yards in 10 plays for another TD, with Wilbur Jackson covering the final four. Davis kicked good and the score was 16-0 with 9:20 left to play in the quarter. The odds-makers who had made Alabama a 16-point favorite were beaming.

Meanwhile, Auburn gave absolutely no hint a storm was brewing. The Tigers had a net of 13 yards of total offense and only one first down. Alabama was not making it a runaway, but the way Auburn was playing, there was no urgency for the Tide to keep the scoring pressure on.

In the last minute of the third period, Gantt missed a 50-yard field goal and Auburn took over at their own 20. For the first time all afternoon, the Tigers got something started. Two Walls' completions (14 yards to Tom Gossom and seven yards to Chris Linderman) spearheaded a drive to the Alabama 24. On fourth-and-eight, Gardner Jett kicked a 42-yard field goal. At the time, the call raised questions among the amateur quarterbacks in the stands, in the press box and in the radio audience.

As Shug Jordan said after the game, "We needed to score three times to win, so I figured that could be one of them."

Even after the field goal, considering Alabama's fat lead and the way they had dominated the play, their position appeared secure—even impregnable. It was 16-3 and 9:15 remained in the game.

Coach Jordan decided not to go with an on-sides kick, and Auburn booted deep. The Crimson Tide knocked out two first downs and had the ball right at midfield, fourth down.

As Gantt stood in punt formation, Auburn put 10 men on the line and eight went crashing through, with Newton as the point man. Gantt slammed his kick into a flying Newton. The ball flew past Gantt, hit the ground and bounced into Langner's hands at the 25. Langner ran untouched for the touchdown and Jett's conversion made the score 16-10. Auburn was alive and in the game. It happened so quickly, many in the stands missed the action. Auburn obliged in a few minutes with the live equivalent of TV's instant replay.

Again Coach Jordan decided not to go with an on-sides kick, and Auburn booted deep. The Crimson Tide knocked out two first downs and had the ball at its own 43, fourth down. The clock had ticked down to 1:34.

Gantt stood in punt formation and Auburn put 10 men on the line. Eight of them went crashing through with Newton as the point man. Gantt slammed his kick into a flying Newton. The ball flew back past Gantt, hit the ground and bounced into Langner's hands at the 20. Langner ran untouched for the touchdown.

The score was tied and pandemonium reigned. It was inconceivable that more drama could be packed into the script. But it had to be because an extra point would put Auburn ahead. A minute ago, any Auburnite anywhere would have been delirious if promised a tie. Now victory was within grasping distance.

And it took a great grasp to pull it off. The teams lined up for the extra point play. They got set—both teams tense, taut, tight and thinking about what they had to do and what it would mean to succeed or fail. The ball was snapped and the lines charged. The snap was low. Much too low. The ball hit the artificial turf and skipped like a thrown rock skips off a smooth pond. Dave Beck, the holder, scooped up the skipping ball, kept a cool head, and rapidly placed it down for Jett. Jett, who had to re-program his rhythm, swung his foot through. The kick was perfect.

The stadium rocked. Approximately 36,000 people who were completely hysterical were making all the noise. The other 36,000 sat in shocked silence—numb with absolute disbelief.

After Auburn's kick-off, Alabama desperately tried to score. But the script called for Langner to take a bow. In addition to his fourth

NEWTON, LANGNER STRIKE

Late AU lightning sinks 'Bama 17-16

The Birmingham News **Sports** For scores, dial 325-2223

Sec. C Sun., Dec. 3, 1972

Final nail in Tide casket: Auburn's Bill Newton (note ball in his hand) blocks Gantt punt, setting up winning touchdown.

BY ALF VAN HOOSE, News Sports Editor

Alabama might still win that national championship. AUBURN, Ala. Home of War Eagles.

After what happened Saturday at Legion Field, anything must be possible in zany football.

Where are those rusty "I Believe" buttons, those that flourished around Tuscaloosa? They now belong in Auburn.

Auburn 17, Alabama 16 — it couldn't have happened. Could it? But, it did.

The Tigers put the blocks to 'Bama.

Some 72,386 saw it. They believe. Ralph Jordan's Auburn scored all in the last 10 minutes, the man's stretch everybody conceded Paul Bryant's ex-No. 2-nationally ranked Crimson Tide, already king of the SEC.

Statistics

	Aub.	Ala.
First downs	7	19
Rushes-yds	40-56	65-223
Pass. yds	30	58
Return yds	120	58
[illegible]	3-6-1	1-7-2
Punts	8-43	7-39
Fumble-lost	0-0	3-0
Pen.-yds	6-57	6-38

Everybody thought that would be 'Bama laughter-time, everyone, that is, except Auburn's defenders, true architects of one of Dixie's all-time upsets.

LINEBACKER Bill Newton — who should have had an S on a flowing black cape instead of drab old 34 on a shirt bloodied with red (Alabama red) — blocked a Greg Gantt punt. David Langner fielded the high-bouncing ball around the Bama 25. He kept running. Six points. There was 5:30 left. Auburn was back.

Time for Alabama to receive, hammer two first downs and expend itself, as most of the gorgeous afternoon, against never-surrendering War Tigers.

Gantt trotted in to punt once more. You've heard about lightning. It strikes, and it can strike twice — if it wears No. 34. Or 38 — that's Mr. Langner who gave a delayed instant replay of his other TD scamper, this time from 20 yards.

Alabama was still visibly moving when Gardner Jett sighted the extra point kick, but Alabama was dead. Jett didn't miss.

JETT HADN'T missed that 16th point behind Langner's first romp, either, nor a 42-yarder capping Auburn's only decent offense of the game, a move from its 20 to the Tide 25, early in the last quarter.

Behind 16-0, only 9:15 to go, Jordan's field goal decision was open to second guess. Two full-blown touchdowns equal 16

Turn to Page C-14

USC, super soph Davis kill Irish

LOS ANGELES — Southern California's super sophomore Anthony Davis ran for six touchdowns, shocking Notre Dame with 97 and 96-yard kickoff returns, and the nationally top ranked Trojans shattered the Fighting Irish 45-23 Saturday.

THE VICTORY gave Southern Cal, which will play Ohio State in the Rose Bowl on New Year's Day, an 11-0 season, and coupled with Auburn's stunning upset earlier in the day of Alabama, left the Trojans as the only unbeaten and untied team in major college football for the 1972 season.

The 5-foot-9, 180-pound Davis, a tailback from San Fernando, Calif., ran the game's opening kickoff a school record 97 yards, then broke Notre Dame's comeback bid late in the third quarter with his second long dash when the Irish appeared to have momentum.

Statistics [illegible]

The 10th-ranked Irish, who finished the season 8-2, fought back to trail just 25-23. Then Davis took a kickoff, slipped away from two defenders at the Notre Dame 26 and completed his 96-yard effort.

Davis, who became the first USC sophomore to gain more than 1,000 yards in a season, also scored on runs of 1, 5, 4 and 8 yards before 75,243 in sunny Memorial Coliseum.

His six touchdowns was one shy of the alltime major college [illegible]

Turn to Page C-17

'This team tops the list,' says Jordan

BY CLYDE BOLTON
News sports writer

For 31 and nine-elevenths football seasons, Shug Jordan resisted calling any victory his greatest.

Saturday he broke that tradition and named Auburn's 17-16 win over second-ranked Alabama his top conquest.

"Oh, yes," Jordan said when asked the direct question.

"I DON'T KNOW that I've ever seen a defense make a greater effort than Auburn's did today," Jordan said.

"You've got to give our defense a lot of credit. They played well all day, but when we were practically out of it they blocked the two punts, and you know the rest.

"I've been on record this season as saying that this is the best coaching staff I've ever had and I think they certainly deserve a lot of credit for the job they did today.

"Twice this season he gave two touchdowns [illegible] here at Legion [illegible] had two great [illegible]

"In 22 years [illegible] hesitated to put one [illegible] teams ahead of any [illegible] others, but today I'm putting this team at the top of the list."

Jordan said Auburn felt it had a chance when the score was 16-0 after three periods.

"I remember the crowd booing when we went for a field goal trailing 16-0," he said, "but those three points turned out to be mighty important.

"WE WENT FOR the field goal to create some enthusiasm on the part of the squad. They had some but they needed more."

Assistant head coach Paul Davis, who leads the defense, said of the two blocked kicks that won the game, "It was the same punt block we have [illegible] all year, we just had a [illegible] more desire to go get it.

"[illegible] hadn't scored on defense all year, and we said we were going after it this time."

"Dave Langner made the big plays, but Dave Beck played some kind of game on the corner," said secondary coach Sam Mitchell.

Defense end coach Jim Hilyer had a word for Danny Sanspree, Auburn's great end.

"Danny is the best end around. He plays technique better than any other end."

Thus Auburn, which was expected to merely spin its wheels all year, finished its season with a 9-1 record. Shug Jordan, who should be the nation's coach of the year, had a final word:

"The boys say we're No. 1. I don't know. But suppose Southern Cal loses later on in the bowl game."

All alone to the endzone: Langner's six-pointer [illegible]

Auburn 17, Alabama 16.	Oklahoma 38, Okla. State 15.
Florida 12, Miami 6.	Sou. Cal 45, Notre Dame 23.
Tennessee 30, Vandy 10.	SMU 35, TCU 22.
Georgia 27, Ga. Tech 7.	Memphis St. 14, Sou. Miss. 14. (Tie).
LSU 9, Tulane 3	Grambling 56, N. C. Central 6.
Tuskegee 19, Ala. State 6.	San Diego 22, Iowa St. 14
Baylor 28, Rice 14.	
Boston C. 41, Holy Cross 11.	
Army 23, Navy 15.	

1 SOU. CAL (11-0) won 45-23 over Notre Dame (8-2).
2 ALABAMA (10-1) lost 17-16 to Auburn (9-1).
3 OKLAHOMA (10-1) won 38-15 over Okla. State (6-5).
4 OHIO STATE (9-1) has completed its season.
5 PENN STATE (10-1) has finished its season.
6 TEXAS (9-1) has completed its season.
7 MICHIGAN (10-1) has finished its season.
8 NEBRASKA (8-2-1) has completed its season.
9 AUBURN (9-1) won 17-16 over Alabama (10-1).
10 NOTRE DAME (8-2) lost 45-23 to Sou. Cal (11-0).
11 LSU (9-1-1) won 9-3 over Tulane (6-5).
12 TENNESSEE (9-2) won 30-10 over Vandy (3-8).
13 COLORADO (8-3) has finished its season.
14 N. CAROLINA (9-2), had an open date.
15 UCLA (8-3) has completed its season.
16 ARIZONA STATE (9-2) has finished its season.
17 LOUISVILLE (9-1) has completed its season.
18 WEST VIRGINIA (8-3) has finished its season.
[illegible]

'WE LET HE DEFENSE DOWN'

Bear says 'put blame on coaching'

BY JIMMY BRYAN, News sports writer

Paul Bryant, losing coach, took a deep drag from a cigarette, collected his thoughts, and put the blame for Alabama's 17-16 loss to Auburn Saturday exactly where he thought it belonged.

"I've always said, and I mean this sincerely, that mistakes are head coaching. And, of course, you saw what happened out there today. The best coached team won," is what 220-time winner Bryant said.

SATURDAY HAD TO be one of the all time disappointing days in 28 years of Bryant brilliance. Alabama got whipped in the fourth quarter, 15 minutes normally reserved for Red [illegible]

a big [illegible] I hate it, of course, for everybody. But I'm particularly sorry to let the defense down that way after they had played so superbly."

COACH BRYANT took time to recognize his conquerors.

"I want to congratulate Coach (Ralph) Jordan, his staff and players for doing an excellent job," Coach Bryant said. "They [illegible] an excellent job all year.

"I thought the entire defense played well," Bryant said. "And some [illegible] in fact, everybody played well most of the time."

[illegible]

right," Bryant said. "There again, it's coaching. I've been teaching punt protection a long time.

"But I've said many times that in any big game you'll find five or six plays that win or lose. I think you'll find that true today.

"We had a 16-0 lead going into the fourth quarter. Auburn's offense didn't score a touchdown and we lost. That goes back to coaching."

AUBURN DID not trick Alabama. The Tigers simply wanted it more.

"Auburn didn't do anything new," coach Bryant said. "I think they might have played one defense they hadn't played before. They gave us a Tennessee [illegible]

Cow College? Those cows kick!

Auburn players were remembering Alabama Coach Paul Bryant's reference to the school as a cow college as they revealed their 17-16 win over the Tide Saturday.

"When those cows get mad they k—," tailback Terry Henley, "I know, 'cause I've been around 'em all my life.

"There won't be enough people going back to Auburn to milk them tonight."

"The cow college hit 'em up 'side the head with our cow bells," tackle Mac Lorendo said.

"OUR DEEP men won the game for us," Henley said. "The first half we just didn't look at nobody. Our other guy wouldn't, I... ...we was regrouped.

"Three and 16 makes 19 and if I'm not mistaken, 17 beats 16.

"I believe we could stay on the field with Nebraska or anybody." Henley continued. "I'm not scared to play 'em and I don't believe anybody else is.

"I haven't seen any team on television that thought could whip us. LSU played us unbelievable game against us, but, I believe if we could d— ever we could whip them."

S— AYS IT'S diff... it to tell just when Henley is serious and when he isn't. "It was a rough game, but not as rough as the Chattanooga game," he said. Alabama like you, but they don't hit like Chattanooga.

"I knew we'd beat Alabama," the quarterback, before we played Florida that I was worried about Florida, but I knew we'd beat Alabama.

"I NEVER got we were out of it," Lorendo said. "I've never felt we were out of any game. I didn't last year until I heard the students count off the final seconds, five, four, three, two, one.

"Jay Casey and I said, we're going to get buy a Southeastern Conference championship ring instead of a senior ring."

Alabama won the SEC title but Auburn Eagles figure they're the league's best, as CLYDE BOLTON.

Alabama * Auburn Photos by...

Newton sums it up
Alabama was too 'cocky'

BY CLYDE BOLTON
News sports writer
Auburn linebacker Bill Newton, who blocked two both punts.

fourth-period punts that beat Alabama Saturday, said he was rushing but daylight on...

"The tackle who was supposed to have blocked out on me said I went inside," he said. "I kept holding by so more field is front of me."

Newton said, Alabama's punt...
"I didn't know what to think," said David Langner, who caught both blocked kicks as the bounce and ran for touchdowns. "It scared me to death.

"Both of the balls looked identical to me. They just bounced into my hands. All I had to do was pick it up and run. It was by far the greatest thrill I've ever had.

"MY NAME is strong for the defense to get started. They never did, so we had to do it for them.

"We were so emotionally ready that nobody ever cried.

"The defense came up with time...once again... said offensive player Jay Casey. "All we did was out-cuss them.

"Our punts all year has been that we just wouldn't have it any other way.

Sophomore linebacker Ken Bernich said it was a victory for the seniors.

"ALABAMA WAS COCKY," he said. "They walked around like, 'Well, let's get it over with.' They are a good team — but we're better."

Former players such as Jerry Gordon and Sonnie McCracken came to the dressing room to toss the celebration. Gordon ended reverently where he sympathetically for Coach Ralph Jordan's hand and rubbed it.

"Yes, deserve everything you've gotten," Gordon said. Berman Mac Lorendo, latter they never wore jersey."
Coincidentally, Gordon wore the same No. 77 that Lorendo wears.
Players and coaches were crying. "I've cried until I can't cry anymore," Lorendo said.

Dave's kicks run back by baseballer

Alabama had a two-man rotating system apparent tactic, hurt a David Bevery Saturday, little used defensive back Buster Carey.

Carey, 5-9, 177-pound junior from Greenwood, S. C., handled David Beverly's morning sprain flawlessly.

The man Carey replaced, however, was Bobby McKinney, one of the SEC's feared punt returners.

COACH PAUL Bryant explained why:
"There was a lot of wind on three today and Carey is a baseball player. He's an excellent pitcher. He has excellent eyes and sees the ball real well.

We just wanted to go with him," Bryant said.
—JIMMY BRYAN

Lightning strikes once: Langner grabs blocked punt and gallops untouched across Crimson Tide's goal line

Triumph-Disaster

Lightning strikes twice: Langner ties score at 16-16; All celebrates; Tidal Blocculla stunned

Lorendo hugs game-winner David Langner

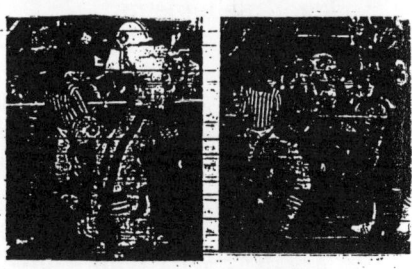

Gardner Jett kicks winning point then roars a "War Eagle"

Shug Jordan consoles Alabama's Bryant

Beverly's foot proved
deadly weapon
against Alabama

That fatal blocked point: Auburn robs Tide of vital victory margin

Bear and Shug meet following incredible 1972 game.

quarter TD's, he had also intercepted a pitch-out in the first quarter. Terry Davis fired a pass to his favorite target, Wayne Wheeler. The ball was overthrown and there stood Langner. Again, he was in the right place at the right time with the interception at the Auburn 41. The curtain began its descent and the 1972 game took its place with the 1942 Georgia game and the 1949 Alabama game as Auburn gridiron monuments.

Although at the time nobody really cared, statistics of the game were preserved. Alabama led in first downs (16-7) and total offensive yards (251-80). Auburn was penalized 57 yards to the Tide's 39. The Tigers were three-for-six in passing, Alabama one-for-seven. Bisceglia was the day's leading rusher with 102 yards in 24 attempts to become Auburn's top running threat. Alabama still held the series lead, 19-17-1, and had scored 611 points—35 more than Auburn.

About Coach Bryant's pre-game "Cow College" remark, Auburn's Henley told newsmen following the game, "When those cows get mad they can kick. I know, 'cause I've been around 'em all my life. There won't be enough people going back to Auburn to milk 'em tonight, though. . . ."

Langner, who scored both Tiger touchdowns, told the press, "I didn't know what to think. It scared me to death. Both of the balls looked identical to me. They just bounced into my hands. All I had to do was pick it up and run . . . we were so emotionally ready that nobody ever got tired."

HEADLINES AS THEY APPEARED OF AUBURN'S UNBELIEVABLE WIN OVER ALABAMA IN 1972

Shug: 'Kicking Could Decide It'
The Montgomery Advertiser

Unreal Auburn Slays Another Giant, 17-16
The Huntsville Times

War Eagles Create Havoc With Tide's Title Dreams
The Montgomery Advertiser

Cow College? Those cows kick!
The Birmingham News

That 'Cow College' Nips 'Bama 17-16
Auburn Uses Two Blocked Punts For Victory
The Mobile Press Register

War Eagle Pandemonium Echos Over Iron Bowl
The Montgomery Advertiser

Tiger Miracle Men Stop Alabama Run
The Tuscaloosa News

'Turning Point Obvious' — Shug
The Montgomery Advertiser

THE OPELIKA-AUBURN NEWS

DAILY and SUNDAY

East Alabama's Complete Daily Newspaper

OPELIKA/AUBURN, ALABAMA, SUNDAY, DECEMBER 3, 1972

AUBURN DOES IT, 17-16

Who's Number One, Coach?

Blocked Punts Key To Victory

Ken Bernich, Auburn's sophomore linebacker, said, "Alabama was cocky. They walked around all afternoon like, 'well, let's get it over with.' They are a good team, but we are better."

An interesting sidelight about the cast of characters of the 1972 drama is that three players who were particularly instrumental in the final outcome had not been recruited by Auburn. They were walk-ons. The three were Bill Newton, Gardner Jett and Roger Mitchell. Truth really is stranger than fiction.

Over on the other side, the Alabama dressing quarters were as still as 3 a.m. in a small town back alley. The players sat and stared into space. There was nothing else to do and almost nothing to say. Nobody believed what had just happened. It wouldn't really "hit" them until the next day, or the next week. Tide lineman Chuck Strickland told a *Birmingham News* reporter, "I guess our blocking just broke down. But give Auburn a lot of credit, they wanted to block them."

Incredibly, one reporter asked Coach Jordan what he thought was the turning point in the game. Shug looked at him, paused, and said in all seriousness, "Sir, I think the turning point in the game was when we blocked two punts."

Auburn met Colorado in the Gator Bowl. It was a time in which the "Big Eight" was synonymous with power. Even though Auburn had lost only one game, and Colorado three, the Buffalos were pegged a big 11-point favorite. It mattered little to the 1972 Auburn Tigers. They took the field in Jacksonville and walloped the Buffs 24-3 to cap a thrilling season with a No. 5 national ranking.

Alabama suffered a second-straight heartbreaker in the Cotton Bowl. Leading Texas 13-3 at the half, the Longhorns bounced back for a 17-13 win by scoring the winning touchdown with just over three minutes left in the game.

Alabama, 10-2-0, wound up No. 7.

By the time of the bowl games, literally thousands of auto and truck bumpers in Alabama were adorned with orange and blue stickers. They read: "PUNT BAMA PUNT."

1973

GAME 38

Revenge

The news folks entered the noisy, steamy dressing room and found Coach Bear Bryant awaiting their arrival with a sly grin on his face. He said, "I've been sitting here trying to remember a little tune. Something about 'punt Bama punt!'"

What Bryant was really grinning about was the resounding 35-0 revenge victory Alabama had just posted over Auburn to conclude an 11-0-0 season and maintain a No. 1 national ranking.

Alabama had been impressive since opening in September with a crushing 66-0 humiliation of California. The Tide proceeded to knock off Kentucky 28-14, Vanderbilt 44-0, Georgia 28-14, Florida 35-14 and Tennessee 42-21. Then came a 77-6 rout of VPI in which Bear's wishbone attack amassed 748 yards rushing and 833 in total offense. Both were NCAA records at the time.

That brought the season to November 22 and a night game with LSU at Baton Rouge. It was not only a game that could keep Alabama undefeated, but it could also become Alabama's 500th all-time football victory. Only seven other colleges had reached the 500-win mark. Yale had 658, Princeton 611, Harvard 600, Pennsylvania 596, Michigan 558, Notre Dame 551 and Texas 536. That Saturday night in Tiger Stadium, Alabama joined the elite group by drubbing the Bengals, 21-7.

In the season, Alabama had scored 419 points, third best in the nation, and its defense had surrendered only 89, fifth from the top.

The Davis brothers, Tim (1961-62), Steve (1966-67) and Bill (1971-72-73) kicked a total of 42 points against Auburn in seven series games. They recorded 24 conversions and six field goals. The Davis boys were 6-1-0 against the Tigers.

Auburn, playing an 11-game regular season schedule for the first time in 34 years, had a 6-4-0 record with wins over Oregon State, Chattanooga, Ole Miss, Georgia Tech, Houston and Mississippi State. There were losses to Tennessee, LSU, Florida and Georgia. The Tigers' 7-0 win over Houston was one of the season's biggest upsets and the Cougars' only setback in 1973.

As the 38th game of the series loomed a week away, both the Tide and Tigers had already accepted bowl bids. Alabama was to meet Notre Dame in the Sugar Bowl and Auburn was going to the Sun Bowl opposite Missouri.

Alabama was made an overwhelming favorite and 71,224 took seats at Legion Field on December 1. It was a contest pitting the Nation's No. 1 rated team against a team that was holding down eighth place in its own conference. But it was Alabama vs. Auburn.

The Tide scored the first time they got the ball, driving 64 yards after receiving a punt. Wilbur Jackson gained six yards in two plays before Randy Billingsley ripped off a 22-yarder to Auburn's 36. Billingsley went to the 34; Jackson to the 26; Billingsley to the 17; Jackson to the 10, and Jackson to the seven. From there, Billingsley circled left end for a touchdown. Bill Davis' conversion made it 7-0 and the game was less than eight minutes old.

Late in the quarter, Alabama's Mike Washington intercepted a Wade Whatley pass at Auburn's 38 and returned it to the two before being run down by Secedrick McIntyre. On second down, quarterback Gary Rutledge scored from the one. With 1:30 showing on the first-quarter clock, the kick by Davis gave Bama a 14-0 advantage.

Auburn regrouped and held Alabama's powerful wishbone attack in check during the second period and the half ended with the score 14-0.

To open the third quarter, Chris Wilson kicked off to Alabama's Mark Prudhomme who returned it 18 yards to the 23. A Rutledge run of 19 yards, Jackson's pickup of 14, and Billingsley's halfback lob to Jackson for 16 more yards highlighted a quick six-play series that brought Alabama to the Auburn 16. Five plays later, Rutledge ran around the right side from the three-yard line for his second touchdown of the game. It was 21-0 after another Davis PAT.

Early in the fourth quarter, Jackson plowed through Auburn's middle to conclude a six-play, 46-yard scoring drive for Bama. Davis made it 28-0.

The Tide's final score came with two minutes left in the game. Taking a punt at their own 33, only eight plays were needed to do the damage against a bewildered Auburn defense. The big gainers were a 26-yard run by James Taylor and a 19-yarder by John Boles.

Taylor scored from the eight. Davis added his fifth conversion of the game for the final 35-0 score.

Bill Davis was the third Davis brother to kick for Alabama over a span of 13 years. The family act put 42 points through cross bars against Auburn. Tim scored 18 points in the 1961-62 series games; Steve booted eight points in 1966-67, and Bill added 16 points in 1971-72-73. Involved were 24 conversions and six field goals.

While increasing its series lead to 20-17-1, Alabama got more first downs 21-13, and more total yardage 405-192. Jackson led all rushers with 89 yards in 15 carries, followed by teammate Billingsley's 66 yards in 10 attempts.

In the last three series games, Alabama had racked up 61 first downs and 1,056 total offensive yards. Auburn had only 27 first downs and 450 yards, although winning one of the three games.

Vanderbilt was the only team in the Southeastern Conference with a lower league record than Auburn's 2-5-0 mark. Even so, the Plainsmen packed their bags and headed for El Paso to meet another group of Tigers from Missouri. The Mo-Tigers had all the fun on the field and beat the Plainsmen, 34-17. Auburn's final record was 6-6-0 — all six losses to teams that were to play in bowl games.

Six teams finished the 1973 regular season unbeaten — Alabama, Oklahoma, Ohio State, Penn State, Notre Dame and Michigan. But the Tide was rated No. 1 and was matched against No. 5 Notre Dame in the Sugar Bowl. It turned out to be one of the greatest bowl games in history. The Irish won, 24-23, in a game that was every bit as close as the final score. The loss cost Alabama the National Championship.

Of the "Big Six" in 1973, two didn't attend bowl games. Oklahoma was on probation, and Michigan (10-0-1) missed out on the Rose Bowl even though it had won one more game than Ohio State (9-0-1). In one of the biggest sports stories of the year a Big Ten committee voted to send Ohio State on the trip to the West Coast. The Buckeyes responded by drilling Southern Cal 42-21, and Penn State (12-0-0) defeated LSU 16-9 in the Orange Bowl. Still, on the strength of its squeaker over Alabama, Notre Dame leap-frogged from fifth to first and was voted National Champions in the AP final poll.

UPI had settled on Alabama as its champion before the bowl games, but the Sugar Bowl loss gave the honor diminished significance.

Time Out For A Trip to Tuscaloosa

Although this book is about Auburn vs. Alabama football, the author has requested permission to inject an account of a personal experience that was memorable to him—and his wife. Permission granted to proceed in the first person.

My only visit to Denny Stadium for an Alabama football game will never be forgotten. I am a University of Georgia graduate and my wife Kay and I decided to go to Tuscaloosa to see "our" Bulldogs play the Crimson Tide in 1973.

On our trip from Atlanta on the morning of the game, Kay suggested that we predict the outcome of the game and the loser would pay for dinner in the near future. That's a favorite "trick" of hers to make certain she gets an occasional evening out.

It didn't matter to her that Georgia had been made an official 20-point underdog to the Tide, ranked No. 2 in the nation that week. "Now don't laugh," she said, "but I have a strong feeling that Georgia is going to win today. In fact, I *know* Georgia is going to win."

"Really?" I said. "You really think so?"

"Yes. And the score is going to be, let's see, the score is going to be . . . 14-13."

I explained to her that Alabama had lost only one game at Tuscaloosa since Bear Bryant had been coaching there. "So what? That doesn't mean anything," she replied.

I predicted the score would be: Alabama 27, Georgia 14.

We had seats behind the South end zone and watched as a weird game unfolded that scorching October 6 afternoon. Alabama led 13-3 at the half. In the third quarter, Georgia blocked a punt for a safety and the game went into the final period with Alabama leading by 13-5. The Bulldogs added a field goal to pull within 13-8. With ten minutes left in the game, the Dogs shocked everybody in the stadium (except Kay) by taking a 14-13 lead on a touchdown. The two-point conversion attempt was unsuccessful.

With just over three minutes remaining to be played, Alabama had reached Georgia's 13-yard line, where it was fourth down. The Tide lined up for a chip-shot field goal and an apparent 16-14 victory.

However, the kick sailed off to the right. I watched as the ball missed its mark and I could see that it was headed in our general direction. It came closer and closer, and suddenly, there was the football. Right there! I reached up and, naturally, made a beautiful catch.

Kay was estatic. She jumped up and down as though she was skipping rope. She screamed: "We beat Alabama! We beat Alabama! We beat Alabama! And I picked the score! 14-13 . . . 14-13 . . . 14-13!"

And to top it all off, I had the game ball. The REAL game ball. In a few moments, a couple of student "ball boys" came to retrieve my treasure. I quickly explained to them that I was from Georgia and that I would like to buy the football. The boys said that I probably could, but I'd have to clear it with one of the coaches after the game. So they squatted in the aisle and waited for the final few minutes to tick off the clock. At the time, I would have waited all night and paid $100 for that football.

Kay was still jumping around. She kept repeating that she had "called" the score . . . 14-13 . . . 14-13.

The Bulldogs took over at the 20-yard line but were unable to pick up a first down and punted. The scoreboard clock now showed 2:23. Alabama scored in three lightning-fast plays, added a two-point conversion and led 21-14. The Tide scored again. Final score: Alabama 28, Georgia 14.

Kay? The tears were rolling down her pretty face. Me? I don't really remember. She later told me that I had turned a strange shade of green. The game ball? I gave it back. It was no longer such a unique treasure.

Neither Kay nor I predicted the correct score that day in 1973. But we both came mighty close.

1974
GAME 39

No AU Luck At All

The 1974 Alabama-Auburn game once again brought national attention to Legion Field in Birmingham. Both teams were ranked in the Top Ten — the Tide No. 2, the Tigers No. 7 — and ABC-TV beamed the game across the country as part of its expanding Thanksgiving weekend package of college football.

The game was played on Friday. For the fourth year in a row, Alabama was to bring a perfect 10-0-0 record into its meeting with Auburn. From the Auburn vantage point, it was the fourth straight year the War Eagles had had to face their big rival when their big rival had not lost a game all fall. The Plainsmen had become accustomed to the situation — and the challenge.

But Auburn, beaten only once in the season, had the horses to stay with Alabama and in an exciting game that saw just about everything, the favored Crimsons escaped with a 17-13 win.

On their way to Birmingham, the Tide has beaten Maryland, Mississippi Southern, Vanderbilt, Ole Miss, FSU, Tennessee, TCU, Mississippi State, LSU and Miami by an average score of 30-7 per game. Alabama ranked eighth nationally in scoring and second in defense against scoring.

Auburn toyed with Louisville and Chattanooga in the first two games of the season before getting down to more serious football against Tennessee, Miami, Kentucky, Georgia Tech and FSU. After seven games the Tigers had a perfect record and had run roughshod over the opposition by an aggregate score of 192-51.

But then came a November 2 trip to Florida Field in Gainesville for the big battle with the Gators, who sported a 5-1 record. The home team pulled off a 25-14 ambush.

The Plainsmen rebounded with four-point victories over Mississippi State (24-20) and Georgia (17-13) and once again turned full attention to the Crimson Tide. At 9-1-0, Auburn was the 10th best defensive team in the country, having given up an average of only 11 points per game.

Two days before the 39th game of the series, another Alabama football team was getting national exposure. The Birmingham Americans, members of the short-lived World Football League, defeated Hawaii 22-19 to gain a spot in the first and last annual World Bowl, a bowl the "Ams" (as they were called) later won 22-21 over the Florida Blazers. So much for the WFL.

Friday, November 29 came and the 71,224 who filled Legion Field were more than ready for the big battle to blast off. Auburn wanted to avenge the licking they had taken the year before, and Alabama wanted to do it again. Alabama scored first.

On their first possession, a 74-yard drive by the Tide was killed by a Richard Todd fumble at the Auburn one-yard line, recovered by Ken Bernich. Auburn took over but had to punt out. On the next series, Todd, faking off the wishbone, hit Willie Shelby with a 45-yard TD bomb. Bucky Berrey added the point-after and Alabama led 7-0. Berrey stretched the lead to 10-0 with a field goal from 36 yards out early in the second quarter.

It was time for Auburn to get back in the ball game. Taking the kickoff, Secedrick McIntyre, Mitzi Jackson and Phil Gargis sparked a 12-play, 77-yard drive that resulted in a touchdown. McIntyre carried six times for 38 yards, Jackson rushed for 31 yards in three attempts, and Gargis gained eight yards in three tries. McIntyre got the TD in a plunge from the one. Chris Wilson's conversion made the score 10-7, Bama.

The Tigers then muffed a great chance to move ahead, or at least to tie the game. On the next series of downs, Auburn's Rick Telhiard popped Todd hard and caused a fumble that Carl Hubbard recovered for Auburn at the Tide 40. Runs of seven and five yards by Rick Neel and McIntyre's 12-yard burst led Auburn to a first down at the Alabama eight-yard line. On the next play, an offsides penalty pushed the scrimmage line back to the 13. It was a costly mistake by Auburn and could very well have been the turning point in the game. Auburn rammed it back down to the three in three plays. On fourth down, Tide end Leroy Cook crashed through the Auburn line and blocked a field goal try by Wilson.

Halftime came and with the score standing at 10-7, the game and the Championship of Alabama were very much still up for grabs.

The second half started quickly. Alabama received the kickoff, couldn't move, and punted. Auburn moved enough to get a punt into the end zone. Alabama started from its own 20 and kept going. Todd carried three straight times and picked up five, seven and 12 yards to the 44. On second-and-eight, Randy Billingsley broke loose for 28 yards, then came back for 11 more as the chains moved down to the Auburn 15. Shelby got two yards and Calvin Culliver the final 13. Berrey's PAT pushed the Tide into a 17-7 lead.

Auburn came back for a quick touchdown — but it didn't count. Gargis got away for a 26-yard run to give Auburn a first down at the Alabama 41. Gargis then swung right and shot a pass to Tom Gossom for an apparent touchdown. But an official ruled that Gossom, in running his pattern, had stepped out of bounds and "re-entered" the playing field before receiving the ball.

The TD was nullified. The Auburn coaching staff hotly disputed the call. They claimed that Gossom had been pushed out of bounds by an Alabama defender. After the words had been exchanged, instead of a 17-13, 17-14 or 17-15 score, the count stood at 17-7.

Auburn, disappointed, was held and had to punt. It was a short one of only 10 yards, and once again Alabama had good field position. This time the Tide went to the Tiger one-yard line before failing to score. On fourth down, Bruce Evans and Mike Flynn threw Todd for a three-yard loss and Auburn got the ball and a chance to come back. The possession didn't last long as Ricky Davis intercepted a Gargis pass. The tough Auburn defense again had to repel the Tide attack down close.

With 7:39 left in the game, Auburn started a drive from their own 38. On third down, Jackson reeled off a 25-yard run to the Alabama 47. Third down again and Gargis was scrambling from a heavy pass rush. He lateralled the ball to Jackson who got to the 33 for another first down. Alabama stiffened and held the Tigers for no gain on the next three plays. Baumgartner came on and Auburn lined up in field goal formation. As Alabama fans chanted "block that kick", Baumgartner took the snap directly and passed complete to Neel for a big 12-yard gain and a first down at the Tide 20. Jackson spurted for 10, then five, then two. He had put the ball on the three-yard line. On third down, Gargis leaped over the goal for the touchdown. Auburn went for two. If successful, it would mean a field goal or a touchdown would produce a win for the Tigers. The try failed and it was still 17-13, Alabama, and just over two minutes remained in the game.

Auburn's kickoff went into the end zone. In three plays, Alabama managed only seven yards. Meanwhile the scoreboard clock had blinked down to 1:07. The Tide lined up in punt formation.

A sea of orange and blue pom-poms fluttered frantically on the roaring Auburn side of the stadium. Alabama's side was subdued. Tide followers were suddenly sweating out another Auburn "miracle". The 1972 game and the two blocked punts were still fresh and vivid images in their minds.

Could it happen again? Could Auburn replay 1972 and beat Alabama again by blocking a punt? It was close. The Tigers stormed in. They rushed Rod Nelson and the kick covered only 27 yards. Mike Fuller returned three yards to the Tiger 49. Auburn, with hopes still high, had the ball — for one play.

On first down, Gargis attempted to hand-off to Dan Nugent on an end-around. Mike Dubose, from his defensive end pass rush position, read the play, slapped the ball away and recovered for Alabama.

The fighting, scrapping Plainsmen had been done in another time. The Tide-Tiger encounter had treated the Nation to a hard-nosed, exciting football show.

Coach Bear Bryant told a *Birmingham News* reporter following the fray, "As I said before the game, I'd be mighty happy with a one-point victory. So now I'm four times as happy with a four-point win."

Alabama's series lead was increased to 21-17-1 and the Crimsons had registered 663 points to Auburn's 589.

The Tide got the best of the 1973 game on the stat sheet as well as on the scoreboard, leading in first downs 20-11, rushing yards 290-228, passing yards 80-12 and total yards 370-240. The winners also led in penalty yards, 31-8.

McIntyre (99 yards), Jackson (69) and Gargis (51) accounted for all but nine of Auburn's ground yards as each carried the ball 14 times. For Alabama, Billingsley had 92 yards in 11 attempts and Calvin Culliver took the ball 19 times for 91 yards to pace the high-powered running attack.

Auburn went to the Gator Bowl to play Texas. The Longhorns had scored over 30 points in seven of their games, including an 81-16 thrashing of TCU. In Jacksonville, the Tigers scored in every conceivable way — touchdowns, one-point conversions, a two-point conversion, a safety and a field goal — and routed the Texans 27-3.

Alabama and Notre Dame had put on such a great show the previous year in New Orleans that Miami decided to rematch the two powers in the Orange Bowl in hopes of another classic. Both had accepted the challenge back on November 16. Notre Dame had lost 31-20 to Purdue early in the season and still had Southern Cal to play. The day after the Alabama-Auburn game, the Irish blew a 24-0 halftime lead and lost to the Trojans 55-24. It was a loss that took a lot of the gloss off the Tide-Irish rematch.

Miami didn't get a classic. In fact, both teams seemed flat. Neither could crank up an offense but Notre Dame put enough together to win 13-11. In addition to the loss, Alabama got a lot of attention focused on its streak of eight visits to bowls with no victories. In the past four seasons, Alabama had recorded an incredible 43-1-0 record during the regular season. But in bowl games those four years, the Tide was winless.

In the same four-year period, Auburn posted a 35-11-0 total record and as strange as it may seem, all 11 losses were to teams that would go on to play in bowl games each year.

"Sure, I'd like to have another time at bat. But it just can't happen. I'm sitting here right now wishing I could come back another year." — Ralph "Shug" Jordan.

1975

GAME 40

An Auburn Era Ends

At Legion Field on Saturday, November 29, 1975, the usual capacity crowd was on hand. A nationwide television audience also looked on. It would be Shug Jordan's 265th and final game as head coach at Auburn. It wouldn't be pleasant. Once again Jordan had to face an Alabama team that was one of the very best in the country. This time around, the Crimson Tide was ranked No. 4. Jordan's going-away party was not expected to be a lot of fun.

Jordan's Auburn, on the other hand, was suffering through the worst season since his second year at the Plains 23 years ago. The 1975 Tigers were 3-5-2 coming into the 40th game of the series.

The disastrous season started on September 13 at home with a 31-20 loss to Memphis State. A trip to Waco, Texas, resulted in a 10-10 tie with Baylor. Tennessee took them in Knoxville 21-17, and then came a 23-16 defeat at the hands of VPI at Jordan-Hare Stadium. The Tigers were 0-3-1. The next three weeks brought three wins — 15-9 over Kentucky, 31-27 over Georgia Tech and 17-14 over FSU.

The FSU game, played on Saturday night, October 25 in Tallahasee, would be Shug's last coaching victory.

Florida beat the Plainsmen 31-14 and Mississippi State was victorious 31-21, both games at Auburn. The Tigers then went to Athens and lost to Georgia 28-13.

Alabama and Missouri kicked off the 1975 season with a Monday night national TV game from Birmingham on September 8. Missouri

Shug, Bear To Meet For The Last Time

The Montgomery Advertiser

came out smoking and won easily 20-7. It would be a year before Alabama would lose again.

The Tide's next nine opponents suffered defeats by an average score of 36-5 and Alabama was second in the nation in scoring (33.3) and first in defense against scoring (6.6).

The experts were saying that Alabama could choose its score against Auburn, but the Tigers fought gamely, trailed by only one touchdown at the half, and held the final score to a fairly respectable 28-0.

The first-half score came with 2:48 left in the initial quarter. Taking a punt at their own 15-yard line, the Tide covered the distance in nine plays. Johnny Davis carried five times for 37 years to spark the drive and Richard Todd threw a short four-yard scoring pass to Jerry Brown. Danny Ridgeway kicked the extra point.

At the half, even though Auburn had not gotten past Alabama's 47-yard line, the Tigers led in possession time, 16:39 to 13:21.

Early in the third quarter, Davis' running (33 yards in five carries) led a drive from the Tide 23 to Auburn's 33. From there, Todd went off right tackle, reversed his field and followed sharp blocking for a touchdown and a 14-0 lead.

Later in the same period, Leroy Cook tipped a Phil Gargis pass that was intercepted by Tyrone King. A 10-yard return put the ball at

Jordan's finale—
And 25 glory years came to this day . . .

Bryant bids a sad farewell to Jordan; 'Sorry we had one of our best games'

the Alabama 46. Davis and Todd took turns on the ensuing drive and it was Todd's turn when he scored from the 14. With 4:53 left in the third quarter, Ridgeway's conversion was perfect again for a 21-0 score.

In the fourth quarter after Auburn missed a field goal attempt, Alabama took over at the 20 and pounded down to the Auburn 24 where Todd passed to Wilbur Newsome for the final touchdown. Ridgeway made it 28-0 and six minutes and 52 seconds remained to go in the game and in Jordan's coaching career.

As the game ended, Alabama substitutes were hammering at Auburn's goal line defense. John David Crowe, Jr. tried twice to score from the three, but the Tigers had decided enough was enough.

For the final time, Shug and Bear met at midfield after an Auburn-Alabama game. It was the 18th time they had greeted each other in this situation at Legion Field. It was the usual quick handshake, but this time thousands of fans—both Auburn and Alabama loyalists, made it a point to watch. It was, after all, a poignant, historic scene worth seeing and worth remembering.

The winners got 22 first downs, Auburn 13. The total yardage was 430-133. Davis' 98 yards in 18 carries led all runners for the day, while Todd had 90 rushing yards and 54 passing.

Alabama's series advantage had now bulged to 22-17-1, and the Crimsons had scored 691 points to 589 for Auburn.

For the 17th consecutive year, Alabama went bowling. It was the Sugar Bowl again and the Tide defeated Penn State 13-6. The eight-year winless bowl streak, about which so much had been written a year ago, was ended.

Alabama's final Associated Press national rank in 1975 was fourth. In the past five years, Bryant's Bama boys had won 54 games and lost only six.

Jordan's coaching career at Auburn spanned 25 years (1951-1975). His teams played 265 games and amassed a 175-83-7 record for a

SPORTS NEWS — **The Montgomery Advertiser** – Journal **D**
Sunday Morning, November 30, 1975

Tide Engulfs War Eagles

THE END: Jordan's Swan Song No Lullaby

Ron Barefield
Assistant Sports Editor

winning percentage of .674. His Tiger teams scored 5,186 points and surrendered 3,520, for an average game score of 20-13.

Against non-SEC opponents, Jordan's Auburn teams racked up an impressive record of 77-17-2. In the Conference, his teams won 98, lost 66 and tied five. As for the Alabama series, Jordan had made the walk to the center of Legion Field feeling the thrill of victory nine times, and 16 times suffering the agony of defeat.

When a Jordan team won a game it was by an average score of 25-9; games were lost by an almost identical 23-9 margin. Of the 83 defeats, 29 were by one touchdown or less; 50 by two touchdowns or less.

Jordan's top team was in 1957 when the Tigers won the National Championship. Eight times the wire services (AP, UPI) voted his teams in the Nation's top 10, and in the top 15 a total of 12 times. In 12 bowl games, his record was 5-7-0. Jordan's four best teams were those of 1957, 1958, 1972 and 1974. The combined record for those editions was 39-3-1.

For an entire generation, Shug Jordan and Auburn football had been one and the same. He was universally respected and when he bowed out, the sadness was inevitable.

1976
GAME 41

Back To The Blackboard

Alabama was 7-3-0. Auburn was 3-7-0. Not in 20 years had the two teams come into the big game with combined records that included 10 losses.

The Tide was heavily favored in the season opener against Ole Miss, but the Rebels surprised everybody by winning 10-7. Three weeks later, Georgia handed Alabama a 21-0 licking. It was the first time Alabama had been shutout in 69 games and only the second in 185 games. On November 13, Alabama journeyed to South Bend for the first time ever. Notre Dame won 21-18.

In between, the Crimson Tide buried seven other opponents 228-75 and that was plenty good enough for a Liberty Bowl invitation. Even having lost three times, the Tide had the fifth best record in the country in holding down point production by opponents.

Doug Barfield had been selected Auburn's 21st head coach. On the average, it had been a high-turnover position. But in the past 46 years, only six men had held the post. As with Jordan, it was a rough break-in year.

The Tigers lost their first two games to Arizona (31-19) and Baylor (15-14). Then came two victories, 38-28 over Tennessee and 10-0 over Ole Miss. Then two more defeats — to Memphis State (28-27) and to Georgia Tech (28-10). A 31-19 victory over FSU preceded consecutive losses to Florida 24-19, Mississippi State 28-19 and Georgia 28-0.

Just over 70,000 showed up on a dull, overcast November 27 for

Tony Nathan, Alabama back, cracked Auburn's defense for 141 yards in 12 carries and scored two touchdowns in the 1976 game.

the 41st game of the series and witnessed a runaway 38-7 Alabama victory.

The first quarter was error-filled and the closest either team came to a score were 47 and 35-yard field goal attempts missed by Auburn.

In the second period, Alabama's Mike Tucker put a vicious hit on Auburn's Joe Cribbs and caused a fumble that Murray Legg recovered for Alabama at the Tiger 40. Thad Flanagan broke free for gains for 12 and 17 yards and Tony Nathan rushed for 10 more. In a flash, the Tide had a first-and-goal at Auburn's one-yard line. The Plainsmen threw them back three times, but on fourth down from the five, Rick Watson blasted over for the touchdown. Bucky Berrey converted and Alabama was off and running.

With time running down before intermission, Auburn's Neil O'Donoghue missed a 36-yard field goal to give Alabama the ball at the 20. In four plays, The Tide had scored again. Nathan went for 20 yards and Jack O'Rear for four. Watson threw a halfback pass to Nathan, good for 42 yards to the Tiger 14 and, on the next play, Nathan took it over. As Berrey kicked good to make it 14-0, the clock stood at 36 seconds.

Alabama received the second-half kickoff and once again went quickly down the field for a score. Beginning at the 20, Nathan carried four straight times for 38 yards to the Auburn 42. Rutledge took the stage and drilled a pass to Ozzie Newsome who caught it at the 30 and fought his way across the goal. After another Berrey point-after, the count had mounted to 21-0.

Auburn got the ball but couldn't move. A punt gave Alabama possession at its own 31. Six plays later it was 28-0. The two big gainers were runs by Davis for 28 yards and the scoring scamper by Nathan for 33 yards.

Still in the third quarter, Auburn got down to the Alabama 29, but on fourth-and-one, a sneak by quarterback Phil Gargis failed and Bama took over. Five plays later, Rutledge scored from the 11. Berrey was once again on target and the score climbed to 35-0.

In the fourth quarter, Berrey slammed a 47-yard field goal to set a new series record for the longest three-point kick. The previous mark had been a 44-yarder by Auburn's Don Lewis in the 1965 game.

Auburn finally got on the scoreboard late in the game. Cribbs ran 31 yards to the Tide nine. Moments later, Foster Christy plunged across from the one. O'Donoghue converted to make the final score: Alabama 38, Auburn 7.

Alabama's five touchdown drives covered distances of 60, 80, 80, 69 and 71 yards, as the awesome wishbone offense crunched out 22 first downs and 302 rushing yards. Rutledge added 139 passing yards on seven completions for a 441-yard day of total offense. Nathan gained 141 yards in 12 carries to completely dominate the personal rushing statistics for the day. Auburn was held to nine first downs and 229 total yards. The Tigers were penalized 30 yards, Alabama 17. The statistical oddity of the game: for the first time in eight years, and only the second time in 16 years, the losing team suffered more penalty yards than the winner.

UCLA, the Tide's opponent in the Liberty Bowl was made a big favorite by the oddsmakers. The Uclans had tied Ohio State 10-10 and had lost only to Southern Cal, 24-14, in the season's final game. Alabama crushed the No. 6 ranked Bruins 36-6.

Alabama ended at 9-3-0 for the year. Auburn was 3-8-0, the first eight-loss season for the Tigers in 24 years.

War Eagle IV

1977

GAME 42

Auburn Can't Hide From Intensified Tide

As the 42nd game of the series approached, it was like tax-time for Auburn; time to take the bad with the worst. The 5-5-0 Tigers had to face another power-packed Alabama team in the regular season's finale. The Tide, at 9-1-0, was ranked No. 3 in the Nation, and was scoring at a 31 points per game clip.

Almost 70,000 turned out on a bright, blustery November 26 afternoon and watched as the game turned out to be almost what the predictors said it would be—a high scoring victory by the heavily favored Tide. The score was 48-21. The fans also witnessed the establishment of two new series records—one for the longest run from scrimmage, the other for the longest pass play—both by losing Auburn.

Alabama didn't really get cranked up until seven weeks into the season. After a 34-13 win over Ole Miss, the Tide lost their only game of the season, 31-24 to Nebraska on national television from Lincoln.

The slow climb back for national honors began with a 32-12 win over Vanderbilt and an 18-10 defeat of Georgia. Then came a close 21-20 victory over Southern Cal in Los Angeles as Alabama stopped a two-point conversion attempt with less than two minutes left in

Charlie Trotman (top), Auburn quarterback, and Byron Franklin, split end, connected on a record 75-yard scoring pass in the 1977 game.

the game. Next, Alabama made it seven straight wins over Tennessee, 24-10 at Birmingham.

It was Roll Tide time.

Louisville, Mississippi State, LSU and Miami were washed away by scores averaging 38-4, and the intensified Tide worked their way up to a No. 3 national ranking behind unbeaten Texas and once-beaten Oklahoma.

Auburn's season was a back and forth affair. The Tigers opened with a win over Arizona; lost to Southern Mississippi; beat Tennessee and Ole Miss; lost to N.C. State, Georgia Tech and FSU; beat Florida; lost to Mississippi State, and beat Georgia. The Plainsmen had scored 183 points and allowed 195.

Entering the Alabama game, Auburn didn't feel deserving of such a decided underdog role. The Tigers were coming off an impressive 33-14 win over Georgia in Athens and were ready and willing to stand eyeball to eyeball with Alabama.

Auburn received the opening kickoff and banged out three first downs before being stopped. Alabama came back with a march to the Tiger 26 but stalled and missed a field goal try. Auburn took over and lost five yards on the first play. On second-and-15, halfback Joe Cribbs made history. Cribbs broke through the left side, twice dodged Tide defenders and headed towards the west sideline. It was an 85-yard dash for a TD and glory—the longest scoring run from scrimmage in series history, bettering by one yard the run off of a fake punt by Auburn's Connie Frederick in 1969.

Cribbs crossed the goal line with 3:49 remaining in the first quarter and after Jorge Portela converted, Auburn had jumped to a surprising 7-0 lead. It was Auburn's first first-quarter touchdown against Alabama in 19 years.

The War Eagles were whooping it up but the joy lasted only until Alabama got its hands on the football again. The Tide drove 80 yards for the tying touchdown. Quarterback Gary Rutledge's run of 14 yards and his 12-yard pass to Tony Nathan, led a quick drive to Auburn's 30. From there Rutledge threw to Bruce Bolton, who made a belly-skidding catch in the end zone for a touchdown. Roger Chapman kicked his first of six conversions for a 7-7 tie.

With just over two minutes left in the half, Alabama managed to take the lead. Johnny Davis and Nathan gained 24 and 22 yards respectively (three carries each) to spearhead a quick advance to the Auburn 12-yard line. Davis scored from there to make it a 14-7 lead.

Alabama received the second-half kickoff and went to work. The drive included a 47-yard option keeper by Rutledge to the Auburn 11.

Joe Cribbs, Auburn back, set a series record in 1977 with the longest run from scrimmage—an 85-yard touchdown streak.

Three cracks by Davis got it to the two before Nathan smashed over for the touchdown and a 21-7 Bama advantage.

Soon it was 28-7. Murray Legg recovered a fumble at the Tiger 21. Three plays later, the Tide was at the one and Davis took it over for the score.

Auburn fans started cheering again as James Brooks took the ensuing kick off and rambled 80 yards to the Tide 20. But on fourth-and-one from the one, William Andrews was nailed for no gain. The Tide then drove 74 yards, settled for a field goal try, and missed.

Auburn had it back at the 20. In two plays, they scored. On second down, Trotman pitched a pass to Byron Franklin and the freshman speedster raced 75 yards for a touchdown—the longest scoring pass play the series had ever seen. The previous record was a 63-yarder from Kenny Stabler to Ray Perkins in 1966. With 13:27 left in the game, Portela kicked good and Auburn pulled to within 28-14.

Three minutes and four seconds later Alabama retaliated to push the lead to 35-14. Two passes from Rutledge to Ozzie Newsome for 24 and 35 yards highlighted a swift march to Auburn's five. Two plays later Mitch Ferguson scored from the one.

It took the Tide only 62 seconds to score again. E. J. Junior intercepted a Trotman pass at the Auburn 42. On first down, Rutledge heaved a beauty into the end zone where Newsome made a sensational catch. Chapman missed his only conversion of the day and the score was now 41-14. The Tide scored another touchdown about four minutes later as backup quarterback Steadman Shealy went over from 15 yards out.

Auburn scored in six plays after the next kick off. Trotman completed three passes covering 51 yards to the Alabama two. Andrews scored and Portela converted. There was still 2:36 left. Auburn had had a long, bruising afternoon of football but wearily held on to prevent another Alabama score.

In the final score of 48-21, the Tigers had surrendered the most points in one game in 26 years.

Alabama had pocketed its fifth straight win over its intrastate rivals. The Tigers hadn't experienced the thrill of victory in the series since the miracle of two blocked punts in 1972.

In the 1977 game, Alabama pounded the spotty Auburn defense for 27 first downs and 515 total yards. The Tigers countered with 10 first downs and 295 yards—160 of those yards coming on two plays. The winners were penalized 26 yards to Auburn's seven.

Rutledge, on 28 run and pass plays, accounted for 295 yards. He rushed for 102 yards in 15 attempts and completed nine of 13 passes for 193 yards. Cribbs had 123 rushing yards in 15 carries to lead the

Auburn offense.

The victory sewed up Alabama's sixth Southeastern Conference Championship in seven years and the Tide's 15th football title since the conference was formed in 1933.

And for the 19th straight year, Alabama followers had a bowl game to look forward to. This time it was New Orleans and the Sugar Bowl, featuring a first-ever meeting of Alabama and Ohio State.

In the pre-game buildup, so much of the news coverage was directed to the Bear Bryant-Woody Hayes angle, that one Buckeye player remarked, "This game is between Ohio State and Alabama, not Woody Hayes and Bear Bryant." He had a point . . . up to a point. After all, the game matched the third and fourth all-time winningest coaches in college football history and the two winningest active coaches. Bryant had logged 272 wins; Hayes 230. Only Amos Alonzo Stagg's 314 wins and Glenn (Pop) Warner's 313 victories topped the rival coaches in this particular game.

The Bear and Bama thrashed Woody and his Bucks by a score of 35-6, to the delight of football fans in every corner of the South, even including some Auburn households. The win also gave Alabama a fabulous 74-10-0 record in the last seven years.

Of the top four teams in the country in 1977, (Texas, Oklahoma, Alabama and Michigan), only Alabama won its bowl game. Notre Dame, clobbering Texas 38-10 in the Cotton Bowl, took a giant "poll vault" all the way from fifth place to first in the 1977 rankings. Washington (with losses to Mississippi State, Syracuse, Minnesota and UCLA) upset Michigan 27-20 in the Rose Bowl, and Arkansas stunned No. 2 Oklahoma 31-6 in the Orange Bowl. Eight major college football teams finished the 1977 season with only one loss, but none escaped undefeated.

1978

GAME 43

"Too Many Chinks In Auburn's Armor"

During game week in 1978 the *Associated Press* polled 23 sports writers across the State who had covered the Tide and Tigers throughout the season. What the AP wanted to know was: who will win, by what score, and why? The vote was unanimous in favor of the No. 2-rated team in the country—Alabama—by an average predicted score of 29-15.

The Tide had lost only to Southern Cal, 24-14, early in the season. Among the team's nine victories were Nebraska, Missouri and Washington. Auburn was 6-3-1, its tie a 22-22 thriller against Georgia that ditched the Bulldogs' Sugar Bowl hopes.

Now, however, Auburn was itching to put Georgia back on the road to New Orleans. And Auburn could—by beating Bama.

Over 79,000 fans, the most ever to cram Legion Field for a football game, were there to see first hand if the Tigers could indeed knock Alabama from a Sugar date with No. 1-ranked Penn State and a National Championship showdown.

Underdog Auburn did put a good case of fear into Tide boosters everywhere, along with giving the Sugar Bowl people some anxious moments.

The game had a shaky start. Auburn received the opening kickoff but had to punt. Alabama punted it right back—a punt that went all

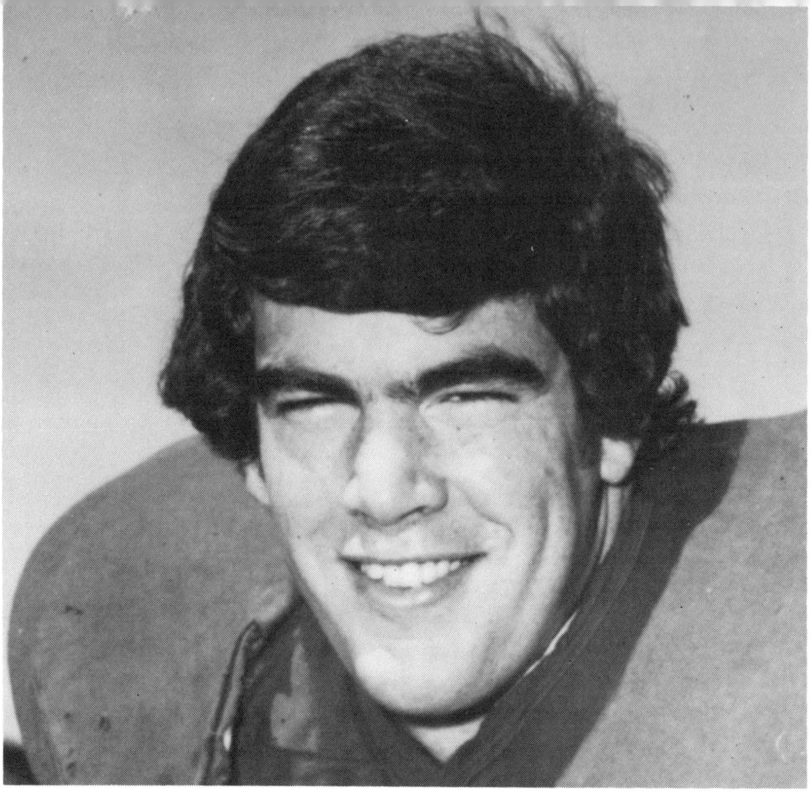

Jeff Rutledge, Alabama quarterback, threw a series-record six touchdown passes — one in '76, two in '77 and three in '78. In all, he completed 29 passes for 506 yards against Auburn. His 30 TD passes was a school record at the time.

Sports

It's Tide vs. Lions for national title

Section B

Shot at Championship!!!

Jeff Rutledge shines as Alabama romps to 34-16 win over Auburn for SEC title

Over Tech, 29-28

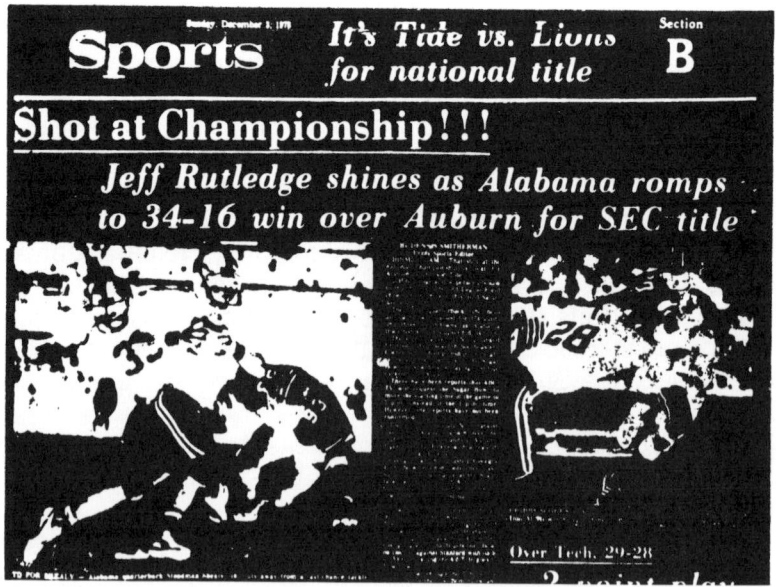

of four yards to give Auburn the ball at midfield. Unable to take advantage of this early generosity, Auburn immediately fumbled it back to Alabama with Marty Lyons recovering Charlie Trotman's bobble at the Tiger 49.

Bama went for a touchdown. On third down from the 47, quarterback Jeff Rutledge, who would have a record-setting afternoon, passed 11 yards to Rick Neal. After two runs gained three yards, Rutledge and Bruce Bolton, a walk-on from Memphis, connected on a 33-yard TD strike. Alan McElroy converted and the Tide had a 7-0 lead 7:40 into the game.

Auburn answered by hacking out an 81-yard drive in 14 plays to get all even. A 16-yard Trotman-to-Byron Franklin pass, plus a Trotman keeper for 17, sparked an advance to Alabama's 32. After three plays could net only seven yards, Coach Doug Barfield reached into his trick bag and came out with a goodie. It was fourth down at the 25 and the Tigers were set for a field goal attempt. Holder Foster Christy took the snap but instead of spotting the ball, shoveled it back to William Andrews, coming around. The surprise caught Alabama's defense napping and gained a 10 big yards for a first down at the 15.

Joe Cribbs then blasted to the 12, to the seven, and to the six, bringing up fourth-and-one. Cribbs got it with a yard to spare. Two more Cribbs carries finally got the ball over the goal line. Jorge Portela converted and with just over a minute remaining in the first period, it was 7-7.

Bama took the ensuing kickoff and marched right back down the field, reaching AU's five-yard line in a fourth-and-goal situation. McElroy broke the tie with a field goal. Tide, 10-7.

Later in the second quarter, Alabama twice turned the ball over, throwing an interception and fumbling, and the second mistake was costly. Starting from their 46, the Tigers got it going with a Trotman pass to Mark Robbins for 21 yards to the 33. Cribbs hoofed it to the 24, Andrews to the 22, Cribbs to the nine and Cribbs for the touchdown. It was just that quick. Portela's PAT attempt was wide and with only 2:46 left on the first-half clock, Auburn was out front, 13-10. Surprise!

The fired-up Tigers kicked off, forced a punt and were ready to "call it intermission" with a 3-point lead. However, on first down from the 17-yard line, Andrews fumbled and Murray Legg recovered for the Crimsons at the enemy 20. Three plays later from the 17, Rutledge once again found Bolton open for a touchdown strike. It was Rutledge's 28th, tying him with Joe Namath as Alabama's all-time TD-thrower. McElroy's kick made it 17-13 with less than a minute left to play.

As the marching bands were "struttin' their stuff" down on the green carpet, the concensus along "press box row" was that Auburn's upset chances had died with the late fumble to let the opposition off a big hook.

They were right. The second half was all-Alabama. On their second possession, the Tide went 75 yards in just six plays, the biggies being a 41-yard run by Major Ogilvie and a 15-yard roughing-the-passer penalty. Rutledge's 11-yard aerial to Neal, an old teammate at Birmingham's Banks High School, capped the drive—and Auburn. It also gave Rutledge "the record," a record that one would think should belong to a Harry Gilmer, a Kenny Stabler, a Steve Sloan or a Namath. But it now belonged to a Jeff Rutledge.

Following the record-breaker, McElroy added another conversion and the score became 24-13.

The scrappy Tigers made one more house call by driving to Bama's 20-yard line before having to settle for a Portela field goal that cut the deficit to eight points. Early in the fourth period, however, Alabama got the points back when McElroy booted a 39-yarder. UA 27, AU 16.

Alabama, on its next possession, tied the ribbon on the 43rd edition of this rivalry, taking only seven plays to go 67 yards against a worn-thin War Eagle defense. Reaching a fourth-and-two at the Tiger 20, Coach Bear Bryant sent in his field goal unit, then called a time-out to reconsider. It was decided instead to go for the first down. Quarterback Steadman Shealy, in for Rutledge, took the snap, glided left on the option, kept the ball and raced for a touchdown. McElroy then kicked his 10th point of the game with just over six minutes remaining.

Auburn was unable to get another first down. Ball game.

Wearing the biggest grins of all late that December 2nd afternoon were the representatives from the Sugar Bowl. Instead of Auburn sending Georgia to New Orleans for New Year's, Alabama detoured the Dogs to Houston, and the Tide would journey to the Cresent City.

Final score from Legion Field: Alabama 34, Auburn 16, not too far off the 29-15 concensus that the State's sports scribes had predicted. Clyde Bolton's (*Birmingham News*) pre-game analysis was as good as anyone's when he wrote, "There are too many chinks in Auburn's armor, and Alabama will exploit them all . . . Alabama, 35-14."

And Alabama did exploit them all, rushing for 253 yards and passing for 174 more on 13 completions in 22 attempts. Overall, the winners led in total yards 427-233 and first downs 22-14.

Cribbs was the day's ball carrying workhorse, rushing for 118 yards on 32 totes. Ogilvie got the call only nine times but responded with 104 yards, a fine 11.6 average. Rutledge accounted for all the Tide's passing yardage.

For the season, Cribbs left behind a new Auburn rushing standard, totaling 1,205 yards in 303 carries, breaking the old record set by Jimmy Sidle in 1963 by 199 yards.

In the "Big Show" under the Superdome, Bama nailed Joe Paterno's No. 1 Nittany Lions, 14-7, thanks to a classic goal line stand in the fourth quarter. Later that New Year's Day, Southern Cal topped Michigan 17-10 in the Rose Bowl, setting the stage for still another "Football Poll War" over the big question of: "Who's No. 1?"

Would it be 11-1-0 Alabama (a 24-14 loser to Southern Cal), or 11-1-0 Southern Cal (a 20-7 loser to Arizona State). Both got a piece of the pie. The AP poll (writers) gave it to the Crimson Tide; the UPI poll (coaches) gave it to the Trojans.

Nobody was happy. Both camps wanted both titles. The outcry from the voting outcome also gave the backers of a national playoff system an arsenal of ammo to fire away with for another year.

Meantime, Alabama's series lead over Auburn went to 25-17-1. And there was no end in sight of the margin becoming even greater.

1979
GAME 44

The December Fumble Fest

"Why us?" pondered Auburn. "What have we done to deserve all of this?" Once more, Auburn had to confront its biggest rival—its most hated rival—in the annual season-ending showdown when that rival was, once again, rated as one of the nation's top teams. This time, in fact, as the *top* team.

Auburn was by no means any pushover in '79, having won eight games and lost only two, good enough for a No. 14 national ranking.

Alabama's top-rated Crimson Tide was also No. 1 in the country in defense against scoring, letting their 10 opponents eke out a paltry five touchdowns and 40 total points. Plus, the Tide was averaging 33.4 points offensively—fourth from the top in that category among major college teams.

Auburn could also score "with the best of 'em," averaging 31.2 points which was seventh best. Auburn's problem, however, was letting the opposition also score, as 213 points had been rung up on the Tigers' defensive platoon.

Alabama won its first five games of the season by an average score of 44-2. In the sixth game, the Tide was on the short end of a 0-17 score against Tennessee before rallying for a convincing 27-17 triumph. After two more runaways, Bama could manage only a field goal against LSU, but the defense pitched a shutout for a 3-0 escape. A week later, Miami fell, 30-0.

Fans needed a pocket calculator to keep pace with Auburn and its opponents' point-production. After 10 games, a total of 525 points had been recorded. The Tigers' losses were to Tennessee (35-17) and Wake Forest (42-38). Among the eight victories were 44-31 and 52-35 slugfests with N.C. State and Vanderbilt, plus a big 33-13 win over rival Georgia at Athens. It marked the second straight year that AU had the pleasure of directly knocking UGA out of the Sugar Bowl. Both times, however, super-rival Alabama was the beneficiary. In that respect, either way, Auburn found itself in a "no win" situation.

It was the first day of December and 77,918 fans filled Legion Field for the 44th renewal of this 86-year old rivalry. Alabama's main concern was stopping (or containing) the nation's most prolific duo in James Brooks (1,153 yards) and Joe Cribbs (1,022). Auburn's main concern was Alabama itself.

Brooks and Cribbs notwithstanding, Bama was still made a whopping 16-point favorite.

It took no time at all for things to start popping in this one. Alabama put up two serious threats early in the game only to come away empty.

The opening kickoff was high and short, one that Brooks couldn't handle and one that was recovered by Randy Scott of Alabama at the 23-yard line. The Tide capped off this drive by punting.

Starting the next series from its 43 after an AU punt, Alabama ripped off a six-play, 47 yard push to a first down at the 10. Three plays later the ball was back at the 15 and Alan McElroy came on and missed a field goal.

It was looking like an Auburn day.

From the 20, the Tigers began to claw. Three Brooks' runs and two by Cribbs, plus a Charlie Trotman pass completion moved the stakes 21 yards before Cribbs broke loose for a big gain of 35 yards to Alabama's 24. The ball was advanced half-the-distance for a piling-on penalty, suddenly giving Auburn a first down at the 12. Aided by a major penalty, the Tide defense pushed the Tigers all the way back to the 30, but Jorge Portela salvaged three points from the situation with a 47-yard field goal, matching a series record for the longest FG with Alabama's Bucky Berrey (1976). With only 44 seconds left in the first period, Auburn had grabbed a 3-0 lead.

It woke Bama up. Taking the ensuing kickoff, the Crimsons began from their 20 and wishboned it to AU's 28. From there, Steadman Shealy and Keith Pugh got together on a pass that was good for six points. McElroy converted and it was 7-3.

MOBILE PRESS REGISTER Sunday, December 2, 1979

Sports

HOUSTON BOMBS RICE, 63-0— Page 2
PITT WHIPS PENN STATE, 29-14— Page 5
NAVY CLOUTS ARMY, 31-7— Page 6

Section **B**

UA march offsets rash of fumbles

Tide rally tops Auburn, 25-18

Auburn came right back with a 49-yard march to Alabama's 35. Here, Portela was short on a 52-yard field goal attempt. The Tide then went 65 yards in 10 snaps for another touchdown, with Shealy getting the final yard on a quarterback sneak. With just under three minutes before intermission, Alabama now had a 14-3 cushion.

On the first scrimmage play of the second half, Shealy fumbled and Ken Hardy recovered for the Tigers at Bama's 21. Auburn blew the opportunity with a personal foul penalty and wound up punting into the endzone. Two plays later, however, Alabama gave the Tigers another good chance when Freddie Smith hopped on a Major Ogilvie fumble at the 28. Still, AU could get only three points from the gift via a 39-yard Portela field goal. That made the score 14-6 with 11:33 left in the third period.

After an exchange of punts, the relentless Tide marched from their 28 to Auburn's 12, only to fumble again, this one by Shealy and recovered by Harris Rabren. But it didn't seem to matter. Brooks fumbled it right back to Alabama's E. J. Junior at the 21. Moving down to the Tiger six, but no further, McElroy upped the lead to 17-6 with a short field goal as only 2:07 showed on the third quarter clock.

School seemed to be out for the frustrated Tigers.

After taking the kickoff, AU ran three plays and punted. Alabama's Tommy Wilcox fumbled it and the Tigers recovered at the Tide 37. After two incomplete passes, Trotman hit Cribbs at the 25 and Cribbs zipped in for a touchdown. After four Tide turnovers in the third period alone, the Tigers finally had a touchdown. Trotman's pass for "2" was intercepted. Auburn had pulled to within five points, 12-17.

Alabama had to punt after only three plays and the Tigers began from their 33 and soon had the Crimson Tiders in disbelief. On second-and-12 from the 31, Trotman threw a bomb that Byron Franklin snagged at Bama's 14—a 55-yard gainer. Two plays later from the 11, Trotman rifled one to Mark Robbins for the go-ahead touchdown. Auburn was going crazy. Trotman was smothered on a

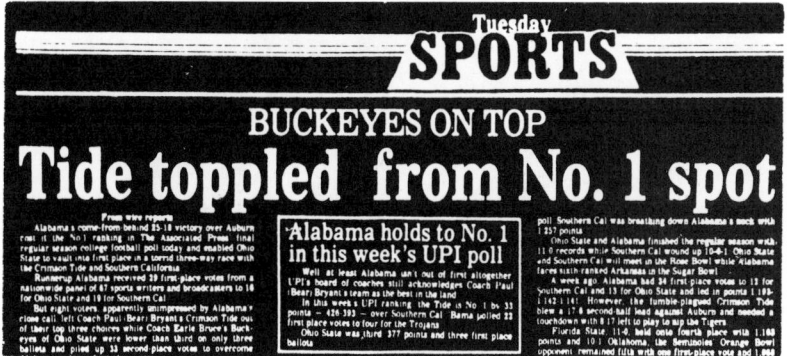

Birmingham News

2-point conversion try, but who cared?

It was now: Auburn 18, Alabama 17. And surely thoughts of 1972 and "17-16" were on the minds of everybody—Tiders and Tigers alike—all across the State.

Just five minutes and 37 seconds earlier, Bama had had a cozy 17-6 lead. Now, it was Auburn's ball game . . . provided it could survive the remaining 11½ minutes of play.

The nation's No. 1 team then showed why it was No. 1. Beginning from the 18, Ogilvie got five yards to the 23. Shealy wheeled for nine, then 16 more and a first down at the 48. Shealy threw to Pugh for nine and a personal foul penalty pushed it 15 yards deeper to Auburn's 28. Steve Whitman then burst through to AU's eight and Shealy scored from there.

Now it was Auburn in disbelief.

With 8:17 left to play, Shealy also pranced into the endzone with two more conversion points to up Alabama's lead to 25-18.

Auburn, however, still wasn't finished.

Brooks took the kickoff at his five and sped 64 yards before being overtaken by Don McNeal and Jeremiah Castile at Bama's 31. On fourth down from the 24, Trotman's pass was tipped and Mike Locklear barely missed snagging it at the Alabama goal line.

Getting the ball back on a punt, the fighting Tigers moved to the Tide's 38 but ran out of downs. Bama then reduced 3:13 off the clock before punting with only nine seconds left. Two long Trotman passes from his own 12 fell incomplete. Auburn had lost a bitter struggle—a struggle it could have won.

Statistically, Alabama had by far the best of it, getting more first downs, 24-11, and more total yards, 394-249. Whitman was the leading rusher with 107 yards (14 attempts), followed by Shealy's 99

Steadman Shealy, Bama QB, scored 26 points (four touchdowns and a 2-point conversion) in the 1977-78-79 games to rank fourth in the all-time series scoring.

yards and Cribbs' 98. In four games against Alabama, Cribbs rushed for 384 yards in 73 carries (5.3) and scored four touchdowns. His 85-yard run as a sophomore in the 1977 game is the longest from scrimmage in the history of the UA-AU series.

When the polls emerged a few days later, Auburn's near-win had knocked Alabama out of the No. 1 position in the AP poll in favor of Ohio State. The Tide, however, did manage to keep the top spot with UPI.

It was a moot point. Bama defeated Southwest Conference co-champ Arkansas 24-9 in the Sugar Bowl, while the Buckeyes lost 17-16 to Southern Cal in the Rose Bowl.

There was no argument in 1979—Alabama was voted National Champ by both polls.

Statistical Highlights the Alabama-Auburn Series, 1970-79

	ALA	AUB
First downs	229	117
Yards rushing	3023	1258
Yards passing	1123	1041
Total yards	4146	2299
Passes attempted	111	162
Passes completed	61	76
Turnovers	27	25
Punts	37	60
Yards penalized	285	298

Score by Quarters

Alabama	66	64	80	90	—	300
Auburn	17	30	19	66	—	132

Alabama won 8 of the 10 games.

The Birmingham News

Metro South Edition

Year—No. 126 — 90 Pages — 6 Sections — Birmingham, Ala., Thursday, July 17, 1980 — Price 15 Cents

The GOP ticket

REAGAN — BUSH

rama builds to stunning
imax: Finally...it's Bush

Shug Jordan, gentleman coach and noted rebuilder of Auburn football, dies

AUBURN — Ralph "Shug" Jordan, the courtly coach who carried Auburn University football from its lowest depths to its loftiest peaks, died early today at his home here. He was 68.

Jordan's family was at his bedside when the nationally-respected coach died, a victim of acute leukemia.

Jordan was Auburn's head football coach 25 years, taking over the program in 1951 and quickly building it back to national prominence. His 1957 Tigers were named national collegiate football champions.

Jordan, known as the "gentleman coach," retired after the 1975 season, having compiled a record of 175 wins, 83 losses and 7 ties. After stepping down as coach, he was named to the university's Board of Trustees, continuing to serve his alma mater until his death.

Coach Jordan: A man to know and to love
— Page 1C

According to the family's physician, Dr. Jim Mathews, Coach Jordan's leukemia was diagnosed four months ago and developed into an abnormal condition of the bone marrow. He said the treatment for the disease consisted of chemotherapy and blood transfusions to which Jordan failed to satisfactorily respond.

"Coach Jordan had previously been treated at Brookwood Medical Center in Birmingham for heart rhythm difficulties which required a pacemaker."

(See Jordan, Page 12A)

Shug Jordan

The Montgomery Advertiser

d Year—No 144 — A Multimedia Newspaper — Montgomery, Ala. 36102 — Friday Morning, July 18, 1980 — 36 Pages

Shug recalled as gentleman

**TOMMY HICKS
MARK J SKONECKI**
rtiser Staff Writers

Ralph "Shug" Jordan was Auburn University's 70-year-old former War Eagle head football ch and member of the school's Board of stees died at his Auburn home Thursday morning of acute leukemia.

had suffered from the disease for almost four hs. He also had a history of heart trouble Jordan's 25 years as head football coach, and the rd accumulated during that span, placed him platoon as one of the game's greatest.

t more than that, his former coaches, players friends said Jordan was a gentleman.

numerous reactions to the news of Jordan's n poured in, that one word — gentleman — rs surfaced.

He was my coach as a player, he was my head when I was an assistant and we were rival es in the conference." Georgia football coach Dooley said. "Through all that span of 30 he was always a gentleman and my friend

Billy Thames a close friend for more 0 years echoed Dooley's sentiments e was a super man, a fine Christian and a

Related stories, photo, page 19

man of honor and character," he said.

Across the state, Alabama coach Paul "Bear" Bryant, a longtime rival, expressed his sorrow.

"He meant a lot to football and to the state," Bryant said. "I will miss him personally."

Auburn sports officials, too, were deeply saddened.

"I can never say how much he meant to me," said AU head football coach Doug Barfield.

Tiger Athletic Director Lee Hayley was "heartsick."

"He was my coach, and I grew up to be his friend," said Hayley, who played under Jordan from 1961-63.

Jordan, whose nickname some say came from his childhood love of sugar cane, compiled a 175-83-7 record and led the Tigers to a national championship in 1957. He also guided Auburn to 13 bowl appearances.

Born in Selma on Sept. 25, 1910, Jordan attended Auburn where he was a three-sport star, graduating in 1932.

See SHUG, page 1

Jordan's 25 years as head football coach placed him among game's greatest
...he led Tigers to national championship and 12 bowl appearances

Reagan, Bush share final salute at convention

1980
GAME 45

Bear Sees Another Change

Auburn came into the series' 45th game with a football program in complete disarray. A beleagured Doug Barfield had become the latest in a long line of coaches—football and otherwise—to pay the price of following a legend. His remaining time as AU's head coach was down to one game.

Barfield's Tigers had hit rock bottom—literally—sharing the position in the SEC standings usually occupied alone by Vanderbilt. Auburn and the Commodores were winless in league action and had the 10th slot all to themselves. Furthermore, one of Auburn's losses was by a 42-0 score against Tennessee, AU's worst defeat since 1948 when Alabama applied a 55-0 shellacking. To say that there were rumblings among the alumni is an understatement.

The season hadn't been a complete washout for Barfield, however, as the Tigers won all five games against non-conference foes.

Alabama, too, was at low ebb—for Alabama. The Tide had lost two games, both close, but losses nevertheless. There was a 6-3 setback to Mississippi State and a shattering 7-0 defeat to Notre Dame in only the second Bama shutout in 21 years. But with Georgia undefeated, there was no chance for a Tide conference title and a trip to the Sugar Bowl. Win or lose against Auburn, the Tide had a Cotton Bowl invitation and would go to Dallas on New Year's.

MOBILE PRESS REGISTER Sunday, November 9, 1980

Sports

MENTON'S FAREWELL — Page 2
DURAN-LEONARD AGAIN? — Page 7
NFL GAMES TODAY — Page 5

Section **E**

Frosh Walter Lewis keys victory

Tide rolls over Auburn, again — 34-18

Alabama was 8-2-0 by an average of 32-8, while Auburn was 5-5-0 by 22-20. The Crimson Tide was favored by 18 points.

Game time came and the 78,549 fans on hand were treated to a wild first half.

Auburn scored just two minutes into the game after Vernon Blackard recovered a Billy Jackson fumble at Alabama's 21 on the first play from scrimmage. The Tigers made it look easy. George Peoples got four yards, James Brooks five, Brooks three more, and Joe Sullivan another three. Sullivan then tossed a six-yard TD pass to Brooks. Al Del Greco's PAT made it 7-0.

Later in the first period, Alabama tied the score when Jeremiah Castille intercepted a Sullivan swing pass and returned it 16 yards to Auburn's 10. Three plays later from the one, quarterback Walter Lewis skirted around the right side for the score. Peter Kim's conversion made it 7-7 with 6:30 showing on the first period clock.

Auburn came right back. On fourth-and-seven from Bama's 35, Del Greco, a freshman, slammed a 52-yard field goal — the longest in series history — and the War Eagles were back on top, 10-7.

A few moments later, Alabama knew it had a "tiger by the tail" on this particular day, as Auburn was back at the Tide's 30-yard line.

Fumble! And Jim Bob Harris recovered for Bama at the 30. After losing seven yards on a sack, Lewis then pulled off possibly the play of the game when, on a QB keeper, he broke loose on a 73-yard dash before being hauled down by Clifford Toney at Auburn's four. Major Ogilvie rammed it to the two, then into the endzone. It was 14-10, Alabama, after a Kim conversion.

The game appeared to be settling into a punting duel when Bama struck for a quick touchdown. Earl Collins streaked 45 yards to cap a six-play, 80-yard drive with 2:48 left in the first half. Another Kim placement made it 21-10, Tide.

Auburn zipped right back. Led by the slashing runs of Brooks, the Tigers reached the Alabama 42-yard line. After two straight incompletions, Charles Trotman hit Byron Franklin in the corner of the endzone. Touchdown. Peoples got the call to add two more points,

Al Del Greco, Auburn kicker, became the first player to score in four series games (1980-81-82-83), his 25 points is among the fifth highest, and his 52-yard field goal in the '80 game is the series' longest. Del Greco's 236 career points ranks second in Auburn history.

James Brooks, Auburn back, left Auburn with the all-time school rushing record—3,523 yards.

and he did.

Halftime score: Alabama 21, Auburn 18—the most points at this point in the history of these UA-AU games.

The third quarter was a complete standoff. Auburn never got past midfield, while Alabama crossed just once, to AU's 34 where a field goal attempt was way off target.

The fourth quarter rocked along the same way. Neither team's offense could maintain any momentum and, with just over four minutes remaining in the game, the heavily-favored Tide was still clinging to the slim 3-point lead. Then, taking over after a punt at its own 47, Bama finally got something going. Jackson ripped off a 16-yarder to Auburn's 37. Ogilvie gained four and the chains were moved an additional 15 yards because of a face mask penalty. It was a first down at the Tigers' 18. Don Jacobs, in at quarterback, scooted to the 10, then to the seven. On the next play he threw to tight end Bart Krout for a touchdown. Kim flubbed the conversion, but Alabama breathed much easier with a 27-18 lead and only 3:03 left to play.

But Alabama wasn't through. Tommy Wilson intercepted a halfback pass thrown by Brooks and ran it back 19 yards to AU's 32. Just ramming it straight ahead and running out the clock, Bama reached the 14. From there, Jackson plowed through the middle and scored with 17 seconds left in the game.

Final score: Tide 34, Tigers 18.

"Of course I'm glad we won," Coach Bear Bryant told newsmen after the game, "but I hated to see Auburn lose. I hated to see Coach Barfield lose. He's had a lot of tough luck this season. I told him that before the game. He's a good person and an excellent coach."

A few days later, Doug Barfield was fired. Barfield had taken over the coaching duties upon "Shug" Jordan's retirement after the 1975 season and, as so often happens, was unable to fill the over-sized shoes left behind by a legend.

Auburn set its coaching sights on Georgia's Vince Dooley by offering him a reported million (or so) dollars to "come home." Dooley, preparing his No. 1-ranked Bulldogs for a Sugar date with Notre Dame, seriously considered the generous proposal but later turned it down. Auburn then went looking out Wyoming way at a former Dooley player and a former Bryant assistant. They would land him.

Barfield was the 35th SEC head coach that Bryant had seen "move on" for one reason or another since he returned to Alabama in 1958.

In the 1980 Alabama-Auburn game, the Tide led in first downs 17-12, and total yards, 365-242. Lewis was the leading rusher with 98 yards in 19 attempts, followed by teammate Jackson's 88 yards, also in 19 carries. Brooks gained 83 yards in 18 attempts to lead Auburn. Bama completed 5-of-7 passes for 49 yards compared to AU's 5-for-14 for 92 yards. In the turnover department, the losers led, 3-1. Bama's series lead was now 27-17-1.

Alabama went on to blast Baylor 30-2 in the Cotton Bowl to finish with a 10-2-0 season (44-4-0 over the past four years). In the Sugar Bowl, Georgia defeated Notre Dame 17-10 to give the Southeastern Conference three straight National Championships—two by Alabama and one by the Bulldogs.

1981
GAME 46

315 In The Beartrap

It began on a Friday night in September of 1945 and was witnessed by only 7,000 fans at Byrd Stadium on the campus of the University of Maryland.

Thirty-six years and 411 football games later, fate had brought the show to Legion Field in Birmingham, Alabama. Over 78,000 people would be on hand for this one, plus there would be millions more watching on television.

It had been a long, amazing road between the two dates and the two events, and one man — Paul Bryant — had traveled every yard of the way. Now, after all that time and all those games, he was on the threshold of collegiate football's most cherished coaching record — more victories than any other coach in the game's history.

Amos Alonzo Stagg, a wonderful name by all standards, had won 314 games over an amazing 57-year career that stretched from 1890 to 1946. Bryant's teams had also won 314. And now it was Bryant's Crimson Tide against cross-state rival Auburn.

Alabama opened the season with an impressive 24-7 win over LSU on national television. A week later, however, Bama and Bryant suffered the most stunnng upset of the college season, a 24-21 shocker to Georgia Tech at Birmingham. The Yellow Jackets had won only once the year before and would not win another game in '81. It was the consumate upset. One of the many consequences, of course, was to help set the stage for the Alabama-Auburn game to be the vehicle for Bryant's ultimate triumph.

After the loss to Tech, the Tide rebounded by beating Kentucky, Vanderbilt and Ole Miss, but "The 315 Express" once again made an unexpected stop when Southern Mississippi pulled off a 13-13 tie. Mississippi State was defeated, tying Bryant for second place on the all-time win list with Glenn "Pop" Warner at 313. Warner coached between 1895 and 1938. That brought the season to November 14 and an Alabama-Penn State matchup at University Park, Pennsylvania. The Tide won, 31-16, and Bryant moved ahead of Warner and had caught Stagg.

Auburn and a possible "315" was next.

The Tigers, under new head coach Pat Dye, who was a Bryant assistant for nine years (1965-1973), got off to a rocky beginning. After a struggling 24-16 win over TCU, the War Eagles lost three tough games—24-21 to Wake Forest, 10-7 to Tennessee and 17-3 to Nebraska. AU won four of its next six games to enter "braggin' rights" time with an all-even 5-5-0 record. Alabama was 8-1-1 and ranked No. 4 in the nation.

Bryant got "315."

But, oh how Auburn made him and his team work for it; sweat for it. Auburn, in fact, *should* have won the ball game. Bryant, most likely, would say the same thing. Dye did say it. After all, the Tigers got inside Alabama's 10-yard line on four different occasions, only to come away with just 10 points from the opportunities. And then there was a devastating penalty that went a long way in swinging things Bama's way.

Alabama received the opening kickoff, soon punted and had to chase down Auburn's Chuck Clanton after a 55-yard return to the 13. On fourth down from the eight, Al Del Greco missed a field goal try.

The Tide took over at the 20 and, after two plays, quarterback Alan Gray turned left end and got away on a 63-yard gainer to AU's 21. Five plays later, it was third-and-goal at the one and Gray sneaked over for the touchdown. After Peter Kim converted, Alabama led, 7-0.

Late in the first quarter, Auburn quarterback Joe Sullivan (brother of Heisman Trophy winner Pat) completed a 31-yard pass to Ed West to Alabama's 19. Driving on down to the eight, where it was first-and-goal, Coach Dye, shuffling three quarterbacks in and out of the game, now had freshman Ken Hobby at the controls. On first down, Hobby threw an ill-advised pass into the endzone. It was intercepted by Tommy Wilcox.

"Drat! Drat! Drat!" screamed Auburn fans.

The 7-0 game rocked along until four minutes remained in the first

MARYLAND MAULS GUILFORD, 60 TO 6

COLLEGE PARK, Md., Sept. 82 —The University of Maryland, scoring almost at will, opened its 1945 football campaign tonight by soundly trouncing an outclassed Guilford College team, 60 to 6, before an estimated 6,000 persons.

Coach Paul (Bear) Bryant's Terrapins, with a starting lineup that included eight players from the disbanded North Carolina Pre-Flight School, tallied in every period, displaying a rugged line that kept Guilford away from the goal on all but one occasion.

This two-paragraph story appeared in *The Birmingham News* on Saturday, September 29, 1945. It was Bear Bryant's first coaching victory.

Inside today's Sports section...
The game...the players...
the coaches in win number **315**

The Birmingham News
Metro Edition
92nd Year—No. 260   270 Pages — 19 Sections   Birmingham, Ala., Sunday, November 29, 1981   Price: 50 cents

Scoreboard lights shine as Bryant walks into history books with dignity

---

Paul Bryant: 37 historic winning years   Sunday, November 29, 1981

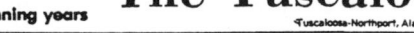

The Tuscaloosa News
Tuscaloosa-Northport, Alabama

Special Souvenir Section

Bryant secures 315th; breaks Stagg's mark

By AL BROWNING
News Sports Editor

Pat Dye, Auburn Head Coach, was on Bear Bryant's Alabama staff for nine years (1965-1973). Dye brought an impressive head coaching record of 54-23-1 (.699) from East Carolina and Wyoming.

half with Auburn at its own 37-yard line. *Wham!* Fullback George Peoples hit off left tackle, broke clean and was gone—63 yards—touchdown. Del Greco's conversion was perfect and, just that quickly, it was tied at 7-7. That's the way it stood at intermission.

On the Tide's first possession of the second half, it was third-and-short at midfield. Auburn held . . . but on the play, the Tigers were guilty of a face mask violation. Instead of an Alabama punt, Alabama was first down at the AU 35-yard line. The Tide quickly advanced on down to the 21 but were penalized five yards. Then came a bit of trickery. Quarterback Ken Coley got the snap, took a few steps back as to pass, and then shoveled a little "basketball pass" to tight end Jesse Bendross who grabbed it at the line of scrimmage and wormed his way to a touchdown. After another Kim conversion, Alabama was back on top, 14-7.

A little later, Auburn punted and receiver Joey Jones fumbled the kick at his own 40. AU's Clanton swatted the ball and, after a mad scramble, Auburn recovered way back at Bama's two-yard line. On second down, Lionel James cracked over for the touchdown, Del Greco kicked good and, with eight minutes left in the third quarter, Auburn had again pulled even at 14-14.

Late in the period, a "replay" occurred when Jones fumbled another Auburn punt and Mike Hicks recovered this one at Bama's 33. After grinding it down to the two, Del Greco finally hit a field goal, sending the Tiger's into a 17-14 lead and Legion Field into a tizzy.

According to the television announcers, that old gridiron ally, *momentum,* had swung to the War Eagles' side.

"Horrors!" thought Alabama fans. It was now a distinct possibility that "315" might have to wait literally until "next year". That would be five weeks away when Alabama would play in the Cotton Bowl against Texas.

But, as so many times in the recent years of this rivalry, Alabama got off the floor with fire in its eyes. After taking the kickoff, the Tide was faced with a crucial third-and-six at its own 29. It was a big first down when quarterback Walter Lewis hit Bendross with a pass good for 12 yards to the 41. Working the ball 21 more yards to Auburn's 38, Lewis heaved one into the endzone. Touchdown. Bendross was there to get his second TD of the day. With just over 10 minutes remaining in the game, Kim's conversion made the score 21-17 and Alabama fans everywhere could now smell "The Record."

Frustrated Auburn, its golden opportunities earlier in the afternoon now gone for good, most likely could also see the "handwriting."

Three minutes later, Alabama scored again, on a 15-yard scamper by Linnie Patrick. Kim tacked on the final point with seven minutes still left to play. It was just a sparring exibition from that point until the final horn.

Final: Alabama 28, Auburn 17. Bryant finally had "315" in the old beartrap.

"Paul (Bear) Bryant looked like a man who just had 315 tons lifted off his back," was the way Jimmy Bryan of the *Birmingham News* put it. And no doubt that's the way Bryant did feel.

The man who was born in a little place in Arkansas that somebody tagged as Moro Bottom, and the man who played his high school football for the Fordyce (Arkansas) Redbugs, was now getting calls from Presidents. President Ronald Reagan phoned in his congratulations, along with former President Jimmy Carter.

Back on September 28, 1945, Bryant's Maryland Terrapins had clobbered Guilford College of North Carolina by a score of 60-6. On November 28, 1981, Bryant's Alabama Crimson Tide had defeated Auburn University, 28-17. In between—at Maryland, Kentucky, Texas A & M and Alabama—there had been 313 other victories in 46 different cities in 23 states and the District of Columbia.

Auburn had played tough, leading in first downs (15-14), total offensive yards (311-279) and possession time (31:30-28:30). Five Tide turnovers (four lost fumbles and an interception) kept the Tigers in the ball game. But, it was Bama's defense that kept Auburn from piling up a bunch of points after those turnovers.

With "315" secured, Alabama lost in the Cotton Bowl. The Tide led Texas 10-0 going into the fourth quarter and seemed on their way to giving Bryant another national record with seven bowl wins in seven years. But the stubborn Longhorns rallied with 14 points, gave Bama a safety, and escaped with a 14-12 victory. Alabama still hadn't beaten Texas in eight games dating back to 1906.

Alabama finished the season with a 9-2-1 record and a final No. 6 ranking. Auburn was 5-6-0.

1982
GAME 47

Bedlam In B'ham

Nine years, they had waited for this. Nine years of humility, frustration, agony and emptiness, nine years of having to plug their ears, and hold their tongues while those big-mouths from across the state could gloat.

Don Kausler, Jr.
The Birmingham News
Sunday, November 28, 1982

Auburn had not beaten its biggest rival since the "Punt Bama Punt" game in 1972. And this was 1982.

Among the pre-season publications which picked Alabama to capture the '82 national championship were *Pigskin Preview* and *Lindy's,* while virtually all of the others pegged the Crimson Tide among its top five. Auburn could hardly be found in anybody's Top 20. However, *Playboy* had the Tigers (14th) rated over the Tide (18th).

Alabama warmed up with wins over Georgia Tech, Ole Miss, Vanderbilt and Arkansas State, was ranked fourth and ready for a national television showdown with No. 3 Penn State at Legion Field. The Tide won 42-21 and moved into the runner-up position behind Washington.

Auburn's schedule that year called for only two games outside the state. The Tigers struggled past Wake Forest 28-10 and Southern Miss 21-19, before taking care of an ordinary Tennessee team 24-14. At Jordan-Hare for the fourth straight week, Nebraska came in and threw a 41-7 spoiler on the fun. Playing two more home games, the Tigers held Kentucky and Georgia Tech TD-less to post 18-3 and 24-0 victories. Auburn had never played six straight games on the Plains.

The rollin' Tide next went to Knoxville for a date with 2-2-1 UT, but the Vols sprang a stunning 35-28 ambush party, toppling Alabama down to seventh place. Then came wins over Cincinnati and Mississippi State, but back-to-back setbacks to LSU and Southern Mississippi. The loss to the Golden Eagles dropped Alabama from the *Associated Press* poll for the first time since October 2, 1976 — an amazing string of 90 straight listings.

The Tigers were next.

Auburn passed the season's first road test with a 35-17 win over Mississippi State at Starkeville, before losing a close 19-17 decision to the Gators at Gainesville. Returning home, AU ripped Rutgers 30-7, but lost a 19-14 heartbreaker to No. 1-ranked Georgia in a game it very well could have won.

The Crimson Tide was next.

Both teams were 7-3-0, marking the first time ever that they met with identical records. Alabama's average score was 30-18, Auburn's 22-15, and over 78,000 crammed Legion Field under cloudy skies, while millions more across the country tuned in via ABC-TV.

And what a drama-packed afternoon of football they'd behold.

Auburn, on its second possession, faced a fourth-and-one at its 48, and Coach Pat Dye said, "Let's go for it!" Fullback Gregg Pratt slammed off left guard. He didn't make it. And Bama would take full advantage of the early decision, moving the distance in only six plays.

Led by wide receiver Joey Jones' 13-yard run on a reverse, and a seven-yard run by Ricky Moore, Alabama was first down at the 22. After an incomplete pass, quarterback Walter Lewis fired one into the endzone to Jones for a controversial touchdown, as many thought Jones was out of the endzone when he caught the ball. But it stood as good, Peter Kim added the PAT, and it was 7-0.

The Tide kicked off, quickly forced a punt, covered 4l yards in only four plays, and was first down at AU's 28. Halfback Joe Carter took a pitchout, was cracked hard by Mark Dorminey, and as the ball popped into the air, it was picked off by cornerback Tim Drinkard who raced 60 yards to Alabama's 14 before being hauled down by quarterback Lewis.

On third down, still at the 14, Lionel James, on a perfectly executed draw play, juked past end Mike Pitts, then broke from the grasp of cornerback Jeremiah Castille at the four, and staggered across the goal line. Al Del Greco converted and it was 7-7 late in the first quarter.

Midway through the second period, Alabama took a 10-7 lead. Back-to-back passes from Lewis to Jesse Bendross covering 49 yards kindled an advance to the Tigers' 26. On fourth down from the 20, Kim kicked a field goal 08:30 before intermission.

Another Tide turnover later resulted in another Tiger touchdown.

From his 24, Lewis was belted as he threw and AU safety Bob Harris intercepted the wobbler and returned it back to the 24. Quarterback Randy Campbell hit Mike Edwards over the middle for a 16-yard gain down to the eight. On third-and-goal from the three, Campbell fought his way in for the score. Del Greco made it 14-10 with 02:55 left on the clock.

Alabama, seemingly in no hurry, used its ground game, until faced with a second-and-10 at its 42 with the clock down to 00:26. Reserve quarterback Ken Coley then completed a 19-yard strike to Darryl White at the Auburn 39. Coley lost a yard. Lewis replaced Coley and hit White with a sideline pass at the l6 with 00:02 left. Kim came on and kicked a field goal.

Halftime: Tigers 14, Tide 13 — their first series lead at intermission in 13 years.

Alabama's Paul Ott Carruth returned the second half kickoff 31 yards out to the 34 and a snappy, six-play scoring series looked easy. It was Lewis to Bendross for 12 yards up to the 46, Lewis to Mike Moore for another 12 to Auburn's 42, Lewis to Bendross for 11 to the 31, Moore to the 24, Moore to the 14, and Carruth for the rushing touchdown. It remained 19-14 when Lewis' pass to Carruth failed to connect.

Auburn knocked out a couple of first downs before punting to the six. The Tide then went 93 yards in 14 plays, but came up two feet shy and forced to settle for the shortest field goal in series history. Along the way, Bama was fourth-and-one at its 48 before pulling off some "back yard" trickery to gain the all-important first down. Lewis lined up in punt formation, moved up behind the center into the Wishbone, then shifted back into punt formation. The last shift pulled AU offsides to keep the drive alive.

Still, though, the Tigers saved themselves — and the game — with a sterling goal line stand, stopping Bama just short of

Auburn ends a nine-year wait

seven points. Kim came on for a successful field goal and a 22-14 lead (instead of 26-14) with 01:19 remaining in the third quarter.

Entering the final period, Alabama led 23-7 in first downs, and 445-132 in total yards, but had only an 8-point lead.

After an exchange of punts, Auburn cranked up. From his 34, a freshman running back — No. 34 Vincent "Bo" Jackson — broke outside and sped 53 yards to the 13. But Bama threw up a stand of its own and, on fourth down from the six, Del Greco kicked a field goal.

Score: UA 22, AU 17. Time left: 09:06.

After the ensuing kickoff, Auburn forced a punt and began once again from its 34.

Time: 07:06.

Campbell got things clicking with a 12-yard toss to Chris Woods at the 46, but was soon faced with a fourth-and-one situation at the Tide 45. Jackson got three. On second down, Campbell was sacked for six back at the 46, bringing up a big third-and-14. Campbell drilled one to Edwards good for 16 yards and a first down at the 30 with 03:19 remaining.

Then came *the* play.

Campbell threw over the middle intended for Woods, but Castille intercepted. The officials, however, ruled *pass interference.*

Auburn's ball, first down at the Bama nine!

An illegal procedure penalty cost the Tigers five yards back to the 14. Jackson gained five. Campbell then swung a pass out to Bo, who plowed down to the one. Jackson then scored. It was now 23-22, the clock was stopped at 02:26, and a 2-point conversion try was no good.

But who cared? Who was even watching? War Eagle! Auburn's portion of the old stadium had gone totally berserk.

The wild-eyed Tigers kicked off and Harris quickly made his second interception of the day, this one at Bama's 31, with 01:45 to play.

Ball game. But wait! Not quite.

On third-and-one at the 22, Jackson fumbled and Alabama's Russ Wood recovered. The Tide moved to their 47, but a sack and an intentional grounding foul finally sealed AU's victory.

The final score in 1972: Auburn 17, Alabama 16.
The final score in 1982: Auburn 23, Alabama 22.

"Auburn fans counted down as the final seconds ticked off the scoreboard clock, and when the game ended, a mass of fans swarmed onto the field and began tearing down the goal posts....A portion of the goal post, strapped to the top of a car, was seen heading off into the sunset....Inside, Dye told his players how much they owed their fans — reminded them how much they had helped them on the field — and sent the Tigers back out for a curtain call....'I've never seen Auburn fans quite like this before,' said Harris. 'It's something I'll look back on for the rest of my life,'" reported the *News'* Don Driver.

Ed Hinton of *The Atlanta Journal-Constitution* wrote, "The emotion rocked Legion Field so relentlessly following the game that 10 minutes after Auburn's players had filed jubilantly into their locker room, they were sent back onto the field, into a sea of orange and blue, for a curtain call....Players and old men wept openly and joyously as they embraced one another and repeated again and again, 'It's about time.'"

It was Auburn's second big Birmingham win in two days. On Friday, the basketball team pulled off a 63-61 upset of UAB, who had finished in the NCAA's Final Eight just eight months earlier.

Back to football, Neal Sims of the *News* wrote, "There was no retirement talk from Alabama Coach Paul Bryant this week, though the question was raised after his team's 23-22 loss to Auburn Saturday. 'I'm damn tired of talking about my future plans,' said Bryant. 'I don't mean to be ugly. I'll think about that on my way home.'"

Coach Bryant's comment on the agonizing afternoon was, "From where I stood, it was an entertaining game — but I can't say that I was entertained."

He couldn't have been, especially after viewing the final stat sheet, showing his team way out front in first downs 27-11, and in total yards by a wide 507-257 margin.

Pat Dye was the first of Coach Bryant's former pupils to beat him in 31 games over a 12-year period. Overall, the professor was 41-6-0 (.872) against his pupils.

The three straight defeats was a first for Alabama football in 25 years, dating back to 1957 when TCU, Tennessee and Mississippi State turned the trick.

Bryant's lingering retirement rumors became reality less than three weeks later. It became official on December 15. Ray Perkins, former Alabama end (1964-65-66) and currently coach of the New York Giants, would replace him.

Both Auburn and Alabama had a game remaining in '82 — the Tigers against Boston College in the Tangerine Bowl at Orlando, and the Tide against Illinois in the Liberty Bowl at Memphis.

This was the 15th occasion that the Tigers and Tide would go bowling the same year and, oddly enough, the first time that they *both* would win.

On December 18, AU topped BC 33-26 to finish with a surprising 9-3-0 record and a No. 14 ranking.

Then, on a bitter cold Wednesday night, December 29 in what became known as the "Bear Bowl," Bama defeated Illinois 21-15 in Coach Bryant's 425th and final game. It was also his 323rd victory.

Maybe it was a headline in *The Commercial Appeal* (Memphis) that said it best: "Cheers, Tears Follow 'Bear' Into Hibernation."

Four Wednesdays later — January 26, 1983 — Paul Bryant passed away.

And maybe it was Woody Hayes who most understood it. He said simply, "Bear coached himself to death."

The Birmingham News

93rd Year—No. 318 · 96 Pages — 12 Sections · Birmingham, Ala., **Wednesday**, January 26, 1983 · Price: **25 Cents**

Heart attack ends life of legendary Bear Bryant

From staff reports

Paul William "Bear" Bryant, who carried the University of Alabama to the heights of football greatness, died this afternoon in a Tuscaloosa hospital.

The 69-year-old Bryant, who retired just last month after 25 years as the Crimson Tide's head coach, reportedly suffered a massive heart attack shortly after noon while receiving an X-ray at Druid City Hospital.

At 12:24 p.m., Bryant had a sudden cardio-pulmonary arrest. Resuscitation measures were carried out — including the insertion of a pacemaker into his chest — but all measures were unsuccessful. Bryant was pronounced dead at 1:30 p.m.

Cause of death was listed as a massive coronary occlusion — a blockage that interferes with coronary arteries supplying the heart with blood.

Lucy Jordan, a spokesperson for the hospital, confirmed Bryant's death.

Further details were to be released at a news conference later this afternoon.

Officials at Hayes Chapel Funeral Home said they would be handling the funeral arrangements.

Bryant had checked into the hospital Tuesday night with chest pains. Bryant's physician, Dr William Hill, told *The Birmingham News* that night that Bryant had been placed in the coronary care unit and that he was under observation "as a precautionary measure."

Earlier today, a hospital spokesman said Bryant spent a restful Tuesday night, and Hill said Bryant's vital signs were stable and that his electrocardiogram appeared normal.

In Montgomery, Lt. Gov. Bill Baxley, an Alabama alumnus and graduate of its law school, broke the news to the Senate at 2:10 p.m.

A moment later, Sen. Ryan DeGraffenried from Tuscaloosa rose and asked that the flag atop the state capitol be lowered to half staff "in recognition of this great man."

"He probably contributed more to the University of Alabama and the education of young men in this state than anyone I've ever known."

Legislators, reporters and state employees had been huddling in the halls and quietly breaking the news to each other before Baxley's announcement in the Senate.

"I'm shocked," said Sen. Charles Bishop of Jasper. "I wish we could adjourn. I really do. My head's just not on straight."

Bishop, who was born in Moro Bottom, Ark., which is also Bryant's birthplace, said Bryant was a close personal friend. "I feel like I've lost part of my family."

Bryant stepped down Dec. 15 as the Tide's head coach, then won his final game, a 21-15 victory over Illinois in the Dec. 29 Liberty Bowl. Ray Perkins, an All-America end for Bryant in the mid-60s, was named as his successor, and Bryant had planned to remain on as athletic director for at least a few months.

Bryant: A winner's journey

By Clyde Bolton
News sports writer

"Arkansas is not my home," Paul Bryant told some friends one day. "Alabama is. Alabama is where I've bought my cemetery lot."

Indeed, the Alabama days were the peak ones for Paul William "Bear"...

Thursday, January 27, 1983

The Tuscaloosa News

2 sections, 32 pages · Tuscaloosa-Northport, Alabama · ★★ 25¢

Warmer Friday
A chance of rain today. Partly cloudy tonight and Friday, warmer Friday. High today mid-40s, low tonight low 30s, high Friday mid-50s. (See details on Page 2.)

City to bid Bryant a final farewell

The loss is great

Editorial

One of these days before long a lot of us are going to realize Paul William Bryant really has gone.

And the missing will begin.

There will be a great deal to miss, far more than most of us likely have thought about. The man has meant so much to so many for so long that somehow it is difficult to believe he is dead.

But he is.

The loss is great.

The Bryant family has lost a loving husband, father, grandfather and brother. We extend our deepest sympathy.

The University of Alabama has lost its most prominent son, our community and state our most revered citizen, college foot...

...others that few of us will ever know about.

And our nation has lost a true hero, a genuine manifestation of the classic American dream. For Bryant started as a humble farm boy in Moro Bottom, Ark., and through ability, brains, courage, toughness and drive achieved fame and fortune of a degree difficult for most of us more ordinary mortals to comprehend.

He made most of it happen his way, too, and surely there is something to be said for that.

Paul William Bryant was...

Cortege will pass Capstone

By JACK WHEAT
News Staff Writer

Tuscaloosans will have a chance to pay their last respects to Paul W. "Bear" Bryant Friday morning as his funeral cortege wends its way past Bryant-Denny Stadium and the athletic complex the legendary coach developed in a quarter century at the University of Alabama.

Bryant, the Arkansas boy who became a towering figure in football and in the state of Alabama, died suddenly Wednesday of a heart attack as doctors were trying to determine the cause of the chest pains that sent him to Druid City Hospital Tuesday night.

Bryant, 69, was pronounced dead at the hospital at 1:30 p.m. Wednesday. Doctors said the cause of death was a massive...

1983
GAME 48

The Pat & Bo Show

Recently, only two people stood as possible threats in keeping Pat Dye and Auburn from ruling the Southeastern Conference. They were Alabama's Bear Bryant and Georgia's Herschel Walker. Both, however, were suddenly gone — Bryant to that great coaches clinic in the sky, and Walker to something they called the USFL and to some team called the New Jersey Generals. It was an expensive attempt at selling the U.S. on springtime semi-pro football. The U.S. wouldn't buy. But any fan on the street could have told them that.

Dye was left holding all the cards, and his deck included the league's ace-in-the-hole in sophomore running back Bo Jackson, along with a stockpile of big and fast talent on both sides of the scrimmage line.

Who, afterall, was left to challenge Dye and his super recruiting ability? He now had the picks of the litters from the states of Alabama *and* Georgia.

In the annual poll of SEC sports information directors, sponsored by *The Birmingham News*, AU received seven of a possible nine votes to capture the league title and placed eight players (four each on offense and defense) on the all-SEC team.

Pre-season publications such as *The Sporting News, Street & Smith* and *Playboy* pegged the Tigers as the nation's top team, while the *Associated Press* started them out at No. 5.

The Tide's average poll position was about 15th.

AU opened with a 24-3 win over Southern Miss even though "looking ahead" a week to a big home bout with No. 3-ranked Texas in a "Battle of the Wishbones." The Steers won 20-7 enroute to an 11-0-0 regular season.

Auburn regrouped and topped Tennessee, FSU, Kentucky

and Georgia Tech, then Mississippi State, Florida, Maryland and Georgia by an average score of 31-17.

The country's top three teams *(AP)* were now Nebraska, Texas and the Tigers.

Among Ray Perkins' multitude of changes soon after his arrival in Tuscaloosa was dropping the wishbone offense in favor of a pro set, and the dismantling of "The Tower" overlooking the practice fields.

Breaking fast from the gate, Bama topped Georgia Tech, Ole Miss, Vanderbilt and Memphis State by a 148-44 combined score and, suddenly, was ranked No. 3 behind Nebraska and the Longhorns. Auburn was seventh.

Next was a trip to State College, Pa., to play unranked Penn State on national television. It turned into a horror show. The Tide trailed 7-34, staged a fantastic rally to pull within 28-34, then scored what would have been the winning touchdowns in the final seconds — only to have it nullified by an *unbelievably* bad call by an eastern official. Actually, it was a carbon copy of what had happened there a year earlier in a 27-24 Penn State win over Nebraska, which directly cost the 'Huskers a national title. In favor of whom? Penn State. Is there little wonder why they call it "Happy Valley?"

For the Tide, it was a devastating defeat, and the following week they lost a wild 41-34 shootout to Tennessee at Birmingham. That was followed by a 35-18 win over Mississippi State, a 32-26 loss to LSU, a 28-16 a win over Southern Miss (UA's 600th on the football field), then a 20-13 loss to Boston College in some Massachusetts rain, sleet and snow.

Auburn's annual trip to Birmingham got off to a lousy start. On Friday night at the Birmingham-Jefferson Civic Center Coliseum, Gene Bartow's UAB basketball Blazers beat Sonny Smith's Tigers, featuring none other than Charles Barkley and Chuck Persons, by a 69-62 overtime score before a crowd of 16,803 — then the biggest basketball crowd in state history.

It was now Tiger-Tide time — No. 3 vs. No. 19.
AU was 9-1-0 by an average score of 28-16 (+12).
UA was 7-3-0 by an average score of 32-20 (+12).
AU was on the boards as a 6-point favorite.

As far as the SEC race was concerned, an Auburn win and it would be the Tigers' title outright. An Alabama win and the title

MOBILE PRESS REGISTER Sunday, December 4, 1983

Sports

Blue Devils won 3A title with strong performance
—*See story on Page 10*

Section **D**

Bo Jackson gains 256 against Bama

Auburn is alone atop the SEC!

would be shared by the Tide, Auburn and Georgia.

And, just like last year, AU-UA staged another nerve-wracker that gave a national television audience (ABC) and a drenched Legion Field crowd of 77,310 all they could ask for.

In 1982, Auburn won 23-22. In 1983, Auburn won 23-20.

It was scoreless early in the second quarter, Jackson streaked 69 yards, and the Tigers were up by seven.

Alabama led by four late in the third period, Jackson streaked 71 yards, and the Tigers were up by three.

Jackson carried the ball 18 other times for 116 more yards.

After Jackson's first long run, Bama answered with a six-play, 80-yard drive to tie the count. The key plays were runs of 13 and 11 yards by freshman tailback Kerry Goode, a nine-yarder by Ricky Moore, plus an 18-yard pass from Walter Lewis to split end Joey Jones, then a 20-yard TD strike from Lewis to Jones. Van Tiffin's conversion made it 7-7 with 11:42 left in the first half.

Midway through the second period, Auburn began from its 41. Jackson got off runs of 13 and 18 yards to spark a march to the 12, where things stalled. Al Del Greco kicked a field goal at 05:35, giving his team a 10-7 lead.

Once again, though, the Tide responded, driving 80 yards in a dozen plays to regain the lead. Along the way, Lewis broke off a 22-yarder and Joe Carter an 11-yarder. And it was a Lewis-to-Carter TD toss of three yards to cap the series. Tiffin converted.

Halftime: Alabama, 14, Auburn 10.

The Tigers received to begin the second half. Keyed by three Jackson runs totaling 26 yards, Lionel James' 12-yard burst, and a 20-yard pass from quarterback Randy Campbell to Chris Woods, Auburn worked its way to Bama's nine before settling for another Del Greco field goal to make it 14-13.

Alabama then missed an excellent chance to take a 21-13

Tigers weather Tide storm

When it rained at Legion Field Saturday, it poured. Auburn quarterback Randy Campbell tries not to let the wet bother him; however, he sprints around right end after blocker David Jordan cuts down Alabama defensive tackle Jon Hand.

...But it couldn't happen without Bo

lead. On first down at its 20 after the ensuing kickoff, Coach Perkins called for "a bomb" and it caught the Tiger defense totally off guard. Jones streaked down the sideline and was about 20 yards in the clear — but Lewis overthrew him.

Later in the third period, AU had UA backed up and punting against the wind from deep in its own territory. Terry Sanders hit a short one that took a 14-yard bounce *backwards*, resulting in an 18-yard kick. The Tigers reached the 17, and Del Greco's third field goal of the game gave his team a 16-14 lead.

But the Crimson struck right back. Three plays after the kickoff, Moore exploded off tackle and raced 57 yards for a touchdown and a 20-16 edge with just over two minutes left in the third quarter. Going for two, Lewis' pass fell incomplete.

Sophomore Bo Jackson buried Bama in 1983 with 256 yards rushing, including touchdown runs of 69 and 71 yards.

Boom! On first down after the kickoff from his 29, Bo Jackson electrified the audience with his 71-yard dash — the sixth longest scoring run from scrimmage in the series. Del Greco converted and it was now 23-20, Auburn.

It had been announced in the third quarter over the stadium's public address system that there was a tornado watch and a heavy line of thunderstorms in west Jefferson County that were heading east towards Legion Field.

And as the fourth quarter arrived, so did a deluge.

"What would have happened at the game Saturday if a tornado threat had really become official?" the *News* reported. "'Something would have been done' answered David Housel, sports information for host Auburn....'We had four men constantly in touch with the weather bureau and the Civil Defense'....Would the game have been stopped? 'The game,' Housel replied, 'was in the hands of the game officials. They would have been informed of what the Civil Defense recommended. We kept the officials well informed of the situation.'"

There were no serious threats on the rain-soaked carpet throughout the last period of play. However, with 02:04 showing on the clock, Alabama was first down at the Auburn 45, but a Lewis pass was tipped by AU's Tommy Powell, and Victor Beasley made a shoestring interception. The Tide's offense never returned to action.

And Auburn could officially whoop it up over its first back-to-back series triumphs in 13 years. There was also celebration over its first Southeastern Conference championship in 26 years.

Alabama led in first downs 19-15, and in passing yards 62-39, while the Tigers were ahead 355-289 in rushing yards and 394-348 in total yards. Auburn also led in penalty yards 25-15, and time of possession, 32 minutes to 28.

Amazingly, three backs — Bo Jackson, Terry Goode and Ricky Moore — rushed for a total of 507 yards in 49 carries for a super 10.3 average. Jackson, of course, led with a series-shattering 256 yards, topping Bobby Marlow's old mark of 233 yards which had stood since the 1951 game (32 years). Goode got 142 yards and Moore 109.

Al Del Greco also set a series record by becoming the first player to score in four games. He kicked for 24 points (six field goals and six conversions) in the 1980-81-82-83 games.

In two years against the Tide, sophomore Jackson had rushed for 370 yards in 37 attempts — exactly 10 yards per carry — had scored three touchdowns and gotten off runs of 71, 69 and 53 yards.

Alabama's series lead was now 28-19-1.

For the second year in a row both teams went bowling and both won. It would be the unranked Crimson Tide against No. 6-rated SMU (10-1-0) in the Sun Bowl at El Paso, and Auburn would play Michigan in the Sugar.

Alabama upset the Mustangs 28-7 to finish 8-4-0 and a final ranking of 15th.

Here was the scenario that January 2 which would bring a national championship celebration to Toomer's Corner:

Auburn Drowns The Tide, 23-20

- Georgia (ranked 7th) had to beat Texas (2nd) in the Cotton Bowl that afternoon.
- Miami (5th) had to beat Nebraska (1st) that night in the Orange Bowl — but not *too* convincingly.
- Then, of course, Auburn (3rd) had to beat Michigan (8th) *convincingly* that night in the Sugar Bowl.

Four of the five happened.

Georgia nipped Texas 10-9, with a touchdown at 03:22.

Miami nipped Nebraska 31-30, on a missed 2-pointer by the 'Huskers at 00:48.

Auburn nipped Michigan 9-7, with a field goal at 00:23.

It was now in the unpredictable minds of the voters.

Glenn Sheeley of *The Atlanta Journal* reported, "After the game, coach Pat Dye preached a fiery and well-documented appeal for the national championship for his Tigers.

"Speaking after the Sugar Bowl and during the final minutes of the Orange, Dye said, 'If Miami beats Nebraska, then Auburn should be No. 1 — it's cut and dried. If you're going to have a No. 1 team in America, and you're going to put any credibility at all in the (full season's) schedule, well, I happen to have my facts here before me.

"'Our opponents this year have a combined winning percentage of 69.5. Texas's opponents, 59 percent. Nebraska's 52 percent.'

"And then he spoke with relish and emphasis: 'And *Miami's* opponents had a combined winning percentage of *51* percent....If Miami beats Nebraska 38-10, Miami deserves the national championship. But Miami won only 31-30, when Nebraska failed on a two-point conversion attempt.'"

Eight of Auburn's opponents went to bowl games that year. Miami had four.

Sports

The Atlanta Journal — TUESDAY, JANUARY 3, 1984

WHO'S NO. 1?

□ The University of Miami, ranked No. 4 and No. 5 in the final regular-season polls, claims the national championship with a stunning upset of top-ranked...

Hurricanes stake their claim by shocking Nebraska 31-30

By Glenn Sheeley
Staff Writer

MIAMI — At 1:45 Tuesday morning, the crowd at midfield at the Orange Bowl demanded to see its new guru. The assemblage pleaded for a chance to toast this man who looks like he should be your neighborhood butcher but today just happens to be the most envied man in college football.

"Howard ... Howard ... Howard," they chanted into the public address system.

Howard Schnellenberger, whose mind still savored a freeze frame of Miami defensive back Ken Calhoun poking away a Turner Gill pass for running back Jeff Smith on a two-point conversion try by Nebraska with 48 seconds left in the 50th Orange Bowl Classic, stepped to the microphone on this, the giddiest night of his life. His hoarse voice, coming out in deep, crackling drawls, became amplified into the balmy evening air.

"We're No. 1, we're No. 1," the Miami Hurricanes' coach said. "No doubt about it."

No doubt about it. Not here anyway. Not after the Hurricanes, 10-point underdogs to what many had considered the finest college football team assembled since they

See ORANGE 2D ▶

To Auburn and Pat Dye, it's all cut and dried: Tigers earned it

---

The voting wasn't even close.

The *AP* poll showed Miami with 1169 points, Nebraska 1109 and Auburn 1079. Fifty-eight members cast ballots and 47 first place votes went to the Hurricanes.

Maybe it was because Nebraska had been tagged with one of those kiss-of-death *"all-time greatest team"* labels. Why? Well, meditate over these nine 'Husker scores of that year — 84-13, 72-29, 69-19, 67-13, 63-7, 56-20, 51-25, 44-6 and 42-10. Their regular season victory margin was 52-16, on the average.

When time boiled down to that two-point conversion attempt for the national championship, the Nebraska football team had amassed 654 points....

1984
GAME 49

"We Beat The Sugar Out Of Auburn"

The 1984 *Associated Press'* pre-season poll was announced in August 26 Sunday sports sections all across the country and Auburn was ranked No. 1. Miami, last year's national champions, was 10th. They would meet the next night in Kickoff Classic II at Giants Stadium in East Rutherford, N.J.

The Hurricanes hopped on top early, then hung on for a 20-18 victory. UM leaped all the way to first place and AU tumbled all the way to eighth.

Auburn also lost its next game, 34-27 to Texas at Austin, and the fans' anticipated "Super Season" was only a memory. But the Tigers rebounded with six straight wins, including one of their all-time football thrillers — 42-41 over Florida State at Tallahassee. With a 6-2-0 record, AU had worked back to 11th, but Florida ruined the surge with a 24-3 triumph.

Frustration? Yep. And the Tigers took it out on the University of Cincinnati by a 60-0 score, the school's most lopsided win in 52 years, dating back to a 77-0 rout of Erskine in 1932. AU then took Georgia again, 21-12, and Alabama was next.

Alabama lost to Boston College and Heisman Trophy winner Doug Flutie for the second straight year, this time 38-31 at Birmingham. UA then journeyed to Atlanta for its 52nd and final game with Georgia Tech in an off-and-on series which began in 1902. The Jackets, only 3-8-0 last year, pulled off a big 16-6 surprise, and the Tide was 0-2 for the first time 28 years (1956).

Alabama later defeated Southwest Louisiana, Penn State, Mississippi State and Cincinnati, but lost to Vanderbilt, Georgia, Tennessee and LSU. Auburn was next and was ready to invoke even more misery upon Bama boosters.

Florida led the Southeastern Conference with a 5-0-1 record but could not represent the league in the Sugar Bowl because of NCAA probation. Auburn was 4-1-0 and would get the bid with a win over Alabama. A loss would send AU to Memphis (Liberty Bowl) and LSU (4-1-1) to New Orleans.

Auburn was 8-3-0 by an average score of 30-20 and ranked No. 11. The Tide was 4-6-0 by an average score of 21-19, and bowless. When was the last time that Alabama had *not* gone bowling? Well, the seniors at the University of Alabama were yet to be born, and the country had seen seven different presidents. To be more specific, it had been 26 football seasons.

The Tigers were a solid 7-point favorite.

"Saturday, 10 a.m.: Legion Field sits like a Queen Bee in her honeycomb. Thousands and thousands of drones flock to her," wrote Bob Blalock of *The Birmingham News.*

"They've been gathering for at least the last few days — first the motor homes and their tailgate parties, then the rest come.

"Most of the drones wear clothes of flaming crimson, or blue and burnt orange.

"Some wear sweatshirts that say 'AUsome.' Others sport red baseball caps with elephant trunks and ears. Or T-shirts featuring a tiger on a surfboard riding a cresting wave. The caption says, "Ride the Tide to the Sugar Bowl!'

"Buses are painted with slogans of 'No Sugar for Auburn,' and 'Liberty Bowl Bound.' Other buses spilling out Auburn supporters say, 'Sugar Bowl Bound.'

"Welcome to the 1984 version of Auburn vs. Alabama, *the* football game."

And the full house and a national television audience would witness the dizziest and most discussed finish in series history.

Auburn kicked off, forced a punt, then strung out a 12-play, 80-yard march. Quarterback Pat Washington completed passes to Trey Gainous (16 yards), to Ron Middleton (12 yards), another 12-yarder to Clayton Beauford, and Bo Jackson had rushing gains of 14 and 11 yards, before scoring from the two with 06:15 left in the quarter. Robert McGinty converted, it was an easy 7-0 lead, and the good times seemed safely tucked away in the orange and blue sugar bag.

But Alabama answered with an 80-yard march of its own. Hanging onto the ball for 13 plays and just over eight minutes, the Tide tied things. Facing a third-and-one from his 29, quarterback Mike Shula, son of Don Shula, coach of the Miami Dolphins, sneaked it two yards. Shula later completed a pass to Preston Gothard for 12 yards, and Ricky Moore got off runs of nine, seven and 14 yards. Paul Ott Carruth scored from the six, Van Tiffin kicked good and it was 7-7 just seconds into the second period.

On the final play of the half, a bad snap from center prevented McGinty from getting off what would have been a chip-shot field goal and a 10-7 Tiger advantage.

Bama quickly grabbed the lead to open the second half, zipping 69 yards in seven plays. Shula, from his 31, rambled for 19 to midfield. Shula was on target to Greg Richardson for 18 more to the 32, and Carruth raced down to the two. However, Bama's first-and-goal quickly became fourth-and-goal. Carruth finally cracked into the endzone. Tiffin converted and it was 14-7.

Later in the third quarter, Alabama put Auburn on "alert" when Tiffin's 52-yard field goal put the underdogs up 17-7 with 05:09 remaining. Tiffin's kick matched a series record for distance with Auburn's Al Del Greco in the 1980 game.

Both offenses were held in check and the game was down to the 09:11 mark when Auburn's Brent Fullwood broke free and bolted 60 yards for a sudden touchdown. Jackson added two more points and, just like that, it was 17-15, setting the stage for loads of late-game drama.

Auburn got the ball right back. Shula's short pass went off the hands of intended receiver Moore and into the hands of Kevin Greene. *Interception!*

Line of scrimmage: Alabama 17. Time left: 07:41.

Auburn was soon third-and-11, but Jackson powered 14 yards and steamrolled All-American linebacker Cornellius Bennett along the way. A dazed Bennett had to clear the cobwebs before pulling himself off the carpet.

First down at the four! But it was soon fourth down at the two-foot line.

Time: 03:44, and running.

A field goal would give Auburn an 18-17 lead.

"Go for the touchdown," was Coach Pat Dye's decision.

Tight end Ron Middleton brought the play into the huddle.

Charles Hollis of the *News* reported, "Pat Washington looked at Bo Jackson.

"Bo Jackson looked at Pat Washington.

"Simultaneously, they seemed puzzled as the play arrived in

the huddle.

"'At first I was a little surprised we didn't go for the field goal,' offered Washington. 'Then I thought, we needed only a yard for the touchdown, we were probably going to run a play with Bo.'

"Jackson, like Washington, seemed surprised, too, jerking his head back as soon as he heard the call from the Auburn sideline — a toss sweep to halfback Brent Fullwood."

The play called was "56 Combo," a simple sweep to the right by Fullwood with fullback Tommie Agee and Jackson leading the interference.

Agee and Fullwood went right, but Jackson went left and brushed Fullwood, who never had a chance. Fullwood escaped incoming linemen Randy Rockwell and Vernon Wilkinson, but he couldn't get past linebacker Rory Turner, who drove him out of bounds back at the four.

Pandemonium in Birmingham!

From Alabama's side of the ball, the *News'* Chuck Finder wrote, "Turner prayed the Tigers would run his way, wide to his left. They did....'When I saw the tight end (Middleton) block down, I saw the biggest hole in the whole wide world, I was blessed for that,' Turner said. 'I wanted to knock his head off, tried to kill him. I just waxed the dude.'"

But the game was a long way from being over.

The Tigers held, forced a punt, and still had a good shot at a field goal victory, starting from their 44 with 01:45 and one timeout remaining.

Auburn reached the Alabama 25 and the clock was down to 00:09.

McGinty, from Neptune Beach, Fla. and wearing jersey No. 13, trotted onto the field. A successful kick and his team goes to the Sugar Bowl to play No. 5 Nebraska. An unsuccessful kick and his team goes to the Liberty Bowl to play unranked Arkansas. And think of the cash payoff difference to his own school. Not to mention "Braggin' Rights" for a whole year. It meant *everything.*

Somehow, it seems cruel that so much would ride on the shoulders of 11 young men, or in this case, on one Robert McGinty.

The official's whistle blew to resume action. Back went the snap from center. Mike Mann spotted the ball. McGinty's kick started out good, but tailed off to the left....

Final score: Alabama 17, Auburn 15. And it goes down as the

Sunday Sports

Troy in Division II finals — Page 10B

Greyhounds/2BB
Jim Martin/2BB
Outdoors/27B
SportsStats/2B

Sun., Dec. 2, 1984 · The Birmingham News

Tide rolls Tigers out of Sugar Bowl

A win over Alabama would have put Auburn in the Sugar Bowl in New Orleans ... but the underdog Crimson Tide capped its worst season in three decades with a 17-15 victory that sends the Tigers to the Liberty Bowl instead.

- Rolling back the calendar, All Van Hoose, Page 8B
- A solid Tide front, Clyde Bolton, Page 8B
- The big surprises, Charles Hollis, Page 7B
- Individual Statistics, Page 4B

By Chuck Finder
News sports writer

Mike Mann tugged and tugged, trying to lift him. But Robert McGinty couldn't, wouldn't get up off his knees. Oh, the agony.

On the flip side, Alabama couldn't get any higher. Mike White slid on his derriere to midfield and writhed in ecstasy. Jim Ivy bolted to the 25-yard line and, facing the North end zone, jiggled his body as if he was either doing the twist or having a seizure. The Alabama sideline went out of line.

So what if that meant a 15-yard penalty for celebrating too heartily? McGinty's 42-yard field goal with nine seconds left in the game Saturday missed the mark, and Alabama was right on it.

The Crimson Tide, after two seasons of *Be Over The Top* and *Over The Rainbo*, after a season beset with a maelstrom of misfortune, had beaten the Tigers 17-15 the final score in stone, 17-15, next to the 5-6 engraving for its worst Alabama record in nearly three decades.

"I know," Auburn Coach Pat Dye said, concedingly, sensitively, "it's might sweet to 'em."

Funny he should say that. With the loss, Auburn let slip its chance of a holiday trip for 117 to New Orleans and a New Year's date with Nebraska in the Sugar Bowl. Instead, as a Sugar substitute, the No. 11 Tigers, 8-4 overall and 4-2 in the Southeastern Conference, will travel north by northwest to play Arkansas in the Liberty Bowl on Dec. 27. *Long distance information, get me Memphis, Tennessee.*

For the Tide, 5-6 in league play, it brought to a gleeful close a season that started so glumly. Ah, but don't call this a salvage job. Alabama (not Tampa Bay) Coach Ray Perkins confessed: "As for the personal aspect of it, the coach whom many condemned when his team was 1-4, he confessed, "damn sure's gonna make it easier to live around here for the next 364 days. But if somebody wants to give me heat, light the fire."

Alabama players lit up in the locker room afterward, puffing on their Hav-Tampa Jewel stogies. Even though the 49th convening of the Iron Bowl had been close, it deserved a cigar.

Outside of Bo Jackson's 111 yards rushing and one touchdown — is making an All-America career out of Alabama or what? — and Brent Fullwood's 60-yard touchdown romp, the rest of the Auburn offense could muster up only 150 yards. Then again, the Tide stumbled as much, committing a dangerous turnover inside its 20-yard line on a tipped pass off Ricky Moore's hands into Kevin Greene's open arms. Yet Alabama repelled a Tigers fourth-down effort for a touchdown (more on that later) and won.

"Shows you how much I know about this game," Perkins said. "I said other day that our team that would make the most big plays and the team that would make the fewest mistakes would win."

■ See Tide, Page

Perkins and two reasons he left the field smiling: kick returner Cedric Vaughns (left), linebacker Cornelius Bennett. | McGinty takes it hard after missing with nine seconds left.

The sun finally shines on Alabama

Neal Sims

Winter will be warmer now for Ray Perkins and his Alabama Crimson Tide. The fourth-quarter sun has shined finally on their side of the street.

It glowed in the head coach's face. It beamed from his players' eyes. It rose brightly from the clinched fists of victory held high toward the Legion Field sky.

Alabama, loser of a bunch and headed nowhere

third-and-11, with barely six minutes remaining, he powered 14 yards to the Tide 4, crunching Cornelius Bennett along the way. The linebacker Taylor spent more than a minute on his back, recovering from Jackson's charge.

SOON, THE TIGERS WERE two feet from the lead, the football pushed up close to the same such goal-line where Jackson had made famous the play now known as "Bo Over the Top." That legendary leap of '82 had beaten

Football Inside

■ Flutie's No. 50!
Odds-on favorite Doug Flutie was officially announced as the winner of the 50th annual Heisman Trophy Saturday by New York's Downtown Athletic Club. Flutie, who passed for more than 10,000 yards in his Boston College career — the first collegian to accomplish that feat — became the first quarterback to win the award since Auburn's Pat Sullivan won it in 1971.
Page

Running back Paul Carruth scored both Tide touchdowns in 17-15 win in 1984.

second biggest upset in series history. The Tigers' win in 1949 remains as the top shocker. Actually, it was the first time in 33 years that a team with a losing record won in this rivalry, and only the fifth time overall (1901-02-49-51).

Coach Dye was, of course, forced to field the "Why didn't you kick a field goal?" question immediately after the heartbreaking defeat. His answer was: "We had a sure touchdown. The ball's sitting on the right hashmark with two feet to go. If we don't make it, we still have time to get the ball back and kick another field goal, which is exactly what happened. If I'd known Bo would've gone the wrong way on the sweep, I would've gone for the field goal."

Generally, Alabama's defensive players said that they were "praying" that Auburn would go for the touchdown. They figured their chances were better at stopping a run than to block a field goal.

Coach Ray Perkins told the press, "It makes living here easier for the next 364 days. It makes it easier to get on that plane and go into that recruit's home. It puts us into the offseason in a better frame of mind. But it doesn't erase those six losses."

As for the reaction of the top bowl representative from New Orleans, the *News* reported, "Elliott Loudeman, president of the Sugar Bowl, just closed his eyes, dropped his chin and shook his head as he watched the final seconds tick away...."

The losing Tigers led in first downs 16-13, yards rushing 215-180 and total yards 328-253. Each team threw an interception and there were no lost fumbles. Jackson led all rushers with 118 yards in 22 carries (5.4 average). Carruth had 97 yards in 23 attempts for Bama. AU was only 8-for-20 in passing, UA 6-for-11.

The hottest-selling item around Legion Field after the game was a bumper sticker that read: *BAMA 17, AUB 15 — WE BEAT THE SUGAR OUT OF AUBURN.*

One Alabama fan was heard to say, "At least we won't have to hear, 'Bo over the top and over the RainBo' for at least another year."

Auburn regrouped and completed a gruelling 13-game schedule with its third bowl victory in three years, topping Arkansas 21-15 in the first-ever meeting of the teams. The Tigers finished 9-4-0 and a final ranking of 14th.

Alabama was 5-6-0.

Six different teams were ranked No. 1 in the *Associated Press* poll in 1984. They were Auburn, Miami, Nebraska, Texas, Washington and Brigham Young. Where was the national championship settled that year? Not the Ohio State-Southern Cal Rose Bowl, or the Washington-Oklahoma Orange Bowl, or the UCLA-Miami Fiesta Bowl. It was settled in the Holiday Bowl at San Diego, where BYU (12-0-0) defeated Michigan (6-5-0) by a score of 24-17 with a touchdown in the final seconds.

1985

GAME 50

The Boy From Red Bay

This is not fiction. It is unbelievable, but it is all true.
In an Iron Bowl that topped all Iron Bowls, both Alabama and Auburn came back from death, again and again. — Wayne Hester, *The Birmingham News.*

This one should be put in a time capsule and preserved for the future so future generations will know what this football game was all about. — Rosco Nance, *USA Today.*

Bo Jackson and Gene Jelks ran wild. Mike Shula and Pat Washington filled the air with passes.
In the end, however, one man and one play decided Saturday's Iron Bowl. — Greg Bailey, *Gasden Times.*

Ray Perkins, the man who committed the unpardonable sin of succeeding Bear Bryant, may be pardoned after all. — Clyde Bolton, *The Birmingham News.*

Electrifying. Stunning. Pulsating.
Throw out all the stock adjectives on this one. None seems adequate. — Al Burleson, *The Huntsville Times.*

Fifty times they've met now, these bitter rivals, and never before had their collision produced anything like this. — Mark Bradley, *The Atlanta Journal-Constitution.*

Pat Dye said this one didn't hurt as much as last year's, but the Auburn head coach carried back home about all the misery one man can handle. — Jimmy Bryan, *The Birmingham News.*

Sunday Sports B

Georgia Tech
falls to Michigan
— College Basketball, Page 16B

Top 20/2B
UNA wins/3B
Outdoors/18-19B
Greyhounds/20B

Sun., Dec. 1, 1985

The Birmingham News

Unbelievable!

Van Tiffin is the last hero in a game of many, as his 52-yard field goal with no time left beats Auburn in a classic Iron Bowl

A photo-finish ... framed in crimson

MOBILE PRESS REGISTER

Sports

Section D

Sunday, December 1, 1985

Bama win leaves 'em gasping

Tiffin's 52-yard
field goal beats
Auburn, 25-23

Four possessions, four scores, a fourth quarter that will rival the best of anything college football has to offer. — David Murphree, *Columbus (Ga.) Ledger-Enquirer.*

Auburn came out Saturday, fell flat on its face and picked itself up, only to have the rug yanked away at the end. There's no shame in that. — Kevin Scarbinsky, *The Birmingham News.*

Both the Tigers and Tide were a pre-season pick as the nation's top team — Auburn by *Inside Sports* and Alabama by *Playboy.* Maryland (*Sport*) and Washington (*Sports Illustrated*) also got No. 1 nods. Oklahoma began as top choice by the *Associated Press* with Auburn second, followed by SMU, Iowa and Florida. Alabama failed to rate.

Auburn's season began on September 7 with a 49-7 wipeout of Southwest Louisiana and, *War Eagle!*, the Tigers moved to *No. 1.* They stayed on top after a 29-18 win over Southern Mississippi, but fell all the way to 14th following a 38-20 loss to Tennessee at Knoxville.

Four wins followed — Ole Miss, FSU, Georgia Tech and Mississippi State — and a climb back to No. 6. But No. 2-ranked Florida escaped the Plains with a 14-10 win, tumbling the Tigers to 13th. AU then topped East Carolina and Georgia.

The Tigers now eyed the Tide.

Alabama opened against Georgia on Labor Day night before a national television audience and 81,000 on-hand fanatics. The Bulldogs blocked a punt for a touchdown with 50 seconds left to grab a stunning 16-13 lead. Quarterback Mike Shula, however, drove the Tide 71 yards in only five plays for a touchdown at 00:15 and a pulsating 20-16 victory.

The Tide then topped Texas A&M, Cincinnati and Vanderbilt and ranked 12th. Eighth-rated Penn State, however, won 19-17 at Happy Valley, then 20th-ranked Tennessee won a 16-14 decision at Birmingham. After wins over Memphis State, Mississippi State, Southern Mississippi and a tie with LSU, the Crimson Tide was ready for Auburn.

The Tigers were 8-2-0 by an average score of 31-15 and ranked No. 7. Bama was 7-2-1 by an average score of 27-16 and was nowhere to be found on *AP's* big board.

The Vols and Gators tied for the SEC title (5-1-0) but, once again, UF was locked out of the post-season picture over its difficulty in following the rules. UT would represent the league in

Alabama's Van Tiffin slams his historic, game-winning field goal of 52 yards on the final play to shatter Auburn's hearts in the 1985 thriller. The Crimson Tide escaped 25-23. Tiffin's FG matched the longest in series history.

the Sugar Bowl.

Auburn had already accepted a Cotton Bowl bid against Texas A&M, while the Tide had lined up a nice little trip to Hawaii to play Southern Cal.

The time had now arrived for the series' Golden Game — the 50th between Alabama and Auburn, and for the fifth straight year a national television audience would tune in for a first hand look at this annual statewide fuss.

"The game plan that (Ray) Perkins brought to Legion Field was one of his best as Alabama's head coach," reported Hester of the *News*. "The Tide offense is normally effective but not flashy. However, Perkins believed more was necessary to beat Auburn. The result was an offensive plan that included a bunch of long passes, runs on pass downs, passes on run downs, and in general bold imaginative play-calling."

Midway through the first quarter, Auburn's Lewis Colbert punted to the six-yard line, but Bama covered the distance in 13 plays, with fullback Craig Turner scoring from the one. Van Tiffin converted and it was 7-0 with 02:52 remaining in the period.

Seconds later, Alabama had the ball again when defensive end Jon Hand roared in and belted quarterback Pat Washington, resulting in a fumble that Bama recovered at AU's 13. On fourth down from the nine, Tiffin kicked a field goal and it was 10-0.

Early in the second period, Alabama's Greg Richardson returned a punt 57 yards to the 18, but AU braced at the 15, and Tiffin added a field goal for a 13-0 score with 12:32 left in the second quarter.

Auburn's first score came at the 08:04 mark, moving 53 yards in only three plays. Bo Jackson, playing with two cracked ribs from the Georgia game and wearing special protection, scored from the seven. Chris Johnson converted.

The teams then traded late field goals. Tiffin's 42-yarder gave Bama a nine-point lead just 62 seconds prior to intermission. Washington, however, superbly used the clock to reach the Tide 32, and Johnson's kick sailed through as time expired.

Halftime: Alabama 16, Auburn 10.

The third period was scoreless.

But the giant football fireworks display was about to explode over Legion Field. And, ready or not, the home viewers and the 75,808 souls at the site were about to be taken on a roller coaster ride of thrills and chills. This was no place for the timid.

The final quarter began with AU's Kevin Porter intercepting a

Auburn's Bo Jackson became the second Heisman Trophy winner to play in the series. He rushed for 4303 career yards in 650 attempts (6.6 average) and scored 43 touchdowns. In four games against Alabama, Jackson carried the ball 90 times for 630 yards (7.0) and scored 38 points (6 TDs and a 2-point conversion). His yardage and scoring are series records. In 89 baseball games at Auburn, Bo batted .335 and hit 28 home runs.

Shula pass in the endzone. Sixteen plays later, Jackson dived over from the one to tie the game and also become the series' all-time top scorer with 38 points. (Bobby Marlow's 36 points had been on the AU-UA books for 34 years.) Incredibly, Johnson missed the conversion — but — Alabama had too many men on the field. Johnson got another try and he made it.

Time: 07:03.

Down by 13 earlier, the Tigers had clawed into a 17-16 lead. But the lead didn't last long — 66 seconds — to be exact.

Alabama's Gene Jelks, on a simple toss-sweep, got outside and raced 74 yards for a touchdown. Tiffin converted and the Crimson Tide was right back on top, 22-17. A pass for the conversion failed.

Time: 05:57.

Auburn then hacked out a five-minute, 11-play drive covering 70 yards, culminated by Reggie Ware's score from a yard out and a 23-22 lead. And it remained that way when Washington's pass intended for Jackson was batted down by Cornelius Bennett.

Time: 00:57.

Alabama began from its 20.

After an incomplete pass, Harold Hallman sacked Shula for an eight-yard loss, and Bama was forced to burn its *final* timeout. It was now third-and-18 back at the 12.

Shula passed 16 yards to Jelks at the 28, bringing up fourth-and-two.

Time: 00:47.

One play! Auburn was on the brink of one of its greatest comebacks ever.

One play!

On a surprise call, flanker Al Bell, on a reverse, shot around his left end for 20 big yards.

First down at the 46.

Time: 00:21.

Shula threw incomplete.

Time: 00:15.

Shula then hit Richardson on a crossing pattern. Richardson grabbed it at the Auburn 45, was hit by Luvell Bivins, but his momentum carried both out of bounds. It was a gain of 19 yards, putting the ball at the AU 35.

Time: 00:06.

Tiffin and the field goal unit trotted onto the field. It would be a 52-yard effort. Tiffin slammed his right foot into the football. There was never any doubt — plenty long and straight through the pipes.

Van Tiffin, 5-10, 160 lbs., from Red Bay, Ala., would *forever* be a Crimson Tide gridiron hero.

Time: 00:00.

Final score: Alabama 25, Auburn 23.

Unbelievable.....

How does one describe such happiness for one side? Or such hurt for the other side? One can't. But all college football fans have, at one time or another, felt both.

Actually, statistics in a game such as this don't mean much, but just for the record, here they are. Bama led in first downs 20-17, yards rushing 239-175, yards passing 195-159, and total yards by exactly 100 — 434-334. UA was 14-for-28 passing, AU 8-for-17. Alabama was also penalized more yards, 37-15.

Jelks led all rushers with 192 yards on 18 carries (10.7), while Jackson gained 142 yards on 31 attempts (4.6). That November 30 was a sad 23rd birthday for Jackson.

But Bo Jackson certainly left his cleat marks on the series. In four games, he carried the football 90 times and rushed for 630 yards (7.0 yards per carry, 157.5 yards per game).

Over 600 yards? Many a moon will drift over Legion Field and Jordan-Hare Stadium before that series record is topped.

The Aloha Bowl landed the nation's two "bowlingest" teams in Alabama and Southern Cal. This would be the Tide's 38th post-season game, the Trojans' 29th. Bama won 24-3 to finish the season 9-2-1 and a No. 13 ranking.

Auburn, unable to shake off its disastrous defeat at Birmingham, got drilled 36-16 by the Aggies at Dallas. It had been a long, hard fall for the 8-4-0 Tigers — from No. 1 to clear off the charts. And to add even more insult, the Crimson Tide claimed themselves "Champions of the Cotton Bowl" by virture of regular season victories over both A&M and AU.

On the national scene that year, the Top Three teams after the regular season were Penn State, Miami and Iowa. All three were beaten in the bowls — by a combined 105-45.

The Hawkeyes lost 45-28 to UCLA in the Rose, the Hurricanes lost 35-7 to Tennessee in the Sugar, and the Nittany Lions lost 25-10 to Oklahoma in the Orange.

The Sooners leaped from fourth to the national crown, followed by Michigan, Penn State, Tennessee and Florida.

1986
GAME 51

Ho-Hum. Another Thriller.

It was Auburn and Alabama in another classic duel in 1986 to go along with a string of classics they had staged over the past several years.

Such as:
1979 — UA trailed 17-18 in the fourth quarter, but won 25-18.
1981 — UA trailed 14-17 in the fourth quarter, but won 28-17.
1982 — AU trailed 14-22 in the fourth quarter, but won 23-22.
1983 — AU trailed 16-20 in the fourth quarter, but won 23-20.
1984 — AU trailed 15-17 in the fourth quarter, but failed on a TD from the 2-foot line, then from the 25 on a FG.
1985 — UA trailed 22-23 in the fourth quarter, but won 25-23.
1986 — Now check this one out.

In early August when the games are played on paper, the numerous publications which crowd the shopping mall magazine racks agreed that "Bama is back." Two of the polls — *Associated Press* and *Football Action* — had the Tide sitting in the No. 4 slot, while *Street & Smith* predicted a No. 5 position.

Auburn, on the other hand, lost 24 players who had earned an amazing total of 69 letters. It's tough to replace that much experience, but Pat Dye still had plenty of talent to call upon. His Tigers were generally picked to land fourth or fifth in the Southeastern Conference.

Alabama and Ohio State kicked off the season in The Kickoff Classic at Giants Stadium in East Rutherford, NJ, on August 27. Crimson Tide 16, Buckeyes 10.

Wins over Vanderbilt, Southern Mississippi, Florida, Notre Dame, Memphis State and Tennessee followed, zipping the Tide

Sports

The Atlanta Journal

SECTION D .... TUESDAY, NOVEMBER 25, 1986

It's clean, old-fashioned hate week

Mark Bradley

Just the facts, Falcons

Sometimes you tire of opinions, even when they're yours and brilliant. Today we rest. Today we traffic in facts. Atlanta Falcons facts, cold and hard and numerical.

Seven: The number of points a team banks when it scores a touchdown and kicks the extra point. Falcon fans have doubtless forgotten.

Three: Number of times the Falcons reached the playoffs under Leeman Bennett, who was fired because

Ray Perkins questions Pat Dye's understanding of fans' emotions when Alabama plays Auburn

☐ MORE COVERAGE .. 5D

By Ed Hinton
Staff Writer

TUSCALOOSA, Ala. — Alabama coach Ray Perkins said Monday that the Auburn-Alabama rivalry is bigger than any bowl game, is the biggest event of any kind ever in Alabama and "affects 98 percent of the lives in this

Ray Perkins

Bulldogs consider Tech their fiercest rivals again after having to stomach two consecutive defeats

☐ MORE COVERAGE 4D

By Thomas O'Toole
Staff Writer

ATHENS — The rivalry might have subsided earlier in the decade, when the Georgia football team had Herschel Walker in its backfield and grander thoughts on its mind than the annual showdown with Georgia Tech.

Vince Dooley

---

all the way to No. 2 behind Miami.

Meanwhile, Auburn topped UT-Chattanooga, East Carolina, Tennessee, Western Carolina, Vanderbilt, Georgia Tech and Mississippi State, and climbed from "nowhere" to No. 5. But beware War Eagles! Those seven teams would win only 30 games that year.

Next for Alabama: No. 7-ranked Penn State at Tuscaloosa.
Next for Auburn: Unranked Florida (3-4-0) at Gainesville.
The Tide lost 23-3.

And in a thundershocker, the Tigers led 17-0 in the fourth quarter, only to lose 18-17 on a touchdown and 2-point conversion at 00:36. Robert McGinty had earlier kicked a 51-yard field goal to get the Gators within striking distance. Robert who? The same Robert McGinty who missed a field goal two years earlier that would have beaten Alabama for Auburn. He had transferred to Florida.

Alabama next defeated Mississippi State, lost to LSU, and topped Temple.

Auburn next defeated Cincinnati, but was upset 20-16 by Georgia (6-3-0) in the infamous "Between The Hoses" game at Jordan-Hare.

The stage was now set for the 51st Tide-Tiger tangle. Alabama was 9-2-0 by an average score of 28-11 and ranked 7th. Auburn was 8-2-0 by an average score of 32-10 and ranked 14th.

Both teams would go bowling, but first things first, and that was the Iron Bowl, where Bama was favored by three points.

Coach Ray Perkins livened things up early in the week when he told the press, "This series is the biggest game there is. It can not mean as much to Dye as it does to me because he went to school at Georgia and did not play in The Game."

Dye replied, "That's like saying playing at Alabama doesn't mean as much to Ray as it does to Jim Fuller (Tide assistant) because Fuller grew up in Fairfield, Alabama, and Ray grew up in Petal, Mississippi."

There was also growing concern for Alabama over Auburn's seriousness in its demand that the series become a home-and-home affair between Legion Field and Jordan-Hare Stadium.

Perkins' reply to that was simply, "It'll *never* happen."

His response — especially the arrogance of it — drew ire from Tiger fans throughout the state.

And, if that wasn't enough pre-game fuel to keep things hoppin,' there were burdensome rumors of marital problems between Dye and his wife Sue, *plus* talk that Dye was leaving Auburn for the University of Texas.

It was a *wild* week.

KICKOFF! Kickoff, and let the boys play football....

Keith Jackson and ABC-TV were on the Iron Bowl scene for the sixth straight year as game day dawned dark, dreary and rainy, holding the attendance to about 76,000.

Alabama took a 7-0 lead in the first quarter on the shortest TD pass the series had ever seen — two-yards — from Mike Shula to Angelo Stafford, and Van Tiffin's conversion.

Auburn tied it on the first play of the second period when Brent Fullwood burst through for 18 yards and Chris Knapp's kick.

The Tigers should have taken the lead on their next possession, reaching the Tide 10, from where Fullwood scored again, but a holding infraction cancelled it. Knapp then missed on a field goal attempt.

Shula's seven-yard scoring pass to Bobby Humphrey and Tiffin's conversion made it 14-7, and that's the way the first half ended.

Tiffin booted a 29-yard field goal in the third quarter and Bama seemed in total control with a 17-7 advantage.

With 11:47 remaining, Alabama reached fourth down at the Tigers' 21-yard line and called upon Van Tiffin to "put the game away" with a field goal. He missed.

Sunday Sports

'Gators upset
Florida State
— Page 4B

War Eagle, hey!

Alf Van Hoose
Sports editor

A pivotal win for the Tigers

Classic battles, contended Clausewitz, expert on war, are lost rather than won.

Classic football games, according to Tennessee legendary coach Robert Neyland, also a military man, are lost, not won.

Those dictums don't have to apply to Iron Bowl 56. It rated only near classic. Let's say Auburn won it 21-17.

Positives beat negatives, anytime, anywhere.

There were errors, fistsful of 'em. There always have been in Iron Bowls, the most intensive of any bowl — for the last five years the most competitive, also.

Auburn blew its script on its most memorable play. You can read of all its snafus on Lawyer Tillman's dramatic, decisive touchdown ramble with 32 seconds left.

For thing right about the results, for Auburn, were six points:

Victory.

So many good things can be written about a murky, then rainy Saturday in famous Legion Field.

From an overview look, by an unbiased judge, it tilted balance in a grand rivalry back toward center. Alabama had won ten in a row, and had its powerful hands on Auburn's throat again.

Auburn was in the same gasping condition in 1982 — Bo Jackson ran the wrong way Alabama survived.

Alabama official pregame propaganda about a football game

Two top Tigers like what they see at end of 21-17 Auburn win: Dye, left, with QB coach Pat Sullivan

---

But on the first play of the final period, it was Fullwood scoring again, this time from 28 yards out. After Knapp's conversion, Auburn was back in strong contention at 14-17.

The Tigers then went 53 yards to Bama's 26, but on second down quarterback Jeff Burger, attempting to hit Lawyer Tillman in the endzone, was intercepted by Kermit Kendrick — Burger's third INT of the game — wasting a good chance for at least a tie.

This would, surely, shutout Auburn's "War Eagle!" shouts for another year.

By now, Legion Field was thoroughly soaked from the steady drizzle and the afternoon of football had ticked down to the 04:54 mark after Alabama punted to the Auburn 33.

On third-and-five, Fullwood got the five to the 43.

On second-and-nine, Burger hit tight end Walter Reeves for six to the midfield stripe.

Burger, on a bootleg, got nothing.

Time: 02:18.

Timeout, Tigers. Fourth down. They needed three yards. It was now fourth-and-game-to-go.

Burger drilled a pass intended for Trey Gainous. And Gainous made a diving, sliding catch for a first down at the Alabama 40.

Auburn caught fire.

Fullwood blasted all the way to the 21, Tommie Agee ripped off 11 yards to the 10, and Vincent Harris got three more down to the seven.

Time: Thirty-something seconds and blinking....

Here's the way Wayne Hester of *The Birmingham News* described the next play:

"Legion Field's 75,808 were screaming. Lawyer Tillman didn't hear the play called in the huddle. As the wide receiver ran out to his position, he saw Coach Pat Dye jumping up and down on the sideline, signaling timeout.

"Tillman, puzzled, looked at Burger.

"'EIGHTEEN REVERSE LEFT' Burger shouted to Tillman, knowing Alabama's defense couldn't hear him because he couldn't hear himself.

"Tillman heard the word 'reverse,' and now he knew why Dye wanted a timeout. Tillman had never run the reverse. That was a play designed for backup wide receiver Scott Bolton.

"Tillman tried to call timeout, but Burger was taking the snap and pitching it to tailback Tim Jessie sweeping right, who gave it to Tillman going the other way, who raced seven yards for the winning touchdown with 32 seconds on the clock."

Ed Hinton of *The Atlanta Journal-Constitution* put it this way:

"Had Alabama fans known of the confusion on the Auburn bench in the do-or-die moments, the crimson-clad ones would have guffawed.

"Alabama defensive players knew Auburn would try to run a reverse in the next few snaps.

"Suddenly, Dye could not remember Bolton's name. He knew he would recognize the receiver he wanted to insert if only he could find him. Dye tried to call time out. On the field, quarterback Jeff Burger saw only six seconds on the play clock. Auburn had to go. Now."

Final score: Auburn 21, Alabama 17.

Auburn's side of Legion was going absolutely bonkers!

Clyde Bolton, popular journalist for *The Birmingham News*,

Trailing 17-7 in the fourth quarter of the 1986 game, Auburn's Brent Fullwood (above) and Lawyer Tillman scored touchdowns for a thrilling 21-17 Tiger triumph.

portrayed the winning play in his own unique style:

"Well, Maw and Them, you'll be tickled to know that when all the chips were on the table, Pat Dye wanted to call on a Bolton to win the game.

"But it will pain you to hear the rest of the story. He couldn't think of his name....Scott Bolton had run a reverse for 21 yards in the second quarter....So Auburn's coach was trying to get Bolton onto the field to carry the ball at the last. But he couldn't think of his name!"

The *News'* Charles Hollis reported, "Some of the Alabama players were still on the ground as they watched Tillman being swarmed in the endzone by his teammates.

"Along the Alabama sideline, heads and hopes seemed to drop at the same time....There were pictures of dejection everywhere.

"There was Cornelius Bennett walking off the field, his head down, and slinging his helmet to the ground.

"There was cornerback Freddie Robinson, still dazed by it all, walking over to an equipment chest and plunking his body on it as he stared into the night."

Bolton reported, "Sue and the kids joined Dye in the postgame press conference. It was a time of wide smiles from them, laughs from them.

"When Dye accidently knocked one of the dozen or so microphones off the podium, he said, 'Well, there goes Channel 19,' and added, 'Everything's funny when you win, isn't it?'

"Told Channel 19 was from Huntsville, Dye looked mischievous and asked, 'Where's the one from Tuscaloosa.'"

That one brought a roar from everybody.

Coach Perkins, who for two weeks had been saying, "The Alabama-Auburn game is a life and death deal for me," most likely wasn't feeling too good.

Auburn led in first downs 25-19, and in passing yards 153-53, while Alabama had the most rushing yards 340-25, and total yards 393-378. The Tide also led in penalty yards 72-31.

Bama's Bobby Humphrey became only the fourth back to rush for 200 yards (204) in a series game. The others are Bo Jackson (256 yards in 1983), Bobby Marlow (233 yards in 1951) and Johnny Musso (221 yards in 1970).

Fullwood led Auburn with 145 yards on 21 carries (6.9). Burger completed 19 of 30 passes, both series highs for AU since Pat Sullivan's 22-for-38 in the 1970 game.

Alabama's Bobby Humphrey became only the fourth back in the series to reach the 200-yard rushing plateau. He gained 204 in the 1986 game.

The Atlanta Journal
THE ATLANTA CONSTITUTION

SUNDAY, JANUARY 4, 1987

Tech's Curry to be head football coach at Alabama

Bill Curry

It was front-page news in Georgia as well as Alabama, and storm clouds quickly began swirling over the Capstone.

The series now stood 30-20-1, with the Crimson Tide also leading on the all-time scoreboard, 999-791.

Both Alabama and Auburn would meet — and beat — Pac-10 opposition in post-season play. It was the Tide over Washington 28-7 on Christmas Day in the Sun Bowl, and the Tigers over Southern Cal 16-7 on New Year's Day in the Citrus Bowl.

Eighteen of Alabama's last 26 games had been televised. The bowl game was its 98th on TV, second only to Notre Dame's 102.

For the fourth time, both Auburn and Alabama finished in the Top 10 rankings. The Tigers (10-2-0) were 6th, while the Crimson Tide (10-3-0) was 9th. The other years were 1963, 1972 and 1974.

On December 31, Ray Perkins, paying the price of following a legend, resigned at Alabama to become head coach of the NFL's Tampa Bay Buccaneers. His four-year record was 32-15-1 (.677), including a split with Auburn.

Perkins was replaced by Georgia Tech's Bill Curry. And it was a toss-up between Yellow Jackets, Bulldogs, Tigers and Tiders over who got the biggest jolt.

1987
GAME 52

Long Seasons End In Auburn's Favor

Alabama-Auburn is not just a rivalry, it's Gettysburg South.

Beano Cook
ESPN College Football Analyst

Ray Perkins' departure from Tuscaloosa last winter directly resulted in a chain-reaction of coaching changes.

Bill Curry went from Georgia Tech to Alabama; Steve Sloan went from Duke to Alabama as athletic director; Steve Spurrier went from the golf courses to Duke; Bobby Ross went from Maryland to Georgia Tech, and Joe Krivak went from Ross' assistant to head coach at Maryland.

Both Alabama and Auburn faced off-the-field strife in early August.

Joab Thomas, president of Alabama, had to defend alumni accusations that he was *de-emphasizing* Crimson Tide football.

First, there was his unpopular hiring of Bill Curry as coach in January. Next was a letter he had recently written to Harvey Schiller, commissioner of the Southeastern Conference, asking about the feasibility of altering the format of the Alabama-Auburn series from an annual affair to a rotating basis.

Alabama-Auburn football on a rotating basis?

Also in August, Thomas said that Ray Perkins would not be athletic director even if he were still at the school. Perkins had told Thomas that he would be willing to hire an associate athletic director, which Thomas flatly refused to accept.

And, of course, there was that on-going and fiery topic of changing the game to an alternating Birmingham-Auburn format.

Meanwhile, Auburn was in limbo over the eligibility status of its starting quarterback.

On August 6, *The Atlanta Journal* reported, "The future of quarterback Jeff Burger at Auburn University remained in limbo today as school and NCAA officials offered different interpretations of NCAA rules and different accounts of a July 14 incident in which an Auburn assistant coach arranged for Burger's release from jail....Burger faces a more immediate threat to his final college season this afternoon. He is scheduled to appear before an academic honesty committee at Auburn on charges of plagiarism. The committee voted last week to suspend Burger from school for three quarters, but Burger requested and received a second hearing."

Jeff Burger was later cleared to the satisfaction of both Auburn and the NCAA, and allowed to play.

The consensus of nine different pre-season polls had Auburn and LSU virtually even for the SEC title, and the A-Tigers as the seventh best team in the country. Oklahoma was an overwhelming choice to win it all.

Alabama was picked to finish sixth — in the SEC.

Both teams won their first two games. It was Auburn over Texas 31-3, and Kansas 49-0; Alabama over Southern Mississippi 38-6, and Penn State 24-13.

The Tigers were ranked No. 3, the Tide No. 10.

But September 19 wasn't a good day. AU and Tennessee tied 20-20, while UA lost to Florida 24-13.

Auburn next topped North Carolina 20-10, then Vanderbilt 48-15, but fell a notch to fourth behind Oklahoma, Nebraska and Miami.

That brought the season to October 17 and a sad day of sorts for football fans around the Southeast. Auburn was in Atlanta to play Georgia Tech for the 90th and final time. Tech, for some strange reason, had cancelled the ancient series, now leaving only two teams — Clemson and Georgia — to fill Grant Field on an every-other-year basis.

The Jackets had beaten only The Citadel and Indiana State, both Division II schools, but led Auburn 10-6 with just seconds remaining. The Tigers, however, scored on a Burger-to-Tillman fourth down pass from the four. The Tigers then intercepted a

NCAA officials disagree on the likely fate of Auburn quarterback Jeff Burger ■ 3D

Sports

The Atlanta Journal — THURSDAY, AUGUST 6, 1987

Bama president to 'step aside' if Curry fails

pass and returned it for a touchdown as a very misleading 20-10 final score went into the record books. Auburn's series lead over Tech froze at 47-39-4.

Meantime, Alabama defeated Vanderbilt and Southwest Louisiana, lost a 13-10 *stunner* to a 1-3-0 Memphis State team, then rebounded with a 41-22 rout of unbeaten and 10th-ranked Tennessee in a night game at Birmingham.

The Tigers then topped Mississippi State and Florida. Next was a national television bout carrying national implications between No. 5 Florida State and No. 6 Auburn at Jordan-Hare Stadium. FSU 34, AU 6. The Seminoles went to fourth, the Tigers to 12th. Putting that big disappointment behind, Auburn handled Georgia 27-11 to even that series at 42-42-7.

The Tide was next.

Alabama defeated Mississippi State and LSU, moving up to 10th place in the polls, but then lost to seventh-ranked Notre Dame at South Bend by a score of 37-6.

The Tigers were next.

Auburn was 8-1-1 by an average score of 29-12 and ranked seventh in the country. Alabama was 7-3-0 by an average score of 25-18 and was rated 18th.

The Tigers were four-point favorites and a victory would clinch an outright SEC crown and a trip to the Sugar Bowl. A Tiger loss would send LSU's Tigers to New Orleans. It was as simple as that.

The 52nd renewal was played on Friday afternoon after Thanksgiving, a full house was on hand, and CBS-TV beamed it across the land. It was "the only game in town" that day.

And this one turned out to be one of those old-fashioned, grind-it-out, in-your-face football brawls.

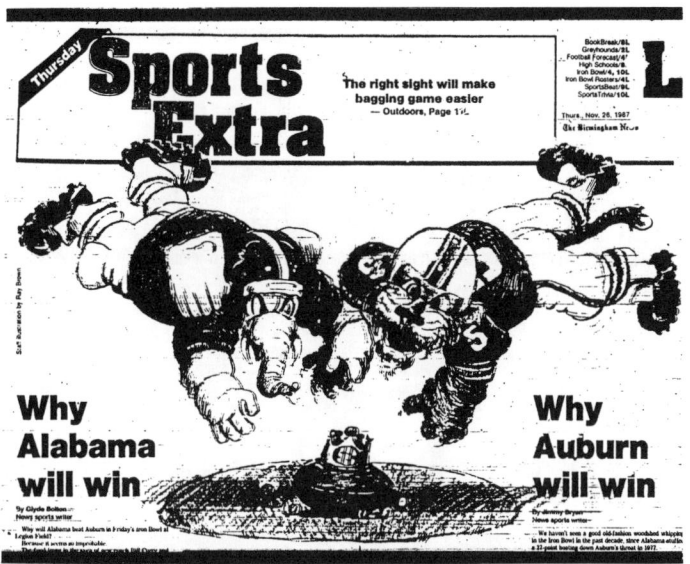

Auburn won 10-0, but Bama certainly had its chances.

On the second possession, UA was fourth down at its 47, and an *inch* to go. Fullback Bo Wright plowed into the line, was stacked up, and didn't make the inch.

In the second period, Alabama marched from its one to a fourth-and-one at Auburn's 36. Philip Doyle was called upon for a 53-yard field goal, and he slammed it long and high enough, but the ball hit the left upright and bounced harmlessly away. It just missed being the longest FG in series history.

The Tigers couldn't move. Bryan Shulman was back to punt, but Derrick Thomas stormed in to block it and the ball went out of bounds back at the nine-yard line.

Three runs netted seven yards down to the two. A fourth down pass never had a chance.

Still, though, Bama had Auburn backed deep. But not for long. The Tigers pieced together a 98-yard victory drive.

On third-and-seven, Burger passed eight yards to Stacy Danley and a big first down at the 13.

On second-and-eight from the 15, Burger let a long one fly intended for Tillman racing down the sideline. Tillman leaped and out-fought cornerback Gene Jelks for the football and, as the play was completed, a frustrated Jelks kicked the football,

Saturday Sports

High school playoffs
— Page 4B

Scoreboard/2B
Greyhounds/3B
SportsDigest/3B
Basketball/6B

Sat., Nov. 28, 1987

The Birmingham News

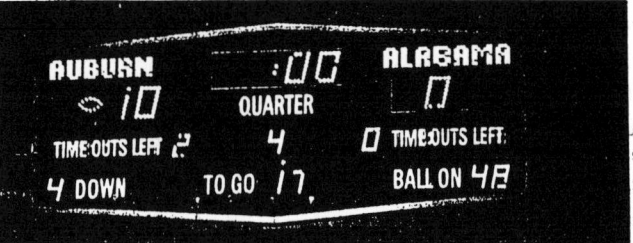

Auburn's big haul:
✓ Shutout of Bama
✓ SEC championship
✓ Sugar Bowl

By Jimmy Bryan
News sports writer

The Auburn Tigers had lived by the forward pass this season, but they refused to die by it Friday at Legion Field.

Coming to the Iron Bowl showdown with Alabama as the Southeastern Conference leader and nestled in the driver's seat on the road to the Sugar Bowl, the Tigers were hoping to get another good, passing performance from quarterback Jeff Burger and fly right on to New Orleans.

However, Alabama shut down Burger and the pass and threatened to block Auburn's path to the Sugar Bowl, as they have done before. But this time the Tigers impressively changed their game plan in the second half.

Auburn made the switch from free-wheeling passing game to ball-control ground game and whipped Alabama 10-0 in an old-fashioned man-to-man showdown before a sellout crowd of 75,808.

With their first shutout of Alabama since 1957, Pat Dye's Tigers won the SEC championship and the trip to New Orleans, where they will play unbeaten Syracuse on New Year's Day.

"We just weren't getting the job done throwing the ball," wide receivers coach Larry Blakeney explained, even though the Tigers led 7-0 at halftime thanks to a massive 99-yard drive — officially 98 yards due to a penalty. "We finally just sold our team on trying to establish the running game and lacing the loom."

Evidence of the switch in strategy:
● Auburn went from 20 yards rushing in the first half to 185 for the game. Redshirt freshman Stacy Danley was the man, slashing for 157 yards on 26 carries.
● After keeping the ball for only 12 minutes and 21 seconds in the first half, Auburn hogged possession for 23 minutes and five seconds in the second.

"We changed (to the run) in the second half because I got tired of Jeff being thrown for losses," Coach Pat Dye said. "That had some influence on it for sure. I don't mind throwing it, but I don't want to take 11-yard losses.

"It was an old-fashioned game, kind of. Both teams tried to run the ball, had good kicking games and jockeyed for position. We just got a little more done than Dye did. It's a game of inches and tonight the inches were on Auburn's side. The breaks went our way.

"I'm mighty proud of this football team. We didn't have the easiest of seasons. But the mark of a champion and a close-knit team is coming together and playing as a unit. I think we have been able to do that."

Alabama had the best of it statistically for two quarters. However, the Tide failed to win a couple of first-half skirmishes and never got back into the flow in the second half.

● Alabama failed on fourth-and-one

Auburn opens a huge hole for freshman Stacy Danley as the Tigers wear out Alabama on the ground in second half

Alf Van Hoose
Sports editor

Inches, mere inches decide the Iron Bowl

The Iron Bowl scoreboard beamed in the gloaming, for history: Auburn 10, Alabama 0.

Ten points of margin, unalterable, forever.

The victory difference computed, however, to teeny-weeny inches, less than the length of a football two admirable teams of young Americans fought for, and with, for three thrilling hours in the maelstrom that was Legion Field.

A football field is 1 32 acres, 691,200 square inches. A measly dozen inches, perhaps, going for Alabama instead of Auburn could have radically affected state society until Nov. 28, 1988.

It definitely would have affected two upcoming

Play a little harder
"Sometimes, when something bad happens, like a blocked punt, they (defense) play a little harder," said Pat Dye.
7B

Go for it
"You can't play a team like Auburn and take half-yard field goals. You need to knock it into the end zone. If you don't, you'll lose," said Bill Curry.
7B

Dye gets a victory ride · Curry dejected

bringing on a 15-yard unsportsmanlike penalty.

It all added up to a big gain of 59 yards to the Tide 26.

Time: Just under two minutes.

Burger was immediately sacked for a loss of 13 yards, but defensive end Phillip Brown came in too late on Burger, costing Bama 15 more infraction yards.

First down at the 22.

Danley dashed 17 yards, and freshman tailback Harry Mose shot around end for the game's first score. Win Lyle converted and the clock was down to 00:53.

Halftime: Auburn 7, Alabama 0.

After a scoreless third quarter, the Tigers' defense just flat buried Bama throughout the final period, leading 27-7 in offensive plays, and 23-7 in possession minutes.

Still, though, the score was only 7-0 with seven minutes to play and, remember, this is the Iron Bowl, where anything can happen.

AU could only think of "7-7" or "8-7" numbers. UA could only wish for them.

Auburn, starting from its 20, then banged out a 13-play drive that reached the Alabama eight. The clock was down to 01:19, and Lyle came on with a field goal that put it away.

Final score: Auburn 10, Alabama 0, and the Tigers had pitched their first series shutout in 30 years. AU also cut its series deficit to 30-21-1.

It would be a *"War Eagle!"* New Year's in New Orleans.

The game was more lopsided than the scoreboard difference, as AU led in first downs 20-10, yards rushing 185-136, yards passing 128-47, and total yards 313-183. AU was 14-for-18 in passing, UA only 7-for-15. UA led in penalty yards 39-36. Danley was the leading rusher with 154 yards on 26 carries (5.9). UA's prize running back, Bobby Humphrey, was held to 83 yards in 22 attempts (3.8).

Auburn (9-1-1) would face No. 4 Syracuse (11-0-0) in the Sugar Bowl on January 1, while Alabama would play Michigan in the Hall of Fame Bowl at Tampa the next day. Both the Crimson Tide and Wolverines were unranked.

In the Superdome, the score was 13-13, the clock was down to 02:04, and Syracuse faced fourth-and-one at Auburn's 21-yard line. Coach Dick MacPherson ordered a field goal, which was good, and a 16-13 lead for his team.

The Tigers then drove to the Syracuse 13 with the clock

Tech-Georgia just a local war this year

By Thomas O'Toole and I.J. Rosenberg
Staff Writers

Georgia vs. Georgia Tech. It means nothing, yet, it means everything.

The country will cast only a cursory look at tonight's neighborhood brawl in Grant Field (7:37, ESPN). Tech (3-8) is still trying to defeat a Division I-A school. Georgia (7-3) is out of the SEC race.

Perhaps the only pocket of real interest outside of the state will be Arkansas. The Razorbacks meet Georgia in the Liberty Bowl in Memphis, Tenn., on Dec. 19.

Though national implications are few, local interest never wanes in this emotional rivalry now heading into its 80th renewal.

"It's the state championship," said Georgia guard Kim Stephens. "In some ways, it's more important than the SEC championship."

"It's for bragging rights," said Georgia linebacker John Brantley.

"This is our last shot this season to salvage some respect," said Tech center Eric Bearden. "We know what we are going up against. But there is no reason why we shouldn't be flying around on that field Saturday."

The main drama will be if Tech can pull off what would rank among the biggest upsets in the history of the series. Subplots abound, too.

Tech coach Bobby Ross said Friday that Darrell Gast will remain as the starting quarterback, though Rick Strom will be available for the first time in five games. Gast became the starter after Strom broke a finger in practice before the Tennessee game.

"We decided that we'll start Darrell, but there is a possibility that Rick will play," Ross said after practice Friday. "He threw better today. Of course, we will not make any change in the game if Darrell is playing well."

Tech's defense, which has been the strength of the team, must overcome the loss of a second key starter. Linebacker John Porter was suspended this week by Ross for disciplinary reasons. The penalty comes two weeks after the suspension of safety Riccardo Ingram, who took money from an agent in violation of NCAA rules.

Eric Thomas, who has not been at full speed since the Auburn game because of a knee injury, will start for Porter.

See RIVALRY, Page 5-D

Sports

SECTION D   The Atlanta Journal □ THE ATLANTA CONSTITUTION   • • • SATURDAY, NOVEMBER 28, 1987

Auburn defense bags the Sugar

Dave
Kindred

A freshman's dream day

BIRMINGHAM, Ala. — When Stacy Danley came off the field, an Auburn functionary squirted water into the running back's mouth, the water both reward and sustenance. Danley had dashed 20 yards to the Alabama 11. Gasping now — early now, 154 yards weary. Tough work becoming a star. Unbuttons that chin strap. Catches a breath. Less than three minutes to play, Auburn up 7-0, victory certain. And this is what Pat Dye says to Stacy Danley:

"Swallow that tadpole water, you're good back in," the Auburn coach shouts, shouting the sweet nothing over the locomotive roar of the orange-and-blue people at Legion Field who came expecting victory, for such is their routine this season, but could not have expected 157 yards from the freshman Stacy Danley, never a 100-yard man until now; our four carries the first six games, a fumbler in practice who says, "I had to earn the confidence of the coaches, as a player and as a person."

Out of the game one play, Danley comes back for more yards out of Alabama's heart. The ball at the yard line. A field goal now. Now 10-0. About five minutes to go. New Auburn has the SEC championship. It has the Sugar Bowl. It has, dearest of all, Alabama at last, beaten again, beaten without a suggestion that this could have gone any other way.

stopped at 00:04. Win Lyle kicked a field goal for a 16-all tie.

MacPherson went into orbit! "How could Pat Dye play for a tie?" He screamed it for weeks.

Pat had snatched Dick's candy away. And Dick was crying. Then, of course, the Eastern press spread its claws, swooped down, and "dug-in."

But get the picture: Syracuse was working on a perfect season, and a possible national championship, while Auburn was working on nothing. With their "16-13 victory" and their "perfect 12-0-0 season" safely socked away — so they certainly thought — Orange rooters were all set to storm the field, as their side of the 'Dome was roaring, "*S-E-C!....S-E-C!....S-E-C!*"

That's all fine and dandy, if the game's over. But this game wasn't over.

At that precise moment, a tie would rip your opponents' heart out. It would be a devastating defeat. And, just an important, it would hush 'em up.

Pat Dye accomplished it all with one swift kick.

What Dick MacPherson, his players and the fans were *really* upset about was the fact that they were unable to *win* the game.

Besides, had Syracuse played Texas, Tennessee, Florida, Florida State, Georgia and Alabama — as Auburn did — the Orangemen would not have won 'em all. *No way!* The average power-rating of Auburn's opponents that year was 107.91, while Syracuse's was a lowly 92.96.

When the final gun sounded, the Superdome was as quiet as church mice.

"We still won," said a Tiger fan to a blue Orangeman, "because tomorrow we're goin' back to Auburn and you've got to go back to New York."

The next day, Alabama fans felt as bad, or worse, than Syracuse had the day before. The Tide trailed 3-21, fought back for a 24-21 lead, but lost 28-24 in the final seconds.

The Tigers finished 9-1-2 and No. 7. The Tide was 7-5-0.

Auburn played six bowl teams in '87 and four won their post-season games. Syracuse played three bowl teams and all three lost.

Top-rated Oklahoma faced No. 2-ranked Miami in the Orange Bowl. The Hurricanes won 25-10.

1988

GAME 53

Bye-bye, Ol' Iron Bowl, As We've Known It

The years of haggling had finally been resolved by cooler heads assembled around negotiating tables.

Last year's Alabama-Auburn match was the last to be played as a "true" Iron Bowl, with each school splitting the allotted tickets on an even basis.

The '88 game was at Legion Field with UA the home team.
The '89 game will be at Jordan-Hare Stadium.
The '90 game will be at Legion Field with UA the home team.
The '91 game will be at Legion Field with AU the home team.
The game will then rotate between Auburn and Birmingham.

Auburn University had *finally* won its long-fought battle.

So, in 1988, AU would be facing a hostile crowd at Legion Field for the first time since the series was resumed in 1948.

The fan ratio was about 6½ to 1 — 65,000 to 10,000.

The *Associated Press'* pre-season poll rated Auburn No. 7 and Alabama 12th.

The Tigers defeated Kentucky, Kansas, Tennessee and North Carolina, and moved up to No. 4 behind Miami, UCLA and USC. But in Baton Rouge, a wounded Tiger with back-to-back losses to Ohio State and Florida, was poised to spring on the invading Tiger. LSU 7, AU 6.

Pat Dye's charges then fashioned five straight wins (Akron, Mississippi State, Florida, Southern Mississippi, and Georgia), worked their way back to No. 7, and was ready to rip into Bama.

Coach Bill Curry's second edition topped Temple, was "weathered-out" of a game with Texas A&M at College Station, then beat Vanderbilt and Kentucky, which was good enough for an *AP* ranking of 12th.

The following week at Tuscaloosa, however, Ole Miss, with only a 1-3-0 record and 18-point underdogs, trailed 7-12 and faced third-and-goal at Bama's 10-yard line with 30 seconds to play. Final score: Mississippi 22, Alabama 12.

That shocker came on October 8, the same day Auburn had lost to LSU, so Tide and Tiger boosters had something to both grieve over and shout about that weekend.

The Tide tumbled off the poll charts.

Bama then topped Tennessee, Penn State and Mississippi State, but lost a 19-18 decision at Tuscaloosa to those pesky LSU Tigers.

It was the first time in 33 years that the Tide had lost twice in a season at Tuscaloosa.

After blanking Southwest Louisiana 17-0, it was once again time to set sights on AU.

Auburn was 8-2-0 by an average score of 32-7, and led the nation in defensive scoring. Alabama was 7-2-0 by an average score of 28-15.

The Tigers were favored by 7½-points — a huge spread for these annual bone-rattlin' functions.

On Thursday, *The Birmingham News* published a box score consisting of 21 "celebs" and their predictions on the big game. Eighteen picked Auburn to win by a consensus score of 19-11. Joe Dean, LSU athletic director, came the closest by picking a 14-10 score.

An Auburn victory would tie LSU for the SEC championship, but AU would get the Sugar Bowl bid because LSU had three losses overall and a much lower national ranking.

For the second straight year the game was played on the Friday after Thanksgiving and CBS-TV was on hand to showcase the series' 53rd conflict to the whole country.

Auburn's awesome "D" allowed the Tide only 12 net yards rushing on 27 attempts, forcing UA to throw 35 times, its third most in the series. Auburn's running game didn't exactly rumble either, gaining only 130 yards on 47 tries for a limp 2.8 average.

But the bottom-line figures, the only ones that really count, went in Auburn's favor for the third straight year. And the figures were 15-10. The game wasn't quite that close, still though, Bama had the Tigers plenty up-tight at one point in the fourth quarter, and the underdogs were still "hanging around" at the end.

Birmingham Post-Herald
Saturday, November 26, 1988

Sports Monday B

Iron Bowl: Auburn 15, Alabama 10

It's the Iron Age for Auburn

Dye's grip on the state is tightening

Tigers win third straight over Tide

By Ray Melick

The Tigers, on their first possession, drove 46 yards in eight plays down to the eight, but settled for a short Win Lyle field goal and a 3-0 lead.

The Tide came right back, going 63 yards all the way to the three. But they had to be content with an even shorter field goal by Philip Doyle to tie things at 3-3.

Before the field goal, Alabama had scored 999 points against Auburn, and Doyle's kick put it over the 1,000 mark. Where did Doyle play his high school football? At Huffman High right there in Birmingham.

Auburn quickly got another drive working that reached the six, but UA's Willie Wyatt put a hit on AU's Stacy Danley, the ball became a free item, and the Tide's Charles Gardner recovered.

On third down still from the 10, Auburn's defensive end Ron Stallworth, who would finish with four sacks for the day, rushed in and dropped quarterback David Smith in the endzone.

It was a safety and the "visiting" Tigers had grabbed an odd 5-3 lead.

Getting the ball right back on the ensuing free kick, Auburn marched 51 yards to the five, but again had to call on Win Lyle for points, and he responded with another chip-shot field goal and a shaky five-point advantage.

Once again, though, Bama retaliated, going 71 yards in 14 plays. But on third down from the Auburn seven, Smith's pass intended for Lamonde Russell was batted by Greg Staples and intercepted by Quentin Riggins.

Halftime: Tigers 8, Tide 3.

The play on the field had been about as bizarre as the numbers on the scoreboard. Auburn reached the five, six and eight; Alabama the three and seven, but no touchdowns resulted.

Just under five minutes remained in the third quarter and Auburn was in real trouble, facing third-and-19 from its 14.

It was time for Lawyer Tillman to don his orange hood and blue cape, dash from the huddle as Captain Tiger — and once again save his team from a Legion Field disaster — just as he had done the last two years.

Quarterback Reggie Slack called the play. It was "X-Take-Off." Tillman, split to the right side, took off on a fly pattern, zigged right to the sideline, then took off again. Slack heaved a long one. But Tillman couldn't shake Bama's rover Lee Ozmint, who appeared to have an interception all to himself. Tillman, Ozmint and the ball all arrived at the same place and the same time, and Tillman just out-leaped Ozmint, snagged the big prize, and was thrown out of bounds at the Tide 33.

It was a sudden gain of 53 yards.

Stacy Danley, who had been sidelined after receiving a vicious head shot late in the first half, ripped off a gain of 18 yards to the 15. Three plays later, fullback Vincent Harris dived over from the one. Lyle's conversion made it 15-3 with 02:43 remaining in the third period. AU finally saw some daylight.

With 10:26 left in the game, Alabama crossed midfield for the first time in the second half, reaching the 22, but a devastating penalty (holding) backed it to the 32. On fourth-and-13 from there, Doyle missed on a 49-yard field goal attempt.

That series of downs — especially the penalty — was quite obviously the game's turning point.

Coach Curry was heavily criticized for that decision. Why try a field goal? Even had it been good, Bama would still trail by a touchdown and field goal. Why not try for the first down?

The game's final points came with only 01:37 on the clock after an 89-yard Tide drive in only six plays. Smith passed to Greg Payne from the 12 for the score, and Doyle converted.

Bama attempted an unsuccessful onsides kick and Auburn ran out the clock.

The Tigers' third straight series victory was a first in 30 years (1956-57-58).

Auburn's top-rated defensive unit harassed Tide QB David Smith all afternoon. Smith ran the ball 10 times, but only one was planned. He dropped back to pass 44 times, got 35 off, mostly while scrambling, and completed 20 for 255 yards.

The Tigers led in first downs 19-16 and total yards 350-267. Slack was 13-for-26 in passing for 220 yards. The 475 combined passing yards by Smith and Slack was the series' most since the 1970 game (529 yards). Danley led all rushers with 97 tough yards in 25 carries. David Casteal's 28 yards (seven carries) led the Tide. Auburn was also hit with 112 penalty yards, the second most in the series to its 114 yards in the 1956 game.

Bama's series lead was 32-22-1, its scoring lead 1009-817.

Coach Dye told the press afterwards, "To be honest, the co-championship is important and the Sugar bowl is important, and we're proud. But winning this game means more than Sugar Bowls and championships. I wish we could play it today, talk about it tomorrow, and then it would be over with. But that's not the nature of this game. It's a game that will be replayed a thousand times before it is ever laid to rest."

Paul Finebaum of *The Birmingham News* wrote, "For Bill Curry, the future is uncertain. Although the Board of Trustees has given him a vote of confidence, saying they will honor his five-year contract, the rumor mill is working overtime....There are those Alabama fans who still talk about salvaging this season. A victory over Texas A&M and a victory in the Sun Bowl would give Alabama a 9-3-0 record.

"There's nothing wrong with that.

"But unfortunately, in the state of Alabama, there is only one thing that seems to matter: the Iron Bowl."

The Tide's game with A&M, scheduled for September 17, was postponed when tornado-like weather began running rampant throughout the Southwest.

They met on December 2, and the Tide won 30-10.

Once again, both Alabama and Auburn went bowling.

Bama, down by eight points in the fourth quarter, rallied for an exciting 29-28 win over Army in the Sun Bowl on Christmas Eve. Quarterback David Smith, a fifth-year senior, set school bowl records with a 33-for-52, 412-yard passing performance.

In the Sugar Bowl, it would be No. 7 Auburn against No. 4 Florida State. The Seminoles won 13-7.

The Tigers have scored a mere two touchdowns in their last three Sugar Bowls but, amazingly, lost only once (1-1-1). But there's a flip-side to that stat: the Tigers have allowed just three touchdowns, but won only once.

Auburn finished 10-2-0 with a No. 8 ranking, while Alabama was 9-3-0 and 18th.

With three straight Tiger victories over the despised Tide, and with next year's game at Jordan-Hare, everything was peaceful and lovely in the Loveliest Village on the Plains.

1989

GAME 54

Home Sweet Home? Yes! Yes! Ohh, Yes!

Auburn proved its point that it could kill the Iron Bowl. Auburn also proved again that it could grandly host a dramatic college football game. The event was carefully planned, details superbly executed for Alabama's historic first visit.

It made mockery of the blustery bluffs by Paul Bryant and Ray Perkins that Bama would never play the Jordan-Hare scene.

Alf Van Hoose
Sports Editor, *The Birmingham News*
Monday, December 4, 1989

For sure, Alabama-Auburn was a *big* game in 1971 when they met with perfect records. But for sheer, all-american hype, the 1989 game at least matched it, maybe even topped it.

The consensus of six pre-season polls had Auburn rated 10th in the country, with Alabama coming in at 16th.

Their memorable 1989 seasons unfolded:

SEP. 9 — Auburn pounded Pacific 55-0, while Alabama had an open date. *Associated Press* poll position: AU 5th, UA 16th.

SEP. 16 — Auburn over Southern Miss 24-3, Alabama over Memphis State 35-7. Poll: AU 4th, UA 15th.

SEP. 23 — Auburn didn't play. Alabama beat Kentucky 15-3. Poll: AU 4th, UA 13th.

SEP. 30 — Auburn lost to 12th-ranked Tennessee 21-14. Alabama got by Vanderbilt 20-14. Poll: AU 11th, UA 13th.

OCT. 7 — Auburn defeated Kentucky 24-12. Alabama trailed Ole Miss 0-21 before rallying to win a wild 62-27 shootout. Poll: UA 11th, AU 12th.

OCT. 14 — Alabama got by Southwest Louisiana 24-17. Auburn got by LSU 10-6. Poll: UA 10th, AU 11th.

OCT. 21 — Alabama won another shootout, this one 47-30 over Tennessee. Auburn lost a 22-14 decision to Florida State. Poll: UA 6th, AU 16th.

OCT. 28 — At Happy Valley, Penn State trailed 17-16, was fourth down at UA's one with the clock down to 00:13, and set for a winning field goal. Bama blocked it! Auburn shutout Mississippi State 14-0. Poll: UA 5th, AU 12th.

NOV. 4 — Alabama topped Mississippi State 23-10, and Auburn edged Florida 10-7. Poll: UA 4th, AU 12th.

NOV. 11 — Alabama doubled up on LSU 32-16, and it was Auburn over Louisiana Tech 38-23. Poll: UA 4th, AU 11th.

NOV. 18 — Alabama topped Southern Mississippi 37-14. Auburn beat Georgia for the sixth time in seven years by a 20-3 score. Poll: UA 4th, AU 10th.

NOV. 25 — Both teams were idle. But results elsewhere would dump even more appeal into the Alabama-Auburn media hot pot.

Top-ranked Notre Dame was beaten 27-10 by seventh-rated Miami, second-ranked Colorado had already completed its season, and third ranked Michigan defeated Ohio State 28-18.

On Monday when the polls were announced, Colorado went on top, Alabama hopped over Michigan into second place, Miami jumped three places to the fourth position, and the Irish fell to fifth. Auburn, meanwhile, dropped a notch to 11th.

Now, the Tide-Tiger clash would carry national championship implications.

Let the hype begin!

TUESDAY — Clyde Bolton of *The Birmingham News* wrote, "Bill Curry played in the first Super Bowl and two more, but he's more thrilled by a game that's coming up in Lee County.

"'I have never been involved in a game that's as exciting as this one. Even those Super Bowls were not,' Curry said."

Also on Tuesday, the *News* reported, "At least two University of Alabama players have been the targets of death threats in the past five months."

SPORTS

TOMORROW: Auburn readies for Tide's visit

TUESDAY, NOVEMBER 21, 1989

Bama players targets of death threats

Curry promises all-out effort to catch those responsible

By Charles Hollis
News staff writer

Clyde BOLTON
News sports columnist

SPORTS

TOMORROW: Dye has Bama on his mind

WEDNESDAY, NOVEMBER 29, 1989

Dye: Behavior, history most important

By Jimmy Bryan
News staff writer

At VAN HOOSE
News Sports Editor

Who has the edge in big one?

Where have the years' hidden? Time is so fleet it couldn't be, but it, more than 30 years since the custodian of this corner established a custom — an Alabama-Auburn game positions analysis.

Penny Marshall was no expert. Neither am I. He did enjoy attention. So do I.

He hewed the tradition. I follow. So, microscope focused, no with the show, Alabama versus Auburn. Offense first, the people's choice

AUBURN — Pat Dye wanted to talk more about civil behavior than civil war when he discussed Saturday's historic Alabama-Auburn football game at Jordan-Hare Stadium.

Alabama-Auburn football may fizz up brother against brother, sister against sister, but Dye tried to convince his audience that it's not who wins the game that's important

It's the behavior of the fans and the historical significance of Alabama's first visit to Auburn, he said. This could be Harvard's first trip to Yale to hear the usually combatative Dye tell it.

This was Pat Dye turned statesman.

"This is a historical game for Auburn and Alabama," he began. "Depending on which side you're on, the game is big enough in itself. Alabama has a great season going. We can make ours pretty good.

"Alabama has already earned at least a share of the conference championship and have the opportunity to win it outright. They also have a chance to win the national championship.

"Our players have an opportunity to win a share of their third straight conference championship, go out as the winningest class in Auburn history and

beat Alabama four straight times. Regardless of who wins, it will be a tremendous victory for that side.

"I hope the fans who come will respect that and conduct themselves in such a manner we don't disrupt the fact it's going to be great for one side or the other."

Despite the emotional flames fanned by this game every year, and particularly this year, Dye said he hopes no off-the-field incidents smear the first game in Auburn.

See Dye, Page 7D

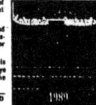

'One of the nastiest rivalries there is ...'

But Tide's Stacy says threats won't bother him on Saturday

By Charles Hollis
News staff writer

SPORTSEXTRA

TOMORROW: Counting down to the kickoff

THURSDAY, NOVEMBER 30, 1989

Dye has Alabama on his mind

Clyde BOLTON
News sports columnist

'I ain't afraid to lose, and I ain't afraid to win'

By Kevin Scarbinsky
News staff writer

I have a bad feeling about Saturday's Auburn-Alabama game.

The last time I had a feeling like this, I was scheduled to be on a morning plane flight.

I canceled the reservation and took an afternoon flight instead

And do you know what happened to the plane I was originally supposed to be on?

Nothing.

Still, I have a bad feeling about Saturday's game.

A few years ago, in a story about the series, I wrote "...It means so much to us that we treat it almost reverently, and it is nearly always a showcase of how college football fans should behave."

But I have detected a change of mood in some fans over recent seasons. The language has become harsher. More seem to wear their feelings on their sleeves when the rivalry is mentioned. Eyes narrow, and teeth grind. It's difficult to explain, but I believe I am correct.

One reason, no doubt, is that the series has become more competitive. Alabama doesn't dominate Auburn, as it once did. Tiger fans are tasting more blood, and Tide fans are tasting more ashes. Neither situation makes for attractive spit.

And boorishness is increasing in the stands at college football games, period. Booing your own players has become routine. T-- filthy language would melt an anvil and embarrass a master sergeant. Missiles fly more frequently. Auburn-Alabama is part of the overall college football picture. And the overall college football picture is part of the abandonment of standards of

AUBURN — Consider the evidence.
● Thursday, July 27: "We've had to throw Alabama a bone. We had to let them play in their sandbox."
● Monday, Oct. 2: "As a coach I'd rather play that game in Birmingham... For the first time I'm going to have to take my team to a motel the night before a home game."
● Saturday, Oct. 7: "Anybody heard a score from Jackson?"
● Saturday, Nov. 11: "It depends on what happens against Georgia, if I can get our people to stop talking about Alabama long enough to get ready for Georgia."

His people? For the past four months, if Pat Dye wasn't selling lumber or lawn tractors or auto parts, he was talking about Alabama.

Back when everybody was undefeated and the heat rose up around Bill Curry, Dye predicted the Tide would make its first visit to Jordan-Hare Stadium without a loss.

He talked about the agreement that brought the game to the Plain. He talked about "all the commotion" that would turn the game into a carnival and force him to alter his normal plans.

Coming off the field in Lexington, Ky., after a win over Kentucky, he wondered how Alabama was faring at Ole Miss after falling behind 31-0.

And two weeks ago he hinted the fans' anxiety to play host to Alabama might hinder his team's performance against Georgia.

Perhaps never before had the leader of one side in this rivalry talked so openly, so often about the game well before it came time to play the game.

From the outside, it looked like a man with his cage rattled. Whoa had Dye last chosen an October morning to discuss his plans for the night before a December game? How could he focus on Tennessee, LSU, Florida State and the rest if he kept talking about Alabama?

The word at Alabama this year has been "focus." At Auburn it looked like double vision.

From inside the cage, it looked different. One of Dye's most trusted and valuable players heard the Alabama talk all season and saw not paranoia but purpose.

"The reason he's been talking about it this year is he's had to talk about it," senior inside linebacker Quentin Riggins said. "Alabama's been winning and they're coming here for the first time.

"He's been put in a situation where he's had to talk about Alabama. And that's probably been for the better because he's been able to relieve some of that pressure by talking about it."

Every Auburn player and every Auburn coach, if he's honest, will admit that every day of the year Alabama lurks somewhere in his mind. "Always," wide receivers coach Larry Blakeney said.

Dye himself admitted in 1988 — before the Georgia game — that "not a day goes by I don't think about Alabama."

See Dye, Page 7D

ELSEWHERE
The quarterbacks Page 3D
Rosters, traffic map Page 4D
Tide, Tiger superstitions Page 1F

NEWS STAFF ILLUSTRATION/RAY BROWN

They were back Siran Stacy and lineman Charlie Dare.

Curry said, "When our players are threatened by those gutless wonders who find some perverse pleasure in making anonymous phone calls and writing letters, I will use every mechanism at my disposal, including the FBI, and prosecute them to the full extent of the law."

About the upcoming bus trip from Tuscaloosa to Auburn on Friday, Curry said, "Our players will virtually be surrounded by security."

And what about this Tuesday announcement: It became official that Gene Stallings would not be returning to the Phoenix Cardinals next year as head coach.

WEDNESDAY — Pat Dye responded to Curry's statements by saying, "If somebody actually threatened those kids, from Auburn or Alabama, if it's serious and not a hoax, I hope they catch them and put them in jail.

"But that kind of thing has been going on for years. I'm not saying this is not serious, but letter writing and phone calls and sending funeral wreaths and caskets is supposed to be some kind of psychological ploy. Most of it is usually by your own folks, trying to get you ready to play.

"The thing that surprises me is that if you hire the FBI to look into the matter, I wouldn't put it out to the public. I believe I would have called us over here and informed us. We certainly want to protect the Alabama players, plus our own."

Kermit Perry, Auburn's assistant athletic director for operations, had not heard from anyone at the University of Alabama about beefing up security.

"It's not like we've never handled a big crowd before," said Perry. "We have emotional sellouts against teams like Florida, Florida State, Tennessee and Georgia every year."

There was also news of another coaching change. Yesterday it was Gene Stallings leaving the NFL Cardinals, and today it was Jerry Claiborne leaving the University of Kentucky. Both, of course, would soon have a bearing on Crimson Tide football.

THURSDAY — The *News'* Kevin Scarbinsky reported, "Every Auburn player and every Auburn coach, if he's honest, will admit that every day of the year Alabama lurks somewhere in his mind ....Dye himself admitted it in 1988 — just before the Georgia

Over 85,000 crammed Jordan-Hare Stadium for the historic '89 game — the biggest crowd to ever see a football game in the State of Alabama at the time.

game — 'There's not a day goes by that I don't think about Alabama.'"

And Alabama's Stacy, who rushed for 1,025 yards and scored 18 touchdowns this season, said, "It's one of the nastiest rivalries there is. I mean that, too. By nasty I mean people saying nasty things about people. And that's not right."

Good things began happening early to Alabama. The Crimson Tide basketball team upset Dean Smith's 11th-ranked Tar Heels 101-93 Thursday night in Tuscaloosa before a sellout crowd of 15,043.

FRIDAY — Alf Van Hoose, sports editor of the *News,* wrote, "How much is too much. Hasn't too much been written and spoken about this football game? Is my reaction lonesome that I'll be happier when it's over?....For the first time I'm receptive to arguments that maybe this rivalry needs a break. Bear Bryant, an expert, kept insisting in his last years that the series had become too divisive in terms of state well-being."

And, of all things, Dye was at the stadium to tape an interview with CBS and was astounded to see a flower arrangement in one of the corners which spelled out "Beat Bama." He ordered the arrangement be dug up. It was. On game day, the flowers read, "Go Tigers."

Another state team also made its first visit to Auburn. The University of Alabama at Birmingham, better known as UAB, was there for a Friday night basketball game, and the Blazers defeated the Tigers 75-65 before a full house at Eaves Memorial Coliseum. All six of their previous games had been played in Birmingham.

SATURDAY — Thirteen members of *The Birmingham News* sports staff gave their predictions. The vote was 9-4, Tide.

Alabama was 10-0-0 by an average score of 31-15. Auburn was 8-2-0 by 22-10. The oddsmakers gave no points and took no points. They said, "pick-it, boys."

The town of Auburn and the campus of Auburn University early on turned into a carnival of orange and blue, with patches of crimson sprinkled here and there.

The first football game played at Auburn Stadium was on November 30, 1939, and resulted in a 7-7 tie with Florida. A capacity crowd of 15,000 was on hand.

Now, 50 years later almost to the day, December 2, 1989, the biggest crowd saw the *biggest* of all the 213 games played there. In fact, it's the biggest game that will *ever* be played there. Nothing else will come close.

It had taken Auburn 97 years to get Alabama to come into its back yard to play a football game.

The largest crowd to ever see a football game in the state, officially announced at 85,319, crammed the place and gazed on in amazement. Only about 11,000 wore crimson.

And, of course, CBS-TV beamed it to millions more across America.

It was finally 1:07 p.m., time to kickoff, and time for the players down on the field to take the spotlight. And, as usual in this series, they gave their vast audience a "*Bravo!* 5-Star" performance.

Alabama's Philip Doyle kicked off to Alexander Wright. All of the hoopla was history.

Starting from his 32, quarterback Reggie Slack connected with Greg Taylor for 12 yards, then a short lob to Wright for four,

THE OPELIKA-AUBURN NEWS, Friday, December 1, 1989

AU-Bama: the drama builds

Frenzied atmosphere expected this weekend

Perry BALLARD

It's an historic weekend, no matter who wins

By PERRY BALLARD
Sports Editor

The indications of a big weekend have been evident for a couple of days.
● More signs around campus.
● More cars and people in town.
● RV's arriving and staking out their territory for the weekend.
● Ticket prices soaring higher

Schedule

FRIDAY
3:30 p.m.—Auburn parade, beginning at Morris Drill Field, proceeding through town and ending at Plainsman Park.

THE BIRMINGHAM NEWS

SPORTS

SUNDAY
Tide, Tigers at Jordan-Hare

Basketball/3C
Football/4-8C
SportsDigest/8C

CLASSIFIED
Page 7C

FRIDAY, DECEMBER 1, 1989

THE GAME

Alf VAN HOOSE
News Sports Editor

Maybe this game is too big

As a wise man commented, "From the mouths of children ... wisdom."
From the mouth of Jon Martin, son of *News* golf writer Jon Martin:
"Gosh, Dad, I sure hope they don't interrupt the (TV) Alabama-Auburn game with President Bush and Mr. Gorbachev."

How much is too much? Hasn't too much been written and spoken about this football game?
● Is my reaction lonesome that I'll be happier when it is over?
● My conscience clangs a bell that a ball contest between 18-21-year-olds should not be Armageddon.
● No game in this series has collected much intensity, apprehension and ticket prices as this one.
● For the first time, I'm receptive to arguments that maybe this rivalry needs a break.
● Paul Bryant, an expert, kept insisting in his last years that the series had become too divisive in terms of state well-being.
● Of course, anything Bryant said propped instant 99.9 percent Auburn opposition. Bryant had Alabama boosters also on this issue.
● Time may add another star in Bryant's crown as a perception master.

Some history

Auburn's David Housel, eminent in public relations, leaped into history in a release the other day. His account of why the Tiger-Tide rivalry began again in 1948, after a 41-year lapse, has weak foundation points.
The athletic rivalry resumed not because of the state Legislature's, Housel wrote. Technically, he's right. All the purse-holder Legislature did was to tell the schools to re-marry, or else — a shotgun marriage sort of threat. Housel presented school presidents Ralph Draughon (Auburn) and John Gallalee (Alabama) as peacemakers without pressure. Neither merited Nobel nomination. Both fresh and historic careers. But, fresh at their posts, no established support bases, both understood a power threat.

State holds its breath as kickoff nears

By Jimmy Bryan
News staff writer

AUBURN — If the 1989 Alabama-Auburn football game was an automobile race, somebody would have announced early in the week:
"Gentlemen, Stall Your Engines ..."
Hey, slow down a minute.
Everything leading to Saturday's historic first meeting of Auburn-Alabama in Jordan-Hare Stadium for a television-concocted 1:37 p.m. kickoff has been full throttle.

Take a minute and remind yourself that it is just a game. Then consider that more attention has probably been directed toward this college football game than any event in the history of this state. In the memory of the living, anyway.
The hype has been extraordinary for a year now. This week it became mind-boggling.
● Auburn Coach Pat Dye says the game transcends winning and losing — it's the playing in Auburn that matters.
● Alabama Coach Bill Curry says he's played in two Super Bowls — but this game is bigger than both of those.

Suddenly, everybody in the state wants to go. Ticket demand is unprecedented. At last count the price to see it has been said the price to see it is $135 to $500 a pair.

Fans numbering somewhere between $1,216 — capacity — and 80,000 — according to how many more fans find a way — will wedge together to watch history in the making. By the turn of the century, 250,000 will swear they saw it or know somebody who did.

It is well documented what is at stake when they push back the sidelines and play the game Saturday.

Alabama (10-0) can finish an undefeated season, have its first SEC championship since 1981 — 19th overall — and put itself in position to at least play for a possible national championship against Miami in the Sugar Bowl.

See The Game, Page 6C

INSIDE
● Smith's Alabama offense vs. Hall's Auburn defense
● Tickets a hot item Page 4C

NEWS STAFF ILLUSTRATION/WAYNE MARSHALL

but the Tigers soon faced third-and-five at their 49. Slack threw long to a streaking Wright, who made a beautiful over-the-shoulder grab at the Tide seven, a big gain of 44 yards. Three plays later, James Joseph dived over the heap for the score. Win Lyle converted and it was 7-0 less than three minutes into the game.

The place was, to say the least, rockin' en'er rollin'!

Midway through the period, Tide tackle George Thornton cracked Darrell "Electron" Williams, the ball came loose, and Thornton recovered at the Auburn 21. On first down, Stacy broke through 10 Tiger defenders and was one-on-one against safety Dominko Anderson at the five-yard line. Anderson brought Stacy down, saving a touchdown.

Still, it was first-and-goal. Stacy tried it wide and was stuffed for a yard loss. Bama quarterback Gary Hollinsworth then misfired twice, bringing on kicker Philip Doyle to salvage three points. He did. With 08:13 left in the period, it was 7-3.

The Tide was soon on offense again and moved to a first down at the Tigers' three. They then pulled a near carbon copy of their earlier blown opportunity. Stacy again tried to go wide and was stuffed for a two-yard loss. Hollinsworth then mis-fired twice, bringing on kicker Doyle. But it was a fake, as holder Jeff Wall threw into the endzone. It fooled no defenders.

It looked like an Auburn kind of day and the thunderous roar of the big crowd could be heard all over Lee County.

What very well could have been a 14-7 Bama advantage was actually a 3-7 Bama deficit.

Things settled down until late in the half, when Slack was intercepted by Keith McCants at the Tide 37. Eleven plays later from the Auburn 18, Hollinsworth drilled one over the middle to Marco Battle. Touchdown. Doyle converted again with the clock down to 01:49.

Halftime: Alabama 10, Auburn 7.

The lights on the scoreboard usually determines the noise level of college football games and, except for the blare of the bands, the mood at intermission among the majority party was fairly somber.

But not for long.

Bama received the second half kickoff and six plays had it third-and-one at the Auburn 30. In "four down" territory, the Tide had two shots at 36 inches and possibly going up 17-7.

A pass play was called. Hollinsworth froze the linebackers

Opelika Auburn News

War Eagle

AU's 30-20 victory shares SEC title

with a play-action fake, put the ball on his hip, then threw to a wide-open Kevin Turner at the 25. The pass hit the grass short of Turner.

Fourth-and-one. A give to Siran Stacy, a 1,000-yard rusher that season? A quarterback sneak? No, a 47-yard field goal try into the wind. Doyle's kick fell well short.

Moments later, Slack connected with wide receiver Shayne Wasden on a bomb covering 58 yards to Bama's 10. Joseph later scored from the two, his second TD of the game, Lyle kicked good, and Auburn had regained the lead, 14-10, with 10:36 remaining in the third period.

Alabama, however, was threatening to move back ahead when Hollinsworth threw complete to fullback Kevin Turner at the Tigers' 26, but a hit by linebacker Quentin Riggins caused a fumble, and AU recovered.

It was soon another long Slack-to-Wright connection, this one good for 60 yards to UA's 14, setting up a Lyle field goal and a 17-10 Tiger lead.

Alabama punted, Auburn drove 80 yards in 13 plays, and Williams scored from the 12. Lyle kicked good again, 13:04 was left to play, and Tiger fans everywhere were whoopin' it up over their 24-10 cushion.

Auburn kicked off, Darrell Crawford intercepted a pass, and this led to a 31-yard Lyle field goal and a 27-10 boon with 09:36 to play. It was AU's biggest series lead in two decades.

Alabama answered that one, going 73 yards in only seven snaps, capped by Hollinsworth's 15-yard pass to Battle. Doyle's conversion made it 27-17 and the clock "just wouldn't move" for Auburn. It still showed 07:51 — plenty of time "for anything to happen!"

The Tide kicked off, got the ball back, and bounced all the way down to the Tigers' six-yard line, where it was fourth down and just under two minutes to play! A TD here and it's suddenly 27-23 or 27-24 or 27-25.

My, ohh, my!

Just 11 minutes earlier the stadium had been trembling from the rumble of a big 27-10 lead. And now....

Alabama instead went for a field goal — much to the delight of Auburn fans and to the disdain of Alabama. The decision brought a heavy round of boos from Crimson zealots.

A successful field goal would still leave their team "two scores" behind — a touchdown and a two-point conversion.

Doyle made it, bringing the score up to 27-20, and the clock down to 01:49.

Auburn recovered an on-sides kick, reached the 17, and kicked a field goal of its own — a 34-yarder by Lyle with 00:33 to play.

Final score: Auburn 30, Alabama 20.

Ol' Shug was looking down and smiling mightily — or was it an old-fashioned belly laugh — as he watched Jordan-Hare explode in jubilation.

The town was a madhouse of happiness through the night and into he wee hours.

Toomer's Corner hadn't seen a fun-loving mob this big and in this kind of spirit in 32 years, or since their Tigers were crowned national champions following the 1957 season.

Jimmy Bryan of *The Birmingham News* wrote, "The emotional runoff of Auburn's victory over Alabama Saturday in the historic first Tide-Tiger game to be played at Jordan-Hare Stadium, was more important to AU Coach Pat Dye than the 30-20 final score....There was the team's Tiger Walk from Sewell Hall to Jordan-Hare Stadium through Auburn fans that had the team running over with emotion.

"There was the electricity dealt from the mostly Auburn crowd of 85,319 that would have nudged the Richter scale.

"But most important to Dye was the fact this game was being played in Auburn at last.

The Birmingham News

SUNDAY, DECEMBER 3, 1989 — **OUR 102nd YEAR** — **9 SECTIONS**

Happy Auburn fans feel the earth move

SPORTS

Tide tamed in Tiger town

AU clock strikes midnight on Bama's Cinderella story

VAN HOOSE
News Sports Editor

THE BIRMINGHAM NEWS — **SUNDAY, DEC. 3, 1989**
THE ALABAMA AT AUBURN GAME

On a historic day at Jordan-Hare, the best team wins

Clyde BOLTON
News sports columnist

SPORTS

MOBILE PRESS REGISTER — SUNDAY, DECEMBER 3, 1989 — **SECTION C**

It's history: Auburn beats Tide!

Tigers win share of SEC title

By PETE ZURALES
Press Register Reporter

Kim Shugart
Press Register Sports Director

Both teams are true champions

"'It has been the most overwhelming experience I've ever been through,' Dye said. 'Alabama coming here to play is much bigger than who won the game. I believe the Alabama people who came here today and saw our stadium will want to come back.

"'There's no way to describe the way this football team felt coming down to the stadium today with all of the Auburn people lining the streets. I tried to stay out of the way, but seeing the look on the faces of Auburn people must have been like the Berlin Wall was coming down.'"

Alf Van Hoose reported, "It's first-grade simple.

"Big plays win big football games.

"Auburn and Alabama played a big, big game Saturday. It had national championship overtones. The Southeastern Conference title was at issue. And more importantly, for peace and comfort, the state title."

From Clyde Bolton we have, "'Come into my parlor' said the spider to the fly.

"Nope. The last thing this game was about were parlors and tiny creatures.

"It was more like inviting someone to your house and then sicking your pit bull on him."

Tony Barnhart of *The Atlanta Journal-Constitution* said, "On a historic day filled with possibilities, Auburn's sweetest dream came true, even if it wasn't Sugar-coated."

Raad Cawthon of the Atlanta paper reported, "And though fans had begun arriving as early as Wednesday, pulling their motor homes into the parking lot of Eaves Memorial Coliseum for the long wait, police said there had been little trouble....'We had about 20 arrests last night,' a policeman said. 'Most of them were DUIs. I went by the emergency room at the hospital this morning, and they had treated about 10 people, mostly college students who had gotten in fights. Broken noses, that kind of thing'....Most of the fans just seemed eager to go about the business of being at a football game....'This doesn't bother me,' said Barry Willard, an Alabama fan, as he sauntered through the crowd. 'I go up to Knoxville and get right in the middle of that Big Orange mess. I can handle this'....'The people here have been great,' said Clay Wiggins, an Alabama fan from Tuscaloosa. 'I think maybe this is something we should have done a long time ago.'"

With Auburn's four straight series wins, and six out of eight,

In Auburn's 1988-89 wins over Alabama, Tiger quarterback Reggie Slack was 27-for-52 in passing for 494 yards.

In the 1989 loss to Auburn, Tide quarterback Gary Hollinsworth passed for 340 yards — second most in the series to Scott Hunter's 484 yards in 1969 — also in a losing cause.

Alabama's lead was now down to 30-23-1.

UA led in first downs 23-21, and passing yards 340-276, while AU led in rushing yards 167-32, and total yards 443-372. The combined 815 yards of offense ranks third in the series behind the games in 1970 (1,074) and 1971 (970).

Hollinsworth was 27-for-49 and his 340 passing yards is second in the series to Scott Hunter's 484 yards in 1969 — both in losing causes. Slack's 274 yards (14-for-26) is fourth best in the series.

Auburn's win over Alabama threw the SEC championship into a three-way tie between the Tide, Tigers and Tennessee.

UA went to the Sugar Bowl to face No. 1 Miami, AU went to the Hall of Fame Bowl against Ohio State, and UT went to the Cotton bowl opposite Arkansas.

Miami took the Tide 33-25 to nail down the title.

Auburn bounced the Buckeyes 31-14.

Tennessee edged the Hogs 31-27.

Both Auburn and Alabama finished with 10-2-0 records. The Tigers were ranked No. 6, the Tide No. 9.

The combination of Joab Thomas as University president, Bill Curry as head football coach, and Steve Sloan as athletic director, lasted only three years.

Six weeks after losing to Auburn, Curry, as they say in the trade, resigned under pressure. His rocky stint at Tuscaloosa resulted in a 26-10-0 (.722) record.

Bill Curry's problem: 0-3 against Auburn.

1990
GAME 55

October: No. 2 In America.
December: No. 2 In Alabama.

It was a high-flying time for Auburn's autumn Saturdays.

In the last eight seasons (1982-89), the team had played a superb .794 brand of football, posting a 79-19-2 record, which was third best in the nation behind Miami and Nebraska. AU had won or shared four Southeastern Conference championships and gone to eight bowls. And with a 5-2-1 post season record, only FSU and UCLA were more impressive.

But Auburn's top accomplishment during the successful period was its six victories, including the last four, over the despised Crimson Tide.

The *Associated Press* revealed in its pre-season poll that Miami, Notre Dame, Auburn, Florida State and Colorado were the cream of the '90 crop. Alabama was pegged 15th.

Auburn opened with a 38-17 win over Cal State-Fulleton, beat Ole Miss 24-10, but was tied 26-all by Tennessee.

Meanwhile, back at the Capstone, Bama was 0-3.

AU nipped Louisiana Tech 16-14 and fell to sixth place. But impressive back-to-back wins — 56-6 over Vanderbilt and 20-17 over Florida State — shot the team all the way back to No. 2 behind Virginia.

Virginia? No. 1 in football?

The Tigers were right back in the hunt — for a few days.

A 17-16 victory over Mississippi State was good only for a tumble down to fourth place in the poll.

Auburn then lost to Florida by a stunning 48-7 score and plunged to 15th. Another defeat, 14-12 to Southern Mississippi, and the Tigers vanished from the rankings. A 33-10 racking of

Georgia did, however, assist somewhat in soothing a season gone sour.

Alabama was next.

Eugene "Bebes" Stallings became the new head coach the previous January. He had played for Paul Bryant at Texas A&M and was a survivor of Bear's infamous "Junction City" training camp in 1954.

"Yeah," he has said, "Bear took us out there in two old school busses, and brought us back in one." It was also the beginning, it has been written, of Bear getting the rest of the Southwest Conference coaches off the golf courses.

Stallings was later an assistant at Alabama for eight years (1958-64), and his most recent position was head coach of the Phoenix Cardinals.

Gene Stallings lost his first three games — 27-24 to Southern Mississippi, 17-13 to Florida, and 17-16 to Georgia.

But the Tide bounced back with victories over Vanderbilt, Southwest Louisiana and Tennessee, before a loss to Penn State. Picking back up, Bama bounced Mississippi State, LSU and Cincinnati.

Auburn approached.

The Tigers were 7-2-1, the Tide 6-4-0. Auburn's average score was 25-18, Alabama's 24-13. But the Tide was coming on strong, especially their defense, allowing only 31 points over the last six outings.

Although Auburn was ranked 20th and Alabama was unranked, the Tide was installed as a 2½-point favorite.

There was an SEC title at stake, plus all sorts of puzzling bowl conditions riding on the outcome. Going into that final Saturday, the league's top teams were Auburn (4-1-1), Tennessee (4-1-1), Ole Miss (5-2-0) and Alabama (4-2-0). Florida's 6-1-0 numbers were tops, but the Gators were still on the NCAA's naughty-naughty list.

What it actually boiled down to was this: A Tennessee win over Vanderbilt (doesn't UT always beat VU?) would send the Vols to the Sugar Bowl and Mississippi to the Gator Bowl. The Fiesta Bowl would take the winner of the Alabama-Auburn game, the Peach Bowl would get the loser.

On Friday night before the big game, both Alabama and Auburn basketball teams ran into trouble in Birmingham. Southern Mississippi edged the Tide in an 84-82 thriller before almost 17,000 fans at the Civic Center Coliseum, while at the

UAB Arena, an overflow crowd of nearly 9,000 watched the Blazers clip the Tigers 71-65.

After a year's hiatus, the game returned to Legion Field and the crowd was about 65,000 to 10,000 in Bama's favor for the 55th match. The CBS television crew was also on the grounds.

It all added up to an impressive attendance figure of just over 100,000 for the basketball and football games that weekend in Birmingham.

This was the seventh series game played on December 1, and Bama had won all but one. Was this a bad Auburn omen? It probably wasn't known, so it probably didn't matter.

The Tigers gave away seven quick points. A play after receiving the kickoff, quarterback Stan White was hammered for a sack by Bryan Holdbrooks back at the 10. On the next play, White was intercepted by free safety Efrum Thomas, who returned nine yards to the five. Three plays later, Robert Jones scored from the one, Philip Doyle converted, and it was 7-0 just three minutes into the game.

Auburn missed an excellent chance later in the period after gaining a first down at the Tide 17. On a reverse, Herbert Casey fumbled the handoff and UA's George Thornton recovered.

The teams continued their game of "kick-back" until just before intermission when they threw 10 fast points up on the scoreboard.

White's pass intended for Fred Baxter glanced off his finger tips into the hands of UA's Brian Stutson who returned it 19 yards to the Tigers' 23. On third-and-one from the 14, Jones was stopped short, and Doyle's field goal made it 10-0 with just 02:14 on the clock.

Bama kicked off and Auburn punted. On first down, Kevin Turner fumbled, and AU's Lamar Rogers recovered at the Bama 38 with less than a minute left.

On third-and-eight, White threw complete to James Joseph down to the eight, then hit Baxter for the touchdown with only 00:05 on the clock. Strangely enough, it was the Tigers' first series touchdown pass in 10 years (1980).

A fellow by the name of Win Lyle had been Auburn's place kicker for the last three years. Lyle was replaced for the next three years by a fellow named Jim Von Wyl.

Von Wyle converted.

Halftime: Alabama 10, Auburn 7.

Both offenses would continue to sputter throughout the

second half. Or was it a condition of just too much defense?

Alabama's Kevin Lee returned the kickoff 61 yards to Auburn's 38, but the Tigers braced.

Late in the quarter, AU got off a short 30-yard punt, giving Bama the ball at its 45. Four carries by Junior Sewell for 29 yards keyed an advance down to the Auburn 23, and Doyle booted another field goal for a 13-7 lead with only 28 seconds remaining in the period.

The Tigers botched a great shot at taking the lead early in the final quarter when Rogers recovered a fumble at the Tide 16, but the AU sideline again failed to dial up the right numbers.

White passed seven yards to Joseph. Tony Richardson got a yard.

Third-and-two at the eight. Another reverse was called, and once again it was fumbled, this time by Baxter. Holdbrooks made his second recovery.

Woe be the Tiger....

The clock kept on tickin' and had reached the eight-minute mark. Flustered Auburn, still trailing only 13-7, was fourth-and-one at its 40. After a long count in an attempt to draw the defense offsides, which didn't work, AU punted.

Starting from its 23, Bama haywired its offense together long enough to reach the Auburn 47, where was also was fourth-and-one.

Would Alabama, like Auburn, punt?

Stallings' order: "Go for it, boys!"

Martin Houston, a 232-pound fullback thundered into the line for three enormous yards.

First down.

Driving on down to the 23, Philip Doyle kicked his third field goal of the day and 77th of his college career to set a new SEC record, previously held by Georgia's Kevin Butler (1981-84).

There was still 02:15 remaining, but this game was over.

Final score: Alabama 16, Auburn 7.

The Tigers *could* have won, but didn't, and their four-year victory party was over.

It had been a long, baffling season.

The game's light offensive stats showed Alabama led 13-11 in first downs, and 92-52 in yards rushing, while Auburn led 185-102 in passing yards and 237-194 in total yards. Alabama's passing game was 14-for-26, Auburn's 17-for-31. The numbers that killed Auburn were 5-2, representing turnovers. Auburn also

The Tide turns

led 65-50 in penalty yards.

The combined 431 yards of offense was the series' fewest since the "Punt Bama Punt" game in 1972, when they managed just 331 yards.

Tennessee captured the SEC title outright for the automatic invitation from New Orleans.

In Atlanta, Auburn scored a touchdown in the final few seconds to get past Indiana 27-23 on December 29. On New Year's Day, both Mississippi and Alabama ran into buzz-saws. The Rebels lost to Michigan 35-3, and the Crimson Tide was shocked 34-7 by the University of Louisville. That night, the Vols scored a TD just seconds from the end to edge Virginia 23-22.

The SEC's all-time bowl record against the Big Ten went to 12-4-0.

Auburn finished 8-3-1 and No. 19. Alabama was 7-5-0.

Following their game in December, *The Atlanta Journal* reported, "Auburn coach Pat Dye will return to the University of Alabama Medical Center next week for more tests on his stomach condition that kept him hospitalized for three days earlier in the season....There has been talk that Dye would retire after this season because of illness....Dye said he would return as Auburn's coach next year."

1991
GAME 56

Bama's Big "D" Pays Big Dividends

Much of the luster which had surrounded the Tide-Tiger clashes of the past several years was missing for the 56th renewal of this harsh old rivalry.

The fact that Alabama was 9-1-0 and Auburn 5-5-0 certainly was a basis. But for Auburn boosters everywhere, the puzzling "Eric Ramsey Tapes" dilemma also weighed heavily.

And a CBS-TV crew would soon be coming to the state for interviews and to gather information on the Ramsey controversy for a "60 Minutes" segment that would be aired in the coming weeks.

More off-the-field controversy hit Tuesday before the game. But this was on Alabama.

Guerry Clegg of the *Columbus* (Ga.) *Ledger-Enquirer* reported, "The Iron Bowl is still four days away, but the first shots in the Auburn-Alabama war already have been fired.

"The Auburn athletic department has filed a complaint with the Southeastern Conference office, claiming that David Palmer, Alabama's standout freshman wide receiver, had another student take his college entrance exam."

This meant his ACT (American College Test.)

Clegg continued, "Alabama coach Gene Stallings said, 'If Pat Dye is going public with something, he must think he knows something....If I were Dye, I think I'd be more worried about things going on down there at Auburn.'"

This, of course, was in reference to the Ramsey thing.

All in all, there was an ample amount of lighter fluid available for both camps to keep the talk red-hot throughout the week.

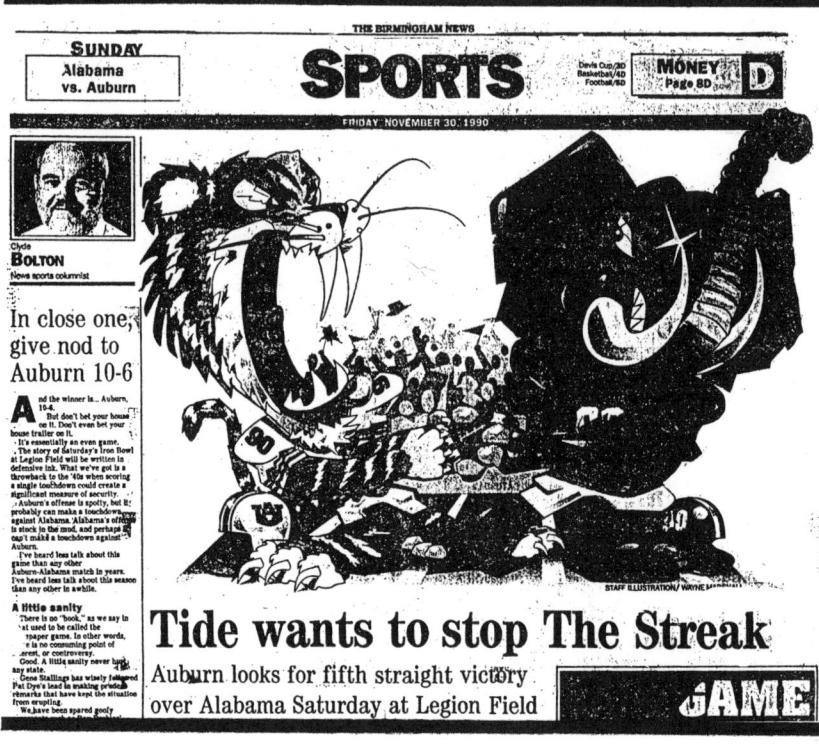

As the pre-season publications hit the stands in August, football fans around the Southeast were wondering, "What has happened to Auburn and Alabama? Why are they suddenly rated so low?"

It's interesting to note that one of the magazines, *Heinrich's College Football '91,* picked its Top 20, then listed another 10 as "teams to watch." It included both the Tigers (21st) and the Crimson Tide (30th).

It seemed strange to see Auburn and Alabama regulated to the level of "teams to watch."

In the *Associated Press* poll, AU began as the 18th-ranked team, UA 20th.

Alabama opened with a 41-3 win over lightweight Temple. But next was a 35-0 battering by the Gators at Gainesville in the Tide's most lopsided loss in 384 games going all the way back to 1957 and a 40-0 ruin to Auburn.

Coach Stallings somehow dislodged his shipwreck from the reefs, got a high tide, and picked up full sails.

Eight straight wins went on the books. Falling were Georgia, Vanderbilt, UT-Chattanooga, Tulane, Tennessee, Mississippi State, LSU and Memphis State, by a combined 240-74 score.

The Tide had worked all the way up to No. 8, and Auburn was next on the schedule.

Auburn got a sample of things to come in its opener against Division II Georgia Southern. The Tigers trailed 17-7 just before intermission, saw Southern drop a sure touchdown pass, then got serious long enough to struggle to a second-half 32-17 win.

After decisions over Ole Miss and Texas, the Tigers were ranked 13th.

Little did Auburn know, but the "good times" were over — for awhile, anyway. Directly ahead was a mine field of strife, controversy, uncertainties — and defeats on the football field.

The Tigers lost to Tennessee and Southern Mississippi, edged Vanderbilt, lost to Mississippi State and Florida, walloped Southwest Louisiana, then lost to Georgia for only the second time in eight years.

Alabama was next.

The Tide was 9-1-0 by an average score 28-11, ranked eighth, and was favored by a touchdown. The Tigers were 5-5-0 by an average score of 23-20.

Clyde Bolton of *The Birmingham News* wrote during game week, "If Pat Dye could rub the magic lamp and have the jinni summon any opponent Saturday, I believe he would choose Alabama.

"Getting to play the Tide at the end of this disastrous season is like having the opportunity to go double or nothing on the last hole of a golf match in which you've lost money."

Right-on. Coach Dye and his Tigers had a whole lot to gain and only a little to lose.

As for the Southeastern Conference race, Florida's 7-0-0 figures had the Sugar Bowl all wrapped up. This was the SEC's 59th season and the Gators had *finally* won a title.

Bama had accepted an invitation to help Colorado break-in the brand new Blockbuster Bowl at Joe Robbie Stadium in Miami on December 28.

As for David Palmer, his test score dilemma was settled and he was allowed to play.

Just over 83,000 packed Legion Field on Saturday, November 30, for Auburn's last "home game" at the old place. It was televised for the 17th time — all national — since the first one in

SPORTS

SUNDAY, DECEMBER 1, 1991

Tide rules the Iron

1964. NBC carried that game, ABC the next 11, and CBS the last four. This one would be beamed via national cable by ESPN.

With all the bizarre circumstances momentarily left behind, it was time to tee it up and kick it off.

The first two scores were field goal trade-offs — Matt Wethington's 38-yarder in the first quarter for UA, and Jim Von Wyl's 26-yarder in the second period for AU.

Bama, starting from its 20 in the second quarter, scored the game's only touchdown. Quarterback Jay Barker lobbed a pass out to fullback Kevin Turner who turned it into a gain of 68 yards, sparking a four-play burst to the Auburn 10.

Coach Stallings then sent in Palmer to replace Barker at quarterback with a play especially designed to take advantage of his speed and quickness.

"If everyone expected Palmer to run a quarterback sweep, no one in blue expected it would be quite that hard to arrest him," reported the *News'* Kevin Scarbinsky.

"'I didn't want to choke,' Palmer said. 'I wanted to come out and prove myself. I think I did.'

"Even after bobbling the snap, even after coming within arm's length of four Auburn tacklers, Palmer found his impossible way into the end zone. Just before Tim Cromartie, James Willis, Corey Barlow and Jon Wilson would reach his way, Palmer would vaporize only to crystallize in an open space."

Wethington converted and it was 10-3.

Early in the third period, UA was stopped at the AU 22, and Wethington booted another field goal for a 13-3 lead.

Later in the quarter, Auburn reached the Alabama 26, but Von Wyl's kick for three missed its target.

The game's turning point occurred early in the final period. Auburn had marched 59 yards to a first-and-goal at the one.

On first down, quarterback Stan White pulled away from center and dropped the ball. He recovered back at the three.

On second down, tailback Joe Frazier tried a toss sweep to the short side, but was hit for a two-yard loss by linebacker John Sullins.

On third down, White lobbed a high one into the endzone for 6-foot-4 tightend Fred Baxter. It didn't connect.

On fourth down, Von Wyl kicked a field goal.

Instead of a three-point difference, it was seven. And that's the way it ended.

Alabama 13, Auburn 6.

It was the first time in 16 years that Auburn failed to score a touchdown in the series.

The Tigers led in first downs 15-14, and total yards 345-286. Bama's passing game was 7-for-18 for 125 yards, AU's 13-for-27 for 113 yards. Auburn also led 3-2 in turnovers, and 100-59 in penalty yards.

It has been remarkable the number of goaline stands this rivalry has seen in the last seven years which, of course, has led to a high number of field goals. During that period (1985-91), they combined for 22 field goals and the line of scrimmage on exactly half the kicks was the *seven-yard line.* The average line of scrimmage on all 22 field goals was only the 14.

In the Blockbuster Bowl, the Buffaloes led by scores of 9-7, 12-10 and 19-16, but Bama pulled out the see-saw battle by a 30-25 final.

Gene Stallings' boys escaped from the "teams to watch" plateau, and rose from their 18th *AP* ranking all the way to a final No. 5 position on the strength of an 11-1-0 record.

And with two straight victories over Auburn, the Tide's series lead went to 32-23-1.

A "team to watch?" Just wait'll next year....

1992

GAME 57

Tuscaloosa Is Again Titletown

The football programs of Alabama and Auburn took entirely different directions throughout the 1992 season. As the weeks progressed, one kept going up, the other kept going down.

It went like this:
SEP. 5 — Alabama topped Vanderbilt 25-8 and remained in its No. 9 pre-season ranking (*Associated Press*). Auburn lost to Ole Miss by a score of 45-21.
SEP. 12 — The Tide got by Southern Mississippi 17-10 and remained ninth. The Tigers stomped Samford 55-0.
SEP. 19 — Alabama 38, Arkansas 11, and a move to seventh. In one of Auburn's few bright spots, it edged LSU 30-28.
SEP. 26 — UA got past Southwest Louisiana 13-0 and stayed put in the poll. Auburn 16, Southern Mississippi 8.
OCT. 3 — Bama hammered South Carolina 48-7 and nudged up a notch to sixth behind Washington, Miami, Michigan Tennessee and Texas A&M. Auburn downed Vanderbilt 31-7.
OCT. 10 — Crimson Tide 37, Green Wave 0. And UA moved up two steps to fourth, as Tennessee got caught "lookin' ahead" a week to Alabama and lost in a staggering upset to 1-4-0 Arkansas 25-24 — at Knoxville, no less. UT had led 24-14 just minutes earlier. Idle A&M remained No. 5. Auburn was beaten 14-7 by Mississippi State.
OCT. 17 — The Tide took Tennessee for the seventh straight season, 17-10. (The UA-UT average score over the period was 32-19.) Bama remained No. 4 behind Miami, Washington and Michigan. Auburn, meanwhile, lost to Florida 24-9.
OCT. 24 — Alabama 31, Mississippi 10, and the top four teams remained the same. Auburn eked out 25-24 decision over Southwest Louisiana.

OCT. 31 — Bama didn't play, but moved up to No. 3, even though Michigan got a 24-17 win over Purdue. Auburn and Arkansas fought over a 24-all draw. Now at the top was the Washington-Miami-Alabama trio.

NOV. 7 — The smooth blend of two "UA" victories sent the Crimson Tide into second place in the polls. It was Alabama over LSU 31-3, and Arizona over Washington 19-3. Auburn welcomed its open date.

It was now Miami-Alabama as 1-2.

The following week had an explosive start for Alabama, as "The Gene Jelks Story" hit the headlines and airwaves, bigtime! Jelks said that he had received large sums of money while playing football at the University during the 1986-89 period.

But for Auburn fans everywhere, it was by far the *best* news they'd heard in months. They wallowed in it. They looked at it this way: "OK, Alabama, we've got our *Ramseygate* and you've now got your *Jelksgate!* Live with it, busters!"

NOV. 14 — The Tide survived a super scare in Starkville and was happy to escape with a 30-21 win. It was *much* closer than that. The win clinched the SEC's West Division title and the chance to play Florida for the conference championship.

At Auburn, the Tigers found an incredible way to lose a heartbreaking 14-10 decision to Georgia. AU was second-and-goal inside the Bulldogs' one, ran a play, didn't make it, then let the final 19 confusing seconds disappear from the clock.

Alabama-Auburn was next. And the 10-0-0 Tide was a whopping 15-point favorite to take care of the 5-4-1 Tigers.

On Wednesday, November 25, the day before the game, Pat Dye dropped a bombshell. He announced his resignation as coach at Auburn.

That, of course, overshadowed even Alabama-Auburn.

NOV. 26, THANKSGIVING DAY — Mike Bolton of *The Birmingham News,* wrote, "If one moment Thursday illustrated that the 1992 edition of the Iron Bowl was going to be a strange one emotionally, it was when Alabama assistant coaches went onto the field before game time and refused to shake Pat Dye's hand. They each hugged him, instead."

The *News'* Charles Hollis said, "Cameras flashed as Alabama coach Gene Stallings place his arm around Auburn coach Pat Dye and embraced his rival Thursday in pre-game warmups at Legion Field....'It was really sad. I told him we would miss him. I told him college football would miss him. It was more of an

emotional meeting than I was expecting.'

"While they embraced, while they put their arms around each other and spoke to their ears only, Dye's Auburn cap tumbled off his head.

"Without the cap, without the security of something that could hide the eyes, Dye's emotions were exposed.

"There were tears in his eyes and Stallings could feel the emotions running through Dye.

"There was a lump in Stallings throat. 'I told him how I felt.' Stallings said, 'I just hate to see him leave the game like this.'"

A crowd of 83,009 was at Legion Field for the series' 57th game and they watched a scoreless first half before the Tide hacked out a businesslike 17-0 win.

Only in 1906 and 1967 had the series failed to produce any points by intermission.

Early in the third period, Auburn drove from its 22 to the Bama 35, where it was second-and-six. Quarterback Stan White

The Birmingham News

Thursday, November 26, 1992 — **Our 105th Year** — **12 Sections**

TODAY SPORTSEXTRA — Dye resigns: 'Relieved' it's over

The Birmingham News

Friday, November 27, 1992 — **Our 105th Year** — **9 Sections**

TODAY RELIGION  Even rivals emotional over Dye's surprise departure

threw a sideline pass intended for Orlando Parker, but Tide cornerback Antonio Langham raced in front of Parker, tipped the ball in the air, made the interception, then raced 61 yards for the game's first score. Michael Proctor converted and it was 7-0.

After the ensuing kickoff, Auburn punted. Terry Daniels got off a 51-yarder to Alabama's 11, but a holding penalty brought it back. Daniels' next kick was 37 yards, and the Tide instead started at their 40.

On third-and-five from his 45, Bama quarterback Jay Barker completed a pass to Curtis Brown for 21 yards to the Tigers' 34. After reaching the 21, Barker was sacked back at the 30, and Proctor popped a 47-yard field goal for a 10-0 advantage with three minutes left in the quarter.

Dye told the press afterwards, "The interception return on our first drive of the second half hurt. And then they got that field goal. But 10-0 is not a big lead unless you've got a defense like Alabama. Then its a monumental lead."

Early in the final period, Daniels shanked a kick that carried only 17 yards, Alabama began 45 yards away, and drove for the

THE BIRMINGHAM NEWS

COMING SUNDAY
Samford begins
I-AA playoffs

SPORTS

MONEY Page 16D

D

FRIDAY, NOVEMBER 27, 1992

Iron Bowl has tears, cheers

Emotional Dye bids farewell

By Neal Sims
News staff writer

There wasn't a dry eye in the house

If it wasn't the most emotional scene I've witnessed in 38 years in the newspaper business, I don't know what was.

As one old reporter said, "If there was a dry eye in that room, it had to belong to Hitler."

Pat Dye stood before the gyrating pencils and humming cameras of the media in his last postgame news conference as Auburn's coach and without hesitation answered the question of whether he will be happy not coaching:

"You're damn right."

Then he asked his wife Sue and their two daughters to join him at the microphone. But if Dye hoped for a chorus of familial delight that he was escaping the meatgrinder, it didn't materialize.

"Wanda, you quit crying, and Missy, you, too," he said as his grown girls broke down. They should be celebrating, he told them, but then his own tears welled over.

"They've been through an awful lot," Dye said in a emotionally charged voice. "Some of you guys put them through an awful lot.

"You ought to think about that when you're doing your job."

Pat Dye, tough coach, was crying as his final press conference ended and he and his family walked out into the Thanksgiving chill and into a new phase of their lives.

Twin pain

Thomas Bailey, the sophomore wide receiver, lingered in a corner of the room. "I wish we could have won it for him," he said softly.

Bailey was hurting from the twin arrows of loss of game and loss of coach.

"Everybody is feeling down," he said. "Coach Dye gave everyone the opportunity to come here and play collegiate football.

"Nine out of 10 of us, he's the reason we came to Auburn."

Dye announced his resignation the night before the game because, in his words, "that's when it was finalized."

I figured the players would be confused and downcast and be at even more of a disadvantage, but after watching them play a better Alabama team to a scoreless tie for more than a half, I think the timing of the announcement may have been beneficial.

"Coach Dye just came in last night and announced he had signed a letter of resignation," Bailey said. "It came as a shock to us. It gave us every reason to try to give him his 100th win."

When the players heard the news "there were a lot of mixed feelings. Some were fired up and some were down. All I could do was go to sleep."

Players tried for Dye

Did the timing help or hurt the team? "I feel we played better," Bailey said. "We had a lot of breakdowns on offense. We couldn't score. But the defense really played well. We were set on giving Coach Dye his 100th win."

After Dye met with the team, the players held their own meeting, without coaches, Bailey revealed.

"We said, 'Coach Dye is gone, and let's win it for him.' We knew what we had to do. There was no use talking about it, just go do it."

Bailey was philosophical in the wake of the 5-5-1 season.

"The best thing that came out of this season was that we learned to love each other, and that's the most important thing in life," he said.

"Coach Dye touched my heart, and he touched my family's heart. I hope we can maintain a close relationship with him, and I can have somebody to talk to. Everybody needs somebody to talk to."

And so Pat Dye strode into football history, and Thomas Bailey said he will support the next head coach of the Auburn University Tigers.

Whoever he is. "I've got to get better next year," Bailey said with a degree of resolution that would have pleased his ex-coach.

The Dye years returned pride, success and fun to Auburn. They weren't perfect, but they were pretty darn good.

A teary-eyed Pat Dye gives one of his daughters a hug after his final game at Auburn.
NEWS STAFF PHOTO/STEVE BURNETT

• Dye's resignation was announced Wednesday night, 1A
See Dye, Page 8D

Dye initiated resignation talk

By Charles Hollis
News staff writer

Auburn coach Pat Dye had a quiet dinner with his attorney on the eve of the Iron Bowl in his Sheraton-Civic Center hotel suite.

Lawyer Sam Franklin of Birmingham said it was just an intimate evening away from the crowd and the 10 p.m. press conference at which officials called at the hotel to announce Dye's plans of resignation.

"He ate in his suite and concentrated on the game. He had been check with his players, just like he always does.

"Everything was going pretty well, as well as you could expect for something as emotional as this, until Pat's two daughters, Missy (19) and Wanda (22), came by the suite.

"They had no idea about the announcement. They didn't know their dad was resigning after 12 years."

"They took the news hard. Dye said 'a lot of tears were shed. But they knew this was the best thing for me, our family and Auburn."

Franklin added that "other than that, there was smile laughing and just a good, uneventful evening for Pat."

Dye returned a phone call from one of his former players, Heisman Trophy winner Bo Jackson.

Jackson called from Chicago to wish the Tigers good luck against their archrival.

"Pat really enjoyed talking with Bo," said Franklin. "I think it helped to ease some of the pain he was going through."

The day before, late in the day, a high-ranking Auburn official said Franklin and Auburn president Dr. William

More on IRON BOWL Pages 6-9

See Resignation, Page 8D

Auburn quarterback Stan White feels the crushing defense of Alabama's Lemanski Hall (left) and Derrick Oden.

Bama's mighty defense marches on

By Jimmy Bryan
News staff writer

The University of Alabama's second-ranked football team proved conclusively Thanksgiving afternoon that great talent is a more powerful foe than emotion.

The Crimson Tide peeled away the emotion of Auburn coach Pat Dye's shocking Wednesday night resignation to punish the Tigers with a 17-0 Iron Bowl shutout at Legion Field Thursday afternoon. A sellout crowd of 83,091 and a national television audience looked on.

It was the first shutout ever of a Dye-coached team.

Winning this most bitter of rivalries for the third straight year would normally be satisfaction enough for Alabama. Particularly when it means an undefeated regular season of 11-0 and extension of a winning streak to 21 in a row.

Yet Thursday's victory advances Alabama tantalizingly within reach of more significant things.

The Crimson Tide moves into the first-ever SEC Championship Game at Legion Field against Florida a week from Saturday unblemished and looking for a national championship.

If the Tide handles Florida, the stage will be set for a Sugar Bowl showdown with No. 1 Miami New Year's Day. The Hurricanes have only out-classed San Diego State Saturday in the way of holding their No. 1 ranking.

Alabama coach Gene Stallings refused any national championship discussion.

"We've won 11 games and still haven't won anything," he said late Thursday afternoon. "I have no thoughts on anybody but the University of Florida. We've been able to concentrate (on the next game) well all year.

"This still haven't played our best game. Maybe we will next week."

Dye, in a final press conference as Auburn coach that became emotionally-charged, paid tribute to his main rival of the past 12 years.

"This was a great day for Coach Stallings, the

Alabama players and fans," Dye said. "If I had a vote for No. 1, Alabama would get my vote."

The Crimson Tide defense stuffed Auburn with a net of only 39 yards rushing and 119 passing. It was Bama's third shutout of the season, but first over Auburn since 1975 (28-0).

But Auburn played the 15½-point favored Crimson Tide to a 0-0 standoff in the first half. It was perhaps fitting the game was turned early in the second half by Alabama's No. 1-in-the-nation defense.

Auburn was proceeding on its most productive drive of the game. It had put together two first downs under its own power for the first time, and moved 36 yards to the Alabama 39.

On second-and-4, Tide cornerback Antonio Langham stepped in front of receiver Orlando Parker and tipped quarterback Stan White's pass in the air. He gathered it in and fled 61 yards to the game's first points.

"Man, I can't explain it," Langham said. "I was in a man-to-man and the receiver ran an out."

See Bama, Page 8D

11-0

W	Arkansas	
W	Louisiana Tech	
W	South Carolina	48-7
W	Tulane	37-0
W	Vanderbilt	
W	Tennessee	17-10
W	Ole Miss	31-10
W	LSU	31-11
W	Mississippi St.	30-21
W	Auburn	17-0

game's final points. Sherman Williams scored from the 15, and Proctor converted.

Daniels' seven other punts for the afternoon averaged a handsome 46 yards.

With the 17-0 final, Alabama had thrown its 13th series shutout overall, but the first in 17 years (1975).

Obviously, Bama had better statistical numbers, leading in first downs 17-8, yards rushing 199-20, and total yards 262-139. Auburn passed for 119 yards (14-for-25), Alabama for 63 yards (5-for-14). Auburn led 74-44 in penalty yards. The game's leading rusher was UA's Martin Houston with 68 yards in 14 carries (4.9).

The series' 57th game was history.

The *News'* Clyde Bolton was there and describes the last moments of Dye's coaching career at Auburn:

"Pat Dye stood before the gyrating pencils and humming cameras of the media in his last postgame news conference as Auburn's coach and without hesitation answered the question of whether he will be happy not coaching:

"'You're damn right.'

"Then he asked his wife Sue and their two daughters to join him at the microphone....'Wanda, you quit crying, and Missy, you, too,' he said as his grown girls broke down. 'They should be celebrating,' he said.

"But then his own tears welled over.

"'They've been through an awful lot,' Dye said in an emotionally charged voice. 'Some of you guys put them through an awful lot. You ought to think about that when you're doing your job.'

"Pat Dye, tough coach, was crying as his final press conference ended and he and his family walked out into the Thanksgiving chill and into a new phase of their lives."

Dye coached 142 games at Auburn with a 99-39-4 record (.711). He and Mike Donahue (1904-22) are tied for the second most wins behind Shug Jordan's 175. Donahue's record in 19 seasons was 99-35-5.

Dye's teams outscored the opponents 3569-2129 (25-15 average). At Jordan-Hare, he was 66-13-2 (.827) and 33-26-2 (.557) on the road. Twenty of his 39 losses were by one TD (seven points) or less. His wins were by a 30-12 score on the average, his losses by 13-23.

Dye split his 12 games with Alabama.

Saturday January 2, 1993 — SPORTS — The Tuscaloosa News — C

TIDE STORMS 'CANES

Alabama sticks to simple plan to dominate defending champs

By CECIL HURT
Sports Editor

Alabama 34
Miami 13

NEW ORLEANS — All year long, Gene Stallings had said that the University of Alabama still had not proved

Vol. 175, No. 2
4 Sections

The Tuscaloosa News

Tuscaloosa/Northport and West Alabama

SATURDAY, JANUARY 2, 1993

25¢

NATIONAL CHAMPIONS!

THE BIRMINGHAM NEWS

SPORTS   B

SUNDAY, JANUARY 3, 1993

ALABAMA

How sweet it is for 13-0 Tide

By Charles Hollis
News staff writer

NEW ORLEANS — Standing in front of the CNN/McDonald's college football championship trophy Saturday in the Big Easy, it finally dawned on Alabama coach Gene Stallings what his team had done.

The Crimson Tide (13-0) was the 1992 national champion, not just in the CNN/McDonald's poll but in the Associated Press writers/broadcasters poll as well, the latter considered the big one among the big ones.

For the first time since the 1987 Fiesta Bowl, No. 1 had played No. 2 for the undisputed national championship.

And just like No. 2 Penn State surprised No. 1 Miami and Heisman Trophy quarterback Vinny Testaverde, No. 2 Alabama (13-0) surprised No. 1 Miami (11-1) and its Heisman Trophy quarterback Gino Torretta in a surprising, even stunning, 34-13 upset Friday night before 76,789 in the Sugar Bowl.

And now the Crimson Tide, the Southeastern Conference champion, is the national champion and joins Brigham Young (1984) and Nebraska (1971) as the only teams to go 13-0 and win the national title.

"I don't have the vocabulary to describe how much beating Miami and winning the national championship mean to me, our football team, our university, our fans," Stallings said Saturday morning at the Sugar Bowl awards presentation. "I know it felt pretty good last night after the game, but it's just now starting to hit me what our team has done.

"We're the national champion and, brother, that's big. That's what you work for all year. That's what our players worked for since spring training. You know, it's great to have goals, but it's a whole lot better when you reach them.

"We talked to our players before the game about what it was going to take to win. I told the team it wasn't enough to just want to win. I told the team it was going to take more than that. We were going to have to leave everything on the field, and we did. I've seen some of our players this morning and they're exhausted.

"They gave it everything they had. Everything."

SUGAR BOWL
INSIDE
- Alabama dressing room/4B
- Statistics/5B
- How they moved the ball/5B
- Miami dressing room/6B
- Best, worst of Sugar/8B
- What the media is saying/6B

THE FINAL TOP TEN
ASSOCIATED PRESS

	Record	Points	Pvs.
1. ALABAMA (62)	13-0-0	1,550	2
2. Florida St.	11-1-0	1,470	3
3. Miami	11-1-0	1,410	1
4. Notre Dame	10-1-1	1,375	5
5. Michigan	9-0-3	1,266	7
6. Syracuse	10-2-0	1,209	6
7. Texas A&M	12-1-0	1,167	4
8. Georgia	10-2-0	1,159	8
9. Stanford	10-3-0	1,058	13
10. Florida	9-4-0	931	14

	Record	Points	Pvs.
1. ALABAMA (60)	13-0-0	1,500	2
2. Florida St.	11-1-0	1,422	4
3. Miami	11-1-0	1,358	1
4. Notre Dame	10-1-1	1,326	5
5. Michigan	9-0-3	1,233	7
6. Texas A&M	12-1-0	1,152	3
7. Syracuse	10-2-0	1,138	9
8. Georgia	10-2-0	1,029	8
9. Stanford	10-3-0	986	13
10. Washington	9-3-0	855	11

As the Legion Field game clock blinked down to 00:00 that Thanksgiving afternoon, all Tide concentration immediately shifted to the Gators, the SEC's East champs.

Back at Legion Field nine days later, Bama and Florida were locked 21-21 with just over three minutes left. Once again it was Antonio Langham picking off a pass for a touchdown, this one for 26 yards and a 28-21 Bama triumph. The Tide, now 12-0-0, won the conference crown and the right to play the University of Miami for the national championship.

Miami, and those mean ol' Hurricanes.

No. 1 vs. No. 2.

Start the countdown, boys! Twenty-six days...25...24...23... Could Bama's vast fandom wait that long?

The Miami Hurricanes. It was a college football team that America had grown to love not to like. But that's the way the 'Canes wanted it. They said so, many times over. They wallowed in their swaggering, jive-bone, bad-boy, trash-talking image.

Like 'em or not, though, Miami had built a phenomenal record over the past several years. For example:

- Won national championships in 1983-87-89-91.
- Last eight years (1985-92) had an 83-5-0 regular-season record, plus a 5-2-0 bowl record (with Bama coming up).
- Overall record during that period was 88-7-0 by an average score of 34-11.
- Won all of its last five bowl games, beating Nebraska twice, Oklahoma, Texas and Alabama by an average score of 29-9.
- Last 13 seasons (1980-92), had an overall 127-20-0 (.864) record, which includes 7-4-0 bowl figures. Six of the 20 losses were to Florida (3) and Florida State (3).
- Another remarkable thing about Miami's super surge beginning in 1980 was that it followed a lowly .385 record (42-67-0) throughout the decade of the 1970s.

That's the recent background of the team Alabama had to play, and beat, for the national championship.

Miami had won 29 straight games and Alabama 22. No bowl had ever landed two teams with 51 wins in a row. The previous high had been 44 by Oklahoma (29) and Maryland (15) in the Orange Bowl following the 1955 season.

FINAL SCORE: ALABAMA 34, MIAMI 13.

By the fourth quarter, it had become a comedy — but the 'Canes weren't laughing.

And the 13-0-0 Tide received a unanimous vote. All 62 of the writers and sportscasters on the *Associated Press* panel said Bama was best. One writer, in fact, had voted the Tide tops from pre-season all the way through. He was Corky Simpson of the *Arizona Citizen,* an afternoon paper in Tucson. He became a real celebrity New Year's Night. Simpson said the next day, "I didn't even get to see the second half of the game because of the phone ringing."

Why Bama all the way? "I knew they had a strong defense," said Simpson. "And I have a lot of faith in the ability of Gene Stallings. I got to know him when he coached the Phoenix Cardinals."

The top six teams were the Crimson Tide, Florida State, the Hurricanes, Notre Dame, Michigan and Syracuse. Miami had played three of those teams and beaten two of them — the Seminoles and the Orangemen — but not the Tide.

The last Division I team with a perfect 13 wins was Brigham Young in 1984.

1993

GAME 58

"The Miracle Season"

This would be the 939th game in Auburn's football history and there's little doubt that it ranks right there with the 1942 Georgia game and the 1972 and 1989 Alabama games as the most memorable.

The '93 classic capped one of the most *unique* seasons in collegiate football history and will forever be known to Tiger fans as "The Miracle Season."

Auburn's '93 campaign actually began the day after last year's Tiger-Tide clash in Birmingham. It was announced on November 27 that Auburn President William V. Muse would form an eight-man search committee to seek a new coach to replace the departed Pat Dye.

The next three days produced three "leading candidates" — Fisher DeBerry (Air Force Academy), Don James (Washington) and Dick Sheridan (North Carolina State).

On December 1, it was reported that Sheridan had the inside track, and that Pat Sullivan, former AU Heisman Trophy winner, was too "pricey" because four years still remained on his $200,000-a-year contract at TCU. Another hat hit the ring, as Tim Stowers, former AU lineman and now head coach at Georgia Southern, called Athletic Director Mike Lude and asked to be considered.

On December 2, Lude said that Sheridan was not the leading candidate. Also, James informed Auburn not to call. He was remaining in Washington.

Everything suddenly went quiet, until December 8, when the name of Miami's Dennis Erickson cropped up. Two days later, Lude denied that a reported $6 million offer to Sheridan had been made. Lude even called it "ridiculous."

By December 15, DeBerry had said "no" to Auburn, while Sullivan and Sheridan officially removed their names. On the 16th, it was hinted that Erickson might be "in."

The bombshell then hit the next day — December 17. It was announced that 37-year-old Terry Bowden had been chosen as Auburn's new coach. He is, of course, the son of Florida State coach Bobby Bowden. Terry's brother, Tommy, was already on the Auburn coaching staff.

Terry Bowden was a three-year starter in football, baseball and wrestling at Morgantown (West Virginia) High School. (He was a First Team All-State running back in 1974.) At West Virginia University, he lettered two years at running back, held a 3.65 GPA in accounting, and graduated Magna Cum Laude. He studied at Oxford University in England in the summer of 1980, and earned a degree from Florida State University School of Law in 1982 while a graduate assistant at FSU.

In 1983, Bowden became head coach at Salem College in Salem, West Va. and, at 26, was the youngest man in the country to hold that position.

Young Terry had a rough beginning, losing his first seven games, before closing with three victories. He followed that up with back-to-back 8-2-0 seasons and a spot in the NAIA playoffs both years.

The next year (1986), Bowden was an assistant at Akron (Ohio) for former Notre Dame coach Jerry Faust. He was then head coach at Samford University in Birmingham for the next six years (1987-92) where he built a 45-22-2 record. His Samford teams averaged 29 points per game.

Then that 17th day of December arrived....

And it was Bill Lumpkin of *The Birmingham Post-Herald* who wrote, "Immediately after being announced as Auburn's new head football coach, Terry Bowden said he realizes that he won't be accepted 'until I beat Alabama.'"

That says it all.

In mid-March it was announced that Auburn had changed the date of the Alabama game, moving it up a week to Saturday, November 21. The original date of November 28 fell on Thanksgiving weekend, and many students wouldn't be able to return for the game. Auburn officials agreed. After all, it was being played at Jordan-Hare Stadium and would certainly be billed as "The Second Coming." The athletic department, players and coaches also liked the idea. They wanted all the vocal support possible.

Alabama also welcomed the change. The Crimson Tide figured they'd be a part of the Southeastern Conference championship game at Legion Field and that it would give them an extra week to prepare for Georgia or Florida or Tennessee.

In *The Birmingham News'* annual SEC spring football review (a poll of the league's 12 Sports Information Directors) Bama was a run-a-way winner, followed by Florida, Tennessee and Georgia. Auburn was picked ninth in front of LSU, Vanderbilt and Kentucky.

Through all these months, however, the NCAA's awesome probation anvil, dangling by a string, slowly swung back and fourth — every minute of every day — over Auburn's head.

Then came the news from the offices in Mission, Kansas. The NCAA wanted AU officials, including President Muse and former Coach Dye, to come on up and personally defend all the problems caused by the infamous "Eric Ramsey Tapes."

They met June 30-July 2. The wait was now on. And the wait would last for 44 days and nights.

On August 15, the sanctions were announced. The most critical were: no post season dates for 1993 and 1994, including the SEC championship game, plus no television for one season. The NCAA gave Auburn its choice for the television blackout period ('93 or '94). AU elected to immediately swallow the giant pill which would result in almost $5 million of lost revenue.

But, at least, the ordeal of the unknown was *finally* over.

By now all of the numerous pre-season publications were in the racks and everybody picked Alabama to field another dominating squad. The top three teams in the only two polls which really count — *Associated Press* and *USA Today/CNN* — were Florida State, Alabama and Michigan, with Miami and Texas A&M swapping the fourth and fifth positions.

Auburn was hidden way away; hidden down there among the Iowa States, Memphis States and Oklahoma States, the Rices, Tulsas and Houstons. AU was projected at about 4-7 or 5-6.

The season kicked off.

SEPT. 2-4 — Auburn found itself in the NCAA penalty box right from the start. Months earlier, cable television (ESPN) had gotten the Tigers and Ole Miss to change their Jordan-Hare date from Saturday the 4th to Thursday night the 2nd. Remember, though, no AU TV. But it was too late to change the change, so a TV-less Thursday night it was. The Rebels were solid favorites, but Auburn scored on its first possession and held a 13-0 lead at intermission. The Tigers then staved off a serious Rebel rally and claimed a rugged 16-12 victory. Two days later, the Tide topped Tulane 31-17 at Legion Field.

SEPT. 11 — Auburn toyed with Samford at home by a 35-7 count. At Nashville, the Tide was unimpressive in a 17-6 win over a weak Vanderbilt club. UA remained No. 2.

SEPT. 18 — The Tigers went to Tiger Stadium in Baton Rouge and knocked around the home 'Cats by an impressive 34-10 score, which resulted in a Top 25 breakthrough — 25th. Meanwhile, Bama bashed Arkansas 43-3 at Tuscaloosa.

SEPT. 25 — Southern Mississippi went into Jordan-Hare, trailed 7-21 at halftime, but rallied for a 24-21 third-period advantage. But AU came back for a 35-24 triumph, controlling the ball all but three minutes of the final period. The Tigers inched up to No. 23. Alabama had some Legion Field fun, like 56-3 over Louisiana Tech. It was still FSU-Alabama as 1-2.

OCT. 2 — The Tigers barely escaped Nashville with their tattered stripes. Vanderbilt led 10-7 at the break, but AU got a third quarter touchdown, then were forced to put up a frantic goal line stand (first-and-goal at the three) in the final stanza to eke out a 14-10 win. Even so, now with a 5-0-0 record, AU went to No. 22. Alabama went to Columbia and left town with a 17-6 win over the Gamecocks. There were no changes at the top.

OCT. 9 — Auburn topped Mississippi State 31-17 at home and moved three more notches in the polls to 19th. Alabama had the afternoon off.

OCT. 16 — Would you believe? Auburn jumped nine places in the *AP* poll. *Nine!* Sure, it had some help. But the Tigers also did more than their incredible share. Auburn's opposition, not including Division II-A Samford, thus far had won only eight of 25 games, so the nationwide feeling was, "Let's wait and see about Auburn. Let's wait until it plays 'somebody.'" Well, on this day, Auburn did indeed play *somebody,* hosting 5-0-0 and fourth-ranked Florida, who was averaging an impressive 41 points a game. Halftime score: Gators 27, Tigers 10. Final score: Tigers 38, Gators 35, as Scott Etheridge kicked a field goal in the final seconds. It sent Steve Spurrier into shock. It will also go down as one of Auburn's all-time great gridiron victories. *War Eagle!* Auburn went from 19th to 10th.

In other parts of the country, four other undefeated teams fell: Penn State (21-13 to Michigan), Oklahoma (27-10 to Colorado), Virginia (40-14 to FSU), and Kansas State (45-29 to Nebraska).

In others parts of Alabama, the Crimson Tide, still ranked second behind FSU, escaped with a "miracle" 17-17 tie against Tennessee at Legion Field.

It's interesting to note here that in August a Big Orange fan had called a radio talk show in Atlanta divulging the many reasons why his Vols were going to the Sugar Bowl. The talk host then said, "Do you realize that for Tennessee to go to the Sugar Bowl, it must beat Alabama *twice in Birmingham?*" There was silence on the other end. The caller quite obviously hadn't considered such a burden — and his day was ruined.

The Tide's tie re-arranged things. It was now FSU, Notre Dame, Ohio State, Alabama and Nebraska as the Top 5.

At this junction, there were only three 7-0-0 teams in the country, and two were coached by a Bowden. The other was coached by a Holtz.

OCT. 23 — Auburn had a much-needed open date. Alabama topped Ole Miss 19-14 at Oxford.

OCT. 30 — The Tigers went to Fayetteville and, surprise of surprises, played the Hogs in the snow. It was Auburn 31, Arkansas 21, which was good enough for a poll move to No. 8. Alabama shutout Southern Mississippi 40-0 at Tuscaloosa and remained in the fifth-place slot.

$2.50 — Iron Bowl Issue — December 1993

TIDE & TIGER

The Magazine of Alabama and Auburn Sports

Alabama
*Sherman Williams:
Shakedown!*
Interview with
Bill Oliver

Auburn
*Stephen Davis:
Worth the Wait*
Interview with
Wayne Hall

NOV. 6 — What an absolutely delightful Auburn day it would turn out to be. It was Homecoming on the Plains and all the War Eagle faithful were still glowing over their big Gator victory and anxiously awaiting their upcoming dates with Georgia and Alabama. There was little thought given to the Aggies from Las Cruces. And once inside Jordan-Hare, AU boosters just relaxed and watched their team frolic past New Mexico State by a 55-14 count. AU moved up to seventh.

Bring on the Dogs!

Meanwhile at Tuscaloosa, Bama was hosting an LSU team which had won only three games — Mississippi State, Utah State and Ole Miss. The Bengals' five defeats had been by an overwhelming 39-10 average score. But in one of the season's headline shockers, it was LSU 17, UA 13, breaking the nation's longest unbeaten streak at 31 games. The Tide had not lost since a 35-0 setback to the Gators at Gainesville back on September 14, 1991.

Auburn had posted a *doubleheader* sweep that November afternoon: the Tigers now ranked No. 7, the Tide No. 12. A few weeks back, who would ever have thought....

NOV. 13 — When the "Latest Line" appeared in the Monday editions it's hard to say which camp — Georgia or Auburn — was more surprised. Or, down right shocked. AU was 9-0-0 and ranked 7th in the land, while UGA was 4-5-0, beating only Texas Tech, Southern Miss, Vanderbilt and Kentucky, certainly not your annual autumn powerhouses. The Bulldogs, however, were *favored* by a point or so. Unbelievable. It certainly couldn't be the "home field advantage" because in this series there is none. In fact, since it moved out of Columbus in 1958, the home team had won only 13 of the 34 games (28%). And the Tigers made it even more lopsided with a 42-28 win. Moving up still another step in the poll ladder, the Tigers now stood sixth. At Tuscaloosa, the Tide took Mississippi State by a 36-25 score. But where had the Tide's awesome defense gone?

The nation's eyes that day, however, were on South Bend, where No. 2 Notre Dame edged No. 1 FSU in a wild 31-24 thriller. A Bowden was finally beaten.

A wild, capacity crowd like the one that showed up for Alabama's first visit to Auburn in 1989 is expected for its second visit.

Drama builds on campus

The Huntsville Times

NOV. 20 — It was the Tigers against the Tide at Jordan-Hare Stadium. Auburn was 10-0-0 by an average score of 33-18 and ranked sixth behind Notre Dame, Florida State, Nebraska, Miami and Ohio State. Alabama was 8-1-1 by an average of 29-11 and ranked 11th. The home team was favored to win by about a touchdown.

"Yes!

"If Auburn wins the big game Saturday, Auburn fans will be allowed to exercise their lengthy tradition and roll the trees, power lines, cars and anything else movable or immovable in the downtown block area where Auburn's main streets intersect, according to Auburn Police Chief Ed Downing." — Penny L. Pool, *Opelika-Auburn News.*

"If, as Auburn football partisans hope, fate already has decreed a Tiger victory today over Alabama, tradition will require a boisterous celebration at the intersection of College Street and Magnolia Avenue, a place far better known as Toomer's Corner.

It's time for the main event

Tide says don't count us out

The Birmingham News

Crowd will be orange and blue

"For War Eagle people, Toomer's Corner is to Auburn what the Arc de Triomphe is to Paris, what Mecca is to the world's Muslims, even what Tiananmen Square is to Chinese Democrats.

"'It's Auburn's Times Square,' former *Auburn Bulletin* editor and publisher Neil Davis said in a speech a few years back." — Tom Gordon, *The Birmingham News.*

"In Tuscaloosa, everything was in place Friday for the world's largest gathering of couch potatoes. A 20-by-28-foot television screen is anchored in the upper southwest corner of Bryant-Denny Stadium, and a field-level 14-foot-by-18-foot auxiliary screen sits in the end zone awaiting 45,000 fans who'll view the closed-circuit broadcast.

"In Auburn, a sign proclaiming 'The Second Coming' — Welcome Back To Your Worst Nightmare," was one of hundreds that greeted severely outnumbered Alabama fans on the eve of what many believe is college football's fiercest rivalry." — Mike Bolton and Doug Segrest, *The Birmingham News.*

"Hi, coach." "Hi, coach."

"Auburn should defeat Alabama by 10 points Saturday. For two reasons. It has the home field advantage, and it has the better team." — Clyde Bolton, *The Birmingham News.*

With about 130,000 looking on — 82,000 "live" at Jordan-Hare and another 47,000 television viewers at Bryant-Denny — the 58th edition of this old gridiron grudge game was here.

Auburn kicked off. It was three-and-out for Bama, then for Auburn, and for Alabama again. Six minutes into the game, Auburn got something going after receiving a punt at its 38. Quarterback Stan White got outside for eight yards and Tony Richardson cracked for two and the game's initial first down at the 48. White, flushed from the pocket, managed two more to midfield. After a yard loss, White hit Richardson for 15 yards to Bama's 36. Three plays could net only a yard and Scott Etheridge's long field goal try was no good — but — the Tide was hit with a big 15-yard penalty for, of all things, an illegal substitution.

First down at the 20.

James Bostic went to the 18, White kept to the 11, then to the seven, and another first down. But Bama braced and Etheridge came on and kicked a short field goal and it was 3-0 with 01:48 remaining in the period.

Early in the second quarter, Alabama began from its 29 and on second-and two, Kevin Lee, on a reverse, raced 63 yards for a touchdown, Michael Proctor converted, and the Crimson Tide had grabbed a 7-3 lead with 10 minutes remaining in the half.

Auburn's next possession resulted in Terry Daniel placing a 49-yard punt back at the Bama six. After quarterback Jay Barker threw incomplete, he was sacked for a safety by linebacker Jason Miska, bringing the score to an odd 7-5.

Following the free kick, AU punted, UA punted, AU punted, and the Tide started operations at its 47-yard line with the first half clock down to 01:30.

Bama struck. Barker and Lee teamed up with a pass play good for 34 yards to the Tigers' 19, and Chris Anderson scored from there. Proctor converted.

Halftime: Alabama 14, Auburn 5.

The Tigers began the second half on offense and after White pitched three incomplete passes, it was punt time. Alabama kicked it back and Thomas Bailey returned it 30 yards to the

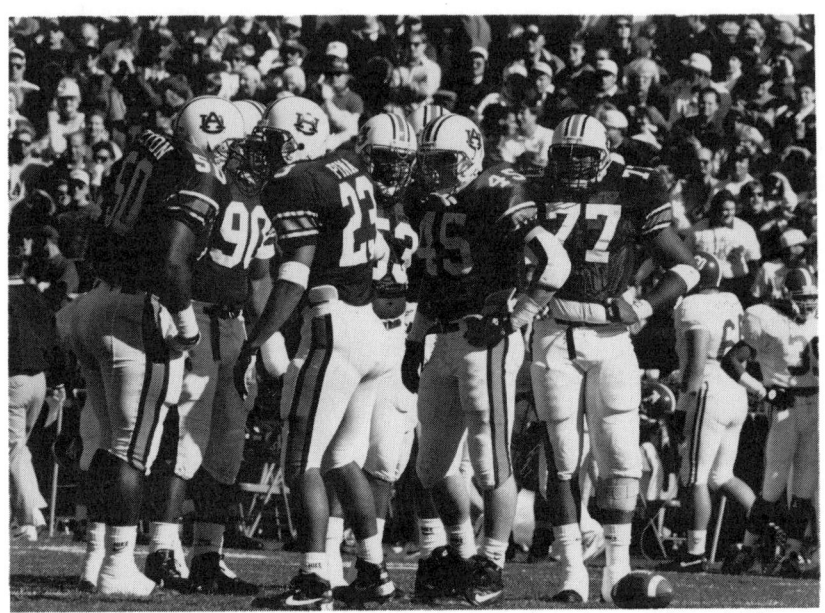

Mike Pelton (50), Willie Whitehead (90), Mike Pena (23), Jason Miska (45), Damon Primus (77) and the rest of the Auburn defense pitched a second-half shutout in the Big Game.

"Auburn should defeat Alabama by 10 points Saturday. For two reasons. It has the home field advantage, and it has the better team." — Clyde Bolton, *The Birmingham News.*

With about 130,000 looking on — 82,000 "live" at Jordan-Hare and another 47,000 television viewers at Bryant-Denny — the 58th edition of this old gridiron grudge game was here.

Auburn kicked off. It was three-and-out for Bama, then for Auburn, and for Alabama again. Six minutes into the game, Auburn got something going after receiving a punt at its 38. Quarterback Stan White got outside for eight yards and Tony Richardson cracked for two and the game's initial first down at the 48. White, flushed from the pocket, managed two more to midfield. After a yard loss, White hit Richardson for 15 yards to Bama's 36. Three plays could net only a yard and Scott Etheridge's long field goal try was no good — but — the Tide was hit with a big 15-yard penalty for, of all things, an illegal substitution.

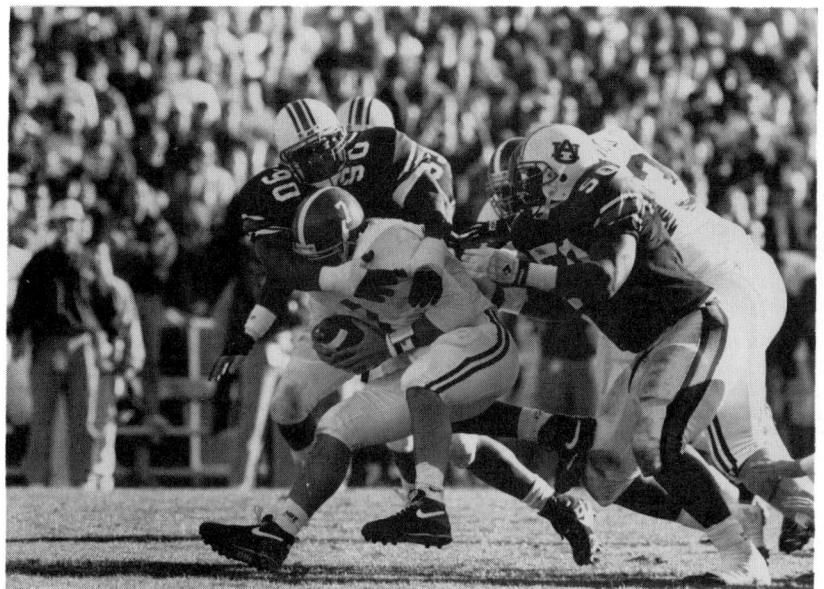
Whitehead and Pelton swamp Tide quarterback Jay Barker.

First down at the 20.

James Bostic went to the 18, White kept to the 11, then to the seven, and another first down. But Bama braced and Etheridge came on and kicked a short field goal and it was 3-0 with 01:48 remaining in the period.

Early in the second quarter, Alabama began from its 29 and on second-and two, Kevin Lee, on a reverse, raced 63 yards for a touchdown, Michael Proctor converted, and the Crimson Tide had grabbed a 7-3 lead with 10 minutes remaining in the half.

Auburn's next possession resulted in Terry Daniel placing a 49-yard punt back at the Bama six. After quarterback Jay Barker threw incomplete, he was sacked for a safety by linebacker Jason Miska, bringing the score to an odd 7-5.

Following the free kick, AU punted, UA punted, AU punted, and the Tide started operations at its 47-yard line with the first half clock down to 01:30.

Bama struck. Barker and Lee teamed up with a pass play

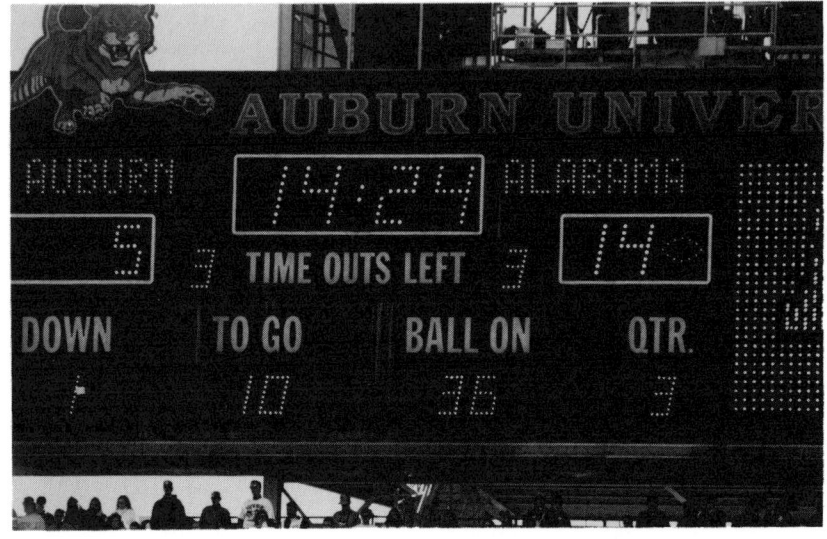

The Tigers' season-long slogan of "AttitUde" came in handy as they trailed eight of their 11 opponents.

good for 34 yards to the Tigers' 19, and Chris Anderson scored from there. Proctor converted.

Halftime: Alabama 14, Auburn 5.

The Tigers began the second half on offense and after White pitched three incomplete passes, it was punt time. Alabama kicked it back and Thomas Bailey returned it 30 yards to the Tide 44. White was again off-target, then threw an interception to Willie Gaston. At this point, things certainly weren't looking too hot for the home team.

But Bama couldn't move and Bryne Diehl got off a great 65-yard punt which Bailey returned eight yards to the Auburn 27.

White, facing third-and-six, spun and fought his way for an 11-yard gain and a huge first down at his 42. Seemingly unimportant at the time, it could have been game's turning point. White then threw to Derrick Dorn for four, Reid McMilion ripped the middle for eight and another first down at Bama's 46. White rolled right and was on target to Frank Sanders for a gain of 16 to the 30. However, on third-and-nine, Alabama's Jeremy Nunley slashed through and sacked White for a loss of six. White was hurt. With a mangled knee, Stan White's AU career was over.

It was fourth-and-15 at Bama's 35.

In a season already crammed with emergencies, Coach Bowden once again had to dial up 9-1-1.

Enter Patrick Conrad Nix, a redshirt sophomore from Rainbow City, Alabama. He had thrown only a dozen passes all season. Suddenly, however, he found himself in the stewpot of what is known as the Alabama-Auburn game. What bigger fix could Nix be in?

Nix took the snap, retreated, and lofted his 13th pass, a floater towards the endzone. Wide receiver Frank Sanders at 6-2, leaped over 5-10 Tommy Johnson, somehow snagged the prize, and stumbled into the endzone.

Touchdown, Auburn! Jordan-Hare exploded.

Etheridge's conversion was good, and with the third quarter clock showing 06:09, Auburn was back in it, trailing only 14-12.

The Tigers kicked off, quickly forced a punt, and went on offense at their 40. Richardson rammed for four before Bostic reeled off a gain of 24 yards to the Tide 32. A Nix-to-Sanders pass got it to the 26. It was Richardson to the 24 and McMilion

This was quarterback Stan White's last collegiate play.

"Somebody please dial me up 9-1-1...."

to the to the 21 and another first down. Bostic then broke free for 13.

First-and-goal at the eight. But Alabama wasn't the defending national champions for just standing around. Bostic was stopped back at the 12. McMilion managed one as the third period came to a close. Swapping ends of the field and back to the action, Bostic gained two, bringing up fourth down at the nine. On came kicker Etheridge to put his Tigers on top, and he did, with a field goal.

It was now 15-14, Auburn, with an eternity of 14:14 still standing there on the big scoreboard clock.

Fired to a frenzy, AU's defense quickly gave the ball back to Nix and the offense when Brian Robinson intercepted a long Barker pass and returned it 17 yards to Bama's 42, but the Tigers clipped on the play and the ball was stepped back to the AU 44. Unable to move, Daniel punted into the endzone.

Time: Still 10:50.

Quarterback Patrick Nix unexpectedly enters the game, about to take the snap from Shannon Roubique — and the rest is history....

The Tide soon faced a fourth-and-one at their 29. Coach Stallings, obviously sensing trouble, made the decision to go for it. Tarrant Lynch smashed into the line. He didn't make it! Auburn's ball at the 29.

Time: 08:55.

Five plays later had Auburn first down at the two. Three plays later had Auburn fourth down at the one. An AU field goal would put UA out of field goal reach, so Coach Bowden called upon Etheridge. But a high snap sent holder Sean Carder scrambling after the ball and he managed to squirm back to where the ball came from — the one. Alabama had escaped a Tigertrap.

Time: 03:51.

Barker pitched Bama up to the 36 before a bomb was intercepted by Dell McGee back at the Tigers' 30.

Time: 02:32.

Bostic, on first down, exploded through the line and was gone to glory — 70 yards — and surely Jordan-Hare would lift

Tailback James Bostic explodes through the Tide line and is gone — 70 yards — and the rest is also history....

off the ground and swirl into orbit like a giant saucer. Etheridge added the conversion, but no Tiger saw it. They were spinning around all upside down in a sea of War Eagle bedlam and thousands of orange and blue pom-poms suddenly looked like a million.

Score: Tigers 22, Tide 14. Time: 02:12.

But Bama still had a chance for a tie. And the Tide went down slinging. They got off 12 plays in the next 111 seconds and reached Auburn's 42-yard line, but when sophomore quarterback Brian Burgdorf, who moments earlier had replaced an injured Jay Barker, missed on a pass intended for Toderick Malone, the Tigers took possession with the clock down to 00:21.

Patrick Nix took the snap and dropped to a knee — for two reasons, maybe. One to keep the clock ticking and the other for a quick little talk with The Man Upstairs.

The game was finally over and "The Miracle Season" had been completed. There will never be another one quite like it. Not at Auburn. Not anywhere.

WAR EAGLE!

The Atlanta Journal-Constitution

Sunday, November 21, 1993

The Atlanta Journal
The Atlanta Constitution

COLLEGE FOOTBALL

FALL FROM GLORY
- HOW THE JACKETS HAVE FALLEN SINCE THEIR CHAMPIONSHIP **G2**
- TRAFFIC TIPS FOR THURSDAY **G2**

A Perfect 11!

THE SEC REPORT

Florida extended the nation's second-longest home winning streak to 23 games and earned a berth in the SEC championship game for the second straight year with a rout of Vanderbilt. . . . The Peach Bowl got a split decision from its participants: Clemson nipped South Carolina, but Kentucky was hammered by Tennessee.

Auburn 22, Alabama 14	G1, 4-6
Florida 52, Vanderbilt 0	G3
Tennessee 48, Kentucky 0	G3
Clemson 16, S. Carolina 13	G6
LSU 24, Tulane 10	Late

THE ACC REPORT

Virginia Tech put the finishing touches on another late season collapse by Virginia as the Hokies turned a pair of Cavalier miscues into 10 points on the way to winning for the fifth time in six games. . . . Maryland rallied from 23-0 and 29-6 deficits to beat Wake Forest. The outcome left both teams with 3-8 records, worst in the conference.

Florida State 62, N.C. State 3	G6
Va. Tech 20, Virginia 17	G6
Clemson 16, S. Carolina 13	G6
Maryland 33, Wake Forest 32	G6

TOP 25 REPORT

Ohio State's dreams of a national [championship] ripped apart by hated rival Michigan. Wisconsin, which hasn't been to Pasadena since the 1962 season, can return with a victory over Michigan State in two weeks. The Badgers topped Illinois on Saturday. . . . Texas A&M won a record-tying 21st consecutive SWC game, placing it in the same company with the 1968-71 Texas teams of coach Darrell Royal.

No. 17 B.C. 41, No. 1 N. Dame 39	
No. 9 W. Va. 17, No. 4 Miami 14	
Michigan 28, No. 5 Ohio St. 0	
No. 10 Texas A&M 59, TCU 3	
No. 12 Wisconsin 35, Illinois 10	
No. 14 Penn St. 43, N'western 21	
No. 16 UCLA 27, No. 22 USC 21	
No. 18 Colorado 21, Iowa St. 16	
No. 20 Kansas St. 21, Okla. St. 17	
No. 21 Indiana 24, Purdue 17	
Details, G7-8	

STATE REPORT

James Williams rushed for 175 yards as Georgia Southern defeated East Tennessee State.

Ga. Southern 31, ETSU 24	G9
Hampton 33, Albany St. 7	G9

Max Howell gives college recruiting reports for ACC, SEC and major independents. Dial 511, enter 3344 and follow the instructions. This is a pay-per-call service. Inside the local calling area the fee is 50¢ for five minutes; the fee is 50¢ per minute outside the calling area. See AJ for details.

Auburn rallies to beat Alabama 22-14 after fourth-down heroics by backup quarterback

By Tony Barnhart
STAFF WRITER

Auburn, Ala. — When the history of this college football season is written, it will state that Auburn University won 11 games with no losers, culminated by a 22-14 victory over Alabama on Saturday. But those few lines will not begin to capture the emotion, the joy, the exhilaration on display on a brilliant fall day at Jordan-Hare Stadium.

Down 14-5 in the third quarter, Auburn rallied behind understudy quarterback Patrick Nix to put the perfect finish on its unlikely season, touching off a wild celebration among the 85,214 fans who came to witness a piece of history.

▶ Complete coverage **G4-6**

Immediately after the game, Auburn's Terry Bowden, who became the first coach to go 11-0 in his rookie season, gathered his troops at midfield to savor the moment. When former coach Pat Dye stuck his hand in the huddle, Bowden grabbed Dye and embraced him, forcing him to share the experience with his former team. It was the kind of moment some wondered if Auburn ever would feel again. Certainly, the experts said, it wouldn't come this soon.

Then Bowden, all 5 feet 6 of him, ran with sprinter's speed toward the Auburn student section, his fists pumping the air. Then he ran to the other side of the stadium to celebrate more. When pressed, Bowden went to the locker room to take care of his media obligations. The Auburn crowd, however, did not leave. They did not want this moment to end. . . . They may still be [there].

First-year Auburn coach Terry Bowden basks in the postgame adulation at Jordan-Hare Stadium.
WILLIAM BERRY/Staff

SO, WHO IS NUMBER 1?

BC kicks Irish to first defeat

FROM OUR NEWS SERVICES

South Bend, Ind. — At the same end of the field where Charlie Ward and Florida State fell short on the final play last week, a little-known Boston College kicker shattered the Notre Dame mystique and ended a 17-game winning streak by the Irish.

David Gordon, who had failed on two game-winning field goal tries in the last two years, kicked a 41-yarder on the final play Saturday as Boston College upset No. 1 Notre Dame 41-39 and upended the New Year's Day bowl picture.

The field goal, the longest of Gordon's career, overcame a brilliant 22-point offensive by the Irish (10-1) in the

Please see **BC, G10** ▶

Boston College kicker David Gordon celebrates with teammate Brian Saxton (above) while Notre Dame players mourn their loss.
Associated Press

Seminoles? Huskers?

Upsets leave picture fuzzy as several teams make case for top spot

By Tony Barnhart
STAFF WRITER

Auburn, Ala. — A funny thing happened on the way to a Notre Dame-Florida State rematch for the national championship. Perhaps not so funny for No. 1 Notre Dame, No. 4 Miami or No. 5 Ohio State, who all lost Saturday, throwing the national championship race wide open with only two weeks left in the regular season.

Just who'll be the top two teams in the nation when the polls are released today is anybody's guess. Notre Dame will certainly drop after losing 41-39 to No. 17 Boston College. No. 2 Florida State, which won impressively over N.C. State, will have to wait Saturday, likely will move back into the top spot followed by Nebraska (10-0), which was No. 3 and did not play.

If Florida State and Nebraska remain No. 1 and No. 2 the rest of the season, they would meet in the Orange Bowl for the national title.

But wait, there is still much football to be played. Florida State must travel to Gainesville, Fla., to take on the Florida Gators next Saturday. No. 8 Florida stomped Vanderbilt Saturday for its 23rd consecutive win at home Nebraska must play its final game at home Friday against No. 15 Oklahoma. If either stumbles, the site of the national title game could again change.

Upsetting

Three of the top five bowl coalition teams lost Saturday, further scrambling the national championship picture.

1 Notre Dame lost to Boston College 41-39
2 Florida State defeated N.C. State 62-3
3 Nebraska had the week off
4 Miami lost to West Virginia 17-14
5 Ohio State lost to Michigan 28-0

Saturday's three big upsets put some other teams within striking distance of the national title. If Florida (9-1) can knock off Florida State and then beat Alabama in the SEC championship game, the Gators could be in the hunt for the title when they reach the Sugar Bowl. West Virginia (10-0), which upset the Hurricanes, still has Boston College remaining and could get a shot.

And then there is Auburn. The Tigers, ranked sixth, could move into the top 3 in today's polls. They finished their season Saturday at 11-0 by beating Auburn 22-14 but cannot go to a bowl due to NCAA probation. However, after Saturday's action, the strong possibility exists that the Tigers could be the only unbeaten team in the nation Jan. 2.

SPORTS
Boston College stuns
Notre Dame /1C
Top-ranked Troy State Trojans explode to rip Samford, remain unbeaten

BUSINESS
KinderCare adapts to market / 8F

FOOD
Relax and enjoy Thanksgiving /1H
Fresh fruitcake great traditional treat for season despite its reputation /1H

MONTGOMERY ADVERTISER

NOVEMBER 21, 1993   MONTGOMERY, ALABAMA   FINAL EDITION $1.00

ELEVEN AND OHHHH!

THE BIRMINGHAM NEWS

COMING MONDAY
How did Bowden turn around Tigers?

SPORTS   B

SUNDAY, NOVEMBER 21, 1993

CLYDE
BOLTON
News columnist

Undefeated
Auburn whips Alabama for 11-0 season

This game too big? No way

AUBURN — Please, don't abuse me with that faddish remark that seems to be on the lips of so many who can't think of anything intelligent to say.

"The Auburn-Alabama game has become too big," they declare. "The teams shouldn't be annual opponents."

The Alabama-Auburn game is too big?

The Smoky Mountains are too big. Yellowstone is too big. A sunset on a clear autumn night is too big. The Statue of Liberty is too big. The Methodist Church is too big. A harvest moon is too big. The Pacific Ocean is too big.

The Auburn-Alabama game is this state at its zenith, and I don't apologize to anyone that it's "just a football" game. I'll admit I don't care for opera, and I expect that many who say they do don't either.

Two squads of young men who have worked harder in their young lives than you and I will ever work,

By the way, it was the *first* Auburn-Alabama football game that Terry Bowden had ever seen.

It was also the Tigers' first perfect finish in 36 years. In 1957, they capped a 10-0-0 season with a 34-0 blank of Bama, and in 1993, it was 11-0-0 after a 22-14 victory over the Tide.

And it's ironic that a "Nix threw for six" both times. In '57, Lloyd Nix and Red Phillips teamed up for a 27-yard touchdown, and in '93 it was, of course, Patrick Nix pitching a 35-yarder to Frank Sanders.

Even after the wild and noisy curtain calls for Terry and his Tigers to re-appear on the stadium set, Auburn fans refused to leave the bowl. But why should they? This was a moment for the AU ages. They had been through a long and bitter period. They had felt the sting and embarrassment of their house out of order. They had expected exactly nothing from their '93 season, except to set things in the right direction. That's all they had asked for. But now, here they were basking in the shocking on-the-field developments which had occurred over the past three months — from their surprise victory over a highly-regarded Ole Miss team to what they had just witnessed — a victory over Alabama. They were also remembering the other nine wins, especially those against Florida and Georgia.

They just stood there. And they soaked up the precious moments which that sunny but chilly November afternoon had to offer. And Ol' Shug, just as he had on that unforgettable Jordan-Hare afternoon in 1989, was lookin' down and smilin' mightily.

And if this hadn't already been "A Great Auburn Day," more astonishing news came rolling in from stadiums around the country. Remember, the Tigers were ranked No. 6 behind Notre Dame, Florida State, Nebraska, Miami and Ohio State.

Well, the Irish were absolutely astounded by a 41-39 mishap to Boston College at South Bend. There goes No. 1.

At Morgantown, the Hurricanes found unbeaten West Virginia more dynamic than advertised, and were stunned by a 17-14 score. There goes No. 4.

And at Ohio Stadium in Columbus, the Buckeyes were blanked 28-0 by four-time loser Michigan. There goes No. 5.

By the end of the day, then, Auburn had advanced all the way up to No. 3 behind FSU and Nebraska.

The Huntsville Times

Sports — Section D

- NFL: D2
- Scoreboard: D4
- Outdoors: D14

John Pruett

AU finishes amazing run in fine style

Auburn turns Tide
Nix, Bostic lead charge
By AL BURLESON
Assistant Sports Editor

11-0, way to go

The Huntsville Times

Sports — Section C

- Scoreboard: C4
- NFL: C5
- Life: C7

John Pruett

Refs didn't cause Tide loss to AU

AUBURN — A few lingering thoughts on the day after the Day After.

It was surprising and disappointing to hear Alabama head football coach Gene Stallings complain about the officiating after Saturday's 22-14 loss to Auburn. He sounded like a man looking for excuses, a trait that is decidedly out of character for Stallings.

In cold black and white newsprint, his words brought to mind Steve Spurrier, not Bebes Stallings.

Doubtless the usually mild-mannered Texan who coached Alabama to a national championship last season was agitated when he compared his team's 12 penalties for 117 yards to Auburn's four for 37. But such discrepancies are not uncommon in college football. Check the statistics from any weekend. The officials didn't beat Alabama, Auburn did.

Upon further review, it seems that Stallings could legitimately argue two calls — a pass interference call against Alabama late in the second quarter in the vicinity of the Tide 30 and the unsportsmanlike conduct call on Willie Gaston after Gaston's interception in the third quarter.

But no backup quarterback

Auburn's defense stops Alabama fullback Tarrant Lynch on fourth down deep in Tide territory late in the Tigers' 22-14 victory Saturday at Jordan-Hare Stadium.

No. 3 AU in national title race

The nation's first-third teams coached by a father-son combo? Nah! Impossible. But there it was.

Back to the Tiger-Tide game, it was much closer than the final stats showed. Auburn led in first downs 21-10, yards rushing 218-113, total yards 351-269, and in possession time 38-plus minutes to only 21-plus. Each team threw 29 passes. Bama completed only 10 for 156 yards, Auburn 14 for 133 yards. There were no lost fumbles, but UA pitched two interceptions, AU one. The Tigers were penalized only 37 yards compared to the Tide's 117 — a series record — topping Auburn's 114 yards in the 1956 game.

Bostic, obviously, was the game's leading rusher with 147 yards in 19 carries (7.7 average). Anderson's 68 yards in 10 attempts paced Bama's ground game.

"The football game was over," wrote Furman Bisher of *The Atlanta Journal*. "In the midst of the circle of humanity that had surged to the middle of the field, the little figure of Terry Bowden, all 5 feet, 6 inches, 160 pounds of him, could barely be made out in the milling celebrants. His head was bare, his face a glowing red. Looking like a Boy Scout who'd just made Eagle. In this case, he had. War Eagle, sir."

Mike Marshall of *The Huntsville Times* said, "Pat Dye saw the score, savored the moment and let the feelings flow. Auburn's old head coach grabbed Auburn's new head coach and planted a kiss on his cheek....Earlier in the week, Dye directed anger towards his former rivals. He said, 'there are some people in this state who tried to destroy me and tried to destroy Auburn and they didn't succeed on either one....Saturday's game 'put a lot of salve on some old wounds.'"

Reporting from Bryant-Denny Stadium, the *Times'* Lee J. Green said, "Bone-rattling tackles, touchdown passes, and nail-biting dramatics were seen by 47,421 fans....'It was weird to see 47,000 people cheering for a TV. There were no players on the field and it still felt like a home game' said Erin Tenbrunsel."

John Pruett of the *Times* reported, "It was surprising and disappointing to hear Alabama head football coach Gene Stallings complain about the officiating....He sounded like a man looking for excuses, a trait that is decidedly out of character for Stallings....In cold black and white newsprint, his words brought to mind Steve Spurrier, not Bebes Stallings."

Bowden's response to the press about that was, "The officiating didn't have anything to do with the game. The penalties did, but not the officiating."

Auburn's big win over Alabama fell on November 20 and only three other times had the Tigers played on that date. They were in 1901 (28-0 over LSU at Baton Rouge), in 1937 (0-0 tie with Georgia at Columbus), and in 1954 (27-6 win over Clemson at Auburn).

Add one more collective miracle to the season. The Tigers trailed in *eight* of their games (all but Ole Miss, Samford and Georgia) by an aggregate score of 47-102, then fired back with an amazing *213-43* rally.

Somebody on the AU sidelines was right there pushing the right buttons when stress-time arrived throughout the grueling campaign. And the buck must begin with Terry Bowden — very likely the best *Saturday Coach* in the country.

Bowden is Auburn's 24th football coach and, as strange as it may seem, ranks 10th in all-time Tiger wins after only one season.

"The Miracle Season" was done.

Alabama, meanwhile, still had two remaining dates that had to be filled — the SEC championship game against Florida in Birmingham, and the Gator Bowl in Jacksonville opposite North Carolina — the first Tide-Tar Heel grid game ever.

Florida 28, Alabama 13. And the Crimson Tide had dropped three of their last four games.

The Auburn-Alabama football fusses began one hundred years ago, and as lively and healthy as the rivalry between the two schools is today, there remains a void in what, despite that void, has become the bitterest collegiate football rivalry in the country.

The only sad feature of the 58-game series is that there were no games played the other 42 years. And, believe it or not, it was all brought about by the disagreement over $34.00.

Some years it's the Orange and Blue. Other years it's the Crimson and White. Every year, though, it's something to see.

After 58 games, Alabama has won 33, Auburn 24, and one ended all even. In the all-time point total, the Tide leads the Tigers 1089-881.

Clyde Bolton of The Birmingham News and author of numerous books, including War Eagle and Crimson Tide, said it best when he wrote, "There was one ticket booth when Alabama and Auburn played in 1893. Now there are none."

Appendix

Records Section

THE AUBURN-ALABAMA FOOTBALL SERIES, 1893-1993
(58 GAMES)

G	YEAR	DATE	PLACE	*AUB REC	*ALA REC	WINNER-SCORE	SERIES
1	1893	Feb 22	BHM-A	0-0-0	2-1-0	AUB 32-22	1-0-0
2	1893	Nov 30	MGM-B	3-0-0	0-3-0	AUB 40-16	2-0-0
3	1894	Nov 29	MGM-B	1-2-0	2-1-0	ALA 0-18	2-1-0
4	1895	Nov 23	TUS	0-1-0	0-3-0	AUB 48--0	3-1-0
	1896	---					
	1897	---					
	1898	---					
	1899	---					
5	1900	Nov 17	MGM-B	2-0-0	2-1-0	AUB 53--5	4-1-0
6	1901	Nov 15	TUS	0-3-0	1-0-1	AUB 17--0	5-1-0
7	1902	Oct 18	BHM-C	1-0-0	2-0-0	AUB 23--0	6-1-0
8	1903	Oct 23	MGM-D	2-0-0	0-2-0	ALA 6-18	6-2-0
9	1904	Nov 12	BHM-C	3-0-0	4-1-1	AUB 29--6	7-2-0
10	1905	Nov 18	BHM-C	1-3-0	4-3-0	ALA 0-30	7-3-0
11	1906	Nov 17	BHM-E	1-3-1	3-1-0	ALA 0-10	7-4-0
12	1907	Nov 16	BHM-E	6-1-1	3-1-1	tie 6--6	7-4-1

1908-1947 — No games

G	YEAR	DATE	PLACE	*AUB REC	*ALA REC	WINNER-SCORE	SERIES
13	1948	Dec 4	BHM-F	1-7-1	5-4-1	ALA 0-55	7-5-1
14	1949	Dec 3	BHM	1-4-3	6-2-1	AUB 14-13	8-5-1
15	1950	Dec 2	BHM	0-9-0	8-2-0	ALA 0-34	8-6-1
16	1951	Dec 1	BHM	4-5-0	4-6-0	ALA 7-25	8-7-1
17	1952	Nov 29	BHM	2-7-0	8-2-0	ALA 0-21	8-8-1
18	1953	Nov 28	BHM	6-2-1	5-2-3	ALA 7-10	8-9-1
19	1954	Nov 27	BHM	6-3-0	4-4-2	AUB 28--0	9-9-1
20	1955	Nov 26	BHM	7-1-1	0-9-0	AUB 26--0	10-9-1
21	1956	Dec 1	BHM	6-3-0	2-6-1	AUB 34--7	11-9-1
22	1957	Nov 30	BHM	9-0-0	2-6-1	AUB 40--0	12-9-1
23	1958	Nov 29	BHM	8-0-1	5-3-1	AUB 14--8	13-9-0
24	1959	Nov 28	BHM	7-2-0	6-1-2	ALA 0-10	13-10-1
25	1960	Nov 26	BHM	8-1-0	7-1-1	ALA 0--3	13-11-1
26	1961	Dec 2	BHM	6-3-0	9-0-0	ALA 0-34	13-12-1
27	1962	Dec 1	BHM	6-2-1	8-1-0	ALA 0-38	13-13-1
28	1963	Nov 30	BHM	8-1-0	7-1-0	AUB 10--8	14-13-1
29	1964	Nov 26	BHM	6-3-0	9-0-0	ALA 14-21	14-14-1
30	1965	Nov 27	BHM	5-3-1	7-1-1	ALA 3-30	14-15-1
31	1966	Dec 3	BHM	4-5-0	9-0-0	ALA 0-31	14-16-1
32	1967	Dec 2	BHM	5-4-0	7-1-1	ALA 3--7	14-17-1
33	1968	Nov 30	BHM	6-3-0	7-2-0	ALA 16-24	14-18-1
34	1969	Nov 29	BHM	7-2-0	6-3-0	AUB 49-26	15-18-1
35	1970	Nov 28	BHM	7-2-0	6-4-0	AUB 33-28	16-18-1
36	1971	Nov 27	BHM	9-0-0	10-0-0	ALA 7-31	16-19-1
37	1972	Dec 2	BHM	8-1-0	10-0-0	AUB 17-16	17-19-1
38	1973	Dec 1	BHM	6-4-0	10-0-0	ALA 0-35	17-20-1
39	1974	Nov 29	BHM	9-1-0	10-0-0	ALA 13-17	17-21-1
40	1975	Nov 29	BHM	4-5-1	9-1-0	ALA 0-28	17-22-1
41	1976	Nov 27	BHM	4-6-0	7-3-0	ALA 7-38	17-23-1

G	YEAR	DATE	PLACE	*AUB REC	*ALA REC	WINNER-SCORE		SERIES
42	1977	Nov 26	BHM	6-4-0	9-1-0	ALA	21-48	17-24-1
43	1978	Dec 2	BHM	6-3-1	9-1-0	ALA	16-34	17-25-1
44	1979	Dec 1	BHM	8-2-0	10-0-0	ALA	18-25	17-26-1
45	1980	Nov 27	BHM	5-5-0	8-2-0	ALA	18-34	17-27-1
46	1981	Nov 28	BHM	5-5-0	8-1-1	ALA	17-28	17-28-1
47	1982	Nov 27	BHM	7-3-0	7-3-0	AUB	23-22	18-28-1
48	1983	Dec 3	BHM	9-1-0	7-3-0	AUB	23-20	19-28-1
49	1984	Dec 1	BHM	8-3-0	4-6-0	ALA	15-17	19-29-1
50	1985	Nov 30	BHM	8-2-0	7-2-1	ALA	23-25	19-30-1
51	1986	Nov 29	BHM	8-2-0	9-2-0	AUB	21-17	20-30-1
52	1987	Nov 27	BHM	8-1-1	7-3-0	AUB	10--0	21-30-1
53	1988	Nov 25	BHM	9-1-0	7-2-0	AUB	15-10	22-30-1
54	1989	Dec 2	AUB	8-2-0	10-0-0	AUB	30-20	23-30-1
55	1990	Dec 1	BHM	7-2-1	9-1-0	ALA	7-16	23-31-1
56	1991	Nov 30	BHM	5-5-0	9-1-0	ALA	6-13	24-31-1
57	1992	Nov 26	BHM	5-4-1	10-0-0	ALA	0-17	24-32-1
58	1993	Nov 20	AUB	10-0-0	8-1-1	AUB	22-14	23-32-1

*Records at game time.

KEYS TO PARK LOCATIONS OF THE EARLY SERIES GAMES:
A - Birmingham Lakeview Park   D - Montgomery Highland Park
B - Montgomery Riverside Park   E - Birmingham Fair Grounds
C - Birmingham West End Park   F - Birmingham Legion Field

Of the 58 series games, four times (1895-1902-1959-1982) Auburn and Alabama have had the same won-lost percentage, and they tied in 1907. In the other 53 games, the team with the better record entering the game has won 77% of the time (41-12). Oddly enough, they have met only once with *identical* records. Both teams were 7-3-0 in 1982.

RECORDS AT GAME TIME:
1948-49 - UA 11--6-2, .632; AU 2-11-4, .235. A 1-1 split.
1950-59 - UA 44-41-10, .516; AU 55-32-3, .628. A 5-5 split.
1960-69 - UA 76-10-3, .870; AU 61-27-2, .689. UA was 8-2.
1970-79 - UA 90-10-0, .900; AU 67-28-2, .701. UA was 8-2.
1980-89 - UA 74-24-2, .750; AU 75-25-1, .747. AU was 6-4.
1990-93 - UA 36--3-1, .938; AU 27-11-2, .700. UA was 3-1.

Since the series resumed in 1948, Auburn has faced Alabama teams (at game time) with an outstanding .767 winning percentage (331-94-18). Auburn has beated Alabama 41% of the time during this period (19-27-0). There are very few college football teams in America that could have won 41% of the time against Alabama over this 46-year span.

AUBURN'S RECORD VS. ALABAMA AT:

	G	W	L	T	POINTS
Montgomery Riverside Park	3	2	1	0	93--39
Montgomery Highland Park	1	0	1	0	6--18
Tuscaloosa	2	2	0	0	65---0
Birmingham Lakeview Park	1	1	0	0	32--22
Birmingham West End Park	3	2	1	0	52--36
Birmingham Fair Grounds	2	0	1	1	6--16
Birmingham Legion Field	44	15	29	0	575-924
Auburn	2	2	0	0	52--34
GRAND TOTALS	**58**	**24**	**33**	**1**	**881-1089**

Auburn's series record is 2-2 in Montgomery, 2-0 in Tuscaloosa, 2-0 in Auburn, and 18-31-1 in Birmingham.

*Every year since 1948, except 1989 and 1993.

SERIES SCORING SUMMARY

	AUBURN	ALABAMA
4-point touchdowns	21 for 84 pts	10 for 40 pts
5-point touchdowns	23 for 115 pts	12 for 60 pts
6-point touchdowns	79 for 474 pts	122 for 732 pts
1-point conversion	83 for 83 pts	111 for 111 pts
2-point kick conversion	18 for 36 pts	8 for 16 pts
2-point run/kick conv.	2 for 4 pts	6 for 12 pts
4-point field goals	0 for 0 pts	1 for 4 pts
3-point field goals	27 for 81 pts	38 for 114 pts
Safeties	2 for 4 pts	0 for 0 pts
TOTALS	**881 pts**	**1089 pts**

Alabama has scored 144 touchdowns, Auburn 123.

SCORE BY QUARTERS

Games 1-12 (game divided into two halves)
AUBURN.................129   125   - 254
ALABAMA.................45   86   - 131

Games 13-58 (game divided into four quarters)
AUBURN..........97   192   128   210 - 627
ALABAMA........190   274   254   240 - 958

Alabama has scored 509 points in the first half and 580 in the second half. Auburn is 418-463. Of the series' 1,970 points, 927 (47%) have been scored in the first half and 1,043 in the second half. Alabama has converted 125 of its 144 touchdowns (87%), Auburn is 103-for-123 (84%). Series: 228-for-267 (85%).

SERIES' 20-POINT CLUB

PLAYER	TEAM	POINTS	YEAR(S)
Bo Jackson	Auburn	38	1982-83-84-85
Bobby Marlow	Alabama	36	1950-51
Rufus Dorsey	Auburn	32*	1893-93
Steadman Shealy	Alabama	26	1977-78-79
Al Del Greco	Auburn	25	1980-81-82-83
Van Tiffin	Alabama	25	1983-84-85-86
Ed Salem	Alabama	24	1948-49-50
Jerry Elliott	Auburn	24	1955-56
Wallace Clark	Auburn	24	1969-70
Tony Nathan	Alabama	24	1976-77
Joe Cribbs	Auburn	24	1977-79
Van Tiffin	Alabama	24	1983-84-85-86
F. R. Yarbrough	Auburn	23**	1900
Philip Doyle	Alabama	22	1988-89-90

*36 and **26 by today's point standards. In the 1900 game, Yarbrough scored 3 touchdowns and kicked 8 conversions.

LONG SCORING PLAYS (50 yards or more)

RANK	YARDS	PLAYER-TEAM	YEAR	TYPE OF PLAY
1	107	Ray Odgen, Alabama	1964	Kickoff return
2	102	George Ranager, Alabama	1969	Kickoff return
3	92	George Wilson, Alabama	1962	Kickoff return
4	85	Joe Cribbs, Auburn	1977	Run from scrimmage
5	84	Connie Federick, Auburn	1969	Run off fake punt
6	80	Benny Nelson, Alabama	1963	Run from scrimmage
7	79	Tommy Loreno, Auburn	1957	Interception return
8	75	Eli Abbott, Alabama	1894	Run from scrimmage
8	75	F. R. Yarbrough, Auburn	1900	Run from scrimmage
8	75	H. A. Allison, Auburn	1902	Run from scrimmage
11	74	Bryon Franklin, Auburn	1977	Pass from Trotman
11	74	Gene Jelks, Alabama	1985	Run from scrimmage
13	71	Bo Jackson, Auburn	1983	Run from scrimmage
14	70	James Bostic, Auburn	1993	Run from scrimmage
15	69	Bo Jackson, Auburn	1983	Run from scrimmage
16	66	Jackie Burkett, Auburn	1957	Interception return
17	65	R. L. Dorsey, Auburn	1893	Fumble return
18	63	Ray Perkins, Alabama	1966	Pass from Stabler
18	63	George Peoples, Auburn	1981	Run from scrimmage
18	63	Kevin Lee, Alabama	1993	Run from scrimmage
21	61	Antonio Langham, Alabama	1992	Interception return
22	60	Brent Fullwood, Auburn	1984	Run from scrimmage
23	57	Ricky Moore, Alabama	1983	Run from scrimmage
24	55	W. L. Noll, Auburn	1900	Run from scrimmage
24	55	Mike Currier, Auburn	1968	Pass from Carter
26	54	George Ranager, Alabama	1970	Pass from Hunter
27	53	Rebel Steiner, Alabama	1948	Pass from Salem

Auburn has 15 long scoring plays, Alabama 12.

SERIES TOUCHDOWN PASSES

NO.	YEAR	PASSER - RECEIVER	TEAM	YARDS
1	1948	Gordon Pettus - Butch Avinger	Alabama	6
2	"	Ed Salem - Clem Welsh	Alabama	20
3	"	Ed Salem - Rebel Steiner	Alabama	53
4	"	Ed Salem - Howard Pierson	Alabama	30
5	1950	Ed Salem - Bobby Marlow	Alabama	26
6	1955	Howell Tubbs - Jerry Elliott	Auburn	23
7	"	Howell Tubbs - Jerry Ellittt	Auburn	9
8	1956	Bobby Hoppe - Jerry Elliott	Auburn	6
9	"	James Cook - Jerry Elliott	Auburn	21
10	1957	Lloyd Nix - Red Phillips	Auburn	27
11	1958	Richard Wood - Jimmy Pettus	Auburn	7
12	1959	Bobby Sklton - Marlin Dyess	Alabama	39
13	1961	Pat Trammell-Richard Williamson	Alabama	20
14	1962	Joe Namath - Cotton Clark	Alabama	15
15	"	Joe Namath-Richard Williamson	Alabama	16
16	1963	Mailon Kent-Tucker Frederickson	Auburn	8
17	1964	Joe Namath - Ray Perkins	Alabama	23
18	"	Tom Bryan - Jimmy Sidle	Auburn	16
19	1965	Steve Sloan - Tommy Tolleson	Alabama	11
20	"	Steve Sloan - Ray Perkins	Alabama	33
21	1966	Kenny Stabler - Ray Perkins	Alabama	63
22	"	Wayne Trimble - Donnie Sutton	Alabama	41
23	1968	Scott Hunter - Mike Hall	Alabama	3
24	"	Loran Carter - Mike Currier	Auburn	55
25	"	Loran Carter - Tim Christian	Auburn	3
26	1969	Scott Hunter - Hunter Husband	Alabama	4
27	"	Scott Hunter - David Bailey	Alabama	7
28	1970	Scott Hunter - David Bailey	Alabama	31
29	"	Pat Sullivan - Robby Robinett	Auburn	17
30	"	Scott Hunter - George Ranager	Alabama	54
31	1971	Harry Unger - Terry Beasley	Auburn	31
32	1974	Richard Todd - Willie Shelby	Alabama	45
33	1975	Richard Todd - Jerry Brown	Alabama	17
34	"	Richard Todd - Ozzie Newsome	Alabama	24
35	1976	Jeff Rutledge - Ozzie Newsome	Alabama	42
36	1977	Jeff Rutledge - Bruce Bolton	Alabama	30
37	"	Charlie Trotman - Byron Franklin	Auburn	75*
38	"	Jeff Rutledge - Ozzie Newsome	Alabama	42
39	1978	Jeff Rutledge - Bruce Bolton	Alabama	33
40	"	Jeff Rutledge - Bruce Bolton	Alabama	17
41	"	Jeff Rutledge - Rick Neal	Alabama	11
42	1979	Steadman Shealy - Keith Pugh	Alabama	28
43	"	Charlie Trotman - Joe Cribbs	Auburn	37
44	"	Charlie Trotman - Mark Robbins	Auburn	11
45	1980	Joe Sullivan - James Brooks	Auburn	5
46	"	Charles Thomas - Bryon Franklin	Auburn	42
47	"	Don Jacobs - Bart Krout	Alabama	7
48	1981	Ken Koley - Jesse Bendross	Alabama	26
49	"	Walter Lewis - Jesse Bendross	Alabama	38
50	1982	Walter Lewis - Joey Jones	Alabama	22
51	1983	Walter Lewis - Joey Jones	Alabama	20
52	"	Walter Lewis - Joe Carter	Alabama	3

TOUCHDOWN PASSES (continued)

NO.	YEAR	PASSER - RECEIVER	TEAM	YARDS
53	1986	Mike Shula - Angelo Stafford	Alabama	2**
54	"	Mike Shula - Bobby Humphrey	Alabama	7
55	1988	David Smith - Greg Payne	Alabama	12
56	1989	Gary Hollinsworth - Marco Battle	Alabama	18
57	"	Gary Hillinsworth - Marco Battle	Alabama	15
58	1990	Stan White - Fred Baxter	Auburn	8
59	1993	Patrick Nix - Frank Sanders	Auburn	35

*Longest   **Shortest

Alabama's 40 touchdown passes average 23 yards in distance, Auburn's 19 touchdown passes also average 23 yards.

MOST TD PASSES: Jeff Rutledge 6, Scott Hunter 5, Ed Salem 4, and Walter Lewis 4. Jerry Elliott has the most TD receptions with 4.

SERIES FIELD GOALS

NO.	YEAR	PLAYER	TEAM	YARDS
1	1906	Auxford Burks	Alabama	+
2	1953	Bobby Luna	Alabama	37
3	1959	Tommy Brooker	Alabama	28
4	1960	Tommy Brooker	Alabama	23
5	1961	Tim Davis	Alabama	36
6	"	Tim Davis	Alabama	33
7	1962	Tim Davis	Alabama	40
8	1963	Marvin Woodall	Auburn	31
9	1965	David Ray	Alabama	27
10	"	Don Lewis	Auburn	44
11	1966	Steve Davis	Alabama	23
12	1967	John Riley	Auburn	38
13	1968	John Riley	Auburn	22
14	"	Mike Dean	Alabama	30
15	1969	Oran Buck	Alabama	33
16	"	Oran Buck	Alabama	21
17	1970	R. Lee Ciemney	Alabama	29
18	"	Gardner Jett	Auburn	26
19	"	R. Lee Ciemney	Alabama	27
20	"	Gardner Jett	Auburn	37
21	1971	Bill Davis	Alabama	42
22	1972	Bill Davis	Alabama	31
23	"	Gardner Jett	Auburn	37
24	1974	Bucky Berrey	Alabama	36
25	1976	Bucky Berrey	Alabama	47
26	1978	Alan McElroy	Alabama	22
27	"	Jorge Portela	Auburn	39
28	"	Alan McElroy	Alabama	37

SERIES FIELD GOALS (continued)

NO.	YEAR	PLAYER	TEAM	YARDS
29	1979	Jorge Portela	Auburn	47
30	"	Jorge Portela	Auburn	39
31	"	Alan McElroy	Alabama	23
32	1980	Al Del Greco	Auburn	52*
33	1981	Al Del Greco	Auburn	19
34	1982	Peter Kim	Alabama	37
35	"	Peter Kim	Alabama	33
36	"	Peter Kim	Alabama	18**
37	"	Al Del Greco	Auburn	23
38	1983	Al Del Greco	Auburn	29
39	"	Al Del Greco	Auburn	26
40	"	Al Del Greco	Auburn	34
41	1984	Van Tiffin	Alabama	52*
42	1985	Van Tiffin	Alabama	26
43	"	Van Tiffin	Alabama	32
44	"	Van Tiffin	Alabama	42
45	"	Chris Johnson	Auburn	32
46	"	Van Tiffin	Alabama	52*
47	1986	Van Tiffin	Alabama	29
48	1987	Win Lyle	Auburn	23
49	1988	Win Lyle	Auburn	25
50	"	Philip Doyle	Alabama	24
51	"	Win Lyle	Auburn	22
52	1989	Philip Doyle	Alabama	24
53	"	Win Lyle	Auburn	22
54	"	Win Lyle	Auburn	31
55	"	Philip Doyle	Alabama	23
56	"	Win Lyle	Auburn	34
57	1990	Philip Doyle	Alabama	31
58	"	Philip Doyle	Alabama	40
59	"	Philip Doyle	Alabama	40
60	1991	Matt Wethington	Alabama	38
61	"	Jim Von Wyle	Auburn	26
62	"	Matt Wethington	Alabama	39
63	"	Jim Von Wyle	Auburn	26
64	1992	Michael Proctor	Alabama	47
65	1993	Scott Etheridge	Auburn	23
66	"	Scott Etheridge	Auburn	26

+Unknown   *Longest   **Shortest

TOTAL FIELD GOALS: Alabama 39, Auburn 27.

MOST FIELD GOALS: 6 by Del Greco, Tiffin and Lyle.

The series' first 44 games (1893-1979) -- 31 FGs.
The series' last 14 games (1980-1993) -- 35 FGs.
The last 8 games (1986-1993) has seen 20 FGs and the average line of scrimmage was the 13.

AUBURN'S ALL-TIME SERIES SCORING

PLAYER	TD	PAT	FG	TOTAL	YEAR(S)
ALLISON, H. A.	3	0	0	15	1902
ANDREWS, William	1	0	0	6	1977
ATKINS, Billy	2	6	0	18	1956-57
BAXTER, Fred	1	0	0	6	1992
BEASLEY, Terry	1	0	0	6	1971
BIEVENS, Frank	1	0	0	5	1900
BOSTIC, James	1	0	0	6	1993
BOYD, W. G.	1	1	0	6	1903
BROOKS, James	1	0	0	6	1980
BROWN, J. V.	1	0	0	4	1893
BURKETT, Jackie	1	0	0	6	1957
CAMPBELL, Randy	1	0	0	6	1982
CHILDRESS, Joe	2	6	0	18	1954-55
CHRISTIAN, Tim	1	0	0	6	1968
CHRISTY, Foster	1	0	0	6	1976
CLARK, Wallace	4	0	0	24	1969-70
CRIBBS, Joe	4	0	0	24	1977-78-79
CURRIER, Mike	1	0	0	6	1968
DANIELS, Bill	2	4	0	16	1893
DAVIS, George	1	0	0	6	1949
DAVIS, Joe	0	2	0	2	1954-55
DEL GRECO, Al	0	7	6	25	1980-1-2-3
DORSEY, Rufus	5	6	0	32	1893-93
DURHAM, J.C.	2	0	0	8	1893
DYAS, Ed	0	1	0	1	1958
ELLIOTT, Jerry	4	0	0	24	1955-56
ETHERIDGE, Scott	0	2	2	8	1993
FOY, Humphrey	2	0	0	10	1904
FRANKLIN, Byron	2	0	0	12	1977-80
FREDERICK, Connie	1	0	0	6	1969
FREDERICKSON, Tucker	2	0	0	12	1963-64
FREEMAN, Bobby	3	0	0	18	1954
FULLWOOD, Brent	3	0	0	18	1984-86
GARGIS, Phil	1	0	0	6	1974
GUINN, J	1	0	0	5	1905
HARRIS, Vincent	1	0	0	6	1988
HATAWAY, Charles	1	0	0	6	1953
HUGHES, C. C.	1	0	0	5	1907
JACKSON, Bo	6	1*	0	38	1982-3-4-5
JAMES, Lionel	2	0	0	12	1981-82
JETT, Gardner	0	6	3	15	1970-71-72
JOHNSON, Chris	0	2	1	5	1985
JOSEPH, James	2	0	0	12	1989
KITCHENS, Billy	1	0	0	6	1956
KNAPP, Chris	0	3	2	9	1986
LANGNER, David	2	0	0	12	1972
LEWIS, Don	0	2	1	5	1964-65
LORENO, Tommy	2	0	0	12	1956-57
LYLE, Win	0	5	4	17	1987-88-89
McGINTY, Robert	0	1	0	1	1984
McINTYRE, Secdrick	1	0	0	6	1974
McLURE, Tom	0	1	0	1	1907

AUBURN'S SERIES SCORING (continued)

PLAYER	TD	PAT	FG	TOTAL	YEAR(S)
MOSE, Harry	1	0	0	6	1987
NIX, Lloyd	1	0	0	6	1957
NOLL, W. L.	3	0	0	15	1900
O'DONOGHUE, Neil	0	1	0	1	1976
PATTERSON, Haygood	1	0	0	5	1905
PEOPLES, George	1	1*	0	8	1980-81
PERKINS, Snow	1	0	0	4	1893
PETTUS, Jimmy	1	0	0	6	1958
PHILLIPS, Red	1	0	0	6	1957
PORTELA, Jorge	0	4	3	13	1977-78-79
REDDING, Author	1	0	0	4	1893
REYNOLDS, James	1	0	0	6	1958
REYNOLDS, R. S.	1	4	0	9	1904
RILEY, John	0	8	2	14	1967-68-69
ROBBINS, Mark	1	0	0	6	1979
ROBINETT, Robby	1	0	0	6	1970
SANDERS, Frank	1	0	0	6	1993
SHACKELFORD	1	0	0	4	1893
SIDLE, Jimmy	1	0	0	6	1964
SLOAN, Matt	3	2	0	17	1900-01
SMITH, Zak	0	3	0	3	1902
STREIT, G. W.	2	0	0	10	1904
SULLIVAN, Pat	3	0	0	18	1969-70
THOMAS	1	0	0	5	1900
TILLMAN, Lawyer	1	0	0	6	1986
TUBBS, Howell	2	2	0	14	1955-56
TUCKER, Bill	0	2	0	2	1949
VON WYLE, Jim	0	1	2	7	1990-91
WALLIS, Johnny	1	0	0	6	1949
WARE, Reggie	1	0	0	6	1985
WILLIAMS, Darrell	1	0	0	6	1989
WILLIAMS, Homer	1	0	0	6	1951
WILSON, Chris	0	1	0	1	1974
WILSON, Gerald	0	1	0	1	1958
WOODALL, Woody	0	1	1	4	1963
YARBROUGH, F. R.	3	8	0	23	1900
ZOFKO, Mickey	2	0	0	12	1969
Unknown	8	8	0	48	1895
Safties (2)	-	-	-	4	1988-93
TOTALS	**123**	**103**	**27**	**881**	---

*2-point conversion

ALABAMA'S ALL-TIME SERIES SCORING

PLAYER	TD	PAT	FG	TOTAL	YEAR(S)
ABBOTT, Eli	2	0	0	8	1894
ANDERSON, Chris	1	0	0	6	1993
AVINGER, Butch	1	0	0	6	1948
BAILEY, David	2	1*	0	14	1969-70
BANKHEAD, Bankman	0	1	0	2	1893
BATTLE, Bill	1	0	0	6	1963
BATTLE, Marco	2	0	0	12	1989
BENDROSS, Jesse	2	0	0	12	1981
BERREY, Bucky	0	5	2	11	1974-76
BILLINGSLEY, Randy	1	0	0	6	1973
BISCEGLIA, Steve	1	0	0	6	1972
BOLTON, Bruce	3	0	0	18	1977-78
BOOTH, Baxter	0	1	0	1	1956
BOWMAN, Steve	1	0	0	6	1964
BOYLES, J. V.	1	0	0	5	1903
BROOKER, William T.	0	1	2	7	1959-60
BROWN, Jerry	1	0	0	6	1975
BUCK, Oran	0	2	2	8	1969
BURGETT, J. I.	1	0	0	4	1893
BURKETT, Jim	1	0	0	6	1950
BURKS, Auxford	2	2	1	16	1904-05-06
CALVIN, Tom	1	0	0	6	1949
CARRUTH, Paul	3	0	0	18	1982-84
CARTER, Joe	1	0	0	6	1983
CHAPMAN, Joe	0	5	0	5	1977
CHIODETTI, Larry	1	0	0	6	1950
CIEMNY, Richard	0	2	2	8	1970
CLARK, Cotton	1	0	0	6	1962
COLLINS, Earl	1	0	0	6	1980
CULLIVER, Calvin	1	0	0	6	1974
DAVIS, Bill	0	10	2	16	1971-72-73
DAVIS, Johnny	1	0	0	6	1977
DAVIS, Steve	0	5	1	8	1966-67
DAVIS, Terry	2	0	0	12	1971
DAVIS, Tim	0	9	3	18	1961-62
DEAN, Mike	0	3	1	6	1968
DOYLE, Philip	0	4	6	22	1988-89-90
DYESS, Marlin	2	0	0	12	1958-59
FERGUSON, Mitch	1	0	0	6	1977
GRAY, Alan	1	0	0	6	1981
GRAYSON, David	1	0	0	4	1893
HALL, Mike	1	0	0	6	1968
HUMPHREY, Bobby	1	0	0	6	1986
HUSBAND, Hunter	1	0	0	6	1969
JACKSON, Billy	1	0	0	6	1980
JACKSON, Wilbur	2	0	0	12	1972-73
JELKS, Gene	1	0	0	6	1985
JONES, B. Sidney	1	1	0	6	1907
JONES, Joey	1	0	0	6	1983
JONES, Robert	2	0	0	12	1982-83
KELLEY, Leslie	3	0	0	18	1965-66
KIM, Peter	0	9	3	18	1980-81-82

ALABAMA'S SERIES SCORING (continued)

PLAYER	TD	PAT	FG	TOTAL	YEAR(S)
KROUT, Bart	1	0	0	6	1980
KYSER, G. H.	0	4	0	8	1893-93
LANGHAM, Antonio	1	0	0	6	1992
LEE, Kevin	1	0	0	6	1993
LEWIS, Tommy	2	0	0	12	1952
LEWIS, Walter	1	0	0	6	1980
LITTLE, W. G.	1	0	0	4	1893
LOFTON, James	1	0	0	6	1956
LUNA, Bobby	1	4	1	13	1952-53
LUTZ, Harold	0	1	0	1	1951
MARLOW, Bobby	6	0	0	36	1950-51
McELROY, Alan	0	6	3	15	1978-79
MELTON, James "Bimbo"	1	0	0	6	1951
MOORE, Ricky	1	0	0	6	1983
MORGAN, Ed	2	0	0	12	1968
MUSSO, Johnny	3	0	0	18	1970-71
McCANTS, Allen	0	3	0	6	1894
Namath, Joe	1	1*	0	8	1962-63
NATHAN, Tony	4	0	0	24	1976-77
NEAL, Rick	1	0	0	6	1978
NELSON, Benny	1	0	0	6	1963
NEWSOME, Ozzie	3	0	0	18	1975-76-77
OGDEN, Ray	1	0	0	6	1964
OGILVIE, Major	1	0	0	6	1980
O'STEEN, Gary	0	1*	0	2	1958
PALMER, David	1	0	0	6	1991
PATRICK, Linnie	1	0	0	6	1981
PAYNE, Greg	1	0	0	6	1988
PERKINS, Ray	3	0	0	18	1964-65-66
PIERSON, Howard	1	0	0	6	1948
PLOWMAN, C. M.	1	0	0	5	1900
PROCTOR, Michael	0	4	1	7	1992-93
PUGH, Keith	1	0	0	6	1979
RANAGER, George	2	0	0	12	1969-70
RAY, David	0	2	1	5	1964-65
RICHARDSON, Jesse	2	0	0	12	1961
RIDGEWAY, Danny	0	6	0	6	1974-75
RUTLEDGE, Gary	2	0	0	12	1973
RUTLEDGE, Jeff	1	0	0	6	1976
SALEM, Ed	2	12	0	24	1948-49-50
SARTAIN, Harvey	1	0	0	5	1905
SAVAGE, Frank	1	0	0	4	1893
SELMAN, Tom	1	0	0	6	1948
SHANKLES, Don	1	0	0	6	1965
SHEALY, Steadman	4	1*	0	26	1977-78-79
SHELBY, Willie	1	0	0	6	1974
SHELLY, J. E.	1	0	0	4	1894
SIMS, T. S.	2	0	0	10	1905
SLOAN, Steve	0	1*	0	2	1964
SMITH, Barry	0	1	0	1	1977
SMITH, D. H.	2	0	0	8	1893
SMITH, Truman	2	8	0	18	1903-05

ALABAMA'S SERIES SCORING (continued)

PLAYER	TD	PAT	FG	TOTAL	YEAR(S)
SPURRILL, Don	1	0	0	6	1948
STABLER, Kenny	1	0	0	6	1967
STAFFORD, Angelo	1	0	0	6	1986
STEINER, Rebel	1	0	0	6	1948
STONE, Bill	1	0	0	6	1953
STURDIVANT, Raymond	1	0	0	5	1905
SUTTON, Donnie	1	0	0	6	1966
TAYLOR, James	1	0	0	6	1973
TIFFIN, Van	0	7	6	25	1983-4-5-6
TODD, Richard	2	0	0	12	1975
TOLLESON, Tommy	1	1*	0	8	1965
TRAMMELL, Pat	1	0	0	6	1961
TURNER, Craig	1	0	0	6	1985
WALKER, M. P.	1	0	0	4	1893
WARD, Lafayette	1	0	0	5	1905
WATSON, Rick	1	0	0	6	1976
WELSH, Clem	2	0	0	12	1948
WETHINGTON, Matt	0	1	2	7	1991
WILLIAMS, Sherman	1	0	0	6	1992
WILLIAMSON, Richard	2	0	0	12	1961-62
WILSON, George	1	0	0	6	1962
Safeties	0	0	0	0	---
TOTALS	**144**	**125**	**39**	**1089**	

HOW THEY HAVE SCORED....

	AUBURN		ALABAMA		SERIES	
Total Touchdowns	123		144		267	
Rushing	98	(80%)	96	(67%)	94	(73%)
Passing	19	(15%)	40	(28%)	59	(22%)
Others	6	(05%)	8	(05%)	14	(05%)

AU others — 3 pass interceptions, 2 blocked punts (who could ever forget), and 1 fumble recovery in endzone.

UA others — 3 kickoff returns, 2 blocked punts, 2 pass interceptions, and 1 recovery of bad snap in endzone.

AUBURN COACHES VS. ALABAMA

COACH	PERIOD	G	RECORD
George Petrie	1893	2	2-0-0
F. M. Hall	1894	1	0-1-0
John Heisman	1895	1	1-0-0
Billy Watkins	1900-02	3	3-0-0
Billy Bates	1903	1	0-1-0
Mike Donahue	1904-07	4	1-2-1
Earl Brown	1948-50	3	1-2-0
Ralph Jordan	1951-75	25	9-16-0
Doug Barfield	1976-80	5	0-5-0
Pat Dye	1981-92	12	6-6-0
Terry Bowden	1993-	1	1-0-0
TOTALS		**58**	**24-33-1**

ALABAMA COACHES VS. AUBURN

COACH	PERIOD	G	RECORD
E. B. Baaumont	1893	1	0-1-0
Eli Abbott	1893-94, 1902	4	1-3-0
M. Griffin	1900	1	0-1-0
M. H. Harvey	1901	1	0-1-0
W. B. Blount	1903-07	5	3-1-1
Harold Drew	1948-54	7	5-2-0
J. B. Whitworth	1955-57	3	0-3-0
Paul Bryant	1958-82	25	19-6-0
Ray Perkins	1983-86	4	2-2-0
Bill Curry	1987-89	3	0-3-0
Gene Stallings	1990-	4	3-1-0
TOTALS		**58**	**33-24-1**

SINCE 1980 (14 GAMES), AUBURN-ALABAMA HAVE SETTLED VIRTUALLY NOTHING....

TIGERS 7 WINS, TIDE 7 WINS.

Here are the close-knit facts:

	AUBURN	ALABAMA
First Downs	227	232
Yards Rushing	2386	2528
Yards Passing	2036	1887
TOTAL YARDS	4422	4415
Passes Attempted	312	325
Passes Completed	158	151
Turnovers	34	31
Punts	85	81
Yards Penalized	696	652

SCORING:
AUBURN.........39 71 44 76 — 230
ALABAMA........54 85 51 63 — 253

SERIES BOX SCORE, 1948-1993

	AUBURN	ALABAMA	PER GAME AVG
Record	17-29	29-17	---
Points	627	958	14-21
First Downs	634	784	14-17
Yds Rushing	7,121	9,408	155-205
Yds Passing	5,089	5,444	111-118
TOTAL YARDS	12,210	14,852	266-323
Passes Att	813	860	18-19
Passes Comp	397	392	9-9
Passing Pct	.488	.456	---
Turnovers	140	106	3-2
Punts	278	257	6-5
Yds Pen	2,046	1,986	44-43

SERIES HIGHS AND LOWS (Since 1948)

MOST FIRST DOWNS			FEWEST FIRST DOWNS		
31	ALA	1970	4	ALA	1969
27	ALA	1977	5	AUB	1960
27	ALA	1982	5	AUB	1963
26	ALA	1969	7	ALA	1963
25	AUB	1969	7	ALA	1971
25	AUB	1986	7	AUB	1972

MOST YARDS RUSHING			FEWEST YARDS RUSHING		
453	ALA	1951	3	AUB	1948
376	ALA	1975	12	ALA	1988
355	AUB	1983	20	AUB	1992
354	AUB	1954	28	AUB	1962
352	ALA	1973	32	ALA	1989

MOST YARDS PASSING			FEWEST YARDS PASSING		
484	ALA	1969	10	ALA	1952
340	ALA	1989	12	ALA	1967
317	AUB	1970	12	AUB	1974
276	AUB	1989	16	ALA	1972
255	ALA	1988	17	AUB	1959

MOST TOTAL YARDS			FEWEST TOTAL YARDS		
541	AUB	1969	48	AUB	1948
533	ALA	1969	80	AUB	1972
515	ALA	1977	126	ALA	1954
513	ALA	1970	131	AUB	1959
489	AUB	1956	131	AUB	1963

MOST PASSES ATTEMPTED			FEWEST PASSES ATTEMPTED		
55	ALA	1969	2	AUB	1949
50	ALA	1989	5	ALA	1967
38	ALA	1968	5	ALA	1973
38	AUB	1970	5	ALA	1974
35	ALA	1988	5	AUB	1972

MOST PASSES COMPLETED			FEWEST PASSES COMPLETED		
30	ALA	1969	1	ALA	1952
27	ALA	1989	1	ALA	1972
22	AUB	1970	1	AUB	1974
20	ALA	1988	2	AUB	1949-52-63
19	AUB	1986	2	ALA	1953-74

MOST YARDS PENALIZED			FEWEST YARDS PENALIZED		
117	ALA	1993	5	ALA	1949
114	AUB	1956	5	AUB	1961
112	AUB	1988	7	AUB	1977
105	ALA	1948	8	AUB	1974
105	ALA	1951	10	AUB	1971-73
			10	ALA	1950-73

SERIES ODDS 'N ENDS....

- The team which scores first wins 81% of the time (46-11). There has been one tie. Alabama has scored first 32 times and went on to post a 27-5 record. Auburn has scored first 26 times for a 19-6-1 record.

- The team leading at halftime wins 88% of the time. Seven times the score has been tied and one game ended in a tie. In the other 50 games, the leaders finished with a 44-6 record. Auburn has lost only one halftime lead (1964), Alabama has lost five.

- There have been 451 kickoffs in the series and only three returned for touchdowns, all by Alabama. They came in 1962 (George Wilson), 1964 (Ray Odgen) and 1969 (George Ranager). That's 1 TD about every 150 kickoffs.

- "Penalties will kill you?" In the 42 series games 1948-1989, the winning team, oddly enough, led in penalty yards by a big margin of 1,909-1,577. In the last four games, however, it has been the opposite. The losing team leads 356-190.

- When Auburn beats Alabama it is by an average score of 27-11, while the Tide beats the Tigers 25-7 on the average.

- Nineteen of the 58 series games (33%) have been settled by one touchdown or less. Auburn has won all three of the series' 1-point games — 14-13 in 1949, 17-16 in 1972, and 23-22 in 1982.

- In 1981, Alabama won 28-17 to take a 28-17 series lead.

- During the Auburn-Alabama football hiatus (1908-1947), who provided each with "season-ending rivalries?" The Tigers closed with 10 different opponents (in a dozen different cities), led by Georgia Tech (12), Georgia (7) and Florida (5). Only twice did they complete their season at Auburn (1941-42 with Clemson). In fact, the Tigers have closed at Auburn just four times ever — the two Clemson games and the two recent Alabama games. Auburn has won all four. Alabama, meanwhile, met 17 different teams in eight locations, including San Francisco, Cleveland and Chattanooga. The Tide's leading opposition was Georgia (11), Vanderbilt (9) and Mississippi State (7). Twenty-four of Bama's season-ending games were played in Birmingham, only four in Tuscaloosa.

EDITOR'S NOTE: All photographs which appear in the 1993 chapter were from the files of Auburn University Photographic Services through the full cooperation of manager Les King.

Auburn has one of the finest photographic operations in the nation, and we would like to thank Mr. King and his entire staff for their generous teamwork and courtesy.

The photographs were taken by King, Van Blankenship, Steve Deckich, Troy Dobbins, Jeff Etheridge, Glenn Miller, Bob Moore, Joel Moore and Tim Phillips.

EPILOGUE

By David Housel,
Auburn Athletic Director

There is a growing school of thought, expressed more and more it seems, that the Auburn-Alabama game, or, if you prefer Alabama-Auburn, is too big, that it has gotten out of hand, that it is no longer healthy for the state of Alabama.

And there may be some truth to that.

Football allegiance is often a factor in political races. Bear Bryant, for example, campaigned against Fob James in the 1982 governor's race because James was a former Auburn halfback, and Coach Bryant, in his infinite wisdom, said it would not be good for the state of Alabama (Alabama football) to have an Auburn man as governor, explaining in part why Auburn faithful took such great pleasure in James' victory, whether they voted for him or not.

Coach Bryant may have known what he was talking about. Auburn did, after all, defeat Alabama 23-22 a few weeks after the November general election and the state of Alabama football has not been the same since, but that is another story for another time.

Clearly, the Auburn-Alabama game, the outcome of it, is often taken to extreme by both sides. Political alliances, family relationships, business relationships, have all been affected adversely by one side or the other taking the outcome of this one single football game too far, to an extreme.

As one visitor to the state noted, "You folks in Alabama tend to take your football rather personally...." Truer words were never spoken.

But that's the way we do things in the South, and in Alabama in particular. It's kind of like eating fried food. What we do might not always be good for us, but we always do it well. Or, as a good Alabama man once said, "It just wouldn't be as much fun if we didn't take it so seriously."

But all of us, Auburn and Alabama fans, should remember Terry Bowden's words prior to the 1993 game. "There won't be any lack of class on that field Saturday," he said, "I can assure you of that...."

He was talking about the quarterbacks, Stan White and Jay Barker, but he could just as well have been talking about all of the players on both sides.

As bad and as misguided as it sometimes is, the annual Auburn-Alabama game also provides the state with one of its finest hours. Young men on both sides, devoting their all, every fiber of their body and the essence of their physical soul as they know it, to one common cause — victory. Victory for their school, for their side and for their people. There's a lot to be said for that. It is the essence of competition, and it is the essence of sportsmanship.

It is no small wonder that immediately following each of these epic struggles — and each meeting is an epic struggle — the players on both sides, the winners and the losers, often embrace in common understanding and appreciation of their uncommon effort in pursuit of a common, singular goal — the goal of winning the Auburn-Alabama game, the biggest game in this or any other year.

All glory is fleeting, and Braggin' Rights are no exception. The one thing that endures is the quality of effort put forth by the players of both sides in pursuit of a common goal.

Right or wrong, good or bad, this is the way we do it in the state of Alabama.

THE AUTHOR

Bill Cromartie is from Leesburg, Ga., and graduated from the University of Georgia in 1958. After spending 25 years in the advertising business in Atlanta, he is now engaged full-time in writing and publishing.

Cromartie's longtime interest in college football has led to the writing of five other rivalry books—Georgia-Georgia Tech (*Clean, Old-Fashioned Hate*), Michigan-Ohio State (*The Big One*), Texas-Oklahoma (*Annual Madness*), Notre Dame-Southern California (*The Glamour Game*), and Duke-North Carolina (*Battle of the Blues*).

He also co-authored *Bear Bryant: Countdown to Glory*, a book chronicling his first 315 coaching victories.

Cromartie has also published two other rivalry books—Georgia-Florida (*War Between the States*) and Florida-Florida State (*Sunshine-Hate*) by Cale Conley, plus *They Wore Crimson* and *Silver Britches* by Clyde Bolton.